WHEN YOUR PARENTS GROW OLD

WHEN YOUR PARENTS GROW OLD

SECOND EDITION

Florence D. Shelley

Original edition by Jane Otten and Florence D. Shelley

Foreword by Robert N. Butler, M.D.

PERENNIAL LIBRARY

HARPER & ROW, PUBLISHERS, New York
Cambridge, Philadelphia, San Francisco, London
Mexico City, São Paulo, Singapore, Sydney

Copyright acknowledgments follow the index.

This work is a revised edition of *When Your Parents Grow Old* by Jane Otten and Florence D. Shelley.

For information address Harper & Row, Publishers, Inc., 10 East 53rd Street, New York, N.Y. 10022. Published simultaneously in Canada by Fitzhenry & Whiteside Limited, Toronto.

Designed by Patricia Dunbar

Library of Congress Cataloging-in-Publication Data

Shelley, Florence D.
When your parents grow old.

Rev. ed. of: When your parents grow old / Jane Otten. 1976.
Bibliography: p.
Includes index.
1. Old age assistance—United States—Directories. 2. Old age assistance—Information services—United States. 3. Aged—Services for—United States—Directories. 4. Adult children—United States—Family relationships. I. Otten, Jane. When your parents grow old. II. Title.
HV1465.S54 1988 362.6'3'02573 88-45059
ISBN 0-06-055010-4 88 89 90 91 92 DT/FG 10 9 8 7 6 5 4 3 2 1
ISBN 0-06-096090-6 (pbk.) 88 89 90 91 92 DT/FG 10 9 8 7 6 5 4 3 2 1

For my mother, Charlotte Dubroff, who has shown our four-generation family how to age with generosity, grace, and spirit and especially how to love and care for each other, and for my husband, children, and grandchildren—all of whose love I cherish

CONTENTS

FOREWORD

We have witnessed in this century an extraordinary increase in life expectancy. People born in 1900 could expect to live an estimated forty-seven years; those born in 1980, seventy-three years; those born in 2000, seventy-five years, and population projections for the twenty-first century promise continuing steady increases. This longevity revolution is a triumph of social and medical progress, but, like most progressive strides, it has brought with it some unexpected problems. More and more people are living longer, healthier, and more productive lives, but increased numbers of older people in our population means that we also have more chronically ill and frail elderly. Public policy has not yet adequately responded to the demands the longevity revolution is placing on society, and so, in this era of limited resources for social and health services, we see a renewed pressure on the family to care for their dependent older members.

How can families cope? How should they deal with money matters, doctors, and hospitals? What kinds of community services are available to alleviate the burden? What should be done when home care is no longer possible, when Alzheimer's disease is diagnosed, when other behavioral changes, diseases, and disorders make caretaking more difficult and stressful? *When Your Parents Grow Old* appeared a little more than a decade ago, and over the years it has helped many families answer these and other questions. In this fine new edition, important additions have been made, including new medical knowledge, new sources of help, new laws and regulations, and new options and alternatives. *When Your Parents Grow Old* is now again a current, comprehensive guide to essential information, resources, and help for children who are facing the problems that arise as their parents grow old.

With this book, Florence Shelley has made an important contribution toward meeting the new challenges of the longevity revolution. Everyone who reads it, and cares for an elderly parent, will not only be comforted by the encouragement and advice it offers, but will learn how to plan for his or her own future.

Robert N. Butler, M.D.

ACKNOWLEDGMENTS

An enormous body of new information has been created in the burgeoning field of gerontology since the first edition of this book was written jointly with Jane Otten. New research, combined with the extended experience of practitioners who provide care and service to the growing body of older people, has resulted in new resources and new ways of looking at old problems. Society has changed, bringing new challenges and new frustrations. Therefore some of the old material has been deleted or restated and as much new material as possible has been added.

The names of everyone I interviewed and a selected list of publications I read to extend my knowledge appear in the Bibliography, but there are a few to whom I owe a special debt of appreciation: Dr. Rose Dobrof and her colleagues; Dr. Robert Butler and members of his department; Diane Lifsey and other staff members of the U.S. Senate Special Committee on Aging; Dr. Kenneth Davis, Dr. Charles Shamoian, and Dr. Barry Reisberg for helping me to understand behavioral changes among the elderly and the new advances in the neurosciences and in Alzheimer's in particular, and the New York City Department for the Aging for making it possible for me to adapt the form used in their publication *Caring* to the information I gathered in the Alzheimer's section; Dr. Edward Fischel, Dr. Ira Gelb, Dr. Steven Mattis, and Dr. Robert Stivelman for additions to their previous contributions; Dr. Simeon Taylor for adding his expertise to the special contributions of Dr. Harold Rifkin to the first edition; Jack Ossofsky and the wonderful staff of The National Council on the Aging: Lorraine Lidoff, Betty Ransom, Cathy Michaelson, Dorothy Gropp, and Carol Forney; Barry Robinson of AARP, who was a constant source of support and hard-to-get information; Marilyn Goldaber, Dr. Natalie Gordon, Janet Sainer, Daniel Sambol, and Ben Warach, who stretched my knowledge of current resources and problems; John Regan and Charles Sabatino, who introduced me to the mysteries of money, law, and entitlements; Victor Kovner, whose wise legal counsel made it possible for me to venture forth into this new edition; Theodore Wagner and Dr. Daniel Sherber, who reviewed respectively some of the legal and medical material; Dr. T. Franklin Williams, Jane Shure, and others at the National Institute on Aging, who gave me time from their busy schedules; Dr. Gene Cohen and many of his colleagues at the National Institute of Mental Health who helped me understand the present status of their disciplines; my patient editor Carol Cohen, who helped enormously in shaping the final text.

All of my dear family—Carolyn, Bill, Phillip, and my grandchildren Natasha and Melissa—were patient with my excuse that I was too busy to be with them as much as I would have liked in this period of their lives. Natasha, indeed, wrote and illustrated a powerful poem always displayed on my wall to exorcise the computer ghost who haunted my early days and, with my husband, helped me to overcome my hesitation at abandoning the typewriter for the new technology. My mother, now 93, put aside her needs to make it easier for me to deal with my conscience when I spent less time with her than I would have liked. I must also salute my friend Tobi Frankel, who throughout her bout with a fatal brain tumor kept suggesting people who might give me important new insights and information and exchanged ideas with me about the role of women to the very last.

Most of all, this book literally could not have been written without the constant, selfless support of my husband, Edwin, who taught me how to use and eventually love my Macintosh, retrieved "lost" material from that mysterious memory, and encouraged me at every turn to do the book first and everything else later or not at all. To all of you who have contributed so much, thank you.

INTRODUCTION

A great deal has changed in the decade or so since the first edition of *When Your Parents Grow Old*. Much is the same.

Our society is more fragmented, facing grave problems that have a serious impact on the older population and their families. For the first time, there is a higher percentage of older people than teenagers in the population, signaling the graying of America. Family structure has changed. Nevertheless the family continues to be the primary source of care and comfort for people as they grow older. While more older people remain in charge of their own lives for a longer period than ever before, more families are taking care of greater numbers of frail older people than ever before.

We are in the forefront of a new development in human history: the prolongation of productive human life. This does not mean an infinite life, nor does it mean that aging is without its decrements but that the span of vigorous years has lengthened. So have the years of chronic illness and the period of frailty, which for most has been postponed to a later age. Your parents' experience growing older is dramatically different from their parents' experience, and yours will be different from your parents'. But you can learn from the events that mark your parents' passage through their later years what you can do to control your own, to take advantage of the gift of longer life and plan realistically to meet your later needs. The information in this book will help you to cope with the problems you are facing now as your parents grow older and to find the resources and assistance you and they require. Information is your best ally as you proceed through these years with them.

Science and medicine gave our parents longer life. Social Security and an expanding economy gave the majority a base of greater financial security. But the rise of new technologies made much of their work experience obsolete. Turbulent world events and social revolutions called many old values into question. As our parents grew older, youth became king. Old bodies, old faces, old people lost currency. Old wisdom had few listeners. The American community forced older people into the shadows. The elderly as a group became largely invisible. Many were willing partners in their own isolation from the mainstream of productive society. They told themselves "It's good to retire early. People get tired when they get older. They become ill, weak, and senile. They end up in nursing homes." These were the myths of the society, believed even by older people who themselves were healthy and vigorous, and despite the fact that the majority do not become senile but live out their years without becoming totally dependent on others.

It has taken time for people to absorb the reality that a longevity revolution has occurred, that attitudes and actions based on old assumptions need review. Maintaining independence and control over one's own life is a universal wish, and loss of autonomy in one's later years is a prevailing fear. To forestall dependence and live more satisfying and productive lives, older people are now thinking twice about leaving the mainstream of life. They are learning new things, working in new ways, and contributing their talents and experience to the larger community. An increasing number of older Americans are coming out of the shadows to live a productive life as long as they are able.

The new consciousness of longer vigorous life is dramatically different from the prevailing attitudes at the time of the first edition. What is the same is the way people feel when they must confront their need for help and care and the way children feel when they are called upon to provide care for needful parents. People still need to cope with their feelings and manage stress and still need information that will lead them to the resources and assistance they require. Among these needs are securing appropriate and affordable medical care, finding or maintaining a favorable environment and housing in which to live, providing long-term care for the frail and incapacitated within the family or in decent nursing homes, protecting economic security, managing finances, maintaining social and recreational opportunities, coping with physical or behavioral changes, assuring safety, dealing with family conflict, keeping up with taxes, making wills, and planning for incapacity. All these and many more are addressed in the following chapters.

An overview of America's older population will help put your parents' situation in perspective. There are now more than twenty-nine million Americans 65 or older, or about one in eight of the general population. The numbers of older people in our country grew twice as fast as the rest of the population in the last two decades. This trend is expected to continue well into the next century. By the year 2050 it is expected that one out of four persons will be over 65. The implications of this dramatic change reach every sector of American life and present unprecedented political and economic challenges that are only beginning to be recognized and addressed by a society so long dominated by a youth culture. Opportunities for the vigorous and healthy to be employed have been broadened by substantially outlawing mandatory retirement. Projected labor shortages before the turn of the century may demand the return to the workplace of a still vigorous older population. The age of eligibility for full Social Security benefits will gradually rise to 67 after the year 2000. Attention is being turned to eliminating disincentives to work that are symbolized by the way earned income is taxed for Social Security recipients while unearned income from such sources as interest or dividends is not. All this will profoundly affect you in your later years and may affect your parent in a few years.

Frailty, disability, and increased need for outside help usually occur near the end of life. Nothing is new in that. It is the age at which frailty appears that has changed. More and more people reach 75, 85, even their 90s before they need call on others for assistance. The group of Americans living to 85 and beyond has been the fastest growing segment of our population.

The vast majority of older Americans live out their lives in their own homes, receiving assistance from their families as their needs increase. Currently, only about 5 percent of the population 65 and older are in nursing homes. These are usually the oldest and most impoverished, about half of whom have no surviving family or "significant other." One out of five of those 85 or older is institutionalized. An increasing number of these are Alzheimer's patients.

About 21 percent of the elderly population are poor or near poor—approximately six million people. For the poor and near-poor older person, life is hard and mean. The choice between being warm or going hungry (heat or eat) is very real. While the majority of older people are in much better economic circumstances than ever before, they are hardly rich. Elderly women, in general, are in much worse financial shape than elderly men. The median income in 1986 for older men was $11,544; for women $6,425, increasing the gap of recent years. People living as families, as couples, or with other family members are better off. Families headed by people older than 65 had a median income of $19,932 in 1986. Median income for whites was $774 higher, for blacks $7,455 lower, for Hispanics about $4,000 lower. More than one-third (38%) of the families had incomes of more than $25,000. The higher incomes are usually enjoyed by the age group 65 to 69. Hardly any can afford the costs of long-term care. The major source of income for older people is Social Security, which accounts for about 35 percent of their income. Almost half of all the elderly poor receive no public assistance. How well off you are in old age is largely determined by race, sex, and marital status.

Most Americans do not move to retirement communities or to the sunbelt. Although about 3 percent of the nation's retirees move to another state, 27 percent don't move more than 25 miles, and 70 percent die at the same address they were at when they were 65. Contrary to popular belief, almost two-thirds of the elderly who have children but are living alone are minutes, not hours, away from a child. About half the American population 65 or older live in eight states: California, New York, and Florida, with more than two million each, and Illinois, Michigan, Ohio, Pennsylvania, and Texas, with more than a million each.

A continuing concern for families is how to deal with the finances of health care. Filling out forms, learning the ropes of entitlements, and talking to doctors, hospital personnel, and insurers are talents it is best for families to develop quickly as parents grow older. Even the most independent old people sooner or later give up on the masses of paperwork or appeal procedures that go along with their entitlements. It is one of the prerogatives of age. Good information is your best protection.

Most older men (77%) are married. Most older women (60%) are not. Most men continue to marry younger women. There are five times as many widows as widowers. The number of divorced older people has increased four times as fast as the older population itself over the last ten years, a phenomenon that brings particular problems to their children. For some families it is a matter of being asked to take sides. For others it is dealing with the emotional and financial consequences. For most it is the problem of accepting a new young wife for father or being called on to deal with a devastated mother. Older women, and the middle-aged women who are also facing dramatically increased divorce rates, are particularly vulnerable to severe economic deprivation. Uncertain medical coverage, pension benefits, and employment, as well as social and personal turmoil, are among the instant problems that emerge for divorced older women.

Life expectancy continues to increase. Women who reached 65 in 1986 could, on average, expect to live another 18.6 years. Men, on average, could look forward to an additional 14.8 years. The gap between male and female lifespan has shortened somewhat. Even with several chronic conditions, most elderly people view their health positively. In the mid-1980s, fewer than one-third of older persons assessed their health as fair or poor, though almost half the blacks did so. If your parent spent as many as fifteen days in bed and restricted his or her activities because of illness or disability for an additional seventeen days in the course of last year, he or she was like the average older American.

The practice of medicine as it relates to older people is changing. In the National Institutes of Health, at the great universities, at the veterans' hospitals, centers on aging are conducting research into the processes of aging and laying the knowledge base that can improve medical and social practice to enhance the quality of life for people as they age. New York's Mount Sinai Medical Center has made geriatrics part of the required curriculum for medical students. In 1988, the American Boards of Internal Medicine and Family Practice for the first time offered an examination for certification of physicians with additional qualifications in geriatric medicine.

Knowledge leaps in medicine have created new problems as well as new opportunities for well-being. Agonizing decisions about life and death are a byproduct of the new advanced technologies. Families, philosophers, religious leaders, physicians, hospital administrators, legislators, and judges are still struggling with these decisions.

New ways of delivering health care and efforts to contain medical costs have made it essential for those needing medical care to stay abreast of their options and have the best available information to make their decisions on how to receive care, from whom, and how to pay for it. People must accustom themselves to the presence in their lives of the "third party" —the insurance company. It is the insurance company that dominates many of the decisions made about health care for older people, that determines how to interpret the Medicare regulations, or establishes the limits on private health insurance. Will Medicare pay? Not as often or as much as most people believe.

With the passage of the Older Americans Act in 1965 and its subsequent amendments, families witnessed a strong federal commitment to improve the life of the senior population and were the beneficiaries of many of its programs. In more recent years we have been witnessing support for some services spreading very thin if not disappearing, and pressure is increasing on families to do still more for their ailing elders. The family has always assumed responsibility for care of the frail and ill elderly. It continues to do so. The idea that the modern American family abandons its old is a myth.

The older woman is the principal giver of care and eventually the principal receiver of care. The average age of persons caring for an impaired spouse is 66, and the majority of offspring caring for an impaired parent are over 50. More than one in three impaired men are cared for by their wives, but only one in ten impaired women are cared for by their husbands. Many women give more than a formal work week of time to their own mother's care, often in addition to their own jobs.

Older women know the personal costs of giving care to others. They do not want to burden their own daughters but often have no other choice. Elaine Brody in a major research study reported that the granddaughter's generation has a continuing strong sense of filial responsibility. Grandmothers, more than their daughters or granddaughters, want to look to the community for care services they might require.[1] Relief for sorely pressed and exhausted caregivers is a pressing need. Respite services are being developed in many communities by volunteers and social service agencies. The Area Agencies on Aging, working in concert with the community, local government, or social service agencies, are developing community-based long-term care and case management programs that may bolster your efforts and help you to utilize the available community services for your parent's benefit.

Home care has become a huge industry, growing in response to the increased needs of older people living in a home environment. Entitlement programs for home care operate under very strict limitations. Families continue to rely largely on their own physical and financial resources to manage what are frequently all-consuming tasks. When you look to home care, whoever pays for it, you are looking into a "black box" where standards remain to be established and enforced and quality is often questionable.

Neighbors are important to the elderly of all economic and social levels. In the absence of family living close by, neighbors assume responsibilities for emergencies as well as for small chores. It is important to learn who your parents' neighbors are.

Not all the giving these days is from young to old. Adult children in crisis are returning home in droves, bringing with them their young children to be cared for, their emotional upheavals, their financial and career woes, their need for some parental TLC. An ugly custody case can lead to a fight over grandparents' rights to see a beloved grandchild. Many members of the older generation are opening their pocketbooks so that their children can buy a first home, open a first office, return for professional education, send the grandchildren to camp or college, or help the younger family to purchase a vacation home. Many retired people on reduced incomes are helping their children—financially or by caring for the grandchildren—more than their children are helping them.

This new edition of *When Your Parents Grow Old* deals with the new circumstances of American society as well as the traditional ties that bind. It can help you with the best new information available as you face and deal with the problems that arise as your parents grow older. Nevertheless, policies, programs, entitlements, and laws change frequently. You should always check with knowledgeable experts about current rules, regulations, and practices before you embark on any course of action that may be affected by them. Legal advice should be sought from lawyers, medical advice from physicians. The information provided here is not intended as specific advice for any patient or family.

The process of providing care for the older person to whom you are connected by bonds of love and loyalty is never simple and is sometimes painful. But if you are armed with information, if you use the outside resources and support available to you, if you understand your feelings and those of your parent, you can achieve a certain clarity of purpose. You and your parent can be in better control of the events that occur and the process will be better than it might otherwise be.

Update on Medicare coverage: A new health care law, passed in June 1988 as this book went to press, limits annual individual outlays for acute illness by expanding Medicare coverage for hospital stays, approved physicians' bills, home health care, and hospice and nursing home stays and adds partial coverage for prescription drug bills in excess of $600 annually, limited respite for caregivers, and protection against total impoverishment of spouses of nursing home residents. Provisions will be phased in between January 1, 1989, and January 1, 1990. Beneficiaries will pay for this through additional monthly premiums of $4, starting January 1, 1989, and higher-income elderly (about 40%) will also pay an income-based surtax. Little changed in regard to long-term care for the chronically frail. Be sure to check a current Medicare handbook to see how and when this new law affects your parents' situation.

WHEN YOUR PARENTS GROW OLD

ONE

FACING UP

According to the law, parents are responsible for minor children and a spouse is responsible for a spouse, while adult children are responsible for parents only in very special circumstances. But following custom, religious mandate, and the inner commands of filial duty, respect, affection, and love, most children do not forsake parents in their old age.

Old age is not merely a chronological state. It comes to some sooner than others. None of us escapes the process of aging, but we live and die according to our own internal clocks, our capacity to deal with disease or trauma, and the impact of our experiences. For the most vulnerable—the ill, the mentally or physically incapacitated, the financially impoverished, the socially excluded—the process of becoming older can be degrading, isolating, and destructive. Among other losses may come "the death of the mind"—the theft of autonomy by Alzheimer's or other insidious brain diseases. The loss of control over one's life may be the most devastating loss of all.

In our society most of us believe that all people, including the old and the sick, are entitled to control over their own lives. The legal system supports this view, and psychiatrists as well as other medical experts know that feeling that you are in control and being in control of your own life are important factors in maintaining good mental and physical health. Except for those mentally incompetent to make rational decisions, the old and the sick have a right to choose how to live and how to die. Even loving children have no right to impose on frail parents solutions the parents are unwilling to accept—whether or not those solutions are believed to be in the parents' best interest.

Each of us with a parent in pain or need, however, knows that life is not that simple. The demands made on us, the decisions we are forced to confront, the pressures imposed on us by circumstances, and our inner emotions and outside expectations drain us of energy, of time, and often, worst of all, of good feelings.

Feelings surround all the actions we take and all the actions we avoid. A family that has everything straight—its inner relationships, its medical and financial plans, its action program for crisis in an emergency—is not the typical American family. The professionals in social service agencies know this because it is they to whom we turn in desperation when crisis strikes and there's no plan to put into operation. The decisions we make under pressure frequently are not the best decisions and may prove difficult to live with. It is often our feelings that put us into these positions. We're reluctant to face up to our parent's mortality—or our own. We deny the need to do anything until it is forced upon us.

The feelings that intrude on our actions have to do with guilt as well as love, stress as well as compassion, fear as well as understanding. Egos are pitted against egos. Sibling rivalries, hostility, resentment, duty, affection, need for approval—a whole tangle of family history and relationships bubble underneath and frequently explode at the very time it would be most constructive for love, patience, and logic to prevail.

So when you get your first emergency call from a stricken parent, or when the demands of dealing with a continuing difficult situation wear on you, don't be surprised or ashamed if some of these feelings rise up in you and others in your family, sometimes seeming to overwhelm. You are not alone; others feel as you do. You will not be the first caught unprepared.

THE BEGINNING OF THE END OF INDEPENDENCE

Let us assume that your parents have been living an independent life. Your lives are separate for the most part, meshing for holiday and family occasions. You visit back and forth. When you can't, you telephone or write. You are in touch.

At some point, sharply or gradually, the situation changes. In regular phone calls or visits, you begin to sense from a parent some new failing or infirmity, and you hear some new fears. Your father is finding it more difficult to climb the stairs. Your mother is worried about your father, who has been growing more and more depressed and now refuses to leave the house at all. A neighbor or even the police may telephone with the news that your father, who has been taking care of your incapacitated mother, has suddenly died. Or your mother calls frantically to say that your father has had a stroke and she doesn't know how long he'll be able to stay in the hospital. What will happen after that? She doesn't drive, nor is she able to maintain their home without his help.

Any of these or similar events are the large signs that foretell the end of the independence you and they have been enjoying. You will be called upon to make new decisions and take new actions that will significantly change your life and those of others you love—your spouse, your children, other relatives. Your parent(s) may be called upon to exchange some independence for necessary care.

What happens from now on depends to some degree on factors you may not be able to change—your financial condition and your parents', the location of their home in relation to yours and those of your brothers and sisters, their actual condition and the kind of medical care they need. The decisions you and your parents make at this point will be influenced not only by your own situation but also by cultural and religious attitudes. Among some groups, for instance, there is a long tradition of extended family. The Amish build an addition to the main farmhouse for the traditional purpose of housing an older generation. Others are concerned for their parents as well but may maintain more physical distance. "Old people are strongly imbedded in family systems," says gerontologist Rose Dobrof. While the myth persists that Americans abandon their elderly parents in times of trouble, the evidence is that they do not. Families provide more than 80 percent of the care extended to the old. Except in rare instances, even adult children still wounded by real or imagined hurts inflicted by a less than perfect parent rise to the need when that parent grows old. It is just more difficult for them to do so gracefully.

So religious or not, alienated or not, rich or poor, no matter what your ethnic background, when your parents need you, you are likely to be increasingly involved in their lives.

Even when you expect to take on the burden of caring for your parents, however, you still have to go through an internal decision-making process. Feelings about old events and your current relationships with your parents can subvert this process and forestall reaching decisions that are practical and effective.

Suppose, for example, that your mother is still telling you that your wife spends too much money on clothes or that your husband spends too much time playing golf or watching television. Or your father is loudly critical because you haven't required your children to adhere to his and your religion and they are with partners of a different faith or no faith at all. Caring for parents who are still critical, still supervisory, will make it more difficult for you to contribute effectively to their needs. You will have to surmount not only your parents' attitudes but your resentment of them to avoid constant collisions.

Outsiders' attitudes may deeply affect your course, especially if the outsiders have great authority in your life. For example, many churches provide excellent pastoral counseling. But what do you do if you are counseled as this woman was? Each day she rose, fed her family breakfast, walked to the next block, helped her disabled parents out of bed, gave them breakfast, installed them in the living room while she straightened up, returned home to give lunch to her husband who worked in a store beneath their apartment, went back to provide lunch and do laundry for her parents, returned to her home to prepare dinner for her family, brought cooked dinner back to the parents, waited to help with baths and get them back into bed, returned to her own home to do laundry and her remaining chores. No one had money for enough outside help, and there was no help except occasionally. This woman had lost 30 pounds and was exhausted and depressed. But her parish priest, to whom she appealed for help, told her only, "You are doing your duty as a daughter and in the eyes of God." The priest was an elderly immigrant governed by the mores of a small mountain village, unsophisticated in modern counseling, unfamiliar with community resources. She was unable to walk away from her own sense of obligation or go beyond her parish priest to seek help and respite from outside agencies. While husband and sons felt sorry for her, they too were of the old school, believed she was doing what a woman is expected to do, and merely hoped no harm would come to her.

While the latter may be an extreme example of how deeply attitudes affect our behavior, it reveals the extent to which children will deny themselves to provide what their parents need when the need is great.

DECISION-MAKING AND FAMILY TENSIONS

The need to make decisions, the ability to make decisions, and the authority to make decisions are often at the center of family disputes and of feelings of guilt or frustration. The complications are not related to the parent-child relationship alone. Brothers and sisters, grandchildren who have deep bonds with their grandparents, and other close relatives have their own ideas of how matters should be handled. Each has his or her own agenda, life history, current life, personal values, and psychological baggage to bring to the problems of caring for older relatives. In life-and-death situations, matters can become intensely difficult. Bickering and tension are not uncommon in the best of families suddenly forced to cope with new or traumatic situations.

Which Child Takes the Responsibility?

A suburban rabbi reports a typical plea for counseling from a member of his congregation:

> My father died last year, and my mother is in chronic heart failure. She really can't live alone. My younger sister lives in Brooklyn. She's a lawyer. My brother says, "You're the one who got the dowry, so you take care of Mother, you're home all day. But if you put her in a nursing home I'll never forgive you. I can't take her—my wife can't bathe her; she has a bad back. She can't stay home with her all day. I'll send you some money." So, of course, I took her in with me. And as soon as I did, they all disappeared. They're too busy and too far away. They don't even telephone. And it isn't fair.

Whether it is the youngest child or the eldest who gives care, the married or the unmarried, the richest or the poorest, a son or a daughter, depends on the family. The relationship between an adult child and a parent may also determine how responsibility is assumed. Sometimes a child feels very close to a parent and does not resent the extra burden of care. Sometimes taking responsibility is the logical outcome of a history of devotion to a parent's needs. Sometimes the child feels guilty about his or her past feelings or actions, and this becomes the motivator for new concern. This child may then act to win approval from a parent whose approval had always seemed beyond reach. The child who feels the most guilty may well be the one who seizes the responsiblity for care, while the most self-centered child may find it easiest to break away from the loving parent. Very few children, however, are so alienated from their parents that they will turn their backs completely.

Whatever the internal dynamics of a family may be, it is usually a woman who takes physical care of the parents, either a daughter or a daughter-in-law. In some families sons are, by necessity, the principal caregivers. More commonly they're expected to help with finances and to offer moral support.

However liberated women may be, the assumption that nurturing and caregiving is their natural role continues to prevail.

What women crave is some recognition of the value of this role, the opportunity to make their own choices, and alternative options so that their responsibilities and burdens do not become overwhelming and ultimately destructive.

Who Makes the Decisions?

It is important to remind yourself that getting older in itself is not a sign of a parent's need for your intervention. It may even be the time when you need to restrain some of your normally courteous behavior because your attempts to help may be misinterpreted as a belief that your parents can no longer care for themselves. It's important that your parent hold on to every symbol of independence as long as possible.

One woman describes the tug-of-war she experiences when she meets her 90-year-old mother returning from a winter month in Florida: "My mother refuses to turn over her hand luggage to me at the gate, while she struggles with her purse, gloves, and hat. 'It's too heavy for you,' she tells me! She won't allow me to be as gracious to her as I would be to any visiting guest. 'I can do it myself,' she insists. I have to stop and remember how important this act of independence is to her, and be grateful she's still in such good shape."

Older people often try to ignore their infirmities and continue to live as they have been living. Many will do this in order not to burden their children. And they struggle keenly between their need for help and assistance and their desire to be independent.

You will have to be watchful. Think about your alternatives, gather your information. Be ready to sit down with your parents and siblings to sift the possibilities of how you can meet your parents' needs when they can no longer really manage on their own. At some point you will sense the need for a change of some sort in their lives, or some incident will point it out to you sharply. Some new arrangements will have to be made.

But is it up to you to tell your parents that they have to revise their habits, up to you to take over with your proposals? Will your parents abide by a decision if you try to force it on them? Or should you wait—even though the signals are clear to you—until they are equally clear to your parents and they ask your advice? How will you feel if they insist on maintaining patterns that you feel dangerous?

Experts differ as to which course you should take. Some authorities believe you should intervene if you feel it is the loving, caring thing to do. Others believe that respect for autonomy is the most important rule.

With conflicting professional advice, you'll have to run your own course. Do what is comfortable for you and acceptable to your parents, as long as there is no serious danger involved in their continuing to deal with the burdens of daily life. If your parent lives too far away for you to keep check on what is happening, ask your parent's neighbors or a local social worker in a family service agency to alert you when the time has come for you to arrange for someone to help with burdensome chores.

Adult children, intelligent and educated as they may be, sometimes have blinders on when it comes to assessing their parents' abilities. They have their own ideas about what is or isn't appropriate behavior. They see their parents through a bundle of emotion, from a distant perspective, not as the older people see themselves or are seen by their own contemporaries: admired for their accomplishments, their vigor, their ability to cope. Children are best advised, say the professionals, to respect the way a parent views the quality of his or her own life and begin with that when considering what should be done and when.

For example, your parent may be living in a deteriorating neighborhood, once safe, now dangerous. He or she has friends and activities in the neighborhood and is willing to take the risks involved in order to maintain these satisfactions. Should you insist, to soothe your own guilt, that your mother or father move to a safe neighborhood? No, say the experts. Don't insist on moving a parent who has expressed a clear wish to stay in a familiar house or apartment among familiar surroundings. You can inquire about a neighborhood crime watch, install strong locks, and remind your parent about sensible precautions on the street. You can hire a teenager or aide to accompany your parent on errands. By seeking out such supports you can try to accommodate their wishes and your fears.

The important thing is not to nag about your concerns, but to talk about them with your parent armed with some reasonable alternative possibilities. Ask: Are you worried about the neighborhood? Do you really want to stay where you are? Would you like to consider some alternatives to living here—a move to a retirement community, closer to me? Would you like to live with me? But don't ask that last question unless you are truly willing to share your home. And don't decide that you are willing without thinking through all the consequences for you, your spouse, your children, and of course your parent. Don't be surprised if your parent prefers independence in a second-class neighborhood to becoming a second-class citizen in your first-class home.

Safety may not be the only consideration. It may, however, be the easiest thing to talk about and give you an opportunity to discuss other important aspects of their lives that may require good planning to insure a positive outcome. The need for help with personal care and household tasks sharpens with age. If your mother or father needs help with bathing or dressing, with grocery shopping or cooking, laundry or cleaning, or just to take a walk and get out of the house, then it's time to sit down together and talk about how to accomplish this in a way that is acceptable to him or her. The solution may be a relatively simple one, or it may require extensive changes in an accustomed living pattern. Whatever the solution, it should be reached with the older person's participation. Except when a parent is severely mentally impaired, "children have no right to jump in, take over, and direct all the traffic," says one geriatric specialist. "When they do, they trade one set of problems for another." As one social worker points out, "You can't break down your parents' survival techniques and expect survival. Your parent may deny the need for help and become hostile. Don't be surprised if that happens."

It's important to remember that your parent will probably

have ambivalent feelings once a change in living arrangements is under discussion. Even if your parent cannot or chooses not to verbalize these feelings, you would be wise to be aware of them. Trained counselors, social workers, and other therapists are experienced in helping older people and their families deal with these feelings. You will find more about this in the next chapter.

Role Reversal?

The term *role reversal* persists in the professional literature as it persists in people's conversations. When you were a small child your parents made decisions for you. You respected their wisdom and judgment and had confidence in their ability to know what was good for you. As you matured, your learning may have gone beyond theirs, especially in specialized areas. While they may not think you know as much about life, they may become willing to consult you about which is a better TV, how to operate a VCR, which is a better airline. Hardly anyone would call that role reversal. Nor is it role reversal when a parent is happy to allow a child to assume some burdensome tasks such as filling out insurance forms or tax returns. As geriatrician Robert Butler says, it's nice after a long hard day to have someone be especially considerate, even make a few decisions for you. The same is true after a long hard life. It doesn't make you incompetent.

When the need for help in making decisions touches the ordinary events of the day, however, when the give and take goes beyond what would be considered a normal relationship between adults, albeit parent and child, then temptations to regard this as role reversal heighten. "I feel like I'm the mother and she's the child," is a typical comment of those dealing with Alzheimer's patients. Some gerontologists, such as Anna Zimmer, question whether *role reversal* is ever a proper term to describe the relationship when older parents become more dependent on children. Giving needed help is not a license to forget that an older parent is a mature adult who nurtured you as a child and continues to regard you as the child. The evolution of this relationship requires the greatest sensitivity and understanding.

In ordinary circumstances, if you unnecessarily usurp your parents' decision-making rights, you increase their dependency and usually also their resentment. Often a "loving" child can be ruthlessly domineering, particularly toward mothers. This happens frequently if the child feels guilty. Fathers are more frequently left to "adjust," though older men confirm that they too are often patronized by younger generations. Unfortunately, many older women have a poor self-image and, without the skills and resources they need to cope on their own, they may be less resistant to authoritarian children. But not necessarily less resentful.

When Taking Charge Is Required

Obviously there can come a time when taking charge is required and a child must make a critical decision on the parent's behalf: when, for example, the parent is incapacitated or mentally incompetent. This can range from a decision about where the parent should live, or who should be hired to care for him or her, to more agonizing questions about life and death in a terminal illness. Only when a parent is incapable of making a decision or participating in the decision-making process should a child take steps to do so alone. Given serious mental deterioration, a caring child will feel impelled to act in the parent's best interest even if there is verbal resistance from the parent or if earlier expressed wishes are contrary to the reality of a parent's present needs. In such situations, before you decide on crucial matters affecting your parent, consult and consider the advice of objective outsiders—a physician, a psychiatrist, a social worker, a member of the clergy, a lawyer.

GUILT FEELINGS ARE INEVITABLE

Adult children often feel guilty. No matter how much or what they do, it's not enough to erase the feeling that some other solution would have been better. "It isn't useful to remonstrate with someone, to tell him or her not to feel guilty," says Dr. Butler. "That is counterproductive. Guilt feelings are inevitable." From infancy on, the child demands total care from parents, but offspring don't want to give that kind of care to parents. When parents reach the stage where they need care and the child doesn't fulfill the demand, the child feels guilty. A parent helps a child to grow, but a child cannot keep a parent from becoming ill and dying, and the child feels guilty.

Overreacting to Guilt

When we feel guilty, we frequently overreact. We do so particularly when death separates two parents. A common overreaction is to move the remaining parent out of his or her home immediately. "Come live with us, or brother John, or Aunt Sue. Come live in this apartment on the next block to ours. You don't have to do anything. We'll take care of everything for you."

This is a seductive appeal to a newly bereaved person who may or may not have been dependent on the lost mate but is certainly in shock. Grief-stricken, seemingly bewildered, the survivor is rushed away from home, friends, familiar surroundings and activities, and perhaps a job, and thrust into dependency. According to psychiatrists, this deprives the bereaved person of the opportunity to pass through a normal and therapeutic grieving period, as well as the right to stay in control of his or her own life and the opportunity to try to make his or her own adjustment. And the take-charge, guilt-ridden person who has summarily applied this solution has bought a bundle of troubles.

A New York nurse tells how she and her sister packed and moved their mother out of her Florida apartment two weeks after their father suddenly died. The parents had retired to Florida, along with a number of their contemporaries, five years earlier. The mother had never learned to drive, having lived all her life in a Manhattan apartment house where everything was accessible by foot, bus or subway. The father used a car for business and drove it to Florida on retirement. When he died, the daughters believed the mother would be stranded. Furthermore, she couldn't handle a checkbook, never having had to. "I live in a studio apartment, but my sister has a small house. The kids doubled up and they made room for my mother. She's driving everyone crazy. All her friends are in Florida. The children are in school or camp. My sister works. Last week I looked at my mother and realized that she isn't that old. She's in her early seventies. I began to think about my grandmother, who *was* a very old, frail woman when she died at 71. My mother is nothing like that. She could have stayed where she was, learned a few new things; her friends were ready to help her. We could have spent some time helping her to continue living down there. It never really occurred to us and now it's too late. We thought we were doing the right thing. It's a disaster."

"Older people," says Marilyn Goldaber, director of social services for the Miami Jewish Home and Hospital for the Aged, "are much more flexible than many people realize. They learn new things. They make new friends. They adjust. Of course, this is not true of every old person. Some very frail old people without close-by friends or relatives need their children and family during the last stages of their lives. They may live with a child, or close by or even enter a nursing home where family can visit regularly." But children need to give their folks a chance and not prejudge their resilience or lack of it.

Money and Guilt

Guilt has another face. A 65-year-old man appeared in the social service department of a suburban county agency, overcome with anguish. For years he had supported his mother as well as his wife. He lived in an old house; his energy costs were sky high. Everything needed repair. He was barely managing. When Medicare failed to cover the real cost of his wife's illness and then his mother fell ill, he was in a tight squeeze. He was torn between using his money for his wife or his mother. He felt he had no right to deprive his wife in order to sustain his mother but was overwhelmed by a feeling of having failed his parent. Never before had this family made a call on government assistance, and he couldn't bring himself to do it then. In time, with the guidance of a social worker, he secured Medicaid assistance and Food Stamps for his mother. This helped his financial problems but not his guilt.

People with money can have guilt problems too. Some give money to help with a parent's care, but nothing more—no time or energy. Then they criticize the decisions made by others involved in coping with their parent's daily problems. All this can lead to divisive family arguments to which guilt—conscious or unconscious—is a major contributor. Witness the wife of a wealthy corporate executive who flew in her private jet to a meeting where problems of coping with elderly parents were being discussed: "I've purposely flown here to ask how I can get my brother to help me instead of making things more difficult. My mother has completely forgotten all the events of her life except her childhood. The servants couldn't cope with her. I've just come from visiting her in a nursing home, where I arranged for her to live. She is comfortable. He is furious at me and won't speak to me. On account of his stubborn refusals we cannot have a conservator appointed. Everything is dreadful and I am at the end of my rope." Money doesn't always help.

Using money to buy services for one's parents is increasingly necessary, however, for those whose jobs make it impossible for them to provide the daytime care or assistance a parent may require. For those who can afford these costs, this is a way to provide for some basic need and erases the pressure of having to be everywhere at once but not the guilt of substituting money for personal care.

These days, the financial burden often falls on the same individual who provides the physical care. Sometimes money earmarked for that person's own children is suddenly diverted for a parent's emergency. Using limited financial resources for your parents may well make you feel guilty about failing other people you love and to whom you also owe responsibility. If at the same time your brothers or sisters fail to help with your parents, there's no question that resentment and conflict may erupt.

Many of us share these feelings of guilt and others equally painful; we carry them inside us, reluctant to air them with our friends and families. If you have these feelings, you aren't unique and alone. It is up to you to sort it all out, to balance your own needs against the legitimate needs of others. You will have to face imperfect solutions. Professional counseling can help in these hard moments. Seek it out. It's available. There is no stigma attached. You will find information in the next chapter on how to find help and use it.

A REMINDER

You're in a new role in relation to your parents. You're probably looking over your shoulder at your own children and wondering how they'll behave toward you when you are older. You may suspect that the way you treat your parents now will affect how your own children behave to you later. If you have no children you may be worried about your own old age and wonder who'll be there for you. If you haven't already started to think about your own old age, today is not too soon to start. Your experiences with your parents at this stage of their lives should alert you to what is most important for your own future.

TWO

FINDING HELP IN THE COMMUNITY

Most people at some point in their later years need help or care that comes from outside their normal life framework. They may need help for a day or two, a week, or a month. They may need help for the rest of their lives. Many older people require just a little bit of help to maintain a largely independent life. Others require all the muscle, energy, and dollars a family can muster to cope with the crises of their old age.

In nearly every community you'll find some help for present needs and some to help you avert or plan for a possible crisis. Use what is available. No matter how much outside advice you receive, the ultimate decisions about what to do and how to do it rest with you, your parent(s), and other family members. Outsiders can help you to reach a good decision. They cannot make it for you. The more you know about your alternatives, the better your decisions will be.

You can complicate your problems by not gathering your information ahead of time. The danger lies in the complexity of legal entitlements, especially in regard to Medicare and Medicaid, the difficulties of securing and assuring good home care on a reliable and compassionate basis, the potential of financial crisis resulting from prolonged chronic illness, and the shortage of appropriate housing for older people and of nursing home beds for those who require them. It is never too early to start gathering the information you may one day need suddenly, nor is it ever too late to use new information to improve a current situation.

An extensive network of experts to help you can be found in private and public agencies, philanthropic and community service organizations, family service associations, religious and social service groups. In addition there are countless self-help and support groups, one for almost every health, financial, legal, social, or emotional problem you are likely to encounter. You will also find educational or activity programs to help prevent problems from occurring and to improve the daily quality of life for older people.

Despite the proliferation of programs and services, you may be reminded often by government personnel that it is your responsibility to care for your elders. In this era of budget crunch, many services are spread very thin. Help is not always at hand, especially for long-term care. Furthermore, you will need help to deal with the different bureaucracies when you try to negotiate the system to take advantage of the assistance that is available. The sooner you become acquainted with the system and the regulations involved, the fewer costly errors you and your family will make. This chapter will guide you to the people who can help and to the services and programs available to older Americans and their families.

MAKING A BEGINNING

Talk to your friends. Those who have been through it can tell you about the good people they've dealt with, the ones who can get action. They know the dead ends. Their good and bad experiences can be guides for you.

Talk to your doctors and your parent's doctors. They can help you define the problem, suggest possible alternatives to consider, and recommend the appropriate social or community service agency for further assistance. A psychiatrist or psychologist can counsel you if your parent's mental status or family emotional problems are becoming troublesome.

Talk to your religious leader or the clergy of your parent's neigh-

borhood. The major religious denominations sponsor a full range of social services. Your minister, priest, or rabbi can put you in touch with facilities or can counsel you about intrafamily or spiritual problems. Many have been trained in pastoral counseling and offer expert advice.

Talk to a social worker specializing in problems of the aged. These professionals are important links between families and the services or resources they require. They can help you deal with small problems and major crises. They can help you to make a plan. You'll find them in your local social service agencies, community and family service organizations, senior centers, and your Area Agency on Aging.

Use your local library. Look for a special section on aging where you can read a variety of books and periodicals for information to help you evaluate the advice you get from others. Directories of housing, nursing homes, recreational facilities, doctors, hospitals, and many other useful resources are also here.

Telephone or visit your Area Agency on Aging. Offices exist throughout the country. Each has an information and referral service to help you find the specific services available in particular locations. Many also publish directories of local services and programs.

THE AREA AGENCY ON AGING

Depending on their size, the Area Agencies on Aging have a range of specialists on their staff who should be able to direct you to anything you need. They may work directly with you or your parent to explore what needs to be done, where specific help can be found, and to help you make a plan for the future. The AAAs also offer specific services directly to older people, such as meals at community sites and delivered at home (Meals on Wheels), transportation, legal services, information on housing resources and residential care, chore services, in-home services, home health aides, respite for caregivers, friendly visiting, long-term care, employment referrals, companions, Foster Grandparents programs, senior centers, adult day-care centers, tips on buying Medigap insurance, tax relief and energy assistance, protective services, and nursing home ombudsman programs.

In the big cities or major counties the Area Agency on Aging (AAA) may be called by the city or county name. In rural areas, several counties may be covered by a single Area Agency on Aging, and a local group may provide local information or services under arrangement with the area agency. If you're unable to obtain the information you require from your Area Agency on Aging, call the state office. Some states have a hot line or toll-free number for this purpose. Consult your telephone directory or ask the information operator. (Also see the Appendix of this book under Government Agencies.) The AAA is the best single source of information on the services and programs available where you need them.

Many states, large cities, and counties publish handbooks to help the elderly understand the state and federal programs available to them. Because of the increasing responsibilities of families for their elders, many states also publish useful handbooks on caregiving. Inquire of your AAA for these.

The amount of help available will vary by state and community and will depend on your parent's entitlements, on the amount of money allocated for help by the various government jurisdictions, and on how generous the local population is to the social and philanthropic agencies it supports.

Chances are that no single community will have everything described in the following pages. Sometimes a service will be open to all, sometimes only to those of limited means. Often services are offered for which people pay on a sliding scale according to what they can afford.

Here you'll find an overview of current sources of help. Later chapters include more detailed discussions of some of these sources.

SOCIAL SERVICE AGENCIES

Some of the best services for the aging are sponsored by the major religious denominations and philanthropic organizations. You do not have to be poor to seek the help of a social worker; you do not have to be Jewish to secure counseling or home care from a Jewish family service agency, or Catholic to get help from Catholic Charities. Neither do you have to be an alcoholic to utilize the Salvation Army.

Most of these agencies, generally sponsored and maintained by a particular faith or group, have become resources for the entire community. Family Service America, which has no religious affiliation, has agencies in almost every metropolitan area. Fees may be elastic, based on income; the religious groups may suggest a small donation. If the agency you select is not an accredited member of a large organization or part of a nationally recognized network of sectarian or nonsectarian agencies, ask whether the counselors are licensed and registered with the state to provide professional services.

Many of these agencies have specialized divisions for services to the aged, whose staff can tell you what help is available, assist you in finding it, and sometimes arrange it for you. Increasingly, these agencies, in response to pressure for their services from an expanding aging population, are teaching family members to help themselves by sponsoring group workshops and specialized training programs for caregivers. As the tasks you perform for your parent become more complex, you will need to learn where you can find help on the outside. These agencies are wonderful sources of help.

Services of a Social Worker

While numerous programs and services exist for older people and their families, it often takes great patience and fortitude to get through by telephone, or even in person, to the correct person for any particular information or assistance. Especially as programs multiply, and despite the best efforts of many dedicated administrators, lack of coordination may cause you to spend many hours and many telephone calls before finding the right person or the information you're seeking.

That's why you might be best off working with a trained and experienced social worker. It's a simple question of efficiency. Many middle-class people still associate social workers with welfare and relief programs, but social workers are trained to help people in crisis, no matter what their economic level. There is no stigma attached to consulting a social worker. Ask for help early and you'll avoid unnecessary mistakes and save yourself a great deal of time and anguish.

Experienced social workers can normally provide you with whatever information and assistance you need. They know what your parent is entitled to from federal, state, and local governments, and they can get you through all the red tape more easily than you can do it by yourself. They can counsel you, or direct you to someone who can, if conflict and stress are invading good family relationships.

A social worker can be particularly valuable if you live in one place and your ailing parent in another. By making arrangements through an established social service agency in your parent's locality for a social worker to check on your mother or father regularly, you'll have peace of mind you could not have otherwise. In places where many older people have retired, such as Florida, California, and Arizona, a number of agencies and private social workers offer this kind of service for a fee. In large cities, the major philanthropic agencies usually perform such services when necessary. The Area Agency on Aging can tell you what is available in your parent's region.

If you and your parent or other family members aren't getting along too well, if you don't understand the puzzling aspects of your parent's behavior and attitudes, if there's undue argument or frustration, then social workers can help you find a support group or a professional therapist for one-on-one counseling. Groups have their advocates and critics, usually depending on whether or not professional leadership is present. An exchange of ignorance is futile, says one critic; others say there is magic in the group per se, that the process of talking with one another provides the treatment. Groups with professional leadership are generally viewed as serving a positive and helpful function. You should do what works for you.

Some people shy away from social workers because they don't want to be "analyzed." Dr. Robert M. Rice, executive vice president of Family Service America, says:

Traditional counseling by social workers has changed. The 50-minute hour is a thing of the past. The Agency programs now are more varied and numerous and are interdisciplinary. Programmatic social workers today do lots of things beyond therapeutic counseling, but they do work with self-help groups and provide them with information. The professional tries to help people use their own strengths. There is greater awareness today of the realistic problems people face. Their problems may not be just emotional, though there can be an emotional overlay to the frustration of solving real problems. The professionals are more sensitive to significant health issues and their effects on the personality. They have a better understanding now of income problems. Our agency people are now trained to help solve problems right now rather than go back to investigate the feelings people carry forth from their childhood. Family service agencies are a good place to start to get help. Families won't be conned into uncomfortable solutions.

Benjamin Warach, executive director of the Jewish Association for Services to the Aged (JASA) in New York, says the majority of people who come to JASA for help are the elders themselves. "So many here in the city live at a long distance from their children. The number within walking distance of their children is modest. One-third of our calls for help are related to managing physical and mental disabilities. About one-third come for counseling on personal management of finances, getting home care. The remainder relate to benefits, housing, entitlements, and help in filling out Medicaid forms —getting through the system.

When you make an appeal for help to a social service agency, they will try to answer your immediate questions and will usually assign a social worker to you and your family to help you work out appropriate solutions. In some instances, the social worker will be the case manager, bringing in other specialists as required. The relationship can be effective if you know how to work together.

Private-Practice Social Workers

Social workers in private practice may prove as helpful as those practicing in the nonprofit agencies if they're experienced in this field. They may also allocate more time to you. When you interview a private counselor, be sure he or she has the professional expertise you are seeking and that you are compatible before you enter into any costly arrangements. Understand beforehand exactly what service this person will offer to you and how much it will cost. For instance, if it involves finding a companion or housekeeper for your elderly relative, ask what will happen in terms of replacement or costs if the selected employee doesn't work out. If it involves help with nursing home placement, know what further services to expect if your parent isn't accepted or if you're unhappy with the choice. If you need someone to help you manage the various aspects of your problems, a private practitioner can act as a case manager.

What You Should Expect from a Social Worker

- an attitude of warmth and understanding, listening and accepting; professional knowledge of and experience with human behavior and family relationships; training and experience in gerontology, or the processes and problems associated with aging; knowledge of and access to the resources that provide solutions
- skilled and sensitive questioning to help you to describe the situation accurately
- help in getting through bureaucratic channels, establishing entitlements and benefits, and gaining admission to special programs, residential facilities, and institutions
- direct consultation with the family as a unit and the individual members concerned

- help in putting everything together and making a workable plan
- emotional support and reassurance when you're taking actions that may be necessary but are painful

A social worker should not:

- make your decisions for you or in other ways take over your life
- sit in judgment on whether what you are doing is morally good or bad
- be cold and officious, or "screen you out" without referring you to a person or agency better equipped to provide the service you need

What a Social Worker Should Expect from You

- as clear and objective a description as you can provide of the particular circumstances of your parent's life and the reasons you are seeking help
- an accurate outline of your parent's financial, health, and living conditions
- an honest description of your feelings about your parent and his or her situation: misgivings, guilts, reluctance, anger, or frustration; your expectations of yourself; the expectations of others
- as objective an assessment of your parent's personality as you are capable of providing and your perception of what you believe he or she would prefer and what his or her reactions are to the current situation
- an honest statement of what you wish to accomplish with the social worker's assistance as well as your assessment of the feelings and attitudes of other concerned and involved family members

- willingness to include in the consultation the older person whose life and problems are the focus of your discussion, either separately or together with you, so long as your parent is competent, able to participate in decisions and solutions, and wishes to be included
- the understanding that the social worker cannot solve the problem immediately unless it is a routine matter to which there is a simple solution

Seek Help Before the Crisis Comes

Most people don't ask for help until they're in a crisis or are frustrated and fed up. Then they want immediate action and total solutions. This usually isn't possible or reasonable. Many social agencies have crisis intervention services, but it's better if you anticipate problems and begin to explore possible solutions with a professional counselor well before the problem becomes acute.

As William Dickey, supervisor of services for the Aging Unit of Catholic Charities in New York, points out:

> Typically we're called in when the older person has fallen, broken a hip, and then the family is thrown into the social service system. Families are spread out these days. The layer of support seems much thinner to many of us working here in the cities. People are probably just as responsible or irresponsible as they've ever been, but they do seem farther away. It would just be better if they gave some thought ahead of time to preparing for dealing with problems. Trying to anticipate is a hard thing to do. It's hard for families, it's hard for individuals to look ahead, to plan for a time when they may not be able to do for themselves what they can do today.

Obviously, you can't anticipate an accident, a heart attack, or the onset of cancer or a disabling stroke. But you can plan for the possibility of an emergency, and learn the names and locations of the people and facilities that will help if an emergency occurs. The social workers at the social service agencies or Area Agency on Aging can help you make a start.

USING THE TELEPHONE BOOK

Different communities have different names for the agencies serving the needs of families and their aging parents. In general, you will find government agencies in the blue pages, private and not-for-profit social service agencies in the white and yellow pages.

In the Blue Pages Look here for village, county, state, and United States government and agency offices: Agency, Commission, or Office on Aging; Social Services; Community Service; Health; Human Resources; Housing and Community Development; Welfare; Office of Consumer Affairs; State Ombudsman; Elderly Assistance Programs; Veterans Affairs.

In the White Pages Look here for names of social service agencies such as Family Service Agency of (name of city or county); Community Service Society; Catholic Charities Family and Community Service; Jewish Family and/or Community Service; Lutheran, Methodist, and other Protestant agencies (by denomination); Mental Health Association; Salvation Army; American Red Cross; Visiting Nurse Association; Volunteers of America.

In the Yellow Pages Look here for Adult Care Facilities, Home Health Services, Homes for the Aged, Retirement Home and Continuing Care Communities, Senior Citizens Service Organizations, Senior Citizens Homes, Social Service Organizations, Nursing Services, Nursing Homes.

Help for specific services may be listed in different ways. For example, for legal help you might need to look in different sections for the state or county attorney's office, the corporation counsel in your city, the local or state bar association, a

Legal Aid bureau, or a list of private attorneys. There's more detailed information in later chapters and in the Appendix about how to find a variety of assistance.

MEALS FOR THE HOMEBOUND OR LONELY

There are all kinds of reasons why older people who can afford to eat three good meals a day don't, but one of the major reasons is their tendency to make do with less and less when they are eating alone.

Fortunately, most communities now offer help in two ways: through home delivery of Meals on Wheels for the frail, handicapped, and homebound, and through meals at a community center for those who can leave their homes. Neither has an income eligibility requirement.

The local Area Agency on Aging can tell you how to arrange for home-delivered meals, or you can check your local telephone directory, a nearby senior center, your religious leader, or the local Y. These meal programs are often supported by both federal and local funds. There's a modest charge for those who can afford to pay, but frequently the state will pay part of the cost. Food Stamps can be used to pay for these meals. Sometimes Meals on Wheels delivers two meals at noon—a dinner to be eaten hot on delivery and a cold supper for the evening. Sometimes only one meal is delivered. Meals on Wheels will even deliver a meal to the older person who has someone at home to provide care, thus relieving the caregiver of that responsibility for a portion of the week.

Communal meals, offered through the National Nutrition Program for the Elderly, are for the older person who is capable of leaving home and who needs and can enjoy the social exchange that takes place. People who can afford to or wish to can contribute to the price of the meal. "That place has saved my life," says one Nyack, New York, woman, who goes whenever possible, not only to eat a meal with friends but to help prepare and serve it as a volunteer. She contributes a dollar or so for each meal she eats. "I have somewhere to go and people to talk to. My daughter was hospitalized and I couldn't go for two weeks; when I returned they all said, 'Ida, we missed you so.' It means everything to me to know there are people there who care what happens to me and who enjoy my company as much as I do theirs."

The solid meal once a day provides needed nourishment for the solitary older person whose interest in cooking has waned. The communal setting stimulates enjoyment of eating. Administrators of the nutrition programs report that about one-third of those who enjoy communal meals are above the poverty level. There are even a few lonely millionaires. The meals are provided in a variety of places—schools, churches, senior citizens' centers—in order to make them easily accessible. Often some form of sponsored transportation will bring the older people to the dining place and then take them home. In some communities the local newspaper features the weekly menus at various locations.

A "market on wheels" brings the supermarket to the older person who can't get to a store to shop. A truck, its shelves and bins stocked with all kinds of food, services neighborhoods where there are heavy concentrations of older inhabitants. There may be one where your parent lives.

Surplus food programs sometimes make quantities of food such as cheese available to the elderly at no charge. This bounty empties overstocked warehouses and provides nutrition simultaneously. If money for food is a problem for your parent, be sure to inquire about this at the local senior center or agency on aging.

HELP IN THE HOME

One of the most common needs of older people is for help in their homes. For example, your parent may need someone to come in for several hours at a time to do the marketing, some cooking, and a few household or personal chores. Many communities and agencies provide such chore and helping services. In some cases, senior citizens themselves help those less fortunate. Call the local department of social services or human resources or the local office on aging for information. Medicaid sometimes provides housekeeping services in addition to medical services to help keep people out of institutions. If your parent's income is too high to qualify, private agencies can usually provide these services for a fee.

If your parent is independent and able to live at home without help but is lonely, he or she may benefit from a friendly telephone call or a visitor on a regular basis or from time to time—something almost any community can supply. Volunteer workers in senior centers, many church and fellowship groups, and Red Cross units are organized to do this. You can arrange for someone to telephone your parent daily or every few days through a telephone reassurance program, and for someone to visit once or twice a week through a friendly visitor's program. The local Area Agency on Aging can help you arrange for this kind of reassurance.

Many public library systems will deliver books, records, and paintings to the homebound.

There may be special radio programming with which your visually handicapped parent can connect. These bring news and features to those who can't watch television or read newspapers. National Public Radio has programs in which books, plays, or articles are read to listeners. Many communities have special television programs for the deaf, and many regular TV programs are captioned for the deaf.

To satisfy your frail parent's need for social contact and recreation, a companion can be employed on a part-time or full-time basis, to read aloud, play a game, write a letter, or escort your parent outside the home.

HOME CARE

Personal care, a part-time nurse, or full-time nursing care at home may permit your parent to continue to live at home in familiar surroundings. Home care can be helpful to you, but it can also be hazardous to your pocketbook and peace of mind. Before you go this route, there are important things for you to know that can make a difference in quality, costs, and in how satisfied you and your parent will be as a result of the experience.

Definitions

Because of the urgent needs for care of an increasingly old and frail population, thousands of agencies have sprung up to supply personnel for various levels of home care tasks. Efforts to regulate the amount of public money being spent on home care have given birth to a flood of rules and regulations governing home care, and private insurers are tightening their reimbursement requirements as well. Home care is now a billion-dollar industry with very specific definitions.

Home care is described by the National Association for Home Care as including "a variety of services viewed from a broad perspective. These include: skilled nursing, occupational therapy, physical therapy, speech therapy, medical social services, physical care, nutritional/dietary services, meals at home, homemaker services, home health aide services, respiratory therapy, I-V therapy, medical supplies, drugs, biologicals, medical appliances, respite care, adult daycare, case management, and a variety of other supportive services."[1]

The duties of *home health aides* are now very specifically defined by various reimbursement agencies and may vary in different localities. They usually include some help with bathing, dressing, and personal needs and may include light nursing services. *Homemaker services* include shopping, cooking, and general housekeeping chores and may include help with dressing but do not include nursing duties. A *companion* may shop, cook, take the older person out for a walk, to a social gathering, or to a recreational activity, and supervise a bath but won't give physical care. Companions aren't usually covered by entitlements or insurance. Fees for these levels of care are approximately the same and depend on the going rate in the locality.

A *licensed practical nurse* (LPN) will give injections and medications and usually will cook for the client but not for the family if others are in residence. An LPN will be more knowledgeable medically than the kinds of helpers described above, be more sensitive to the client's health condition and any changes that may occur, and can discuss this with the doctor. Naturally the fee for an LPN is higher. A *registered nurse* will provide only skilled nursing services and may be essential for certain acute situations or to provide those services otherwise only available in hospitals or skilled nursing homes. Fees are very high.

The Visiting Nurse Association (VNA), in existence since the turn of the century, is a national, voluntary, nonprofit agency whose services include home nursing and health care. The VNA charges a fee, but sometimes this is covered by entitlements, or the patient pays only a part of it.

Responsible Agencies

To secure homemakers, home health aides, or professional health care services at home, you can look in the yellow pages or ask for help through a social service agency or the Area Agency on Aging. You can also call or write one of the national associations that have state or local affiliates for information about home services in your location (see Appendix).

In any case, you will want to be sure that the agencies you are dealing with meet the standards of some responsible group or authority. This is somewhat difficult since standards are not universally applied. The National Association for Home Care (NAHC) includes organizations that represent both nonprofit and commercial homemaker or health aide agencies. The nonprofit agencies, grouped in the National HomeCaring Council Division of the Foundation for Hospice and Homecare, accredits agencies that meet their standards, and the names are available to consumers through NAHC. The profitmaking agencies belong to Home Health Services and Staffing Associates. They also list their membership, available through NAHC, and are in the process of setting standards. Each of these groups will try to help you find a reputable agency. But many agencies do not belong to them. (See Appendix under Home Care.)

There are other concerns: some but not all states have licensing requirements for various home care workers. Professional accreditation and/or licensing requirements exist for some but not all professional health care personnel. Nurses and speech, physical, occupational, and respiration therapists may be individually licensed but work for agencies that are neither licensed nor accredited.

What to Expect

The American Bar Association Commission on the Elderly in its 1986 report to the House of Representatives Select Committee on Aging called the quality of home care in the United States a "black box"—"an unknown both to the consumer and to policy-makers."[2] The dedicated, loving, responsible person you are looking for may or may not exist where your parent lives. Instead you may find that widely advertised agencies are providing minimal training to a large number of people who may or may not show up and who may or may not be kind, considerate, trustworthy, and responsible. The agency may promise you that if one doesn't come, someone else will. To the frail and dependent elderly who have a difficult time adjusting to strangers, a stream of "someone elses" makes life hell, as anyone who has been through it will tell you.

Ben Warach, whose agency, JASA, administers the largest home care program in the country for the New York City Department for the Aging, says:

> There is no substitute for the personal care and concern of the family, no matter how much one pays for the service. If you work through personal care agencies, work is supposed to be supervised by the agency. The worker is presumed to have had at least one week of training. If this training doesn't result in satisfactory performance, the agency is supposed to supply a replacement. All this must be carefully discussed and agreed upon in advance, and even then it is up to the family to see to it that what is promised actually takes place. Many find these arrangements honored in the breach.

Difficulties, moreover, are not caused by the helpers alone. Resentful, hostile, or paranoid older people may fire the people you have hired, no matter how nice and responsible they are: "It's too expensive. I don't need anyone here. She steals. She doesn't do anything except look at TV. She's nasty. I don't like the way she cooks." These are among the common complaints you may be hearing from your needful parent. He or she may be absolutely right or absolutely wrong. How can you tell? And if your parent doesn't complain, how do you know he or she is not being terrorized by the aide and is afraid to complain? You must be constantly vigilant, pay unexpected calls, help establish a trusting relationship—and keep your fingers crossed. You may have to try several different people before you've made the best choice, and no matter how satisfied you and your family are with your selection, be sure you have made arrangements for emergency backup help.

The Omnibus Reconciliation Act of 1987 established a set of rights for recipients of home care provided by home health agencies certified by Medicare or Medicaid. These rights are similar to those described for nursing home patients in chapter 5. (Also, see the Appendix for the Home Care Bill of Rights prepared by the National HomeCaring Council and Better Business Bureau.) Remember that it will take several years for this federal legislation to be put in place. It puts providers on notice that they can be punished for violations, but it really does not relieve you of your continuing need to pay close attention to the people who come into your parents' home and to the details of how they assist your mother or father at home. Your Area Agency on Aging can tell you how to proceed if you wish to complain.

If you are about to embark on a period of securing home care for your parent or other elderly relative, know what you are getting into. Ask clear questions about the entitlements from the social worker or hospital discharge person with whom you are dealing, and discuss the possible alternatives. Find out ahead of time what regulations pertain to your situation. If you don't understand what you are being told, persist politely in asking for an explanation that you *can* understand.

Choosing an Agency: Questions to Ask

The National Association for Home Care suggests the following questions to help you decide whether a particular agency is for you:

- How long has this agency been serving the community?
- Does my physician know the reputation of this agency?
- Is it certified by Medicare?
- Is it licensed by the state?
- Does the agency provide written statements describing its services, eligibility requirements, fees, and funding sources?
- Does it protect its workers with written personnel policies, benefit packages, and malpractice insurance?
- Does a nurse or therapist conduct an evaluation of your needs in the home? What is included—consultations with family members? with the patient's doctor? with other health professionals?
- Is the plan of care written out? Does it include specific duties to be performed, by whom, at what intervals, and for how long? Can you review the plan?
- Does the plan provide for the family to undertake as much of the care as is deemed practical?
- What are the financial arrangements? Can you get them in writing, including any minimum hour or day requirements and any extra charges to be involved?
- Does the professional supervising your home care plan visit the home regularly? Are your questions followed up and resolved?

- What arrangements are made for emergencies?
- What arrangements are made for patient confidentiality?
- Will the agency continue service if Medicare or other reimbursement sources are exhausted? Under what terms?[3]

The Better Business Bureau and National HomeCaring Council have published *All About Home Care: A Consumer's Guide*, which you can purchase through the National Association for Home Care (see Appendix under Home Care). It is full of excellent tips to guide you through this maze.

TRANSPORTATION HELP

Local governments and church and other groups offer a variety of transportation services to the aged. Many communities have a dial-a-bus or dial-a-cab service for older people, and a telephone call in advance will bring transportation to the door. There may be regularly scheduled minibuses following planned routes to take older people for weekly shopping and recreational excursions and visits to senior centers. Volunteer drivers may chauffeur for visits to doctors and other necessary trips, by appointment. In some instances these programs have been curtailed because of insurance and liability considerations. Check in your locality for their current status.

Some communities have medicabs, health cabs, or invalid coaches, vehicles specially outfitted to permit a person in a wheelchair to be rolled in directly. They may have automatic lifts or steps so that the handicapped can enter without difficulty. Some big city buses are similarly equipped, owing to federal laws mandating equal access for handicapped persons. Hospitals and rehabilitation centers, the Red Cross, or a volunteer ambulance corps may offer these vehicles. Be sure to check on the availability of this kind of service before you or other family members engage in cumbersome lifting for a handicapped older person.

SENIOR CENTERS

There are thousands of senior citizens' centers all over the country. Equipped originally to provide social and recreational opportunities, they are now organized in most instances to serve as multiservice centers for older people. They offer everything from the ubiquitous bingo game to organized travel, from medical to nutrition services, from supervising medication to monitoring blood pressure, from counseling to education, from social services to legal services, from volunteer activities to paid job connections.

Senior centers may be located in freestanding buildings of their own, in churches, schools, local recreation department buildings, apartment houses, or extensive residential complexes. Look in the phone book under Senior Citizens' Centers or call the local office on aging to find a center convenient to your parent.

Older people whose energy, abilities, and social needs require continuing outlets can find fulfilling activities and companionship at these centers every day of the week. In more elaborate centers you will see artists and sculptors, photographers, wood carvers, poets, and musicians along with sewing and quilting, knitting and carpentry buffs. Some centers sponsor food-buying coops. Some sponsor lectures and courses in a variety of subjects. Museum trips, theater and opera, and trips abroad are on the schedule for one large city group, while a rural center promotes snow-shoveling programs, friendly visiting, card games, and regular trips to nearby metropolitan centers for educational and cultural programs.

"It's my lifeline," said one user of a senior center, and many of her fellow members feel the same way. Whatever a person's interests and preferences, there is likely to be a senior center that can provide stimulating social and recreational activity as well as on-site professional service for particular problems.

DAY-CARE CENTERS AND DAY HOSPITALS

Only a decade ago there were scarcely twenty-five centers in the nation to which families could bring the frail and ill elderly for recreational, medical, and therapeutic services: places where the older person could be safely cared for while the family caregiver had respite. There are currently about 850. Most are freestanding, but others are situated in nursing homes, hospitals, senior centers, board and care homes, senior housing, and mental health centers. They are a major source of help to the elderly and their families. Most participants are over 65; the average age is 74.

Betty Ransom, coordinator of the National Institute on Day Care, a constituent unit of the National Council on Aging, describes what a good adult day-care center should include in its programming:

- *Social stimulation* through activities with others. For example, it may offer programs such as a trip to the zoo, a walk through the neighborhood, a trip to the supermarket for shopping, or a visit to the swimming pool. These are not random, unplanned events but are designed to help the person function better, to maintain better health or some independent function as long as possible. People have a snack, lunch, even dinner together. It is a time to be stimulated by others, to talk together. All this overrides the social isolation of the person at home.
- *Individual health services.* The client's health and behavior are monitored, blood pressure is taken, medication dispensed. A plan of care, health education and individual exercise program is designed for the individual's needs. Staff is in a position to bring changes in the client's status to a doctor's attention and help the family work with the physician. A few centers have a physician on the regular staff; most have a doctor on call. Physical, occupational, speech, and other ap-

propriate therapies, and sometimes diagnostic services, are available on site or are accessible to clients.

- *Recreation* is an extremely important ingredient in a good adult day-care program. If you are visiting a facility and observe a vigorous program of singing, dancing, and music in action, this is a sign of a good program.
- *Activities of daily living* need to be bolstered. The center should help the clients perform for themselves as much as possible the tasks of eating, bathing, and dressing. Some help participants do their own laundry.

Costs

The cost, on a national average, is about $30 a day. Attendance may vary from two to five days a week. Less than two days, says Ransom, does not afford the older person the opportunity to take advantage of the program, or make it possible to gain from the restorative therapies. The desirable amount of time for the client to spend at the adult day-care center should be arrived at as a joint decision of the family and staff. On a long-term basis, patients may stay a few months or a few years. Discharge usually comes as a result of death, institutionalization, moving to another location, or because the costs are unaffordable. Participation may be reimbursed, depending on the state in which you live, through Medicaid or other programs. "The poor do get help," says Ransom. "The rich who can afford day-care attendance often prefer to hire help at home. If not bed-bound, the more affluent person might nevertheless be better off at an adult day-care center, because participation overcomes social isolation and provides more stimulation than staying at home with a housekeeper." The middle-income family has the most difficulty in meeting the financial burden of adult day-care and therefore suffers the greatest stress managing care for an impaired parent. Given the burden and the need for respite, the decision in such families is how to use their available resources to greatest advantage. It is a tough decision.

When Is Day-Care Appropriate?

It is time for you to investigate the possibilities of day-care in your vicinity when you begin to realize that serious help for your parent is necessary or when:

- the activities required to provide such care are so time-consuming for you that they are incompatible with other family requirements, such as employment, children, or another sick member needing atttention
- the physical burdens of lifting a patient who has had a stroke or suffers some other handicap become too onerous
- the older person is suffering a depression or other mental illness with which you and others in the family are unequipped to deal
- you observe a gradual deterioration in the older person for which you need help
- there is a sudden and possibly short-term need following an acute illness. The hospital discharge planner may suggest to you that, following discharge, a day-care center is the best place for this patient
- a chronic illness has gone on for so long and the patient's deterioration has been so gradual that your increasing burdens have become overwhelming

Says Ransom, "Often, the family physician may not even know that day-care is available. But a telephone call to your local Area Agency on Aging or the county health department, the local senior center, or the social services department in your community will tell you whether there is a day-care center available for you."

Before you commit yourself, inquire about the facility, make an appointment to visit, and bring your elderly relative with you if this is possible. Some day-care centers require the client to appear for the first visit, others will talk with you first and then schedule an appointment with the potential participant. In some cases, the staff social worker will visit the older person at home to see how and whether adult day-care can help.

Sometimes an older person will not be admitted; for example, an Alzheimer's patient may be too far advanced for this setting or at too early a stage to require day-care (see chapter 9). The potential participant may be unmanageable and incontinent or exhibit behavior that is too disruptive or can be harmful to others. Most participants, says Ransom, can handle their own toileting, even if they require a little assistance. In some centers incontinent patients may be admitted. People who are unable to transfer themselves in or out of wheelchairs, given a little assistance, as to sit at a table or to use the toilets, might not be admitted. Those with communicable diseases will not be admitted. Usually a medical examination is required for admission.

Adult Day-Care Checklist

If you believe adult day-care is a possible option for you and your family, investigate the facility most convenient for you, using the following guidelines.

- Check the physical environment for safety, sanitation, and accessibility for the handicapped. Does this center meet local fire regulations and sanitary codes established by the health department? Are there clear emergency procedures? Are doorways wide enough, tables or toilets at the right height for wheelchairs? Check with the office on aging to determine whether your state has established standards for day-care and whether this facility meets them.

- Check the program to determine if it is suitable for your parent's needs.

- Check the qualifications and experience of the staff and how sensitive and caring they are.

- Check the scheduled hours of the facility to be sure they match your needs. For example, if they are from

8 A.M. to 3 P.M. and your job is not over till 6 P.M., this will not help you. Some centers make an effort to vary their hours to suit clients' needs.

- Spend some time at the center to observe what is happening there and get an idea of what to expect. The facility should have a homelike atmosphere, not look like an institution. The staff should be caring and kind, but experienced and knowledgeable. Observe how other clients are faring. Talk to them and ask questions. Drop in at different times of the day. Says Betty Ransom:

> If everyone is having a nap at the same time, or everyone is watching TV incessantly, this may not be where you want your parent to be. A good adult day-care center tries to keep a participant active, not napping during the day, so that he or she is more likely to sleep during the night, when it does the family the most good. An occasional nod-off is to be expected, but not scheduled napping for all. A recliner in one of the common rooms for an occasional rest can be therapeutic, a bed for special situations in a different room is to be expected, but the facility should not look like a ward.

- Remember, if you bring your parent to an adult day-care center, you are paying for a planned program, not for "baby-sitting." The activities are supposed to be relevant to your parent's individual needs.

HOUSING ASSISTANCE

The Area Agency on Aging or local housing authority or community development agency will have information about just what senior housing or alternative housing exists where your parent lives. They can also tell you whether your parent is eligible for a rent subsidy, and what regulations exist to protect older people if the apartment house in which your parent lives is going coop or condo. They can inform you about the status and regulation of life care communities in the state where your parent might like to live. They usually have a directory of all levels and types of special housing for the aged, describing the facilities, requirements, and costs of each particular residence. You may find it worth your while to pay a small fee to a private social worker or one from a social service agency to investigate specialized housing with you and advise you. You might especially want to have this kind of assistance if you're looking into nursing homes. These often appear better on paper than they actually are, and even a visit or a series of visits may not reveal the true quality of the atmosphere and services. Nursing homes are licensed by state departments of health, and your county or city health department will give you a list of all approved homes in its area. Then you can investigate.

You will find more information on housing and residential care in chapters 4 and 5.

LEGAL ASSISTANCE

Older people frequently need the advice of a good lawyer, sometimes more often than they believe. This is particularly true now that their lives are enmeshed with enormous bureaucracies that determine what they are entitled to and whose decisions may be open to question. Because they don't realize the legal implications of their actions, older people may take steps that will have an adverse impact on their income, security, and ability to maintain their independence. They need legal advice for all transactions, such as contracts, leases, and transfers of assets or property, that customarily require an attorney's attention as well as to protect themselves in case of future incapacity or incompetence. For all these reasons, and for events that may unexpectedly occur, you should know whether or not your parent has a personal lawyer and can afford one and where you can find legal assistance when it is required.

Be cautioned that legal advice to the elderly is becoming a specialty; regulations are complex and change frequently. The government, through the Older Americans Act and Legal Services Corporation, and the legal profession, through various national and state bar committees and specialized institutes, have in recent years put in place a number of programs to provide legal assistance to the elderly. They have also sponsored educational and technical assistance programs to enhance the public or private lawyer's ability to deal with the special legal problems of the elderly. Of particular help to lawyers and other professionals serving elderly clients are the Institute on Law and Rights of Older Adults at the Brookdale Center on Aging in New York and the National Senior Citizens Law Center in Washington.

As a result of these efforts, older people and their families can seek and obtain legal services through a variety of sources. *The Law and Aging Resource Guide,* compiled by the American Bar Association's Commission on Legal Problems of the Elderly, lists services and programs available state by state. Many private firms provide free services or reduced fees for the elderly who could not otherwise afford their services. They will help deal with Social Security problems, powers of attorney, administration of small estates, guardianship, and nursing home problems. Many states and large cities publish handbooks on legal problems of the elderly. An example is one prepared by the Bar Association of Baltimore City—*Know Your Legal Rights: A Basic Guide to Laws Affecting the Elderly.*

Each state has a Long-Term Care Ombudsman to protect people in nursing homes, and in highly populated states there are ombudsmen at city and county levels (for more about this, see chapter 7).

Your local Area Agency on Aging, through federally funded programs, now provides some direct legal services for people over 60 who cannot afford private lawyers, and will provide information and referrals for others seeking legal help. Social workers can also help you find and arrange for legal services.

Your congressman has a local office that will help if your problem is with a federal agency.

See Appendix under Legal Problems.

MONEY: SAVING AND SPENDING WISELY

Most retired and older people need to be careful with their money and save what they can. Whatever special breaks are available to your parent in the state where he or she lives, the Area Agency on Aging should know about them. Following are some reminders on money-savers:

- All states give home energy assistance to qualified low-income seniors under a federal program called HEAP. Call the state energy office or the state energy extension service for information. There are also programs that provide minor and emergency home repairs for older people and help modify a home and make it accessible for handicapped individuals, or provide financial assistance for such repairs to those who are eligible. Some Area Agencies on Aging keep lists to match home maintenance chores with willing workers. Check your AAA.

- A number of states give some relief to renters over 65 by protecting them against rent increases if they have limited incomes and/or by providing subsidies to landlords for rentals when the tenant cannot manage the whole rent independently. In some states, landlords are not permitted to evict elderly tenants when buildings are converted to co-ops or condominiums.

- Most states have consumer affairs offices to protect people against fraud, which also provide tips on how to shop wisely to save money. The Extension Service of the Department of Agriculture helps people to plan low-cost nutritious meals and to make budgets.

- Most communities offer older people special discounts on goods and services. In almost a hundred metropolitan areas around the nation, people 60 and older can obtain a senior citizen discount directory, *The Silver Pages*, prepared by Southwestern Bell in cooperation with the National Association of Area Agencies on Aging. Individuals are issued a "passport," which is honored by participating merchants, locally and nationally. The directories also include community resource guides. Many other discounts, such as reduced transit fares and tickets to entertainment events, are available by showing a Medicare card or senior citizen's card available from the local AAA.

- Banks in many areas offer free checking accounts to older people or reduce the minimum balance requirements.
- Pay particular attention to allowable tax deductions for drugs, medications, and medical expenses. These may expand as your parent grows older and requires more medical treatment. Keep receipts for these expenses. Here are a few you may not have thought of: transportation for medical care is deductible and so are health insurance premiums; special telephone equipment for the deaf; the cost of an air-conditioner prescribed by a physician; modifications in the home essential for medical reasons; unreimbursed home health services; and the cost of liquor prescribed by a physician for medicinal purposes.

Savings on Drugs and Medications

Buying medications by their generic names rather than by their trade or brand names can produce savings of up to 50 percent. A generic drug is one called by its basic chemical name instead of by a manufacturer's commercial name. For example, the generic name for Diuril is chlorothiazide; for Valium, diazepam; for Serpasil and Reserpoid, reserpine.

Pharmacists are required by law to give the medicine prescribed by the doctor but may select a generic equivalent, with the same chemicals and same medical effect, unless the doctor asks for a specific brand-name drug. Not every drug has a generic equivalent on the market, because some drugs are protected by patent and available from only one company. About half the drugs on the market now are available generically, however. Your parents should let the doctor know that they want the most effective drug at the best price and ask the doctor to write a prescription permitting substitution of a generic drug product whenever appropriate.

Local pharmacies in many communities offer discounts on all prescriptions for senior citizens, and discounts on other items one or two days a week. They may also offer free blood pressure checkups. Some associations also offer drug-savings programs for members. For example, AARP offers discount prescriptions, vitamins, sick room supplies, and health care products through its mail-order pharmacy service. Finally, some states, such as New York, now have programs to reduce prescription drug costs for qualified older citizens.

HEALTH AND MEDICAL ASSISTANCE

Most communities through their health departments offer some medical assistance in addition to that provided by private physicians and hospitals. Many have hospitals and clinics where patients are treated for no cost or a small fee and that provide free information and services to older people who have chronic conditions. In remote areas the Public Health Service provides medical assistance. Some communities feature free dental care. Multiservice senior centers now offer health and medical assistance as well. There may be mobile medical units in neighborhoods where older people live, which give free general medical checkups and refer patients to doctors for needed care.

See chapters 7 and 8 for more on medical care.

NATIONAL ORGANIZATIONS

Health

Surveys show that most people over 65 have an average of three chronic conditions. The national health agencies devoted to research and dissemination of information about particular diseases, through their local chapters, help with counseling, guidance, and home care and facilitate other aid for patients or their families. For example, the American Cancer Society local units assist with care, rehabilitation services, financial help, counseling, and transportation to and from treatment centers. They also send helpful printed materials on various aspects of the disease and its management.

Other examples of national organizations whose local chapters may be able to help you are: the American Diabetes Association, the National Lung Association, the American Heart Association, the Arthritis Foundation, the American Foundation for the Blind, the Association for the Visually Handicapped, the American Speech-Language-Hearing Association. (See Appendix under National Health Organizations.)

The National Institutes of Health sponsor clearinghouses for information, some with toll-free numbers. From them you can learn more about a variety of mental and physical health problems or you can write the National Institute on Aging for their easily understood materials.

Service

If you can't find a listing for a local organization in your phone book, try the nearest American Red Cross office. The Red Cross also helps in other ways: transportation to doctors, clinics, rehabilitation services, and shopping; Meals on Wheels; friendly visitors to the homebound; telephone reassurance to shut-ins. Some Red Cross chapters give courses to train older people as homemakers, home health aides, companion aides, nursing assistants, and patient-sitters. Your parents may be interested either as potential trainees or as users of trained personnel.

Don't overlook local chapters of fraternal, benevolent, and special interest organizations, whether your parent is a member or not. Many have strong public-service-oriented volunteer programs for medical needs, and you may find help there for transportation, friendly visitors, telephone reassurance, and other needs. For example, check the Elks, Kiwanis, Rotarians, Junior Chamber of Commerce, Lion's Club, Altrusa, and B'nai B'rith.

Organizations of Older People

Many national organizations of retired and older persons offer extensive services and varied programs: travel, discounts, insurance, educational programs, support groups, and information of interest and importance to older people through newsletters, magazines, and books. They also issue directories on housing and nursing homes and provide help with financial planning and other critical matters. These organizations are also advocates for older people and may lobby actively before Congress and state legislatures on national and local issues affecting older people. Membership in any of these groups costs only a few dollars a year.

The American Association of Retired Persons (AARP) has the largest membership and has developed an extensive national network of local chapters. AARP offers a broad spectrum of programs and services. In addition to its travel, cultural, recreational, and insurance programs, AARP fills prescriptions at a discount through its pharmacies and publishes excellent books and guides for older people. The National Council of Senior Citizens is composed of more than 3,000 senior clubs across the country. Among other activities, it publishes a guide to long-term care and informs seniors about how to obtain information and set up a nursing home directory in areas where they live. The Gray Panthers is a highly active organization with chapters in cities across the country. Members are both old and young. They are active lobbyists on matters concerning older people, particularly age discrimination.

Blacks, Hispanics, Asians, and Native Americans are among those who have formed their own organizations to advocate the special needs of their elderly and to provide information and services. Compared to the majority many of these populations have less education and money, have held fewer jobs that offer good pensions and health benefits, and have been unemployed for longer stretches of their adult lives. Their health is poorer, their housing worse, and their life span somewhat less than that of the white majority. Some suffer language barriers that interfere with their access to the services to which they are entitled; some are suspicious and fearful of becoming entangled in bureaucratic processes. Among the organizations that serve the minority communities are the Asociación Nacional Pro Personas Mayores, headquartered in Los Angeles and particularly concerned with the Hispanic aged, the National Caucus and Center on Black Aged, which has been in the forefront of focusing attention on the black elderly, and the National Indian Council on Aging and others concerned with Native Americans. The new influx of Asians has spurred new organizations, such as the National Pacific/Asian Resource Center on Aging, working on behalf of their senior citizens.

The Older Woman's League (OWL) focuses on the middle-aged and older woman, sponsors workshops and training, and is an advocate for women on important issues of income, legal rights, and pension reform.

Anyone interested in working with the professionals in the field of aging can become an individual member of the National Council on the Aging (NCOA) or the American Society on Aging (ASA), both of which provide research information, technical assistance, and resource services to those dealing with the aged. Publications highlight current issues in the field of aging, and national conferences bring thousands of professionals together with legislative and community leaders to disseminate new knowledge and programs for the aging. Both NCOA and ASA welcome older people who enjoy putting their intellectual and creative energies and organizational experience to work in this field.

Mental Health and Counseling Organizations

In well-populated regions, you'll generally find community mental health associations or clinics staffed by trained social workers, psychologists, and psychiatrists to help older people and their families. Psychiatric clinics and special hospitals treat those with mental disorders or serious emotional and behavioral problems. The clinics or hospitals are often associated with a university medical school, but some are free-standing. State mental hospitals are often considered institutions of last resort. The clinics are sometimes supported in part by United Way or United Givers funds, and their fees are based on a sliding scale related to income, or they may be free. You can find them by calling the Mental Health Association, and Area Agency on Aging, the local social services department, or United Way.

Remember that social service agencies may also provide counseling for individuals or groups or refer you to a psychiatrist, psychologist, or social worker in private practice. The local hospital will have a psychiatric staff from whom you can select someone. Or your doctor or your friends can recommend someone to you in whom they have confidence. There are also pastoral counseling centers, staffed by clergy trained in counseling and therapeutic techniques. Some medical insurance policies cover therapy and counseling costs under certain conditions.

Many communities now have a crisis or counseling hot line —a telephone number you can call 24 hours a day, seven days a week for immediate information and help or for actual crisis intervention. This might be listed in the telephone book. If in doubt, call the operator or look in the front of your telephone book for Emergency Services.

Also see the Appendix under National Health Organizations and specific listings.

WIDOWS AND WIDOWERS

Special needs arise when a long-married couple is suddenly separated by death. Grief, loneliness, financial problems, and estate tangles face many newly widowed people, men or women. Many Ys, social service and mental health agencies, and the AARP sponsor support groups for the recently bereaved. Telehone to find a convenient group. The meetings are led by other widows or widowers, and emotional support comes from people who understand what it's like. Some of the groups provide practical help about legal and financial matters, housing decisions, job counseling, and family relationships.

Some local offices on aging have a widowed person's service or a widowed-to-widowed network. The AARP has a particularly good book, *Survival Handbook for Widows and for Relatives and Friends Who Want to Understand,* which might help your widowed parent. This and other booklets and guides will answer many questions on dealing with grief, moving to a new home, and preparing for life without a partner.

See Appendix under Widows.

COMMUNICATION AND ALERT SYSTEMS

Almost all telephone companies can install special devices for people disabled in various ways. For the person with some hearing loss, the phone company will put an amplifier on the receiver, which can be adjusted to various levels. (Portable telephone amplifiers can be purchased at modest prices at some electronic gear shops, which allow the hard-of-hearing to use phones away from home.) A flickering light can be added, also, to attract attention when the bell rings. Telephone bells can be installed in rooms without phones to attract attention. For the completely deaf or the speech impaired, there are now telecommunications devices (TDDs), which permit communication with other TDD users (including other utilities or emergency services) via the telephone lines. The phone receiver fits into an acoustic coupler and a typewriterlike device, and users type messages back and forth. Other arrangements can be made for people disabled in other ways. For example, a paralyzed person might have an open line that is voice activated.

Some states may have a Senior Citizens Hotline, like New York's, which operates toll-free, statewide, Monday through Friday, and is plugged into a tape recorder at other times to answer questions on programs and services.

Alert Systems for Elders Living Alone

One of the great advances in the electronic art now makes it possible for older persons living alone to call for help, or be monitored, through various "alert" systems. By wearing a pendant or bracelet, which requires only the touch of a finger, or having a button to push for help installed on the telephone, an older person in trouble can signal a central station that help is needed. Then a prearranged system of notification to you, another family member, a neighbor, the police, an ambulance, a doctor, or a hospital is put into action so help can arrive quickly. Even if your parent is unable to speak and explain the problem, some systems will, after trying to make voice contact, proceed with the notification. Failing to find a relative, neighbor, or friend, they will call the local police who will break in to discover the problem. If your parent leaves home for more than a day for a vacation or other purposes, it is important to inform the alert service; otherwise they go through their protocol. Also be sure to inform your parent's neighbors or friends about the system. Otherwise they may simply call 911 if an emergency occurs. You may then find your parent in a large city hospital emergency room, awaiting treatment without benefit of his or her own doctor, and your planning will have done no good.

Electronic alert systems vary in sophistication in different localities. Usually there is an initial installation fee and a monthly charge. In some communities they are installed free as a philanthropic service of local organizations. The local AAA will give you the names of companies in your parent's locality from which you can select the system best suited to your parent's needs.

To help strangers help your parent in an emergency, you can tape all pertinent medical information and important telephone numbers on a wall near the telephone, or use the "Vial of Life" kit some supermarkets are offering to the elderly. Included is a Red Cross label to stick on the refrigerator to alert an ambulance driver or paramedic that essential medical information is in a vial taped under a refrigerator shelf, where it doesn't interfere with normal food storage but is instantly available when needed.

Paying Bills: Third Party Notices

The public utilities and other companies that provide essential services to customers will now inform a third party if service is to be shut off for nonpayment of bills. You should arrange for this. For older people who become forgetful, frail, or are hospitalized for a long period and are unable to take care of their financial obligations, a third party program is protection against sudden loss of service. The older person can choose you, a friend, other relative, a church, social service organization, or community group to receive a copy of the warning letter that is sent prior to drastic action. A telephone call, a letter, or a visit to the local offices of the utilities serving your parent will bring you the necessary forms to put the third party program into action. You should also inform the utilities of any special health or life-sustaining devices in use by your parent so that special arrangements can be made should there be a service emergency or a financial problem in continuing service.

RURAL AREA SERVICES

Although a large proportion of the country's aged live in high-population, nonrural states, the proportion of the aged to the general population is greater in rural areas. Many rural expatriates retire from their city jobs to return to their origins, either in or close by their home towns, increasing the presence of the elderly in rural areas. Margaret Carlson, director of the Riley County Senior Service Center in Kansas, says, "More people are coming from California to Kansas than the other way around. We're seeing a return to family roots."

Those elderly who remain, those who return, and those who come to rural areas to live for the first time find that, in addition to a sparse population, rural regions have a great scarcity of doctors and of public transportation, essential needs of the old.

"When rural people are in trouble," says Betty Ransom of the National Council on the Aging, "they can rely on a strong network of informal, neighborly supports. They're noted for this. This may not be enough help for those with severe functional problems. They can't afford good home care, which is virtually nonexistent in these areas anyhow. If necessary, they go to the local retirement home, which tends to be like a real home, not an institution, with a dozen or fewer people in residence, and they receive relatively compassionate care."

The AAAs, the Cooperative Extension Service, and public health nurses combine to provide some supports, but it is still the family and the neighbors who bear primary responsibility for the elderly individual in need of help. "The real fallout of the farm crisis," says Ransom, "is that businesses in the nearby towns are failing. People have to travel for services 30 to 50 miles away as local services become scarce. The farm crisis is having a domino effect on a system that was already short on comprehensive services for the aged."

Nevertheless, rural counties do have some social, medical, and volunteer support services, even though they may not be so numerous or accessible as their urban and suburban counterparts. In some rural communities, adult day-care is beginning to be available, but it is expensive. The Area Agency on Aging may cover a broad territory, or there may be only one covering the entire state. The AAA will then send teams to various locations in the course of a month to provide rural citizens with as many of the basic services as possible, or arange with some local organization to provide the nutrition program, or provide transportation. Mental health services are sparse and insufficiently staffed, and more stigma is attached to psychological or psychiatric problems than in urban areas, though this is said to be changing.

If you have a parent in a rural community who insists on remaining there, investigate what is readily available so that you can get help on an emergency basis if necessary, and prepare for ongoing help if that is the need and it is available. Know the people you can count on for cooperation. Keep a list of telephone numbers handy.

Specific help for specific problems can be sought from:

- the Area Agency on Aging. They will tell you what is available in the older person's community or nearby, and may help you with setting up a support system, if necessary.
- your parent's religious leader. This person can perhaps help you decide whether your parent's independent stance should be honored or whether the time has truly come for you to persuade your elder to move into town, into a supervised residential setting or near you. This person may also be able to arrange for an able parishioner to make regular calls or visits to your weakened parent, perform some housekeeping or chore services, or even sleep overnight. The church is a strong connection in rural areas.
- the county social services, human resources, or welfare department, for information about Medicare, Medicaid, SSI, Food Stamps, and local supporting services
- the county health department for special care and help in your parent's home. Some rural counties with populations over 600 have a comprehensive health center. The county health department and the AAAs should know about state-licensed nursing homes in the area.
- farmers' organizations such as the Grange. Through its thousands of chapters, the Grange conducts a varied program of volunteer activities for the elderly, including transportation, reassurance telephone calls and friendly visitors, Meals on Wheels, and clinics for eye and hearing tests. Green Thumb, administered by the Farmer's Union, trains older people and finds jobs for them as homemakers and nurses' aides, carpenters, renovators, and refurbishers.

Cooperative Extension Service

The rural elderly can receive a great deal of help from the U.S. Department of Agriculture's Cooperative Extension

Service, with which they have been dealing in one way or another for most of their lives. The well-trained and competent home economists who are part of the Extension Service have been working increasingly on programs for older people.

The home economist is a good source for almost any information you may need if you are concerned about an older person. Extension staff will help you find the network of public and private services in the rural areas where your elders live. They organize and sponsor support groups and respite care workers and provide educational programs for the aging and their children; for example, Growing Older in Rural America: A Preretirement Planning Program for Farm Couples, with materials on financial planning, family records, and turning the farm over to the next generation. The emphasis in educational programs varies from state to state, depending on local citizens' needs.

In addition, local units of the National Extension Homemakers Council, Inc., an organization of volunteer women advised by Cooperative Extension Service home economists, often augment local meal and transportation programs for the aged. Texas and Georgia provide training for family members and volunteers or paid workers through an Adult Sitter program. Missouri trains Extension Homemaker Club members and others to serve as information sources for caregivers.

FOLLOW-UP

Wherever your parent lives, follow-up is essential for the services you want and those you actually obtain.

Bureaucratic agencies are sometimes rigid, often disorganized, and these days frequently understaffed. Employees might not look for loopholes or the small print unless you prod them. If a Social Security spokesperson tells you your mother doesn't qualify for certain benefits, don't give up until you have talked to a second and perhaps a third person. Your parent's physician may have forgotten to sign the forms required to obtain certain services, or the clerk or nurse may not have mailed them. People are busy and need to be reminded.

Push for everything you would like to have. After you're told that you'll have it, watch to be sure you get it. Don't be afraid "they" will think you are a pest if you persist in trying to get what you're entitled to.

Solid information is your best protection. Know what is available for your elders. Know what his or her entitlements are. Learn how to appeal for what is rightfully theirs. Don't be intimidated. You don't have to be obnoxious to assert your family's rights, but you don't have to be a pussycat, either.

SELF-HELP GROUPS

Taking charge of your own life is a current theme of American life. When in trouble, we are urged by professionals to use our own resources, find others in similar circumstances, share information, and develop our own solutions insofar as possible rather than to rely solely on professional and/or government assistance. Controlling one's own life is a powerful way to enhance one's own life. For good results, however, it is essential to have accurate information on which to act. And it is important to know the limits of your own resources, and when to call on others for guidance and help.

The Area Agency on Aging can direct you to the relevant local groups for your parents' or your own needs. A directory, *Self-Care and Self-Help Groups for the Elderly,* published by the National Institute on Aging, is available to you. The Public Affairs Committee and the Clearinghouse on Self-Help are other good sources of information about groups to join or use as models for initiating your own group.

RESPITE

> **Respite** *A temporary cessation or postponement, usually of something disagreeable; an interval of rest and relief.* —American Heritage Dictionary

Most of this chapter has been directed toward helping you find the information or specific services you need to help your parent live at home despite problems. This section is for you, the person or persons providing the care, sometimes at great cost to your own lives. A life of sacrifice is what some people expect of themselves and what some parents expect their children to endure, as they may have had to in their own time. Memories of selfless devotion, of the overburdened wife catering to her mother-in-law, of the spinster daughter shunning marriage to care for her aging parents—these collective memories trickle down through the generations and now nourish our guilt if we do less. But in the past it was a rare individual who lived years beyond the norm. The life expectancy of adults was so short that few children had to care for aged parents for more than a year or two.

Today, the period of old age has lengthened. While most acute illnesses have been tamed by antibiotics and hi-tech interventions, the pain and deficits associated with chronic illnesses and the explosion of such devastating diseases as Alzheimer's have imposed a new period of prolonged caregiving on American families. Whoever assumes prime responsibility for this care needs relief and respite.

Programs and services are springing up throughout the country directed at relieving the pressure on the pivotal family member who is the caregiver. For example, the National Council of Catholic Women (NCCW) respite program works through individual Catholic dioceses to back up local programs and provide training assistance for respite workers. The workers are all volunteers, trained to understand the processes of aging and to learn a few technical skills, such as how to lift a frail old person and transfer that person from a chair or bed. They do not provide health care services. When grateful caregivers give them some donation in gratitude, they're urged to turn this money back to the respite program to increase the pool and quality of other volunteers. In general, their respite programs flourish in smaller communities. There are fewer volunteers in the large cities. The volunteers are men or women of different faiths; their services are available to the entire community, not just to Catholic parish members.

Other respite programs, also flourishing, are based on respite work for pay. For example, in California, the San Mateo Senior Corporation, a technical service agency, developed respite programs for five area hospitals. The training program initially focused on a small number of local people but quickly tripled in size and has steadily increased since. Your Area Agency on Aging can inform you about the particular options for respite in your community. After January 1990, Medicare will cover up to 80 hours annually for allowed cost of respite for caregivers. Check to see if you're eligible.

Respite services include:

- volunteers organized through the Area Agency on Aging or a local community group such as a church auxiliary to come into your home for a designated period so that you can leave
- private families who take an older person into their own homes for a few hours, a day, or a week for a fee so that you can have private time for yourself
- adult day-care, which combines respite for the caregiver with structured programs for the older person
- respite units in hospitals with a surplus of beds where a frail older person may stay for a designated period, usually not more than two weeks; rates vary with the locality
- special respite houses established through public or private efforts where an older person can come for short or longer stays while the family has relief

Take advantage of what is available to you.

THREE

IMPROVING THE QUALITY OF YOUR PARENT'S LIFE

For a study conducted some years ago in San Francisco, a group of elderly people listed the factors they believed influenced their morale. While these factors may not coincide precisely with your parents', they can provide clues to improving the quality of your parents' lives.

Factors conducive to *high* morale, in order of their importance, were entertainment and diversion, socializing, productive activity, physical comfort (other than health), financial security, mobility and movement, health, and stamina.

The most significant causes of *low* morale were financial or physical dependency, physical discomfort or sensory loss, loneliness, bereavement or loss of nurturance, boredom, inactivity, immobility and confinement, mental discomfort or loss, loss of prestige or respect, fear of dying, and problems of others.[1]

It may be beyond your ability, no matter how much you care, to change some of these factors in your parent's life. But there are things you can do, some of them seemingly small, to raise your mother's or father's morale.

COMMUNICATIONS

Your attitude, of course, comes first. How you go about offering help will have a great deal to do with maintaining your parent's self-respect and dignity. Try to see things from your parent's point of view. Respect your parent's knowledge and experience. The best-intentioned adult child sometimes has an insulting way of talking down to a parent.

As the deficits of aging take their toll on your elder's hearing or eyesight, you may find it increasingly difficult to convey your concern and desire to help without offense. It isn't easy to sound kind and considerate when you are raising your voice to be heard. Your concern may come across as anger, and this won't help the situation. Your parents don't like peremptory directions any more than you do.

Communications Breakdowns

All of us have experienced communications breakdowns in talking to other people. Sometimes our thoughts are elsewhere. Sometimes we truly don't hear something said. But sometimes we don't want to hear it; it is too painful or embarrassing. These conditions are especially common in conversations between a parent and adult child.

The way you talk and listen to your parent is very important. It is easier if you have been accustomed to frank and open dialogue since you were a child; you're probably continuing this pattern now that you're an older adult. So when your parent says "I don't feel well," you know that he or she really doesn't feel well, and you can sympathize and make suggestions. You know the reported discomfort is not a reflection of your parent's anger with you or a device to gain your attention or sympathy or to make you feel guilty.

Bad communications between parent and child probably start early in the child's life. Sometimes they never get better. Kids typically start to screen their parents out of their private thoughts and lives in early adolescence. Then, unaccustomed to treating their parents as adults with the usual range of adult feelings, adult children's conversation may remain perfunctory. As one old woman said to her daughter, "I much prefer to talk to you when Judy is with us. When she's here you tell what really happened and how you felt. It's much more interesting than when you tell the same story to me."

Perhaps your mother asks question after question about you, your spouse, and your children. She's prying, you tell yourself, just the way she always pried about your friends and your dates and your life. You clam up or you get angry. Perhaps your father complains ceaselessly about his health. You're bored and don't respond or you get angry. Beneath their monologues lie real fears that their futures may be dark and an almost frantic need for reassurance and affection from you. They are trying to communicate it.

And if they are silent, no trouble to you, do not take that as a signal that they don't need you or want to hear from you.

Talking to Your Parent

An 85-year-old man was confined to his home. He could walk with difficulty from room to room. Poor eyesight prevented much reading or television, but his mind was keen, his reactions lively. His son, who lived nearby, came to visit at the same time as his daughter, who had driven from a city 250 miles away. The son talked about his wife, his children, about two interesting law cases on which he was working, about several of his office colleagues, about recent encounters with law school classmates his father had known. The father listened, commented, responded, reacted.

"You're marvelous," the sister said to her brother later. "You tell him everything. Why do you do it?" "I'm trying to bring some of the world to him," the brother said. "I know he can't get to it any other way."

You can bring some of the world to your parent too. Talk about the events of the day and of your life that you know will be of special interest. Don't feel you have to shield your parent totally from the problems you or your spouse or children face. By bringing news of your life, you assure your elder that he or she is still needed, still has resources to be a parent, and possibly can even help with your problems.

If he or she is very ill, you might not want to tell distressing news, but otherwise keep your parents abreast of the details of your life. Not to do so is to reinforce their feelings of being old and discarded, useless, out of the action. Even if you try to cover up, your parent, who has known you for so long, will sense when something is troubling you. Not discussing it will only increase his or her uneasiness about what might be wrong. Some very old or ill people will protect themselves from distressing events, detach themselves, and appear to you to be unconcerned. You need not share every pain with them; be sensitive to their needs as well as your own.

If your elder is intellectually impaired, has a poor memory, or has limited ability to deal with information or cope with disturbing events, then impart your information on a selective basis. Figure out what is important to him or her and what he or she needs to know about the world. It's often a good idea, in relationships where the dialogue is so often charged with emotion, to talk about impersonal subjects as much as possible.

Listening to Your Parent

Good listening is a skill. If the talker is a parent whose complaints, worries, nagging, accusations, constant repetitions, or even silence persist, you may wish to cut and run. But if you can concentrate on the reality of your parent's situation and not just on the emotion it generates in you, then you may be able to respond with some suggestions that can improve the situation. Don't allow the conversation to deteriorate into a harangue. Your parent will appreciate being treated as a person, not "just a parent."

Most older people, especially if they live alone, don't have enough relatives and friends with whom to talk. Older people are in jeopardy when they lose their "old-shoe friends," the ones to whom they could pour out their hearts or with whom they could share some happy event. No matter how old one becomes, social interaction with other people is essential for good health—it's as important as taking the right medication at the right hour of the day.

Old people often complain that no one listens to them. If their lives are boring, so is their conversation—often little more than a litany of complaints and grievances. Some of these may well be justified, but they also reflect an increased turning inward. Encourage your parents to talk to you and to have some social contact with others. You can build on their previous interests to help bring some variety to their lives and some new zest to their conversation. If your parent is withdrawing from normal conversation, be sure growing deafness, depression, or illness is not the problem. Then make the extra effort to include your silent elder in family conversations.

When your parents reminisce, don't cut them off. Older people need to go over events that troubled them or that brought them joy. Recapturing parts of their past lives can give meaning to the present one, and if you listen, perhaps to yours as well. Professional staffs working with old people now encourage reminiscence instead of admonishing elders not always to talk about the past. The "life review" carried on through these recollections, says psychiatrist Robert Butler, is a way for a person to validate his or her life. When you listen to your father or mother, you are acknowledging that here is a person of substance, whose life was not useless, whose presence was and is significant. Your listening can be an emotional shot in the arm.

When parents are mentally impaired or very ill, communicating can be difficult. With little or no response to continued remarks or questions, you may become tongue-tied or uncomfortable. But only in extreme cases does a parent not know that his or her child is sitting there, and just the presence of the child, the stroke of a hand, the touch of a kiss, is a satisfaction and a morale builder.

Visiting Your Parent

Visit your parent as you would a dear friend. Bring a small gift sometimes—a newspaper or magazine article, flowers, or some special food. Accept the offer of food or drink. Bring a child with you; bring a friend.

In the course of your visit you may observe that the house is not as tidy as it once was, that the refrigerator needs attention, that the food supply is too heavily weighted in favor of cookies, that fruits or vegetables are in short supply. Your parent is more than a friend. If you notice your formerly immaculate parent living in conditions he or she would have scorned in younger days, then you should consider how you can remedy the situation. Is a little help in order or are there more serious implications that require a physician's attention?

Your parent's feeling in control of his or her own home is essential to maintaining an independent life, so don't poke. If you are sensitive in your approach, your gentle offers of help may be welcomed. If you ask questions that begin "Would you like—" or "May I—" instead of "You should—" or "You had better—," you can help your parent continue to live in an environment that is at once clean and under his or her control. Then you can continue to visit as a guest, with your parent's dignity intact.

Make your parent's visits to your home a special occasion from time to time. Invite other people—your friends, your parent's friends—for lunch or dinner or a holiday celebration. Your guests will enjoy your parent's company—perhaps to your surprise and pleasure—and he or she will enjoy theirs. One 85-year-old woman delighted a dinner party with her comments on Henry Miller's *Tropic of Cancer*, a book banned by the censors in her youth. Don't be surprised if your parent has a few things to say on matters you've never discussed before, because it may never have occurred to you that this parent could share your interest in them.

Conquering Isolation

Television helps older people stay in touch with the world, but you can help even more. Be sure your parent has a good supply of other sources of information and entertainment, especially if it's hard for him or her to get out. You can order newspapers and magazines by mail, subscribe to a book club, and recruit a high school student or a volunteer from the senior center to pick up and return library books. You can spend time together at a ball game, a concert, or a movie or playing cards—doing something that's enjoyable for each of you.

Help your parent stay in touch with other family members. Provide a good supply of birthday cards and note paper and the stamps to mail them. Younger family members and your parent's old friends will enjoy this correspondence. Send your parents an amusing card or gift from time to time to lift their spirits. Remember, there is no such thing as too many pictures of children or grandchildren. Keep them coming. When space to display them becomes a problem, provide photo albums.

Some adult children have gone to great expense to buy a VCR for an aging parent, with the thought of bringing tapes of faraway great-grandchildren or of buying the older person a subscription to an in-home movie series. This is a good idea *only* if your mother or father can learn to operate a VCR. Many a 60- or 70-year-old has found the designations too small to read comfortably even with glasses. For an 80- or 90-year-old, the gift may become a source of anguish instead of pleasure. Better, think of investing in a cable subscription, which can probably be accessed more easily by an older person. You can always bring your own VCR for family videos if you go for a long visit, or save these treats for the time when your parent is visiting in your home.

Try communicating by audio tape recorder. In some ways these tapes provide more real contact than letters and are a boon to those who'd rather talk than write. Assure yourself that the technology will not be a source of stress. If it is unsuitable, take the equipment back home with you. Families everywhere are using tape recorders to make personal oral histories. Older people relish speaking about the past, and younger ones enjoy hearing stories about long ago. If the eldest members of your family are unable to operate the recorder on their own, then use visiting time to tape their recollections, which you can stimulate with provocative questions.

Attractive long-distance telephone rates make it possible to have long telephone visits without too much expense, and a social call rather than just a check-up call will improve your parent's morale immensely.

All forms of communication, continued without too great lapses of time between them, contribute to your distant parent's sense of well-being. Your parent's state of mind will affect yours as well.

When Adult Children Are a Problem to the Parent

Some parents are enjoying the fruits of their lifetime of work and good planning when suddenly everything goes awry. Grandchildren need care, divorce impels a daughter to go back to school, unpaid child support creates a financial crisis, single parents are overwhelmed, jobs are lost, custody cases become ugly—Middletown U.S.A. was never like this. Some older folks may joke about the never-ending stream of crises. "Give me back my empty nest," they cry. But they roll with the punches, see their neighbors in the same fix, and resign themselves to yet another phase of advanced parenthood. They take their grown offspring back into the parental home, help them over the transitions, get them started again, and hope they'll still have time for themselves before they die. They may complain a lot but nevertheless make a positive contribution to a child's life. They may not complain at all but resent the intrusion on what was supposed to be "their time." How they respond to these continuing family challenges is of course different for different people, but there is no question that the continued close involvement with their adult children's lives so often thrust upon them in today's society is not what they expected when they looked ahead to their children's maturity and independence. Don't complain, advises Great-Grandma, you'll have plenty of quiet when you get really old. They wonder.

Some problems are generated by changes in the society; some are peculiar to a particular child's life. Some are beyond the child's control. Some are caused by children who are insensitive to their parents' needs and desires, place their own interests first, haven't a clue to an older person's reduced energy level, and think it's just as easy to chase a 2-year-old at 70 as it is at 35. If you are unwittingly causing your parent undue stress, consider how your problems reverberate in your parents' lives.

Whatever it is that stems from your life and grows as a blight on your parent's life needs to be considered as a family problem, not as your individual problem. What can be changed should be changed. What can't be changed should be faced and decisions made that are the least destructive to all concerned.

MARITAL PROBLEMS

This is a tough and touchy subject.

Increasing numbers of middle-aged and old men are leaving their wives, after years of marriage. Society's pressures to keep families together have loosened, and the divorce rate has zoomed. The tragedy lies in the devastating effects these "liberating" patterns have on many middle-aged and older women. They are frequently left with inadequate income, often without medical or health insurance protection. They may have little marketable work experience. Even middle-class women in these situations are suddenly plunged into the ranks of the poor. In some instances it is the older women who are taking the initiative to leave unsatisfactory marriages, but by and large they are fewer in number and the effects on the men are less economically devastating, even if they are emotionally painful.

You can't change what has already happened, but you can help your mother in this situation by introducing her to one of the newly emerging programs designed for "displaced homemakers." The Older Women's League (OWL), which pioneered these programs, provides a support network for women who need to learn new skills to function independently. OWL has local chapters and a national office in Washington. Other community groups, social service agencies, and the AARP also sponsor special programs for women. If you believe your mother can benefit from participation in such groups, encourage her to take the first step toward her own self-renewal.

Bear in mind that your mother may be too proud or ashamed to discuss her plight with you. Conversely, she may believe it is her children's duty to take over the responsibilities her husband abandoned. If you find yourself in this bind, you will have to use all the resources and counsel available to develop the least destructive life pattern for all the family members involved. If your father has really not been fair or responsible while seeking a new life for himself, and if you cannot persuade him to provide some economic protection for your mother after a long marriage, then you can help her secure legal assistance to assure that the couple's economic resources are fairly divided.

If you are square in the middle of your parent's marital problems or are observing from a distance the fragility or hostility of their relationship, you'll find yourself in a real emotional quandary. There may not be much you can do to change the situation, but sometimes a few tactful suggestions may help. Be a good listener. Don't be judgmental. Ask some questions: Do you really want to live like this? Have you considered talking to a counselor?—others have found this helpful. Perhaps you can help them find some activity or volunteer job each can enjoy without the other. If your father has just retired, your parents may need time apart. Either or both may need to feel useful again and would welcome the opportunity for a part-time or volunteer job. If a lifetime of unresolved marital problems is now bubbling up, you might be able to persuade them to try counseling at a family service agency. Remember, however, that people who are constantly arguing are not always on the road to disaster. Children are famous for not understanding the true basis of their parents' relationship.

Sometimes sharp events—illness, a drop in income, retirement, or other psychological blows—can shock an older spouse into more sensitive and thoughtful behavior toward the other and draw them closer. Sometimes these events can exacerbate the situation, making the spouse less sensitive and more hostile. Then the pot boils.

Sometimes a change in behavior is a sign of a medical problem. "Don't tell me what to do," a man yelled at his wife when she pleaded with him to make a medical appointment. "I'm too busy in my office right now; can't you understand there's nothing wrong with me?" He died of cardiac arrest a week later. "There's nothing wrong with me except your nagging and criticizing," said another man to his wife when she expressed concern about his increasing fatigue. "*You* make me tired." But he was harboring an as yet undiagnosed kidney problem. Any unusual behavior should trigger questions in your mind, not just resentment at the offending person. Physical causes should be ruled out before other factors are assumed.

Sexual difficulties can result from certain medical conditions as well as certain medications. Couples should be cautioned about this by physicians. Understanding all the factors that are affecting their sexual lives is the first step in solving such problems. Sexual desire, activity, and satisfaction can continue until very late in life, for some till the very end of life, bringing rewards comparable in value to those of younger years. If they don't continue, it may be because of mutual agreement, or one partner may be disinterested or impaired, or there may be emotional or physiological impediments that didn't exist before.

It is very unlikely that your parent will voluntarily indicate any sex-connected problem to you, whether it's frustration with an unsatisfying partner or with his or her own performance, but if you pick up any clues in this direction you should explore them further if you are comfortable doing so. Experienced counselors can approach this sensitive subject, or a caring physician can help. With enlightened techniques and understanding, the sex problems of middle and late age can be overcome or ameliorated. But your parents may resist anything you say as an intrusion, and you may just have to sit back, listen sympathetically, and be there to pick up the pieces.

See the Appendix under Sex and Marriage.

MAINTAINING GOOD HEALTH

Wellness, in contrast to illness, has become the focus of national attention in recent years. The aim is to help people feel better, to improve quality of life, to prevent illness, and to reduce the ever-escalating costs of health care. Older people as well as younger ones can gain enormous benefits by participating in one of the many wellness programs available through senior or community centers, hospitals, HMOs, Ys, schools, and places of employment.

Many factors go into maintaining good health. Most of them are simple. Good eating and sleeping habits are basic; appropriate exercise is a vital ingredient; and climate and clothing contribute. Learning how to manage stress, meet the emotional challenges that accompany aging, prevent premature disease, and use medication or drugs judiciously are among the elements of formal wellness programs.

Wellness is not only a state of physical well-being, it is also one's attitude. "How much or what an older person can or should do should be determined only by what that older person thinks or feels, not by the attitudes or strictures imposed by the family," counsels Susan Abbott, former director of health promotion and wellness programs for the National Council on the Aging.

There are strong indications that maintaining a sense of control over one's life enhances good health."There are detrimental effects on the health of older people when their control of their activities is restricted. . . . With increasing age, however, variability in preferred amounts of control also increases, and sometimes greater control over activities, circumstances, or health has negative consequences, including stress, worry, and self-blame," according to researcher Judith Rodin.[2] In other words, there is a delicate balance between recognizing that your parents may be old but are also quite capable and willing to regulate their own lives, and knowing when a point of frailty has been reached where they would prefer that you assume all or some responsibility for important aspects of their lives.

Don't say "Oh, you shouldn't be doing that at your age." What is appropriate is viewed differently at different points on the age ladder. The 25-year-old may well believe that 60 is the end of the road. The 60-year-old may try to stop the 85-year-old from taking much-loved long walks in the rain. Even young physicians are susceptible to this kind of age-behavior blindness. Overheard in a Florida restaurant one evening were three young interns discussing an attending physician in the local hospital: "He had a bypass at 63! Can you imagine? If I were in his position at that age, I'd just throw in the towel. Why go through all that just to try to live a normal life at *that* age?"

What you should be concerned with is how to enhance your mother's or father's life, at whatever age they are. If they haven't already discovered how to keep vigorous and healthy, you can guide them to better nutrition, a reasonable diet, and exercise. Don't assume that they are incapable of working out their own lives as a matter of personal choice, but make your points by relating what you have discovered is useful for you. Find out where a community senior health promotion or wellness program is in progress and arrange a visit there for your parents. If it is appealing, your mother or father may wish to join.

As Susan Abbott points out, "We are just learning what it's like to be old. At the beginning of the century, people got old and died at 45. The current healthy generation of people past 60 is the first such healthy generation in history. They are really pioneers. We don't know enough yet about how to handle this stage of life. If children say 'You shouldn't do that because you're 70 or 80,' they're making assumptions they shouldn't be making. Most older people are healthy, although they may have chronic ailments that may interfere with their total independence."

She illustrates how your attitude and actions can help promote your parents' independence. Suppose your mother has arthritis and complains of problems fetching her pans from a bottom shelf. Finding household help does less to enhance her independence than helping her to rearrange her utensils so they are accessible and encouraging her to participate in an exercise course designed for those with arthritis. Or you can consult her physician to see whether something more can be done to improve her physical condition or whether physical therapy is indicated. The local chapter of the Arthritis Foundation may sponsor a self-help group and provide useful information. Whatever you do, don't rush a feisty parent into being an invalid.

The older relatively healthy people become, the more likely they'll want to continue doing things their way. This may be valid in many cases, but it can be a real health hazard if smoking is the problem. If you can convince your parent to stop smoking, despite a lifelong habit, you will make an enormous contribution to his or her wellness. A good doctor or one of the many stop-smoking groups may make the difference. Don't turn into a nag if your parent refuses to heed yours or others' advice, however. You may be powerless to alter the path of your parent's choices, even when they are destructive. And if your parent has consciously decided to continue enjoying the pleasures of smoking or other frowned-upon habits, despite the risk, remember that autonomy also has benefits and that good relations are sometimes more important than "being right."

See Appendix under Health and Wellness.

NUTRITION

Nutrition and diet are important at any age but even more so for older people, because an inadequate diet can not only reinforce some of the infirmities that tend to come normally with age, but can also produce symptoms that may be wrongfully attributed to the aging process. If your parent's diet has been inadequate over a period of time, behavioral and psychological changes can occur. Marginal malnutrition, resulting from unsatisfactory levels of protein, calcium, vitamins, and other minerals, can cause weakness, irritability and erratic or irrational behavior mimicking senility. A balanced diet can often reverse these symptoms.

Your healthy parent's nutritional needs are basically no different from yours or those of your adult children. You all need a diet that provides a daily balance among the five basic food groups—protein, fruits and vegetables, breads and cereals, milk and cheese, oils and fats—in amounts suitable for your current level of activity. In general, however, older people's calorie intake may need to be reduced to win the war against weight gain, unless their work load or activity level is as high as it has always been. Also, older people sometimes feel more comfortable when they eat smaller quantities of food at a time; smaller meals taken at more frequent intervals make sense for the body whose digestive processes may have slowed down.

With the high cost of food today, many older people feel they can't afford to buy some of the foods that would be most nutritious for them. This is particularly true of protein, which older people require in greater proportion than when they were young. In fact, the elderly suffer more from protein deficiency than any other deficiency.[3] If you know that your parent is under financial pressure, you will want to make sure that his or her basic diet is adequate. Encourage your parent to use Food Stamps or other entitlements. You may want to send a gift each week of nutritious but costly food items such as meat and fish, or ask the local market to deliver such a package for you on a regular basis. Make sure the meals you serve when your parent visits feature something he or she would enjoy but not buy because of the cost. And encourage your parent to take advantage of the hot meals served at the local community center each day.

Sometimes cost is not the only problem. Appetites fall off, especially in advanced age. Dentures, or a need for them, may create an eating problem. Fewer taste buds and a less keen sense of smell may erode the enjoyment of food. Depression and anxiety affect the appetite; so does loneliness.

Living and Eating Alone

Especially if your parent lives alone, you should devise some system of keeping watch on eating habits, monitoring for regularity and content. If you visit frequently, you'll have a pretty good idea of what is happening. Long distance, you may have to depend on a neighbor or friendly visitor to do some judicious checking. If you talk regularly with your mother by phone you may engage her interest in food by asking about recipes, meals she's planning for the day, and the specials in her supermarket. If it's your father who is living alone, you may have more trouble. Older men, who have lived their lives waiting for wives and daughters to call them to the table, are not as likely to cook nutritious meals for themselves, once living alone. Frozen meals, of course, are a way around this obstacle, but they are expensive.

Eating is generally regarded and experienced as a social act. Parents and children come together at mealtime; large families join for festive dinners; friends meet over lunch or afternoon tea. Sharing meals with others is a large element in the lives of most of us. When asked, "Would you like a cup of tea?" a common response is, "If *you're* having one." Having a cup of tea *together* is more important than having it at all.

Food is often the medium through which older women, especially, express love. It may be a vehicle for their creative energy and talent, a way to relax, sometimes a device for exercising authority over their children and impressing their husbands. Many older women, robbed of this role, recollect it nostalgically and are unable to reconcile themselves to the shrunken ritual of preparing a meal for one and eating it without company. There are ways to get around this.

Most lonely people who would like to share a meal aren't sure how to do it. Some women present their specialties to the postman, or the doorman. Many older people help each other in a neighborly way with shopping or other chores and then close their doors to eat their meals alone. You can help open the doors by encouraging your parent to give the first invitation. This has the double virtue of motivating your parent to maintain good nutrition and fend off social isolation.

Your father alone may have to start from scratch, learning the map of the supermarket and the use of kitchen equipment, learning what to buy and how to cook it. He may be glad to be introduced to some basic cookbooks or some simple cooking classes at the Y or senior center. Inspired by the great tradition of male chefs and the numerous TV cooking shows, he may become quite interested in cooking. If he does, accept his invitations gladly, bring a bottle of wine to accompany the meal, and praise the cook.

Loss of Appetite

If you notice that your mother or father has been eating poorly and irregularly over a long stretch of time—not just a few skipped or meager meals—then you may wish to intervene directly and take the necessary steps to avoid prolonging a poor diet to the point of serious deficiency.

If your parent doesn't seem interested in meals or is refusing food, try to find out the reason. Gum, teeth, or denture problems may make chewing difficult or detract from the enjoyment of food. These are conditions a dentist can readily treat. There may be more complicated reasons. People who are de-

NUTRITIONAL CHECKLIST

- Fruits, vegetables, and milk in good supply will provide most necessary vitamins and minerals. Fruits, vegetables, and foods with fiber and bulk prevent constipation.
- Fried foods, highly seasoned foods, dishes prepared with large amounts of fat, gravies, and heavy sauces are difficult to digest. Steamed, poached, baked, and broiled foods are lower in fat and easier to digest.
- Smoked foods and those processed with nitrites, such as bacon, hot dogs, and sausages, have been linked to increased cancer. Except for the occasional treat, these should not be included in the regular diet.
- Heavy meals are a mistake any time but especially in the evening or just before bedtime.
- A steady fluid intake is vital. An older person should drink six to eight glasses of liquid a day, especially in warm weather when there is a tendency to dehydration, and especially if taking medication.

pressed often don't care about eating, and those who feel angry or hurt may refuse food as a punishment for themselves or to others who are close to them. Sometimes people deny food to themselves as a symbol that they are denying life. Or a physical condition may be causing appetite loss. You should not let this go unattended. Try to learn from your parent what the cause is, and discuss it with your parent and with the doctor.

Special Diets

Some chronic conditions of older people—arteriosclerosis, heart disease, diabetes, high blood pressure, and ulcers, for example—require special diets. The presence of more than one chronic condition—common with older persons—can create a dietary conflict. The regular use of diuretics to reduce the accumulation of fluid in the body can dramatically lower the body's essential potassium level, but foods high in potassium can be high in calories.

If your parent has a chronic illness, the matter of a proper diet should be discussed thoroughly with the doctor. You can also consult a trained nutritionist who can map out a diet and weekly menus. Be sure to find out just how restricted the diet should be. Must some foods be stringently avoided, or can they be used moderately or occasionally? Diets are tricky vehicles and require expert guidance. They should be rigorously followed.

The national health organizations doing research on specific diseases can be of great help here. The American Heart Association and the American Diabetes Association give nutrition counseling and suggest specific diets. The Heart Association has a cookbook, available in the library and bookstores, to guide the cook to tasty but appropriate recipes. Nutritionists in the county health department or U.S. Agricultural Extension Service and visiting and public health nurses will help with special diet needs or suggest someone who can.

There's a great deal of printed material available on nutrition and diets for older people in general and for those who have chronic conditions requiring special diets. Check your library.

EXERCISE

Exercise is a key ingredient in good health. But any older person who wishes to start an exercise program should first consult a physician, take a stress test, and then, with the doctor's advice, begin in a limited fashion, gradually increasing duration and intensity. If persistent pain occurs, or undue stiffness lasts more than several hours, the exercise should be cut down or stopped and the doctor informed.

New research reveals the potential of reversing some of what was until recently considered the automatic physical losses of aging. It has recently been reported that with *careful* training and exercise older men can partially regain lost muscle strength. "It is astonishing," says Swedish gerontologist Dr. Alvar Svanborg, "to find now that even at age 81, through training, muscle strength and muscle fibers can be affected. The rate of increase in such strength is the same as at age 30, though the level of strength achieved by the older man will be less than that of the 30-year-old." There is, of course, danger in placing an excessive load on these muscles, but in general, says this physician, "no exercise is more dangerous than too much."[4]

Walking is probably the best exercise for older people. It is the least taxing, requires no skills and no equipment, and the passing scene often pleases the eye and stimulates the mind. A walk taken at a steady pace, arms swinging, has all the advantages of more complex aerobic exercise. How much walking is appropriate for your mother or father should be determined by a physician. Except in special cases, a mile or two a day, at least three or four times a week, will be appropriate. Any exercise that causes undue shortness of breath, persistent fatigue, pain in arms and legs, or any kind of chest pain should be stopped. The aging population has caught on to the benefits of walking and you can see purposeful walkers in the cities, the suburbs, and along country roads. Encourage your parent to walk for a newspaper, to the market, or to some other form of transportation. Except for slippery or icy conditions, weather should not be a deterrent.

People of any age can swim and enjoy it. Whatever swimming can be accomplished comfortably will be good exercise and a good tonic for the body and soul. Except for remote areas, most communities have swimming pools for winter or summer enjoyment; some schedule special swimming hours for older people. Some colleges and universities open their swimming pools to senior citizens at specified hours. Encourage your parent to use these facilities on a year-round basis.

Almost all Ys, community centers, senior centers, and retirement housing complexes now sponsor exercise or social dancing programs for older people. To the tune of the latest music or old jazz, and with the leadership of an experienced exercise professional, older people are enjoying the pleasure of exercising or dancing in the company of friends.

A tennis game with contemporaries, rather than a highly competitive game with a young opponent, is in order for the tennis buffs. Golf, the sport of choice for many older people, is companionable as well as good exercise. Its moderate physical demands are not taxing to the body, and the teasing challenge to better one's score perks up the mind.

Even if your mother or father is physically handicapped and in a wheelchair, there is no reason she or he cannot have a regular exercise program. Check with a nearby senior center or adult day care center to learn what is available, or to learn for yourself how you can help your parent exercise at home. Katherine Dunham, the distinguished dancer, devised a series of chair exercises for older people that allows them the pleasure of moving to music and exercising whatever parts of their body they are capable of moving. Similarly designed activities are now included in many special exercise programs.

Dr. Raymond Harris, a cardiologist, expert on physical activity and the aging, and president of the Center for the Study of Aging in Albany, New York, offers this regimen for older people who wish to minimize injuries and get the best out of exercise:

- an initial warm-up period of at least 10 minutes or more in which you stretch, perform light calisthenics, and walk at a leisurely pace
- a more vigorous exercise period of at least 20 to 30 minutes three times weekly in which you raise your heart to an age-adjusted target training rate
- a cool-down period of 10 minutes or more in which you walk or perform other light exercise that permits your body to return gradually to a resting physiological state[5]

See Appendix under Fitness. See also Chapter 10.

STRESS

Learning how to cope with stress is a life-improving strategy. Some people do it naturally. Others need to be taught. Tranquilizers may temporarily relieve symptoms; they do not solve anything and used to excess can be dangerous.

Understanding the root of stress is the first step in learning how to manage it. Managing it means taking positive steps to improve or accept a situation, in small or large ways. You may not be able to alter the specific situation that has caused your parent's stress, but you may be able to help change how your parent deals with it.

Change is a frequent cause of stress in the aging person. Anticipating change and planning for it reduces stress. But life's events don't always fit neatly into a package, and many stress-producing situations erupt without notice. Trying to pretend everything is fine when it's not is hard on both body and mind. A time of stress unleashes strong emotions, and it's healthier to express them than to repress them.

Talking out the problem helps; so does crying, or expressing anger. "Being brave" is no virtue if it causes subsequent physical disorders, depression, or other emotional difficulties. Studies have shown that cancer patients who become angry and proclaim "I'll beat this thing" do better than those who stoically accept their bad luck and resign themselves to the devastations of the disease. Of course, any response taken to an extreme is bound to be a poor one. Prolonged beyond a reasonable period, the responses of the screamer, talker, crier, or stoic may signal the need for help from a professional therapist.

Stress reduction programs can help enormously. Try to persuade your mother or father to participate in one. They're available throughout the country—at community centers, schools and colleges, and health fairs. Inquire from the local mental health association or Area Agency on Aging. Under professional leadership, participants in the stress reduction programs are helped to cope with change that can come from role changes, retirement, appearance, lessened mobility, living arrangements, income changes, memory changes, death, injury or illness, and sensory changes.[6]

Here are some tips for coping in time of stress:

- Stress causes muscles to tense and teeth to clench. It can cause a real pain in the neck, in the lower back, the jaw, or the head. Careful exercise or gentle massage can help to relax the muscles. Try to relax the muscles that bind one at a time, by making a conscious effort to do so.
- A regular exercise program can help relieve stress.
- Be extra careful in all physical actions. People under stress tend to be accident-prone. They drop and break things, hurt themselves, burn themselves, dent automobile fenders, bump into things, trip and fall.
- Until your elder undertakes his or her own efforts to relax or be entertained and understands that it is healthy to enjoy oneself, provide relaxing diversions to divert his or her anxious thoughts from the immediate problem.
- This is not a time for making major decisions. One Florida widow, a year after her husband's death, said, "I'm so glad I wasn't able to sell my house last year when I tried. I must have been crazy then, though I didn't know it. I'm so glad now I still have my home; it would have been such a mistake to move."

CLOTHING

Most people try to look as attractive as their circumstances allow, no matter what their age. They purchase new clothes to lift their spirits, to celebrate an occasion, to keep up with the fashions. If your parent can afford to do this and has the confidence to carry off a new wardrobe with panache, be happy he or she is interested in maintaining an attractive appearance. On the other hand, many older people keep and wear clothes for a much longer time than younger ones—to save money or because they're more comfortable. How your parents feel about themselves will have a great deal to do with how they dress. When you see sharp changes in how your parent dresses, pay attention and try to discover the causes.

Getting to the shops may become difficult or dressing well too much of a physical or mental effort. They may say to themselves, "I'm too old to care about how I look" or "Nobody cares about how I look."

It's up to you and your family to try to understand what your parent is feeling about appearance and respond appropriately. If your father always wears the same baggy sweater and your mother continues to use your father's old bathrobe (which is not so unusual), you can give a replacement for a birthday or for Christmas. The recipient may decide to "save it for good," put it away, and not wear it, but you will have done all you can—or should.

Be alert to your parent's clothing as an indication of physical well-being or emotional tone. Food and other spots may remain because the wearer simply doesn't see them; then a trip to the ophthalmologist is in order. You can also help by making some regular laundry or dry-cleaning arrangements, either taking care of the situation yourself or finding someone who will. If you find that your formerly meticulous parent begins to neglect his or her appearance and continues to be quite disinterested in it, some form of depression or dementia stemming from emotional or physical reasons could be the cause. You should discuss this with his or her physician.

A physical hindrance may require careful selection in clothing. Garments should be comfortable and fairly loose, easy to put on and take off. Zippers, buttons, and snaps should be readily accessible, preferably in front of blouses or dresses for easy reaching. You can find a special device to help your mother pull back zippers up and down in a sewing or novelty shop. It might be difficult for your parent to see very small snaps, hooks, or buttons or for arthritic fingers to manipulate them. If you can replace these with more usable fasteners, you'll be helping your parent to remain independent. Slippery soles lead to falls. You can replace laces on shoes with Velcro closings.

SAFETY IN THE HOME

Of fatal accidental injuries to persons 65 and over, 40 percent occur in private homes. . . . Most falls occur in the victim's home during common everyday activities, and two-thirds of the falls resulting in death happen at floor level rather than from a height. The most common trigger of these accidents is a rug or the floor itself, which is sometimes slippery. . . . Frequently older people are the victims of falls precipitated by failing eyesight, muscular strength and coordination, and a degenerative condition of the bones known as osteoporosis. Often broken bones lead to terminal complications.[7]

The older the person, the more likely that a fatal accident will result from a fall. Rugs, carpets, slippery floors or bathtubs, and thoughtlessly placed objects that present obstacles in a path are the principal villains. But accidents in the home result as well from fire, from poor lighting, and from poorly maintained or worn-out equipment. Choking on dentures or food or ingesting poisonous foods or vapors are other safety risks. Extra safety precautions are essential in homes where older people live. If your parent cannot safety-proof his or her own home, then you should make this a first priority for yourself. The following are among the suggestions from the U.S. Product Safety Commission's *Home Safety Checklist for Older Consumers* (see Appendix under Safety):

- Remove any rugs or runners that can slide. Buy rugs with nonskid backing or apply double-faced adhesive carpet tape or rubber matting to the backs of rugs or runners. Periodically check for wear. Pile rugs that are too thick can trap an older person's slower, heavier foot, or the rubber-soled shoes they wear. High or worn edges of rugs increase the danger of tripping.
- Paint outdoor steps with rough paint or apply abrasive strips to give them a rough texture.
- Check lighting of hallways, stairs, and any narrow passages.
- Electric stoves are probably safer than gas stoves from which unburned gas can kill if the flame is accidentally extinguished, but neither is safe if left on and forgotten. A timer with a loud bell, turned on when the stove burner is ignited, will remind the cook there's something on the stove that must be turned off. This will help avoid kitchen fires as well as ruined pots and meals.
- Add grab bars or rails next to the toilet and the bathtub. Only nonskid mats or rugs should be on the bathroom floor. Keep a nonskid mat in the bathtub or attach nonskid appliqués. Showers should have a small stool, with nonskid protectors on the legs, so the older person can sit, if necessary, while washing.
- Check the temperature of the water heater. Hotter than 120 degrees, water can scald.
- Electric blankets should be in good condition, *not* tucked in, have *no other coverings on top of them,* and never be turned up high enough to burn anyone. No pets should be permitted on these blankets.
- Pets can be a great comfort but can be a hazard if they sleep on the floor next to an older person's bed. Move a pet's sleeping place out of the way so your mother or father doesn't trip over an animal on the way to the bathroom.
- Make sure a lamp or light switch and the telephone or other alert system are within arm's reach of the bed.

- For the frail, install a handrail between the bedroom and bathroom.
- Install a smoke alarm on each floor and especially near the bedrooms. Be sure the batteries are fresh.
- Have a plan for exit if there is a fire. It's a good idea to rehearse your parent(s) on what to do and where to go if the alarm goes off or if they become aware of fire in their homes. Keep it simple and consistent.
- Discourage your parents from using stepladders or stools. If they must have a way of reaching a high place, purchase a sturdy step stool with a handrail to hold while climbing. Someone else should change ceiling light bulbs.

An experienced public health nurse suggests a buddy system for people living alone. Your parent should check each day on someone in a similar situation; someone should call your older parent daily. Each buddy should have emergency telephone numbers for the other—a close relative and a doctor, the nearest hospital and ambulance service. Your parent should have a list of emergency telephone numbers posted near each telephone, for personal use and for those who come to help.

DRUG ABUSE

Overmedication, drug allergies or toxicity, or conflicting medications can alter behavior, cause physical problems, and even threaten life. You should know what medications, prescribed or self-selected, your parents take.

If your parent is taking prescription sleeping pills and you are concerned about possible addiction, speak to the doctor, and read the section on sleep in chapter 9.

It's not a good idea for older people to exchange medication with each other, which they sometimes do. "Try this," says one to another. "It helps my backache." Impress upon your parent that this can be dangerous because of unsuspected drug interactions.

If your parent needs several different pills regularly for a variety of ailments and is becoming a little forgetful, he or she may be taking some of the medication too frequently or not frequently enough. You can help in two ways.

- You can make a chart. Have your mother or father make a check mark on the chart each time he or she takes a pill. This will answer the question "Did I take it this morning or not?"
- You can purchase a specially designed container, which contains a one-day supply of whatever is prescribed. The container is filled each morning and should be empty at night. If it isn't, at least you won't have to worry about overdoses. Check with the physician about what to do if insufficient medication is taken on any given day and make sure your parent knows what to do in this situation.

Even if your parent is hospitalized or institutionalized, you should check on medication. Unfortunately, it is quite possible for your parent to be given someone else's medication. Your mother or father should understand clearly from the doctor what has been prescribed and how frequently it should be taken and then, each time a pill is delivered, ask "What is that?" If your parent is too ill to do this, then someone in the family should do it during visits. The question should alert the staff to pay close attention.

Above all, be observant about your parent's behavior. Report any concerns directly to the physician in charge of your mother or father's case. If you aren't satisfied with the responses, you may have to take further direct action. Some nursing homes abuse patients with tranquilizers, oversedating them to keep them from being troublesome. If you suspect this is happening, investigate the possibility of a transfer to another facility.

Always inform a doctor about what medication your parent is taking, including over-the-counter drugs, especially if the doctor neglects to ask the question. (See chapter 9.)

ALCOHOL ABUSE

Alcohol abuse among older people can be a serious problem, partly because alcohol can produce stronger effects as metabolism slows with age. Many older people drink less as they age because they are conscious of uncomfortable effects, or because drinking is expensive. Problem drinkers have usually either been chronic drinkers for most of their adult lives or begin drinking late in life to offset stress.

The National Institute on Aging cautions older people about the following physical effects of alcohol:

- Alcohol slows brain activity, impairing mental alertness, judgment, physical coordination, and reaction time and increasing the risk of falls and accidents.
- Heavy drinking, over time, can cause permanent damage to the brain, central nervous system, liver, heart, kidneys, and stomach.
- The effects of alcohol can make it difficult to diagnose certain medical problems. For example, it can mask pain that might warn of an impending heart attack, or cause forgetfulness and confusion, which may be mistaken for symptoms of dementia.

Even the occasional drinker should know that alcohol mixes unfavorably with many other drugs, those bought over-the-counter or by prescription. These include tranquilizers, painkillers, barbiturates, and antihistamines. If your mother or father is sensitive to aspirin, it is important to know that the bleeding some people suffer from aspirin can be aggravated by alcohol. The combination of diuretics and alcohol can reduce blood pressure in some cases, producing dizziness. When combined with alcohol, many drugs lose their therapeutic value. For example, certain medications prescribed as anticonvulsants, anticoagulants, and for diabetes may be metabolized too rapidly if the patient uses alcohol. Some drugs increase the intoxicating effects of alcohol. Finally, some drug-alcohol combinations can be fatal.

Urge your parent to discuss with the doctor whether or not

an occasional social drink may be harmful, and under what conditions.

Some older people are told by their physicians to have a small drink on awakening "to stimulate the circulation." Double-check this and make sure your parent's doctor is aware of all the medication your parent is taking.

Detecting Drinking Problems

How can you tell if your parent is an alcoholic? Your father has retired, hasn't made plans for the rest of his life, is restless, depressed, unhappy. He's accustomed to having a drink before dinner, sometimes two. Now he often takes three. He says a drink helps him go to sleep. Or your mother is lonely, recently widowed. She is accustomed to a little wine with a meal, an occasional cordial after. You may notice that if you call early in the day you can have a coherent conversation with her, but from 4 P.M. on she's "too busy" to talk, sometimes befuddled and sometimes hostile. "I'll talk to you tomorrow," she says.

You can help an alcoholic parent by facing up to the problem, not pretending it isn't there.

The good news is that elderly problem drinkers can be treated with a high rate of success; they are regarded as easier to treat than younger alcoholics. The National Institute on Aging lists the following symptoms as frequently indicating a problem:

- drinking to calm nerves, forget worries, or reduce depression
- loss of interest in food
- gulping drinks and drinking too fast
- lying about drinking habits
- drinking alone with increasing frequency
- injuring oneself or someone else while intoxicated
- getting drunk often (more than three or four times in the past year)
- needing to drink increasing amounts of alcohol to get the desired effect

- frequently acting irritable, resentful, or unreasonable during nondrinking periods
- experiencing medical, social, or financial problems caused by drinking

You can get help for your parent with a drinking problem from Alcoholics Anonymous, the National Council on Alcoholism, and the National Clearinghouse for Alcohol Information.

SAFE DRIVING: THE ELDERLY DRIVER

"My father has cracked up three Cadillacs in the last two years. The one last week never made it past the dealer's driveway. How can I get Dad to stop driving before he kills someone else or himself?" This kind of question is a regular when families attend sessions on coping with the problems that arise when your parents grow old.

If your parent's driving worries you, try a heart-to-heart talk. Express your concern for his or her safety. Some modest limitations might be acceptable for starters: avoid driving at night, during rush hours, in bad weather, while taking strong medication, for too long a stretch, or after a sleepless night.

Prompting a parent to give up driving is one of the more painful intrusions children make on their aging parents' lives. Driving a car is a sign of independence, power, and control over one's own life. But there comes a time in almost every life when driving is no longer appropriate. That time is almost always traumatic for everyone concerned.

Having an official revoke a driver's license is one way of taking the burden off family members. Controversy persists over special testing of elderly persons to determine whether their licenses should be revoked. Those opposed believe such tests would discriminate on the basis of age. Others point to the increasing visual, auditory, and other physical impairments of many elderly people and to their slower reaction time. Some states require special testing at license renewal time; others do not. Depending on where your parent lives you may have to intervene even when you dislike what you have to do. You can inform the motor vehicle bureau if you truly believe your parent's physical or mental condition makes driving a serious hazard. Trying to enlist the aid of a physician in such cases may work because in many states physicians are supposed to inform motor vehicle departments if they become aware that a patient's condition makes driving dangerous. But doctors don't like violating their confidential relationships with patients, don't wish to be sued, and may not help you.

The AARP sponsors a 55 Alive/Mature Driving program. Adult education courses in many communities feature safe driving courses, and insurance companies in some states reduce premiums for drivers who take renewal courses in safe driving. You can suggest your parent participate in one of these programs.

If you are unwilling to confront your mother or father directly on the driving question, you may find it easier to introduce the touchy subject through printed information (see Appendix under Safety). Even if your parent denies that the information is relevant to his or her particular situation, at least you will have opened the subject for discussion. Nobody really wants to become a public menace, and most older people will themselves withdraw from driving when they become uncomfortable with it.

Some older people with vision problems will describe to you their difficulties in making out signs, the problems of glare in bright sunshine, their lack of depth perception at night, their feelings of being uncomfortable at the wheel. Others will insist that all is well, and for some this may indeed be true. But it is hard to deny the evidence that the aging process robs most of us of the quick motor responses that can be crucial when faced with driving emergencies.

Drivers more than 65 years of age have a higher accident rate, on a per-mile basis, than all others except the group 25 years of age and younger. They are more vulnerable to injury than younger drivers, even in minor collisions. Most of their accidents occur "under ideal driving conditions—on clear days, straight roads, dry pavements. Most occur within 15 to

25 miles of the driver's home. Many take place at crowded intersections controlled by signal lights. That's understandable. Heavily trafficked intersections are often confusing and demand special alertness and extra-quick decisions. But there are too many drivers who don't respond to those extra demands."[8]

If your parent continues to be a safe driver, don't hassle him or her. If you see signs of trouble, suggest some alternatives. Figure the costs of maintaining the automobile and see how this compares with hiring a driver for needed transportation, or taking a taxi more often than usual. If one or both of your parents must finally give up the driver's seat, then do all you can to insure their continued access to activities outside the home. Reevaluate where your parents live and consider how convenient it is to shopping, services, and recreation without the use of an automobile.

SAFETY FROM CRIME

Fear of crime keeps many an older person imprisoned in the house or apartment as soon as the sun goes down. Fear of crime is higher among the elderly than among younger people. Although senior citizens are victims of crime less frequently than younger people are, they are more vulnerable to certain crimes: purse snatching, mugging, and fraud. They are also more likely to suffer injuries from an assault that in a younger person might produce no injury at all.

Purse snatchers, muggers, and mailbox thieves know that older people can be thrown into confusion more readily than younger ones and are less capable of defending themselves against sudden attack. The 80-year-old woman who chased a thief racing away with her purse and batted him to the ground with her umbrella was the exception, not the rule.

For this reason, many local police departments mount organized educational programs for older people, to help them not only avoid possible criminal assaults but deal with one should it occur. Here the elderly are taught how to pinch and kick, how to break strangleholds and grips, even karate. While a deputy sheriff at one seminar said that a man of 105 could fight "like he's 25" if his life depended on it, most of the seminar participants were skeptical of their ability to restrain panic under attack or to use force even when they were taught how. Increased civilian and police patrols, teen escort services, neighborhood visits and watch systems, and a good supply of whistles and horns to call for help were considered more realistic safety measures.

So are the safety tips publicized by the National Crime Prevention Council (see Appendix under Crime). For example:

- Protect Social Security or pension checks by having them sent directly to your bank.
- Do not display large amounts of cash in stores, elevators, or any public place, and be discreet with credit cards.
- Do not resist, if you are attacked on the street: better to give up a purse or wallet than your life. Do not pursue the attacker, but call the police, immediately.

The criminal justice system is, unfortunately, not especially sensitive to elderly victims of crime. In testimony before the House Select Committee on Aging, Assistant Attorney General Lois Haight Herrington stated:

> The cruel irony is that elderly victims are one of the most poorly treated clients of the criminal justice system.
>
> After a crime the victim is often interviewed, photographed, maybe physically examined; the house may be dusted for fingerprints. The police may call them to come down for a lineup at odd hours. The victim's name and address may appear in the media. And their address and phone number may be given to the defendant and the defense counsel.
>
> The victim many times must find affordable transportation to court only to learn that the case has been rescheduled for the convenience of the judge or the attorneys.
>
> Moreover, their physical infirmities are often mistaken for mental incapacities. Many elderly have poor hearing, slow motor reflexes,

impaired vision. These natural aging processes are often interpreted by criminal justice professionals as senility.[9]

If your elderly parents are victims of crime, make sure they are not left alone to deal with the consequences. Either you, another relative, or a lawyer should be in regular communication with the authorities. Try to be present for any encounters your elderly parents may have with the police or other authorities. Be in immediate touch with the Crime Victims Bureau in your parent's locality (call the Area Agency on Aging, the local police department, or the attorney general in your parent's state for information about this organization). The National Victim's Resource Center (U.S. Department of Justice) has information on relevant laws and services throughout the country. The National Crime Prevention Council has information on 400 programs for the elderly. The AARP publishes a book *Keeping Out of Crime's Way,* which you can find in the local library or purchase directly.

See the Appendix under Crime.

YOUR PARENT AS A CONSUMER

Not all consumers know how to avoid purchasing problems ahead of time, how to deal with complaints to their own best advantage, or where to go for help when they fail to get satisfaction on their own. Good consumer protection information for your parent can be obtained from *The Consumer's Resource Book* (see Appendix under Consumers). In addition to advice on how to be a smart consumer, this resource book provides a comprehensive directory to names and addresses of agencies that provide consumer assistance.

The Consumer Credit Counseling Service and many social service or nonprofit organizations offer help on understanding and using credit. There are even Debtors Anonymous clubs for those who can't resist.

Protection from Quacks and Shysters

Older people are often easy prey for con artists and swindlers—door-to-door salesmen, promoters of get-rich-quick schemes, dishonest home renovators and repairmen, and fraudulent mail schemes. Persuade your parent not to sign any contracts without consulting a lawyer first. Dishonest hucksters can cost your parent large sums of money at best, and endanger his or her health at worst.

The U.S. Public Health Service and Food and Drug Administration estimate that Americans spend millions of dollars each year on medical device frauds to fulfill their hopes: to look younger, to cure arthritis, to sleep better, to lose weight, to make love better, to live longer. Promoters of fake medical devices peddle false hopes to the sick or dying and laugh all the way to the bank. Furthermore, they sell the kind of hope that can turn a patient away from proper medical treatment that may diagnose early stages of cancer or relieve the pain of arthritis. To guard against this kind of charlatanism, your parents are advised to follow this rule: If it sounds too good to be true, it probably is.

Not every advertised product is fraudulent, but extreme skepticism is called for. Check with the doctor about anything your parent wants to try or has tried. Check advertised medical devices with the national health organizations, such as the Cancer Society or Heart Association. Report any problems to your local, state, or federal consumer protection agency or to the Food and Drug Administration (FDA). The FDA will send you *The Big Quack Attack: Medical Devices,* which lists the brand name, manufacturer, or distributor of each device, a description of the device, the principle of its operation, and a clear statement of its false or misleading claims in labeling or advertising (see Appendix under Consumers).

Funerals and Burial Plots: Consumer Rights

Many families investigate and choose burial plots together or discuss alternative arrangements to burial so that younger members are not left to guess what a parent prefers on death. Your parent may make arrangements and then inform you or may take it for granted that the traditional family plot will be used and the funeral service will conform to family traditions. But if no arrangements have been discussed or made and your parent becomes anxious, he or she may be vulnerable to the sales pitch of a persuasive entrepreneur selling cemetery space or a vaguely defined prepaid funeral.

So pervasive are the opportunities to exploit the elderly or their families in the highly charged emotional atmosphere that accompanies the death of a loved one that the House of Representatives Select Committee on Aging has published *Consumer's Choices to Funeral Planning* (see Appendix). This pamphlet emphasizes the importance of planning, exploring the options available, knowing the preferences of the people involved, and determining the costs that will be incurred. It informs you of consumer protections provided by the Federal Trade Commission's Funeral Rule, which went into effect in 1984, under which the provider must give you prices, terms and conditions, and answers to any reasonable inquiries you make in person or over the telephone. Beware of fraudulent claims regarding state requirements for embalming, cremation, or quality of caskets. Funeral directors are required by the FTC rule to provide you with written statements of what the law does or does not require in all these respects.

The pros and cons of prepayment for funeral arrangements are listed in the pamphlet, and consumers are cautioned that prearrangement does not have to be accompanied by prepayment. If your family prefers prepayment, be sure that the seller has a sound reputation, that the price is guaranteed, and that the funds are adequately safeguarded (placed in trust). Consult an attorney before signing any document.

Consumer Reports has this further caution about prepayment: You may not be able to get your money back if you change your mind and want to back out for whatever reason, such as moving to a different part of the country, and you probably won't get the accrued interest even if you succeed in getting a refund. It also notes the possibility that survivors may still be subjected to a pitch for a more expensive funeral by being told that "prepayment covers only frugal arrangements."[10]

Be sure your parent understands all the implications of body or organ donation before filling out donor cards; then respect his or her decisions. (A contribution to medical research can involve unanticipated costs for transportation or necessitate alternate arrangements if the donation is refused.) Donations can be made legally binding on survivors when the donor completes a Uniform-Donor Card, though some institutions will not accept bodies or organs without the consent of the next of kin. (See the Appendix under Living and Dying.)

ANTICIPATING CHANGE

The prospect of change can be a threat to any individual, but it can be particularly upsetting for old people. Changes in habits, customs, or living arrangements may frighten your parents. And the possibility of change in their lives and its effect on yours may upset you as well.

This is natural. You may have reached a point in your life where things are almost orderly. The demanding years of early professional advancement may have leveled off for you and your spouse. You are probably no longer tied to the full-time care and supervision of growing children. You may be less pressed by other responsibilities and be enjoying life in a new way. Then suddenly you feel the weight of a new and scary situation; you may feel you've lost control over your life just when you thought you had regained it.

Or you may have been going through a period when other facets of your life have been plaguing you—and now here comes something else to plague you. Or perhaps you are already in a caregiving relationship with your parent; you have established a support system and it has functioned well. Now a new development creates a strain on that system.

One of the problems of situations like these is that few people have thought about them in advance. The tendency of most people is to go along, living as they have lived. Some life events are universally accepted as change makers—going away to school, the first job, marriage, the birth of a child, a move to another city—but one knows about these in advance and anticipates them, preparing to meet them as they occur. Yet the process of growing old, with the demands it may place on the aging individual and his or her family, is no complete surprise, either. Some preparation is possible, but few of us want to think about it until we have to.

Try to anticipate the change impending in your parent's life. Try to investigate and plan a little beforehand. Try to have some options lined up for the time when you will actually have to deal with a new situation. Then you will have participated to a degree in the change, and it will not catch you unaware.

Discuss with your parent, if you can, how he or she would like to handle certain circumstances, should they occur. If he or she were left alone, where would they like to live? What if they are sick and can't manage alone, what living arrangements would they prefer? What are your parent's thoughts about the future? You can discuss this in a casual way, long before the necessity of making any decision arrives. Get a head start—even though you may never have to run the race.

FOUR

WHERE CAN YOUR PARENT LIVE?

The Range of Housing Possibilities

Proper housing for an aging parent is a universal and overriding concern. It can also be a problem you will face more than once if your parent's situation changes. Lacking better alternatives, many older people are living in houses that are too large, too difficult, and too costly to maintain properly. Except for the growing number of fairly expensive life care communities, housing for the elderly is in short supply at every level of need in most communities. This makes it even more urgent that those growing older and the families of the elderly start early to consider the options. Furthermore, since a move can be a traumatic event for an older person, gathering information, discussing, and planning in advance with your mother or father can smooth the way and make both the move and the adjustment easier.

Where and how your parents live will be of the utmost importance in determining whether their later years will be enriched or lonely, independent or dependent, financially perilous or secure. It's generally best to look ahead not only to this year's requirements but to those of future years. No one should be rushed into the first step of a total-care situation, especially because only a small percentage of older people ever need to be institutionalized. It is likely, however, that your parent will suffer some future erosion in his or her ability to live independently. You should try to plan for some of the dependency that may occur. No plan can be permanent, as conditions change, but each decision along the way will count.

MOVING

Any new housing at an older age should be examined with an eye to the older person's physical and social requirements, not only at the time of the move but over the next several years. If both of your parents are contemplating a new home, they and you should think about its suitability if one of them becomes widowed or handicapped. Look for housing in a pleasant neighborhood within easy walking distance of stores for basic shopping and close-by transportation for other needs and recreation. Examine safety features—basements, tricky staircases, fire hazards. Consider proximity to family and friends. In today's housing market these positive features may be difficult to find, but they should be considered before a final choice is made. If stores and transportation are accessible, the neighborhood may not be safe. If it is pleasant, as in the suburbs, your parent may not be able to shop without an automobile, or the nearby supermarket may close. If everything is as you would wish it, housing may be extremely expensive. And, of course, family or friends may move.

Classic errors can be avoided by some advance planning or tryout. The reality of living in a warm climate may be different from the dream. The concept of living in an apartment with built-in services, freed from having to shovel snow-covered walks or fix leaky faucets or put up screens, may not translate well to actuality. The parent who decides he or she wants to move to another city to be near children and grandchildren may be looking for trouble. Proximity to family, dear though it is, may not compensate for the loss of friends and social activities in the neighborhood left behind.

Carefully research a new state, and certainly a new community, in advance. A subscription to the local newspaper for several months will give some insights into the local life and atmosphere. Local chambers of commerce are good sources of information. Some states will send a summary of state features related to retirement living. You can write to the state office on aging for information about types of housing, the cost of living, special advantages for those over 65, job opportunities and available services, benefits and entitlements. These may vary dramatically from those where your parent currently lives and be considerably less generous. Special restrictions may also apply concerning length of residence. Friends already living in the area can share their judgments.

A trial living period is the best test of what the future will bring. Although this may be somewhat more costly in the short run, it may be much less expensive financially and emotionally in the long run. At least the climate and resources of the new location can be tested. Particular choices, such as one apartment house or retirement community over another, are somewhat more difficult to test, but a short-term rental can help determine if this is a compatible location.

If your parents haven't had a trial living period in a new location, you may find yourself getting frantic phone calls after they have sold the old homestead and gone to live in a sunny climate: "Why did we do it? Its a terrible mistake. Your mother cries all the time. She's lonely and wants to see the children. I'm sick of playing golf. I should never have retired." Or worse, you may not hear because they think you're too busy to be bothered.

Barring chronic ailments, which can be aggravated in extreme climates, an older person can live anyplace. Some of our coldest states—Vermont and Maine, for example—have high percentages of people over 65. Nevertheless, the greatest number of retirees who move to a new community move to Florida, California, Arizona, Texas, or New Jersey. The Ozarks of Arkansas have enjoyed a little boomlet, and the Carolinas have appealed to those looking for a mild winter climate. New Jersey has captured many a retiree's interest because it is relatively close to major metropolitan centers such as New York and Philadelphia and not so far away as Florida. It is estimated that of those who move to the Sunbelt, about one-quarter, or 100,000 a year, go to Florida. People east of Michigan tend to go to the southeastern states, those west of Michigan to the southwest and California.

However, Charles Longino, a sociologist and demographer who investigates retirement migration patterns, reports that an increasing number of people are returning to their native states in their later years. Says Longino, "The stream of residents into Florida is higher proportionately among the people in their late fifties, early sixties, people who are economically independent. The counterstream of those going home is among the oldest, poorest, and most frail, principally widowed elderly women in their seventies. These are people most in need of services, who want to be closer to their children.

No matter where your parents choose to live—if they are buying a house, a condo, a co-op, or a mobile home—the following guidelines apply:

- Thoroughly check the quality of construction, utility services, water, sewage, and electrical supply.
- Check monthly costs and accessibility of services and medical care.
- Check the lending institution that provides mortgages and the state attorney general's office to determine whether there are any reported problems or lawsuits associated with the property.
- Ascertain whether maintenance charges are commensurate with the services provided. Is the management good?
- Talk to some of the residents and owners to find out if they are congenial and if the development has any special problems.
- Find and use a lawyer who specializes in condo sales, subdivision sales, or land sales, who can guide your parent through these and other matters.

Planning for a move after retirement is like planning for retirement itself. The most successful planning begins in middle age."

Help your parents be realistic about costs. Suggest they keep a daily diary of expenses, then make a checklist that includes every expense where they presently live and compare these to costs where they want to go. Be sure to consider:

- all the costs of living: housing, repairs, taxes, insurance, utilities, new appliances, clothing, food, medical care, and necessary services. Include the costs of transportation for shopping, laundry, cleaning or other services, health care, recreation, and employment. Remember to consider how much it will cost family members or friends to visit if parents move and whether added costs will result in fewer visits or a better location will increase visits.
- special health needs—whether physicians, hospitals, and other health-care services and facilities are better in one place than another.
- availability and cost of help, at all levels of need.
- recreation, cultural, library, and educational opportunities. How accessible are these and how much does it cost to enjoy them in each location? Are people of similar interests, tastes, and religious preference nearby? Is there enough diversity? How much is a meal in a restaurant, a movie, a football game, a play, and a concert? How about TV reception?
- employment and volunteer opportunities.
- climate and weather patterns: pollution, allergies, preferences for seasonal change, and dangers of earthquakes, floods, tornadoes, and hurricanes.

Uprooting is an expensive process. Be sure your parents can afford what they would like to have. Remember that their financial flexibility is likely to be reduced as they grow older, so every effort should be made to conserve some of their funds for emergency situations.

THE WIDE RANGE OF HOUSING CHOICES

You can help parents who wish to move consider their options by helping them find the best new information available for their consideration. A good place to start is the retirement living shelves of the local public library. For example, you will probably find there a copy of AARP's *Planning Your Retirement Housing,* an excellent detailed survey of available alternatives in housing throughout the country, with a first-rate checklist. *Places Rated Guide* is another good volume that provides informed comparisons of living costs, climate, and other details of living to help people think about the important factors in making housing choices. The American Association of Homes for the Aging has directories for those needing protected living. Directories not found in the local public library can be bought from the associations that publish them. Usually these describe facilities, services, and costs; they give no ratings or judgments. See the Appendix under Housing.

Public and private social agencies where your parents presently live, or in the community to which they plan to move, can also tell you what is available. The local Area Agency on Aging should be able to provide you with a housing list or a directory or refer you to special housing programs for elderly people in the desired area. These may range from apartments for independent living to nursing homes.

Despite a critical nationwide shortage of affordable housing for people of all ages, there are increasing numbers of alternatives for older people in some special situations. Following is a range of potential options.

Retirement Communities

These offer totally independent living in an organized setting. They free the older person of the responsibility of maintaining the exteriors and grounds of their homes and of worrying about security on a daily basis or when they leave for vacations. They usually feature recreational facilities and planned social and recreational programs. Depending on location, facilities, and services, costs range from moderate to very expensive.

Private developers are building such retirement housing all over the country, mainly in the South and Southwest, but increasingly within an hour or two of major metropolitan areas. This makes it possible for residents to be closer to families and friends, to continue to work part or full time till a later age, and to enjoy the life of the cities they are loath to give up. Some of the older retirement communities are now adding medical services to their social and recreational packages for residents who have "aged in place."

In some instances, middle-aged couples are buying housing in these communities and renting to older people who do not wish to tie up their capital, with a view to having something for themselves when they are ready to use it. They are counting on continuing inflation to protect their investment and to make their housing a relative bargain when it comes time for them to move in.

Nonprofit retirement communities sponsored by religious, fraternal, labor, or philanthropic organizations offer the same benefits and kind of living. Costs may be high, and there's generally a long waiting list for occupancy. There is a great lag between the demand for and the availability of such housing.

Public Housing

This is in short supply, so waiting lists are long. The benefits of living among peers and having access to social and recreational activities are similar to those found in private housing but at a lower cost. This housing may have the extra advantages of good design: small apartments the right size for the individual, wide doors, grab rails in bathrooms, good lighting, efficiently arranged kitchen facilities, and other features important to older people. Security and maintenance of the physical environment may be questionable, however, especially in large cities. Because so many residents continue to live to a very old age, with accompanying infirmities, many of these housing projects now feature multiservice centers where medical, nutritional, counseling, and other services are offered on-site.

Mobile Home Communities

These abound in states with warm climates. Less costly in general, and with a peer population, they may or may not offer organized social or recreational opportunities or programs. They vary from the stark and unattractive to beautifully planned and landscaped parks. Costs vary accordingly.

Residential Hotels and Motels

These offer both furnished and unfurnished apartments, usually with kitchenettes, for residents who come and go as they please. The benefits are relief from all housekeeping chores, a dining room on the premises for meals at will, companionship in communal rooms, and switchboard service. This can be expensive. In large cities many residential hotels are being converted to co-ops and condos, and older people who rely on them may find themselves suddenly faced with no place to live.

Using Home Equity

The majority of older Americans own their own homes free and clear. For most, these houses are their major, sometimes their only, asset. At the beginning of 1987, the median value of an American home was just under $81,000. Since most older people do not have a large supply of cash, innovative ways of unlocking the cash value of their houses have been devised for their benefit.

Reverse Annuity Mortgage One such is the reverse annuity mortgage (RAM), which works like this: The lender appraises the house, determines its value, and issues the RAM providing the owner with either a lump sum or monthly payments for a specified number of years—or even for a lifetime. Depending on the particular contractual arrangement, the lending institution gets its money back, plus interest, either at the end of the period specified for the mortgage, or when the owner sells the house or dies. When payments are to continue for a lifetime, an initial down payment from the lender to the borrower is often used to purchase an annuity out of which the payments are made if the borrower outlives his or her life expectancy at the time the deal is made. RAMs are fine, *if* all the arrangements are clearly spelled out, *if* the lender is financially responsible, *if* your lawyer has investigated and approved all the details of the contract, and *if there is no danger of encountering unknown risks.* Tax matters involved in these mortgages have not been firmly resolved to date. The AARP, which urges older people to be very cautious, has a fact sheet on home equity conversion. Write for one to find out more about this option.

Because of concerns about abuse in home equity mortgages, new federal legislation authorizes a three-year demonstration program to protect elderly home owners and lenders from default (through insurance) and to permit elderly owners to obtain cash advances against their equity that don't have to be repaid for as long as they live in their homes. The Federal Housing Administration (FHA), starting in 1988, will insure 2,500 reverse mortgages against the risk of defaults. The National Center for Home Equity Conversion (NCHEC), an independent nonprofit group in Wisconsin, is a good source of information on home equity and offers (for $15) a packet of information on the new legislation and a national directory of RAM programs. The NCHEC or your local Area Agency on Aging should be able to give you information about which lending institutions, if any, offer reverse annuity mortgages where your parent lives. See the Appendix under Housing.

Sale/Leaseback Through this arrangement, the owner sells the house to a buyer but does not turn it over for a specified number of years or until death. The initial down payment to the seller is used to buy an annuity to insure payments for a lifetime—no matter how many years that is. The seller then receives payments each month for the balance of the sale price, out of which he or she pays the buyer rent. The rent to the buyer is less than the monthly payment to the seller, leaving the seller extra cash. The buyer assumes all the responsibilities of maintenance and repairs, taxes, and insurance. Buyers, expecting property values to increase over time, count on being able eventually to sell the property for more than they paid.

There are variations on sale/leasebacks in different communities. Here again, it is essential that the arrangement be made with a reputable buyer and that a good lawyer scrutinize and approve the contract. As with RAMs, tax consequences at this date are not yet clear.

Pros and Cons The benefit of equity plans for older people is that homeowners can continue to live in a loved and familiar place till the end of their days, while using their own money to sustain the expenses. The risk is in becoming involved with shaky institutions or unscrupulous people. Another factor to consider is that your parent may no longer be able to pass the house and property on to the children, which can cause considerable emotional anguish to older people. You can discuss the pros and the cons of this together. If it appears to be the best solution for your parents, you can help make the decision a great deal easier by indicating your willingness to accept it. If the symbol of the house as inheritance is too important, and giving that up causes too much stress, then an alternative solution must be sought.

Again, no invasion of equity should be undertaken without the advice of a good lawyer. It is best to ask what protections exist, in the state where your parents live, against fraud or abuse in transactions involving home equity, and to insure that the lending institution can carry out its obligations without financial risk to your parent.

Accessory Apartments, Mother/Daughter Houses

Another option, for older people who want to remain in too-large homes, is to create an apartment within the structure or attached to it that can be rented for income. Although zoning laws may prohibit converting one-family structures to two-family living, special regulations for senior citizens have been enacted in some communities, which permit the addition of an "accessory apartment." In these special situations, either the owner of the home or the renter of the apartment must be more than 60 or 65 years old. If either party leaves or dies and is not replaced by another senior citizen, the house must be converted back to one-family status and conform to the original zoning requirements. Some communities permit building new "mother/daughter" homes as long as one of the occupants fulfills the age requirement.

In most American towns, zoning and safety regulations are difficult if not impossible to satisfy for accessory apartments. As a result, it is estimated that there are two million *illegal* accessory apartments in America. These often represent sanitation and fire hazards.

For many families, it makes good economic sense and provides peace of mind to consider purchasing a home together in a community that permits accessory apartments. Here's how one family solved the problem of privacy and divided a house in a town that allows senior accessory apartments: A daughter and her husband and children are in the main section of the house, while her parents occupy a ground-level, one-bedroom apartment below. The children come down for a cookie, a kiss, or a sleep-over in a sleeping bag, but the families have adopted formal rules for visiting. No one drops in on the other without telephoning first, to assure privacy and independence. In case of need, however, someone is always there for the other. The older folks say, "It's taken all the anxiety away." The younger ones report, "This is much better than having to travel a distance to help them out if they need us."

Check the local zoning regulations if building an accessory apartment for your older parents seems to make sense. If renting to a stranger, it is important to know what landlord/tenant regulations prevail in the community. Thirty days may be the minimum notice you must give to a tenant to vacate the apartment should he or she prove to be undesirable or your parents change their minds. A lawyer should advise you or your parents about rights and obligations and draw the lease.

Shared Housing

Building on to a house may be costly or difficult. Renting a room or a part of the house is an increasingly necessary route for many older people seeking to reduce their housing costs or to have someone share the chores or upkeep. In some instances, groups of individuals pool their resources and buy or rent a house or apartment together. The advantages and disadvantages are obvious: You must balance the financial and social benefits against the possibilities of personality clashes and unfulfilled responsibilities.

Many social service agencies are now sponsoring shared housing programs to help their clients meet pressing housing needs. Once again, zoning regulations can stand in the way of what seems a reasonable solution to your parent's needs. Some communities have regulated against a specified number of unrelated people living under the same roof, even if the group meets other standards, such as using a common kitchen. Some of these regulations were instituted to protect communities from the wild behavior of young people who summered in large old houses; some were to protect the standards of neighborhoods fearful of deterioration if single-family ownership or occupancy was diluted. Nevertheless, a report by the Senate Special Committee on Aging in 1985 states, "Shared housing will become a more necessary option for older Americans in future years as the cost of maintaining a single residence becomes a larger burden than many elderly can afford."[1]

In San Francisco, ABLE (Action for Better Living for Elders), a project initiated by the Unitarian Church, registers people who want to share and tries to make suitable matches. Dee Bergman, director of ABLE, says, "It's challenging when you move in on someone else's turf. It doesn't work when one tries to take over the other's life. People need emotional space as well as physical space when they live in the same house. I know some people sharing who are really searching for the emotional intimacy of a family. If they all agree on that, it works. Others succeed better when they keep their distance from each other."

If you believe this may be a good idea for your mother or father to consider, you can obtain more information from the National Shared Housing Resources Center in Philadelphia (see Appendix under Housing). It publishes a directory of hundreds of shared housing programs across the country, pinpointing communities where experts are available to assist in the matching process. In all instances, it is best to write down, as in a lease, how much will be charged the tenant, and what is expected from each party, to avoid misunderstandings.

Lifetime Care Communities

These complexes, developed and operated by nonprofit groups such as religious organizations and increasingly by commercial developers, are designed for older people still independent but concerned about the future and the possible need for long-term care. An older person or couple can buy into one of these communities while still active and able. Personal quarters, furnished with personal possessions, may be in a town house, villa, cottage, or apartment. Residents may be required to sign in and out, and usually one meal must be taken at a communal dining room. The monthly costs customarily include this daily meal, communal recreational and social activities, housekeeping and linen service, and transportation for shopping, medical, or social needs. Daily checks insure that the resident is not in need of help; alert and alarm systems within the private quarters summon help as needed. Residents can have a private physician as well as access to the on-site medical and nursing staff and health care facility. If a person becomes frail, handicapped, or dependent on nursing care, he or she can continue to live within the complex, in the long-term or nursing care facility. Costs are the same as for the private quarters, with added charges for the two additional meals a day and all medication or physician's and outside hospital bills. But not all contracts include these services, so check specifically for what is offered and covered by the stated fees. Also, determine whether the health care units are certified by Medicare or Medicaid. Old friends can continue to visit without difficulty, and some continuity can be maintained with the patient's former life amid familiar surroundings.

This is an appealing option for those who can afford the costs, which may increase over time as a result of inflation or other factors listed in the contract. Couples who fear the impact of the death of one on the other, couples who wish to remain independent and not bother their children with their frailties, single or widowed older persons, or those without children determined to control their own lives are among the growing number of Americans who see these communities as the answer to problems of long-term care. The older American's average equity in his or her home now approximates the entrance fees in many lifetime care communities. In the Philadelphia vicinity, the Friends have sponsored life care communities for many years; their residents are frequently retired teachers and other middle-income professionals.

Costs vary considerably; the range in 1987 was from $22,000 to several hundred thousand dollars. Operation of these facilities is based on actuarial and economic assumptions. Costs for those requiring longer care are thus paid in part by the residents who don't require much care. If the sponsors err in their estimates, if residents live longer than expected, if entrance fees are not securely protected in special funds, if management is not efficient—all these and other factors can skew the results and put the establishment into financial jeopardy, thus posing a personal financial risk to the residents. It is for this reason that older people and their families are cautioned to investigate thoroughly any continuing care community before signing a contract. Know their track records and have a knowledgeable financial person check into every aspect of the operation. Some commercial developers now offer money-back guarantees under various conditions, or just charge large monthly rents without any capital paid in. These also must be thoroughly investigated. Do not be fooled by handsome brochures or too-good-to-be-true promises. Rather, know the basis on which it is reasonable to expect that promises can be kept. Fewer than two dozen states have regulations governing life care communities.

In 1986 the AARP sent out an alert, cautioning older people against the possible loss of their lifetime savings because of the number of life care communities facing bankruptcy. They could not sustain their promises in the face of long-living residents, increasing costs, uncertain economic conditions, or inexperience. This does not mean that every community is a bad risk. It is important to know which is which and how to select wisely.

When is the right time for your parent to move into a continuing care community? Opinions vary. At La Vida Llena, in Albuquerque, New Mexico, a fireside discussion among residents elicited striking differences: "Don't come until you have to," said a vigorous 72-year-old, whose children had persuaded her to buy her apartment there. "I'm too young for this and it costs me a fortune to travel to other parts of the world from here. I love to travel. Even though there's plenty to do in town, and at the university, it's not the same as living in a large cosmopolitan city. But I do love Santa Fe and it's not that far from here." "Come in while your spouse is alive and get used to living this way," said a widow. "Then when one dies, it's easier for the other. You already know your neighbors and have friends. I made a mistake and lived in an adult community first. When I needed help, my husband was already gone, and then I had to make another move."

At Godwin House in Arlington, Virginia, some of the crafts rooms and photography shops are open all night. "That makes all the difference to me," said one resident. "I'm not a good sleeper. This way I can come down for a few hours and work. When I go back to bed, I don't turn and toss. It's wonderful that everything doesn't just close down in the evening. It's better here than it was at home, where I tossed all night."

Senior Residences

These are like retirement hotels with some additional attention paid to health and medical needs: a doctor or nurse on call, a bell near a bed to summon assistance, a staff member who checks on residents periodically. There may be a requirement to sign in and out, but no restrictions are placed on individual mobility. These homes may be sponsored by a religious denomination or be privately operated.

Board and Care Facilities

Primarily operated by the private sector, these serve more than a million low-income persons, most of whom receive some form of public assistance. It is estimated that there are about 300,000 such foster homes, adult homes, or domiciliary care facilities in the country. The Senate Special Committee on Aging reports that "such homes have often been criticized for inadequate safety and security measures, poor care, abuse of the residents, and even financial fraud."[2] All states now have some health and safety provisions in law, but abysmal conditions persist. To find decent accommodations for your parent, inquire of reputable homes for the aged or nursing homes, which often have lists of acceptable board and care facilities in their environs. Social service agencies or the Area Agency on Aging may also be able to help. If you are worried about a parent who needs sheltered living, cannot or should not be admitted to a nursing home, and for various reasons needs to live at a distance from you, a board and care facility might be the answer.

Homes for the Aged

These give protective, custodial, and personal care to older people who are somewhat dependent but still functioning at a good level. Homes are operated by religious, ethnic, professional, or labor organizations and by private interests. In many communities, the original intent has been made increasingly difficult as residents live longer to become more frail and dependent and lose function but stay on, with more services brought in, because of a shortage of nursing home beds. *Home for the aged* has thus become a euphemism for a nursing home in many instances. In some parts of the country, however, homes for the aged remain just that—places where older people can live in sheltered circumstances and maintain a good quality of life with active social, educational, and recreational activities and the opportunity to come and go at will.

Supervised Housing in Homelike Settings

In some well-populated communities, a philanthropic agency or large geriatric center may rent or buy apartments or houses where two or three older people can live together in one unit, each usually with his or her own bedroom but all sharing the other facilities. Housekeeping services are usually provided by agency employees. The residents may share cooking chores on a scheduled basis, and a social worker visits once or twice a week, or at the request of the trained household help, to solve problems and make needed changes. An arrangement like this provides some independence for the older person along with companionship and supervision. The Philadelphia Geriatric Center and Jewish philanthropic agencies in Chicago and Rockville, Maryland, have pioneered this kind of sheltered living for some of their clients, and the idea is taking hold in other localities.

Call the family service agencies where your older parent lives to find out if they sponsor this kind of sheltered housing. Otherwise you may be able to make your own arrangements with other families that have similar needs. You can do the friendly visiting cooperatively and/or engage a geriatric social worker privately to monitor the situation, take needed action, and alert you to significant changes in physical or mental status of any of the house-mates. The advantages are many: companionship, someone on the premises for emergency situations, and a big economy in living and home help costs. A potential disadvantage, of course, is personality problems—but the advantages may be sufficiently compelling to smooth these over if they occur.

Health-Related Facilities

These offer total shelter at several levels for those whose physicians prescribe some form of nursing care. Persons requiring 24-hour skilled nursing care would live in a skilled nursing facility (SNF); those requiring nursing supervision but who are ambulatory would be in an intermediate nursing facility (INF). INF residents can also come and go for outside medical or therapeutic services or social occasions with friends or family. These are both costly options unless the patient is on Medicaid. They are discussed in detail in the next chapter.

FIVE

AS DEPENDENCY GROWS

From Care at Home to Choosing a Nursing Home

Sometimes a family is stronger than it thinks it is. Even if you've dreaded an accident, a handicap, or a severe illness, you may find that you manage better than you thought you could when you are forced to deal directly with your parent's immediate needs instead of the excesses of your imagination. Sometimes it's your adrenaline that comes to your assistance; sometimes it's your advance thinking and planning; sometimes it's knowing when to call on someone else for help. All of these plus your common sense help you manage.

If you're coping, you're not in crisis. Any situation that upsets normal routine, however, is capable of becoming a crisis unless the people involved draw on all the internal and external resources available to develop and maintain a practical solution. A practical solution takes into account the physical, financial, and emotional limits of the person(s) giving care as well as the needs of the elderly parent. If you're not doing this, you're flirting with crisis.

STAGES OF DEPENDENCY

The professionals chart the course of an older person's need for functional assistance based on ability to accomplish the tasks of daily living. These tasks include bathing, dressing, eating, using the toilet, getting in and out of a chair and in and out of bed, walking, going out of the house, shopping, cooking, cleaning, using the telephone, paying bills, and taking medicine. A few years ago, almost 20 percent of noninstitutionalized people between the ages of 65 and 74 and 46 percent of those 85 or older required some kind of functional assistance to perform one or more of these tasks.[1] As the older population increases, the need for help with personal care and home management will increase.

At first, helping may be necessary only a few hours a week, then for a short time daily, then for longer periods each day. As needs intensify, real home care—regular housekeeping, personal care, and some medically related health care—becomes a necessity. Eventually, if health care and homemaking assistance do not satisfy your parent's need, some other living arrangement is in order. Most families cannot afford the costs of health-related facilities. Most institutionalized elderly end up on Medicaid. But only 5 percent of those over 65 live in institutions—2 percent of those 65–74, 7 percent of those 75–84, and 23 percent of those over 85. The majority live in a family setting, some independently, others with smaller or larger amounts of assistance, the need for which increases dramatically with age.[2]

DECIDING WHAT TO DO

Professionals agree that it's wisest, theoretically, not to wait to move a parent until he or she is old and sick. There are pages of articles in academic journals citing the evidence of harm done to frail older people by late life moves unless extensive efforts (not always successful) are made to ease the process. Plan ahead and move while your parents are still functioning normally and can participate in the selection—better sooner than later is the thrust of this advice. But it is often impossible to carry out. The numbers of people who need to be served, and the accommodations or services available to meet their needs on a timely basis, do not always match.

Nursing homes now are occupied almost exclusively by very old, very sick patients, who arrive old and sick, says Dr. Natalie Gordon, director of social services at the Jewish Home and Hospital for the Aged in New York City, and there is a shortage of good long-term facilities for the many patients who require 24-hour care. There's a domino effect, forcing each group, from the most to the least needful, to postpone what would otherwise be the most desirable placements for the older person's psychological and physical well-being. Those with lesser needs are served in other ways—by home care, day hospitals, day-care centers, community services, hotels, sheltered housing, boarding homes, or some combination of these—and often not served at all. It is difficult and sometimes impossible to accomplish the best for your elderly parent. You can only do the best you can.

There is a great tide swelling that makes home care the first and sometimes the only option available to families whose elderly parents can no longer take care of their own daily needs. Whether that care is in the parent's home or a child's home then becomes a matter of family choice and family economics. The older person may prefer to stay in his or her own home, but the logistics may make it almost impossible for the child to manage the necessary care at a distance.

If you are middle class—above the poverty level but not wealthy—you probably cannot afford to pay the enormous costs of comprehensive home care for a needful parent. It is you, or no one. Remember that it is your parents' financial eligibility, not yours, that will entitle them to Medicaid-assisted home care, even if it is provided in your home. At present, only the established community support system or others in your family can reduce your burden. Community support systems may help a great deal or hardly at all. Sometime they exist largely on paper—inadequately funded, poorly staffed, and of little practical use to you. This can be a source of great frustration to you if you expect too much. But others can make all the difference in your life and your parent's, and you should use every source of help you can find. (See chapter 7.)

Suitable care for your parent is the central issue. Your father or mother, you, and all members of the family who are concerned with and involved in the solution, and who take responsibility for the outcome, should be included in the circle of people working out the plan for care.

Before you decide, you should have a very clear idea of your parent's practical needs and how well each alternative satisfies these needs. Make a list that is very specific: physical, nursing, and medical needs; social and emotional requirements; financial and other assistance. What is available? Where can you get it? Then discuss preferences and examine which are, or are not, acceptable alternatives. For example, if your parent's desire to remain independent, with help in the house, is no longer feasible, because no one in the family has the physical or emotional resources to be on 24-hour call when emergencies arise, then this is not an acceptable alternative. If your mother's presence in your house is sure to result in constant conflict with your spouse and put your marriage in jeopardy, then this is not an acceptable alternative. If you want to bring your parent into your home but cannot provide essential nursing services or therapy, then this is not an acceptable alternative. If you cannot find a decent and humane nursing home in your locality, then nursing home placement is not an acceptable alternative.

In every family there will be particular circumstances that make one or another choice a better one.

Choices—The Ladder of Long-Term Care

You can:

- bring additional help into your parent's home: homemaker/chore services, home health aides
- invite your parent to live with you and bring in additional help
- enlist someone else in the family to share a home with your parent and be responsible for his or her care: one of your brothers or sisters, an uncle or aunt. If your parent shares housing and services with another el-

derly family member, the joint household may relieve several family problems at once
- enroll your parent in a day-care center and take advantage of Meals on Wheels and other community services to relieve the pressure on the person giving care
- call on a social worker from a family service agency for help or pay one in private practice to take on the management responsibilities, including that of engaging and supervising aides who come into the home
- arrange for your parent to live in a group home sponsored, staffed, and supervised by a social service agency
- arrange for your parent to live in a boarding home that specializes in caring for frail or elderly people in a homelike setting
- consider whether this is the appropriate time for your parent to move to a more sheltered environment with some nursing and medical care
- consult with the physician to determine whether this is an appropriate time for you to apply for your parent's admission to a nursing home

YOUR PARENT IN HIS OR HER OWN HOME

Maintaining your parents in their own home when they need a great deal of help to remain there is a mixed bag, with advantages and drawbacks for each of you. There's the advantage to your parents of a familiar environment, with the security-giving symbols of their lives in plain sight. Many services can be brought in to sustain this kind of life at home, paid for out of your parents' pocket and those of other family members, or paid for in part by local government social services, Medicare or Medicaid, depending on the situation. Yet a feeble person with a narrowed circle of friends and relatives who may not visit or telephone can become very lonely, especially if he or she can't leave home for companionship. And the situation can be hard on the caregiver.

"I spend all my time taking care of my father," says a Chicago woman who lives a 20-minute drive from her ailing parent. "I do his marketing and most of his cooking. Someone comes in every morning to help him get bathed and dressed, to fix his breakfast, and do a little housecleaning. But I have to check to see if she's there every day, and if she isn't I have to go over myself. A medi-van comes to take him to the clinic and the doctor. He can still go to sit on the park bench, but there is no bus to the part of town where his two friends live, and I have to drive him there. When I'm not with him, he's on the telephone with me all the time, wanting to know when I'll be over. He may not be ready for a nursing home, but I sure am."

Even the most independent person at some point in his or her declining life may want or need to be dependent on a child. The child must have the sensitivity to discover when the need to be dependent has been reached and to offer the opportunity. This is the time when the parent is ready to be taken in to a child's home or the security of a sheltered residence or nursing home where someone is always there.

It's not always easy to recognize this time. Judith Altholz of Duke University's Center on Aging said, "There's a gray area between the older person who is clearly capable of making it and the one who is incompetent. That's the time when families and parents can all be wretched, and no one seems able to make the right decision. Sometimes an outside person, the doctor or a social worker, can help. 'I,' says the expert, 'think you should move to change your life because these conditions are becoming overwhelming for you.' The older person may sometimes gladly follow the suggestion."

YOUR PARENT IN YOUR HOME

Finances, compassion, or custom often lead to the decision to move an ailing parent into a child's home. Two households may be too costly, as may a nursing home; helping services in the home can be performed by the unpaid labor of family members or by part-time help brought into the home at far less cost than by an institution. Just as often, there are emotional reasons paralleling the financial ones. A father may refuse to enter a nursing home, accusing his children of wanting to be rid of him, claiming that he will never survive the experience, clinging resolutely to the live-in support of the family. A mother may cry tearfully that she will be no trouble, that she will go when it's necessary, but meanwhile she'll stay where she is. The anticipated burden of guilt is too much for the child. After all, her mother took her grandmother into her home. The child confers with spouse and children, who agree to the decision that Grandma or Grandpa, or sometimes both, will come to live with them.

Many children bring a parent into their home without any conflict. Love and affection, relaxed temperaments, and self-discipline on the part of all the participants can help. Taking advantage of all the supports and services of the community can help. Sometimes the experience is a joy. The children like listening to the grandparent, playing cards and games with a built-in companion. Grandma or Grandpa feel the same way.

"My mother lived with us for 18 years," said a woman from Madison, Wisconsin. "We had to take her in because she couldn't afford to live by herself. She followed me around from room to room, always asking me what I was doing. I grabbed every opportunity I could to get out of the house. But my husband was a saint with her. My eight children loved her. And believe me, when she died, every one of them came from all over the world to her funeral."

Caring for your parent in your home can be the most practical and most desirable solution for satisfying his or her needs and your wish to do all you can to help.

Advance Arrangements

You will want to have the proper setting when your parent comes to live with you. Try to think it through in advance with your parent: What factors will be important to your parent, to you, and to other household members? Planning for these will help: privacy for him or her and for all other family members; time for everyone's physical and emotional requirements; some form of social life for everyone involved;

availability of good medical care for your parent. Sounds like the neatest trick of the week, doesn't it? But without setting some such standards as a goal, you may be licked before you begin.

You may have considerable problems if your house isn't well organized and tranquil. If your physical space is limited, it will be more difficult. Your mother or father may be unusually resilient and flexible and really enjoy a lively household. On the other hand, most older people prefer a predictable routine: slamming doors, groups of people in and out, and meals at irregular hours disturb them. It may be easier to provide a separate, regular routine for them than to force everyone in the household to a schedule that satisfies no one. It isn't fair, nor will it assure long-term tranquility, to require younger members to restyle thier lives completely to accommodate a grandparent's presence. There should be a quiet place to which Grandma or Grandpa can retreat and have a meal, on time, to satisfy everyone's requirements.

If your parent is frail and/or handicapped, evaluate your home in terms of steps, bathrooms, and other practical necessities that may require you to rearrange your living space. In one Michigan city, a hospital discharge planner told a daughter who protested that she could not take her disabled mother from the hospital to her home because she had no downstairs bedroom or bathroom: "Move out your dining room furniture, bring down a bed, and get a portable commode."

If your parent is so frail that comprehensive care is required, which you cannot afford, and if your parent is not eligible for Medicaid, which might pay for such home care, then you must decide whether you or someone else in the family will need to give up a job in order to provide this care, even if it involves great personal and financial loss.

Maintaining a Healthy Climate

You can only be in control of your own behavior, not your mother's or father's or your spouse's. If tension and conflict erode the good feeling in your household, then it is time to consider alternatives. Can you reestablish good, healthy relationships by an open review of each other's irritating habits? Perhaps an outside counselor can help, or participating in a support group with others in the same situation. Maybe it is better for everyone to separate and make another arrangement. If that is not financially possible, you may have to sweat out the situation. Marriages have broken up when elders came to stay, not because the partners were evil or uncompassionate but because the stresses became too much to handle and the practical solutions for change too elusive or impossible to attain. Some general rules may help:

- Do not discourage your parent's financial help. It will help your father's or mother's morale to be able to contribute to household resources.
- Encourage whatever contribution your parent can make to help with family chores. Productive activity will maintain his or her feeling of independence and worthiness and relieve others in the family of extra burdens. Don't be so rigid you cannot accept your helpful parent's way of doing things. Don't hasten dependence and listlessness by constantly removing tasks the older person can do perfectly well. Even a chairbound or bedbound person may be able to snap beans, sew on a button, play a game, or read to a child.
- Respect your parent's privacy and encourage his or her independent social life from the beginning, so everyone knows what to expect. Invite your parent's friends to visit. Go out for the evening. Not every moment, event, or friendship needs to be shared.
- Don't give your parent any more advice than you are prepared to accept for yourself.

Friction Points

Even a frail and sick parent for whom you feel sorry can irritate you by being bossy, demanding, unreasonable, or intrusive. "Ignore it," says one husband to his wife who cannot seem to run fast enough to satisfy the commands her mother issues from her wheelchair. "Just do what you know she needs and don't pay attention to what she says." His advice proves good as long as the old woman confines her remarks to her daughter. With the first incursion on the son-in-law's prerogatives, he complains to his wife and turns sullen. The daughter rises to the mother's defense, and trouble brews.

If the parent is a permanent member of the household, husband and wife need to talk to each other, understand the stresses, and try not to victimize each other. At an advanced age, a parent is unlikely to change. If his or her presence is too destructive and the family is unable to deal with it, even after seeking help with the situation, then they must consider another plan for care.

The four-generation family presents different problems. The roles of two generations of older parents and one younger adult generation are still being explored as the individuals involved jockey for position, for authority over younger members, for control over their own lives. But when the eldest becomes physically dependent, even if otherwise competent, and lives in one household with another, tensions can rise. Two matriarchs in one household are too many. When and if the eldest relinquishes her prerogatives and defers increasingly to the next generation down, tempers may dwindle. The feelings of relief that follow, however, may well be tempered by sadness, even remorse, about the struggles that no longer seem so important. The contest may be over, but soon, too, may be the life that energized the power play. Fathers and sons are not immune to the same tensions. They are just less likely to play them out in kitchens.

A severe personality clash may be eliminated by changing the place where your parent lives. Moving in with another relative with whom there is less emotional history can sometimes help, but not necessarily. Any friction that arises in your home will probably be paralleled with someone else if your parent is blind to his or her own provocations. Siblings who love and admire each other can become less tolerant in old age. Their childhood rivalries, submerged through years of independent living, suddenly reemerge in very old age; ancient jealousies, feelings about long-dead parents, and competition for "smartest, nicest, most successful" intrude on present efforts to do the right thing for each other. Some opportunities to blow off steam for everyone involved, making some adjustments and accepting some compromises, can make living together tenable. Outside counselors may also help.

See also chapter 2.

LONG-TERM CARE IN A NURSING HOME

At a critical time, when the older person's condition takes a sharp turn from better to worse, family members may turn to each other and say, "Well, maybe it's time for a nursing home."

Maybe it is and maybe it isn't. Current professional advice is to maintain older people in their homes as long as possible, using whatever battery of helping aids is needed and whatever community-based long-term care programs are available. Many old people fear nursing home placement and many extract promises from their children that it will never happen to them. Children volunteer such promises to aging parents, often long before they have a notion of what the reality of need will be. Then if the necessity arises for such placement, the emotional toll is enormous. Extreme impairment, incontinence, confusion and disorientation, and physical conditions that require almost constant nursing care present situations where a nursing home is the best solution not only for the older person but the family. But even if the need is clear, this is a traumatic period. Furthermore, even if emotional conflicts are resolved, admission may be difficult or impossible.

The decision to institutionalize a parent is a highly complicated one. The doctor's evaluation, the possible alternatives for care, your family's financial capability, and your parent's possible eligibility for Medicaid, now or later, will be important ingredients in the decision. Your attitudes and emotions, your parent's, and those of other family members who are closely involved will undoubtedly influence the outcome of your explorations. Moving a parent to a nursing home is a decision you cannot make alone or even in concert with other members of your family so long as your parent is intellectually competent. Then you must know his or her own wishes and discuss the problem forthrightly. You will need the evaluation of a physician and/or psychiatrist who understands your parent's physical and mental condition and, knowing what kinds of care are available in the area, can compare these with the kind of care presently being given to your parent. If you then know that a nursing home is the best place for your mother or father, you can take this step with the knowledge that you are doing what is best and need not flail yourself with guilt.

Because the majority of nursing home placements are made directly from or shortly after hospitalization, most families are not prepared to make informed choices. It is a good idea to explore homes long before you need them. You may never need them. But if you do, at least you'll be making the wisest choices when the time comes.

But remember, if your parent is a Medicaid patient, nursing home placement may be in the first available Medicaid bed available within a radius of 50 miles of your parent's present location. The wonderful geriatric center you know about may not have an opening when you need it, unless your parent is presently enrolled in their long-term care program and has been benefiting from their community services. If your parent or family can pay privately for residential care, you will probably have a wider choice of better facilities. But admission to the outstanding nursing homes may be delayed by long waiting lists, and you will have to balance the quality of the available facilities against the need for institutional care at the time you are making your decisions.

To be assured of humane and appropriate care for their elders, families must be aware of the hazards, look for the good institutions that do exist, and remain involved. Still, it doesn't take much probing to discover a family's guilt, or their disappointment in themselves that they somehow have failed a parent who now lives in a nursing home. One Massachusetts woman says, "My mother is never out of my thoughts. I visit her in the home three times a week, more than I did when she lived in her apartment. I am divorced. I must work. I cannot stay with her. She cannot stay by herself. I know and she knows that the nursing home is the only solution. But it is eating me alive."

What Is a Nursing Home?

Most of us tend to lump together under the catch phrase *nursing home* all institutions where old people live and receive care. Behind that phrase are many different kinds of places offering many different levels of care and services, but they are all facilities where an older person can live somewhere outside the personal family environment on a long-term, usually permanent, basis and receive care ranging from minimal assistance to round-the-clock skilled nursing care.

The terms and labels that describe facilities within the overall grouping of *nursing homes* can be confusing. The states name, define, classify, and license homes in very different ways, and the federal government includes personal care and other residential facilities along with skilled nursing homes in its surveys of nursing homes. You should know about these labels because you will probably hear them from doctors, hospital staffs, discharge planners, social workers, and other professionals who are involved with you in trying to find the best situation for your parent. The important thing is to find out exactly what kind of services a home provides for exactly what your parent needs.

Descriptive labels have developed because nursing homes are (or are not) certified by the federal government to receive Medicare and Medicaid funds. In order to be certified, homes must offer facilities and services and conform to standards that comply with Medicare or Medicaid regulations. To qualify for *Medicare* benefits, the patient must use a nursing home designated as a *skilled nursing facility* and certified by Medicare. To qualify for *Medicaid* benefits, a patient must meet income eligibility requirements and use a nursing home designated as either a *skilled nursing facility* or *intermediate care facility* and certified by Medicaid. Medicaid beneficiaries can receive benefits for a lifetime. Medicare will permit eligible beneficiaries 150 days in a skilled nursing facility per year, starting January 1, 1989. Check the new rules. (See chapter 6.)

- A *skilled nursing facility (SNF)* is at the level nearest hospital care. It's for those who require ongoing medical supervision, skilled nursing services, and professional rehabilitation therapy. There should be, in addition, a total range of other kinds of services for the physical and mental health of residents. Normally a physician must prescribe admission. These facilities are designed for patients recovering from acute illnesses or suffering from serious medical problems. Increasingly, some nursing homes are accepting seriously afflicted Alzheimer's patients, who may be placed in special sections. Patients no longer in need of skilled nursing care will be asked to leave or will be moved to a lower level of care. Medicare will not pay for a lower level of care, or even for custodial care at the skilled nursing level, but Medicaid will. Private patients usually become Medicaid patients after they have exhausted their personal funds. Continuing care retirement communities generally have a skilled nursing facility on the premises, as do some other retirement complexes and old age homes. Medicare and Medicaid rules also apply to these facilities. A registered nurse must supervise the licensed practical nurses and aides in a skilled nursing facility.
- An *intermediate care facility (ICF)* cares for people who are neither well enough for independent living nor sick enough to require constant medical and nursing attention, but require some medical or nursing supervision. Patients are usually expected to be ambulatory, or capable of getting around in a wheelchair, and to come to meals except at times of acute illness. An ICF should give residents help with personal care, including bathing, dressing, eating, and walking as needed, and provide a full program of social and recreational activities. An ICF will generally supervise medication and provide nursing and rehabilitative services as needed. A licensed practical nurse (not a registered nurse) may be in charge and supervise the aides.

Facilities in each category usually have agreements with

nearby hospitals and other health-related agencies in the area to provide services the facility itself may not offer. Be sure to check this when you investigate.

In general, it is better to find a facility that offers care at both levels, so that the resident can be cared for on an appropriate basis as needed. In addition, although many nursing homes that do not accept Medicaid give excellent care, if your parent should eventually need Medicaid assistance, he or she will then have to move. If your parent is entering a nursing home at a level that requires minimal care, it might be wise to choose one where he or she can move along the care continuum without having to change residence because of personal and health care needs or financial pressures.

There are other kinds of homes known by other names and geared to caring for the older person whose medical and health needs are not demanding. The names vary from state to state. They may be called old age homes, homes for the aged, board and care homes, or domiciliary homes. They may be operated by state agencies, by private agencies, or by special groups. Psychiatric hospitals are also sometimes called nursing homes or rest homes.

Finding a Nursing Home

Nursing homes vary in bed capacity, staffing, services, quality, and the cost of care. Many institutions have been adapting or converting their facilities to meet national Medicare standards, but a great many do not qualify.

Policies on these homes and facilities vary from state to state, but almost everywhere in the country all institutions caring for the old at any level must be licensed by the state department of health. Boarding foster homes, which are sometimes not licensed, are the exception. Your city or county health department can supply you with a list of licensed homes in the area. Citizens may request from them, or the state health department, the official reports on individual nursing home compliance with regulations. These reports will tell you what kinds of infractions have occurred and whether or not they have been eliminated. Federal inspection reports relating to Medicare and Medicaid certification from the previous year can be secured from your regional office of the Health Care Financing Administration. The National Center on Health Statistics will answer requests for information on nursing homes based on its 1986 survey (see Appendix under Nursing Homes). A federal guide on quality of care in nursing homes was published in 1988. To receive one, check with your AAA.

Most nursing homes are privately owned and operate for profit. Chains of nursing homes owned and administered by large corporations, some trading on the stock exchanges, are now springing up across the country. The American Health Care Association has among its members about 9,000 licensed nursing homes and allied long-term care facilities, 80 percent of which are proprietary; the remaining are nonprofits, owned by churches, government, and fraternal or other membership groups. The association publishes a directory of its members (see Appendix).

About 3,100 licensed nonprofit nursing homes and homes for the aged are members of the American Association of Homes for the Aging (AAHA), which also publishes a directory. The nonprofit homes generally claim to have a higher ratio of staff to residents and offer broader social and other programs and services than those run for profit. The quality of life in these homes is often on a high plane, and they normally have long waiting lists, but not all are superior. AAHA has also initiated an accreditation process for nursing homes associated with continuing care communities. A call or letter to AAHA will give you information on accreditation standards and a directory of continuing care communities (see Appendix).

If you're looking for a home affiliated with a religious denomination or a fraternal order, inquire of the local church, synagogue, temple, or order in which you're interested. There are many of high quality located around the country. They may offer space to some people who are not members of the denomination or fraternal order. They will of course have waiting lists. Check with Protestant denominations, Catholics,

Christian Scientists, Quakers, and Jews; Elks, Masons, Eagles, Kiwanis; the Salvation Army and Volunteers of America.

You can also ask the state ombudsman in the state office on aging for information about the quality of homes in your area.

What to Look For

When you begin to search for a nursing home, it is important to look beyond the labels at the human aspects of the home in which your parent will live. Visit all the homes in your locality that seem to fit the picture, talk to their administrators and staff members, and observe keenly. What you find in some homes will surprise you pleasantly; in others you'll be intensely displeased.

Try not to react to the severe disabilities of some of the residents. There will be many whose state will be pitiful. Frequent visitors to nursing homes learn to overcome their initial shock and appreciate the compassionate care some institutions provide for such patients. Your judgment should be directed to the quality of life and the care and services that the home tries to give to its residents, whatever their individual condition.

Your parent should participate with you in this investigation to the limit of his or her ability. There is no point in taking your mother or father to see every home you visit. Make a preliminary survey and pinpoint those you think would be best. Then take your parent to visit these, several times if possible.

On one initial visit, a daughter asked the social services director who was taking her on a tour, "Are these residents tranquilized?" "Oh, no, we don't use drugs to quiet them," was the reply of the social worker, new to her duties. The daughter persisted and inquired of the nurse at the floor nursing station. "Of course, they're tranquilized," was the reply. "We couldn't control them otherwise." Know what the policy is in every institution you visit, then ask your parent's doctor very specifically whether tranquilizers are medically indicated for your parent—how much, how often, and why. In some cases, a tranquilizer may be an important part of your parent's care plan. In other cases, it may not. You had better know the difference and be sure the institution you choose is rigorous in carrying out the physician's orders.

After a few visits to several homes, you can tell which are warm, professional, comfortable, and staffed by concerned people, and which are staffed by officious, cold, and uncaring people, even if they are in spanking new quarters. First visit a home without making an advance appointment; visit a dining room at mealtime and an activity room in session to see for yourself how patients are fed and treated. Talk to residents in the social rooms to find out how they feel about the home. You'll learn a great deal this way before you get the official tour. Then make your appointments for talks with the administrators.

Use your eyes, ears, and nose when you visit. "Look, Listen, Smell, Question" is the advice of the Nursing Home Information Service, a nonprofit information and referral service providing information on nursing homes and alternative community and health services (see Appendix). They suggest that the best time to look around, in addition to meal times, is between 4 and 8 P.M. and over weekends. Notice whether the patients are clean and well-groomed, dressed in street clothes, and happy or drowsy and listless, which may indicate excessive use of drugs and tranquilizers. Look at patient rooms in different sections of the nursing home, not just the one offered on a tour. Look to see if the staff are neat, clean, well-groomed, and working with patients, not clustered at nursing stations. Is there a nurse (LPN or RN) on the floor or wing of the home? Listen to the patients and to the staff and pay attention to how the staff speak to the patients. Are they condescending or respectful? "Be suspicious if the administrator does not allow you to talk freely with the patients and staff," is the advice of the Nursing Home Information Service.

Smell will sometimes tell you all you need to know about a nursing home. Strong urine and body odors present throughout the building can indicate poor patient care or poor housekeeping. Strong chemical deodorants should not be a substitute for prompt attention to patients unable to toilet themselves.

Costs

Nursing home placement can bankrupt a person or a family. If your parent's medical and financial condition warrant it, Medicaid may provide financial support for nursing home care. If your parent is ineligible at first but uses up his or her own financial resources in a year or two, Medicaid will then pick up the tab if the home is Medicaid-certified, but not for frills or luxuries. For example, your parent would probably have to give up a private room. Facilities that take only Medicaid patients, such as county nursing homes, provide only basic and minimal services.

Individual state Medicaid eligibility can be determined at the Social Security office or Area Agency on Aging. If your parent isn't eligible for Medicaid and if family funds can provide support for a time but not forever, a sensible approach is to start spending your parent's money on all needed services. This applies to community-based support services as well as to nursing home costs. Your parent may object strenuously that he or she doesn't want money spent this way but wants it saved for the children or grandchildren. This is an emotional stance and not a practical one. It does not take long to exhaust most older people's assets to the point where they become eligible for Medicaid's long-term care benefits, and doing this will not imperil your own family's financial security. Most families are not drinking from the public trough when they do this; they have few other choices.

Nursing home costs will depend on many variables: geographic location, level of care, range of services, ratio of staff to residents, and other considerations. Small homes located in small communities and with care that is primarily supervisory or custodial will probably charge about $1,000 a month. In large metropolitan communities, nursing homes providing complete care through sophisticated services in private rooms may charge over $5,900 a month. The average national cost of nursing home care was $22,000 a year in early 1987. In addition, some nursing homes "suggest" a large gift. It is against federal law to coerce contributions as a condition of entrance to a nursing home.

These figures are indeed staggering. They are propelling a national movement for long-term care insurance. Spotty efforts are in process. The premiums are high, and benefits may be more than are otherwise available, but there are still no panaceas. Older Americans have indicated they would be willing to pay for this added security, but young Americans who cannot project themselves into such a state of need are not yet willing to start paying premiums at the age that makes the process actuarily viable. Alternatives continue to be debated. (Catastrophic insurance is not the same thing as long-term care insurance—it is to cover extended hospital stays not presently covered by Medicare, not continuing or custodial care.) For most people, Medicaid is still the only way to pay for long-term care.

Any agreement signed for nursing home care, whether it is with an individual proprietary or nonprofit home or as an adjunct to buying into a life care (continuing care) community, should be examined carefully by a lawyer. Some nursing homes still have entrance agreements under which the patient pays a lump sum on entry and is guaranteed care for life regardless of changes in condition. Sometimes entrants are asked to turn over all their assets and assign all their income to the home in return for lifetime care. Sometimes the fine print allows the home to ask residents to leave if their condition worsens drastically—with no obligation on the part of the home to refund any of the resident's unused money. Be sure you know exactly what the refunding procedures are, and be knowledgeable about state regulations.

There are hidden costs in nursing homes. Private duty nursing, if it's required, is usually an extra cost. Boxes of tissue purchased from the nursing home may be many times the supermarket charge; shampoos and hairsets may be exorbitant, as may other special supplies and services. Often you can supply these yourself. The Nursing Home Information Service has prepared a long-term care directory for citizens of the

CHECKLIST FOR NURSING HOMES

- Accreditation, licensing, and certification for Medicare or Medicaid should be current.
- The physical premises should be well located, attractive, cheerful, clean, uncrowded, safe, meet federal and state fire codes, and assure appropriate privacy (for instance, pull curtains between beds).
- Nursing, medical, social services, physical therapy, and all rehabilitation services should be consistent with your parent's needs. Each patient should have a plan of care that is regularly evaluated and updated by a physician and other professionals attending your parent.
- Food should be prepared with careful attention to special diets in clean kitchens and should be served in pleasant surroundings with appropriate help if necessary. (The majority of complaints to the ombudsmen relate to poor food and service.)
- A full range of recreational and social activities under proper supervision should be available in activity rooms. These rooms should be attractively furnished and supplied with materials suitable for the highest level of activity your parent can perform and enjoy.
- The staff should be professionally trained and adequate in number to provide the level of care your parent requires. You should know who is in charge of what so that you know exactly where to go should you have a problem.
- You and your parent, if possible, should meet and talk with the administrator and department heads before you make your final decision.[3]

Washington, D.C., area, which clearly states which services are covered and which aren't in homes there (see Appendix). Among the extra costs listed in the directory are physical, speech, and occupational therapies, lab tests and drugs, dental services, podiatry services, hand feeding, catheter, and physician's services. Some even charge for soap, linens, and towels; others for wheelchairs and walkers. Almost all charge extra for private telephones, TV, and radio. You must ask specifically about each thing you can think of to find out what the prospective charges will be and what Medicaid will cover in the nursing homes you are investigating.

Your questions should be very specific:

Services: What is the activity program? Is there recreational therapy? Physical and occupational therapy? Speech and hearing therapy? Social psychiatric and psychological services? Are there religious services? How often?

Fees: What are the extra charges? (Ask for a written list.) What is the policy regarding changes in charges? Is a deposit required? Is it returnable and under what conditions? May patients handle their own funds? What if they are unable to? Will it be necessary to move if the patient goes on Medicaid or if more or less care is needed in future?

Complaints: How are they handled? Is there a resident council? Is there an ombudsman?

If your parent is mentally competent, find out whether patients who are mentally impaired or have behavior problems are mixed with general care patients. If your parent is suffering from Alzheimer's, you'll want to know whether he or she will be in a segregated section and what particular means will be used to handle his or her behavioral difficulties.

Making the Move

Daniel Sambol, director of services for the aging for the Federation of Protestant Welfare Agencies in New York, says, "The decision to seek admission for a parent to an institution is not lightly taken in most families. But once done, families begin to move like lightning because the whole procedure is so painful for them."

Don't let speed interfere with your best instincts. Review your options. Be sure you're not pushing your parent into an institution unnecessarily. On the other hand, don't deny him or her the security and safety of an institution when that is really the best place for your parent to be. And don't leave your own needs out of the calculations if you are stretched to the breaking point. When you make your choice, you may want the further advice of professionals on how to make the move as comfortable for everyone as possible. Social workers on the nursing home staff should be able to advise you well.

Except in emergencies, where immediate placement is essential to health and safety, allow a little time for your parent to get used to the idea, to think about disposing of his or her possessions, to select a few precious things to take along to maintain his or her link with past life. "Families should discuss the disposal of possessions with the older person before a crisis develops. In this way, the older person can maintain a central role in the process. He (or she) might derive pleasure and satisfaction from giving possessions to friends, or donating them to charities. . . . Knowing that one's former possessions will be used and appreciated is not as traumatic as not knowing what happened to them. . . . Increased death rates have been linked to involuntary relocation for which no preparation has been made."[4]

"Transfer trauma" and "transplantation shock" are among the terms used by researchers and professionals to describe the stress experienced by older people when they are moved to unfamiliar environments. To reduce the chances that your parent will suffer these traumas, if it is at all possible, go together several times to the home you have chosen and walk through the spaces in which he or she will live, finding your way from parent's room to bathroom to dining room and social areas. Give your parent an opportunity to talk to the staff and fellow residents a number of times before moving in. Ask the administrator for permission to do this. If time does not permit such familiarizing routines, then stay with your parent as much as possible during the first days to ease the transition.

The Family and the Nursing Home

It's important to have a good relationship with nursing home staff. The arrival of a parent in a nursing home doesn't mean his or her departure from your life. On the contrary, you will visit, spend time there, and have many dealings with many people on the staff. One nursing home administrator offers this advice to families:

- Understand clearly what the institution has to offer—precisely what services are and are not available.
- Strive for mutual confidence between you and the home's administration that they will do their job and you will not interfere as long as they are doing it.
- Maintain regular communication with your parent. Follow the normal pattern you had when your parent was at home: regular telephone calls and visits. Knowing that you are very much involved will give the staff a better attitude toward both your parent and you.
- Protect your parent's connection to the family. Bring children to visit, if appropriate. Bring tapes of family celebrations if the home has facilities for viewing them. Bring plenty of pictures.
- Listen if your parent complains, but don't assume the worst until you talk to the staff and hear their side of the story. Try to play a positive role in erasing the problem. If you are really displeased with something, talk to the administrator, the resident council, and then the ombudsman if the matter hasn't been resolved.
- If, over a period of time, you decide that this is not the place for your parent, you may have to make other arrangements.

The Ombudsman

Federal legislation mandates an ombudsman program in each state to protect the interests of the institutionalized.

Ombudsman is a Swedish word for an official who investigates citizen complaints. In this country, it has come to mean a person who listens to complaints, investigates, and intervenes to help resolve the problem. An ombudsman for a nursing home is a patient advocate.

There is no uniformity in the ombudsman program because funding varies significantly from state to state, beyond the federal minimum. As a result, citizens get very different kinds of protection depending on where they live. Amendments to the Older Americans Act added in 1987 are intended to strengthen the state ombudsman programs. They increase residents' protection against abuse and include regulations to protect residents or employees who complain from reprisals and assure the ombudsman access to the long-term care facility and to the residents as well as access to appropriate medical or social records (with consent of the patient or legal guardian). Volunteers provide 80 percent of ombudsman services throughout the country. If your parent is in a nursing home and you have an unresolved problem, call the state ombudsman. You can get the number through the Area Agency on Aging if you cannot find it in the telephone book.

Patient Rights in Nursing Homes

All Medicare- and Medicaid-certified nursing homes must now adhere to the federal standards for patient rights established by legislation in 1987 in response to years of "shockingly deficient care" in many nursing homes across the country.[5] The new law requires nursing homes to train, for at least 75 hours, the nurses' aides who provide most of the patient care. Homes must also employ licensed nurses on a 24-hour basis. A registered nurse must be on duty for at least 8 hours each day of the week. There are specified exceptions. Patient rights now written into law include the right to quality care, to participate in planning their own care and treatment, to have a yearly evaluation to assess how well their needs are being met, to freedom from "physical or mental abuse, corporal punishment, involuntary seclusion and any physical or chemical restraints imposed for purposes of discipline or convenience," and to protection against abrupt discharge or transfer. Patients are entitled to meet with fellow residents and voice any grievances. The family, government inspectors, and ombudsmen cannot be barred from "immediate access" to patients. Violators are subject to penalties of up to $10,000 a day. The new requirements are to be phased in over a two-and-a-half-year period. While this legislation gives you more strength to protest against shoddy or inhumane treatment and to report violations, you cannot relax your own close involvement in the institution where your parent resides. See the Appendix for the Nursing Home Patient Bill of Rights prepared by the American Association of Homes for the Aging. You may request a copy from the administrator. You should become familiar with these rights for your parent's protection and call the ombudsman if they are being violated (see Appendix).

Families should remember that an ombudsman cannot change everything. Suppose the complaint relates to meals. The ombudsman volunteer will come in at mealtime to see if the meal is served on time, is properly hot or cold, and that someone is there to help if feeding is necessary. Some confused patients will say they haven't eaten for a week, while a just-finished meal tray is still in the room. On the other hand, some patients are afraid to complain for fear of retribution, and the ombudsman must be keenly observant. In a well-funded program, the ombudsman makes periodic rounds and checks on the day-to-day quality of the patient's life. The ombudsman evaluates the complaints and then tries to remedy the problems with the nursing home administrator. Many complaints are serious and warrant prompt intervention, but "Remember," says one ombudsman trainer, "that most residents don't want to be there. They may be angry with the family for placing them there; therefore they make many complaints. The family is full of guilt; therefore they complain about all sorts of nitty-gritty things. The complaints can be secondary to the anger and the guilt—what is going on between the parent and the child—and the ombudsman has to tread very carefully in these situations."

Families who want guarantees that their elders are in good hands should be prepared to keep close check on their parents' daily lives and visit frequently. No solution will be perfect if your parent is ill and old and tired. But whatever you do, if it is done with love and compassion, with respect for your parent, for yourself, and for others in your family, it will be the best you can do. That is all you can ask of yourself.

SIX

MONEY MATTERS

Government Benefits, Insurance, Taxes, Estates, Protective Services

Money problems between generations are widespread and for more than economic reasons. Sometimes it's a parent's ingrained attitude that a child has no business knowing the extent of the parent's resources—even an adult child. Or a parent may be squirreling away assets to surprise the child with a legacy, or be ashamed at how little there is, or be expecting the child to provide support while the parent is alive to assure that there will be something to leave on the parent's death. Sometimes it's the child's reluctance to bring up money matters for fear of seeming overly interested in how much will be left. Sometimes it's superstition that any discussion about wills and estates is bad luck. For whatever reason, if you haven't talked to your parent about money before now, you may be reluctant to begin.

Being old—like many other things—costs much more than it once did. It's legitimate for you and your parent to discuss where the money will come from. Will there be enough to live on after retirement for the foreseeable future? Will there be enough for medical bills, for long-term care at home, in a nursing home, or in some other kind of supervised setting? Because most children sooner or later become entwined with their parents' financial needs, it's best to begin talking together early, so there will be fewer unpleasant surprises. The aim is to meet your parents' needs and protect their resources.

But how to begin?

You can begin to overcome the obstacles by being forthcoming about your own affairs and by being sensitive to your parents' wish to remain independent and in control of their own lives. Your parents are entitled to do what they wish with their resources. No matter that your mother is more frugal than you believe necessary because she wants to leave something for the children, or that your father spends more for his own pleasure now than you think suitable. (One bumper sticker reads "I'm spending my children's inheritance.") Only extremes that indicate your parent may no longer be competent to make reasoned judgments require your direct intervention to protect your parent's well-being. Few old people willingly part with whatever they consider the essential resources for their own old age. You can help by talking about actions they can take or avoid to assure that they are protected and that their wishes—whatever they are—are accomplished.

This chapter deals with the major government programs and entitlements, health insurance, taxes, wills and estates, and problems of incompetency that can affect your parent's financial status. Private investments and private pensions are not included. Information on these can be sought from older persons' organizations, adult education courses, private financial counselors, or from articles and books on the library shelves. Some senior centers also sponsor seminars in financial planning. The information here is not comprehensive but will give you and your parents some background so that you can better understand some of the major pitfalls and possible remedies for common problems.

The major federal programs that can help pay for the living costs and high medical expenses of people who are 65 and older include Social Security, Supplemental Security Income, Medicare, Medicaid, Food Stamps, and veteran's benefits. Knowing about them may mean extra dollars for you and your parent. If your parents are among the poor but proud, remind them that they contributed through their taxes to making these programs available to low-income people. They are entitled to all the help these programs provide and should have it. Sometimes eligibility for one program depends on applying for another.

It is not possible here to give you all the rules and regulations that apply to the various programs. Consult the local Area Agency on Aging; be prepared to bring documents to prove your parent's financial status; if necessary, seek legal advice. Legal assistance may be essential, for example, if one of your parents is in a nursing home and the other cannot meet expenses at home with the small portion left from Social Security.

SOCIAL SECURITY

The Social Security system is intended to provide a base of continuing income when earnings stop or are reduced as a result of retirement, disability, or death. In varying ways, Social Security protects dependent minors, seniors, the widowed, the disabled, and anyone suffering permanent kidney failure who requires dialysis—under particular regulations. But its major contribution has been to improve the quality of life for America's oldest citizens.

Social Security provides the major portion of income for most people over 65. Many older Americans have income in addition to Social Security; many have only Social Security to sustain them; some are not covered at all. Within the range of elderly people—from the starving and impoverished to the wealthy—lie the vast majority of America's seniors, who are largely better off than they were in the past, but whose budgets are nevertheless tight, whose medical bills are about twice what Medicare provides, and who have little or no protection against long-term frailty.

Earnings record and marital status are the basis for determining Social Security benefits. Life earnings are adjusted for inflation in calculating benefits. Maximum benefits to a 65-year-old starting to collect in 1988 were $828 a month. There is no longer a minimum, though people with minimal incomes may be entitled to SSI. Full benefits are available currently to the earner at age 65. This will change within the next decades to age 67; the change will be phased in gradually after the year 2000. A person who has worked at a job covered by Social Security is eligible to receive monthly benefits at age 62, but only at 80 percent of the amount he or she would receive by waiting until age 65. There is a formula that establishes the applicable rate between 62 and 65. It is complicated to figure out when it is most beneficial for one or both partners in a marriage to start collecting benefits, but staff at the local Social Security office or a good tax lawyer can work with your parent(s) to arrive at the best solution.

If one parent has never worked but is an eligible age, she or he can receive Social Security benefits amounting to half the spouse's benefit while the spouse is alive, then the full benefit at the spouse's death. Under these circumstances, while both are alive, a couple may receive one full benefit and one half benefit of the earner's maximum benefit. If both spouses have worked, each is entitled to the maximum benefit based on his or her record. A wife, for example, might then receive full benefits based on her own record rather than half based on her husband's. The system allows you to receive the highest benefit, whichever that is.

At present, your parent's Social Security benefits are reduced if he or she earns more than a specified amount in any given year, up to age 70. This amount changes each year; in 1988 it was $6,120 a year, or $510 a month, for those between 62 and 65 and $8,400 a year, or $700 a month, for retirees between 65 and 70. The law provides a periodic increase in this amount, just as it provides automatic cost-of-living increases in the monthly Social Security payment. If your parent earns more than the allowed amount, his or her Social Security is reduced according to a formula. Until 1990, the formula calls for returning $1 of Social Security income for each $2 earned over the allowed amount. After that year, under present regulations, it will be $1 for every $3 earned in excess. The law may change again, so it is always wise to check each year to know what regulations prevail.

If your parent chooses not to retire from work at age 65, his or her Social Security benefits will be increased by a credit of 3 percent a year till age 70, and the benefits will be calculated on a higher earnings base. In 1990 this "delayed retirement credit" will increase to 3.5 percent. If your eligible mother wishes to start collecting before your working father does, or vice versa, the nonworking spouse is entitled to half the earner's entitlement at age 65, and this does not rise, even when the earning spouse is eligible to receive a greater benefit later. Check with the local Social Security office to learn what the monthly benefit will be.

Other factors to consider, when deciding at what age to start collecting benefits, include how much income tax your parent will pay on income earned if he or she chooses to continue to work; whether or not your parent *wants* to continue working after 65; and how much other income is available. Only earned income—not interest, dividends, or profits—counts in determining how much Social Security benefit will be retained if your parent goes over the earned income limit. Income tax, however, is based on total income, and Social Security income is now partially taxed. There is considerable pressure building to tax all Social Security income for those above a certain total income.

An unmarried, divorced spouse may start to claim benefits at age 62, based on the previous partner's earnings record, so long as the marriage lasted at least ten years, no matter how long ago the couple was divorced or whether the partner is collecting Social Security or has remarried. One practical effect of this is that older women with no significant work record of their own, who are divorced after a long-lasting marriage, have a claim to Social Security benefits based on their previous husband's earnings record (a record to which the excess earnings deductions mentioned above do not apply). Another effect is that older divorced people have taken up the live-in relationships their youngsters pioneered, without benefit of marriage, so as not to jeopardize their Social Security payments.

Widows are now permitted to remarry without losing their widow's benefits on a dead spouse's earning record. After a year of marriage, if the new husband's entitlements are higher, she is then entitled to an additional amount that brings her the benefit of his higher rate.

Social Security benefits do not arrive automatically when a person reaches the eligible age. Your parent must apply for them at the local Social Security office. People are urged to do this three months in advance of their 65th birthday, or before the date set for retirement in advance of age 65, so that all papers can be processed and benefits begin on time.

Applications for Social Security can be arranged by telephone through Social Security's Teleservice. This is a good way to save time, energy, and the expense of a trip to the office. They'll send the necessary forms, and your parent can return these with the necessary documentation: proof of birth, marriage certificates, Social Security numbers, and income tax records from the previous year for the self-employed. (Keep copies.) Once in the system, your parent can continue to use Teleservice for questions or problems. The telephone number is listed in your local directory under Social Security Administration or U.S. Government. Call for information after the middle of the month, unless it is urgent, to avoid long waits. Offices are open Monday through Friday during regular business hours. Expect phone lines to be very busy at the beginning of the week and month and on the day checks are received and the day after.

Your parent's check can be sent directly to his or her bank; this can be arranged when application is first made or at any time thereafter. This arrangement saves trips to the bank and worry about mailbox thefts or muggings.

Social Security pays a lump sum death benefit, generally $255, to an eligible surviving widow or widower or an eligible child. Application for this must be made within two years after the death.

Special Social Security Benefits

Some other Social Security benefits, less well known, can go to older people under certain conditions. Your parent must apply for them; they don't come automatically. It's well worth a call to the local Social Security office if you think any of these conditions pertain. Benefits can go to:

- a person who becomes severely disabled, mentally or physically, before age 65, if the condition prevents the person from working, is expected to or has lasted 12 months, or is expected to result in death
- the spouse of a Social Security–eligible person who is disabled, retired, or has died, if the spouse is more than 62, even if not covered in his or her own right
- a divorced woman who had been married at least 10 years, is 62 or older, and has not remarried, or has survived her husband (beginning at age 60) or is disabled (beginning at age 50)
- a divorced woman who marries a man eligible for Social Security and has been married, generally, for at least one year. She may apply for benefits under the conditions that usually apply to married couples.
- those 62 or older completely dependent on a child who has died
- any widow or widower, 60 years old or more, of a deceased person eligible for Social Security

These benefits are sometimes larded with complicated requirements and conditions. The Social Security office can explain these requirements to you. Unfavorable decisions can be appealed.

The Social Security Administration in Washington and its local offices have many pamphlets discussing all aspects of benefits. You can pick these up at any convenient Social Security office or write away for them (see Bibliography). For further explanations, talk directly with a local office staff person or use the Teleservice.

SUPPLEMENTAL SECURITY INCOME (SSI)

Supplemental Security Income (SSI) goes to people over 65 who have limited financial resources. Half the states add their own money (in varying degrees) to what the federal government allocates for SSI payments; consequently, the amount an older person may receive differs from state to state. Eligibility requirements also vary. Only people already on Social Security are eligible for SSI.

The basic Federal SSI payment in 1988 was $354 a month for a single adult with resources of less than $1,900 and $532 for a couple with resources up to $2,700. In New York in 1988 the basic SSI check for an individual living alone was $425.91 and for a couple $624.91. Massachusetts and California make bigger state contributions, others less. The amount paid may also be less or more depending on various factors that are reviewed at the time of application. The amount is determined anew each year.

Check with the Social Security office to determine what the resource limitations are in your parent's state. A person who is on the borderline of eligibility may be advised to "spend down"—use up assets in order to become eligible. For example, people who have been living off a lump sum of capital from an insurance policy or inheritance and are down to their last few thousand dollars can benefit by spending that amount for necessities and becoming eligible for the more helpful SSI benefit rather than hanging on to the small amount of money and trying to make it last. Even a person whose resources are above the stated ceiling may be able to get some monthly payments based on a sliding scale related to income. Blind and disabled people are eligible for SSI even under age 65, if they meet all the other criteria.

MEDICARE

Medicare is indeed a boon to older Americans, but it is not the total answer to medical bills. Despite the facts, most older Americans continue to misperceive what Medicare does and does not pay for. The benefits and coverage it promises must be examined carefully in advance for the actual value they may hold—or withhold.

Medicare is available to virtually everybody at age 65, as well as to victims of advanced kidney disease requiring regular dialysis or kidney transplant at any age and to certain other disabled people under 65. If your parents are covered by Social Security or railroad retirement benefits, they will also get automatic hospital insurance under Part A of Medicare, whether or not they are retired. At 65 they also become eligible for Part B of Medicare—the part that covers doctor's bills and some other medical expenses—on payment of a monthly fee. In 1988 this basic premium was $24.80 a month. There is a schedule of deductibles and copayments. If your parent plans to continue working, he or she should apply for Medicare three months before the 65th birthday month, so that coverage starts the month the birthday is reached. If your parent neglects to apply for Medicare until a later year, premiums will increase, unless your parent is enrolled in an employee medical plan and other rules apply.

The basic costs of Medicare are constantly increasing. Expanded coverage, taking effect between 1989 and 1990, limits individual total annual outlay for hospital stays to $564 and approved physicians' fees to $1400, reimburses partially for annual prescription bills of more than $600, increases home care, nursing home, and hospice benefits, provides for some respite, and protects spouses of nursing home residents against total impoverishment. To pay for this, the monthly Part B premium will increase $4 on January 1, 1989. A surtax will also be charged to higher-income elderly. Check with the IRS or Social Security to determine whether the surtax applies to your parent. Medicare Part B pays only 80 percent of the *allowed* cost of medical services; the individual pays the rest unless he or she holds Medigap insurance (discussed below). The discrepancy between a medical fee and what Medicare allows can be large. Not all physicians accept Medicare *assignment*—that is, the amount allowed by Medicare for a particular service. If they do, of course, this is to the patient's advantage. Medicare has paid for only about 46 percent of its recipients' annual medical costs. Many costly items, such as eye examinations and glasses, dental bills, and hearing aids, are not covered.

If your parents are not covered by Social Security, they can buy Medicare hospital insurance (Part A) by paying a premium; this monthly basic premium in 1988 was $234. People who buy Medicare hospital insurance (Part A) must also enroll in medical insurance (Part B).

After 65, working people have the option of staying with an employee health plan or choosing Medicare as the primary payer. Some stay with an employee health plan—if the premiums are not too high—for primary coverage and use their Medicare, to which they continue to be entitled, as the secondary payer, to supplement the employee plan. Employers are required to explain the options to employees when they become eligible for Medicare. Not every office fully understands the options, however, so it is wise to check personally before deciding on one or another. Enrollment for Part B is limited to certain periods of the year.

Medicare is not administered by the Social Security Administration but is part of the Health Care Financing Administration, which sets the rules and regulations. When your parent, the doctor, the hospital, or the home health providers send a bill for treatment or services, it goes to an insurance company selected by the government to process and make Medicare payments. *Hospital* claims are handled by *intermediaries. Medical* claims are handled by *carriers.* These intermediaries and carriers are sometimes referred to as third parties. They are different in different parts of the country, and you are subject to the third party's interpretation of the rules and regulations in your local area.

Once you become enmeshed in your parent's Medicare affairs, an event that usually occurs as older people feel less and less able to deal with the system and the endless forms involved, you should make yourself as knowledgeable as possible about the processes and start a well-organized file to keep track of the papers. *Keep copies of every bill, every filled-out form, every piece of correspondence.* You won't be sorry about the extra time this takes initially. People who can afford it sometimes pay a person to follow through with all these papers from beginning to end—it's that bad. People who can't afford this route and aren't careful may lose significant amounts of money.

How the System Works

Medicare may or may not pay your parent's medical fees. This fact is often ignored, and a majority of America's older population continue to be lulled into a false sense of security by the Medicare promise. The fact is that the elderly pay a substantial portion of their medical bills out of their own pockets. Medicare pays only according to its approved charges, and it pays only if services are delivered by a Medicare-certified institution, agency, or health care provider.

There are several reasons why personal health costs are so burdensome.

- Hospital and doctor's bills continue to escalate dramatically, despite efforts to curb them.
- Nursing home costs can wipe out a family's savings in two years or less. It's worse for the single elderly person. According to a Massachusetts Blue Cross and Blue Shield study, 63 percent of unmarried residents of nursing homes ran out of money within thirteen weeks, and 83 percent were impoverished within a year.[1] Moreover, most of the nation's nursing homes are not Medicare-certified.
- Approved charges are usually less than actual charges by doctors and health care providers.
- Older people and their families often don't inform themselves in advance of exactly what Medicare will and won't pay for.
- Hospital and medical services are reviewed by committees (Peer Review Organizations, or PROs) before Medicare payments are made. If the review committee feels that the services, treatment, charges, or length of stay in the hospital weren't reasonable and necessary, Medicare may pay none of the bill or only part of it.

- Medicare-reimbursable hospital stays are now limited by the prospective payment system and Diagnosis-Related Groups (DRGs). This system calculates ahead of time how much a hospital stay for a particular condition should cost and pays a fixed amount to the hospital. Whether the hospital discharges the patient sooner or later than the DRG specifies, it receives the same amount of money, except in special cases. Costs for posthospital home care for still sick patients can be considerably higher than Medicare will cover.

Familiarize yourself now with just what Medicare can and cannot pay for. Each year a *Medicare Handbook* is issued. You can obtain the current one from a local Social Security office or by calling the Teleservice. Don't wait until you're in the middle of an emergency—by that time, you may already have paid an ambulance service that isn't certified by Medicare or a nursing home that doesn't qualify for Medicare posthospital benefits. Medicare will not reimburse you for these outlays.

The *Medicare Handbook* is more than 50 pages long and includes information on who can provide services and supplies, what is or isn't covered for Medicare hospital patients, the restrictions on inpatient care in skilled nursing facilities, the requirements for care in certified facilities or by certified personnel, hospice, limits on home health care, and blood coverage. The medical insurance section explains what doctor's and outpatient services are covered, such as physical therapy, speech pathology, and outpatient surgical procedures. There are directions for filing claims and notification of your rights to appeal. Pay careful attention to each of these items.

The names of the Medicare intermediary and carrier in each state are also listed in the handbook. Read the material carefully and talk in person with the third party about any item you do not fully understand, in advance of the need, if possible. Also listed is a toll-free Fraud and Abuse Hot Line: 800-368-5779 (800-638-3986 in Maryland). Use this if you have reason to believe that a doctor, hospital, or other health care provider is performing unnecessary or inappropriate services, or if you believe charges are being made for services not performed.

If you are having trouble with appeals from unfavorable Medicare decisions, consult the local Area Agency on Aging or bar association to obtain legal services, if necessary. It is important to use lawyers who are experienced in these matters or who will consult experts in this field on your behalf. See the Appendix under Legal Assistance.

Reading the *Medicare Handbook* is only the beginning of your self-education. When your elderly parent is actually in a situation where medical expenses are about to be incurred—as when a hospital stay is indicated or when the doctor says home care is necessary—then ask the doctor, or the staff person who deals with Medicare forms, how much Medicare will pay for each step and service along the way. Your rule should be: *Always ask in advance.* Then if you find Medicare won't pay for something, or will only pay for part of it, perhaps you can find a less costly alternative. If that isn't possible, at least you won't have a shock when the bill comes in.

Medicare Pitfalls

Some of these rules may have changed by the time you read this. Check the current regulations.

- The doctor says your parent needs certain laboratory tests. Medicare will pay only if these are done in a laboratory certified by Medicare. Not all laboratories are certified, or certified for all kinds of tests. *Check this with the doctor.*
- Your parent needs someone to take care of him or her at home after a hospital stay. Medicare will pay only for part-time skilled nursing care, physical therapy, and speech therapy, not for personal care or housekeeping services. Additional services such as occupational therapy, home health aides, medical social services, medical supplies, or durable medical equipment are *not* covered, on their own, unless the part-time skilled nurse, physical or speech therapies are also needed. *Medicare does not pay for full-time nursing care at home* or for other home health needs such as drugs, delivered meals, or blood transfusions.

▪ The doctor says your parent should go to a nursing home after a hospital stay. Medicare will *not* pay unless *all* its criteria are met: The home must be a skilled nursing facility (SNF), be Medicare-certified, and give the required kind of service. Then the following five conditions must be met: (1) your parent must have been in a hospital at least three days in a row, not counting day of discharge; (2) reason for admission to the SNF must be treatment for the same condition for which hospital treatment was required; (3) admission to the SNF must be within a short period after the hospital stay (generally within 30 days); (4) a doctor must certify that skilled nursing service or rehabilitative service is required on a daily basis; (5) the SNF's Utilization Review Committee or a Peer Review Organization does not disapprove the stay. Finally, your parent must require skilled nursing or rehabilitation on a daily basis, not just a few days a week. Medicare will *not* pay for what it calls *custodial care.* A legal expert, John Regan, in his book *Tax, Estate and Financial Planning for the Elderly,* warns that the nursing home or SNF benefit "is fraught with pitfalls to coverage. . . . Advocates for Medicare beneficiaries report that many cases that fall well within the regulatory standards for skilled care are denied coverage by the Medicare administration."[2]

▪ Your parent is admitted to a nursing home after hospitalization. If all criteria are met, Medicare will *help* pay for up to 100 days in each benefit period (if 60 days elapse between hospitalizations and all criteria are met anew). It pays for all covered services during the first 20 days; after that until the 100th day, it pays for part and your parent pays for part. This amount changes periodically. In 1988 the part for which patients were personally responsible was $67.50 a day.

Your parent needs psychiatric care. *In a psychiatric hospital:* Medicare will pay for only 190 days of care in a lifetime, and only in a participating hospital. *On an outpatient basis:* treatment for mental illness is covered for a maximum of $250 a year (less than that if these charges are used to meet the annual deductible).

Some things Medicare won't pay for at all:

- a private room in a hospital or nursing home, unless it is deemed medically necessary; otherwise it will pay only for a semiprivate room
- private duty nursing
- personal conveniences: TV, radio, telephone
- dental care, unless it involves surgery of or setting fractures of jaws or facial bones; it will cover hospitalization, but not the dental care, if procedures are severe enough to require this
- routine foot care and optometrists' services

Assignment

This is the magic word that controls your parent's medical budget. Ask the physician if he or she accepts payment on *assignment*. Many doctors won't, but your parent will end up ahead of the game if the doctor will. If the doctor accepts assignment (the approved amount), Medicare pays 80 percent of that amount to the doctor directly. Your parent is then billed only for the remaining 20 percent. Doctors and suppliers who are willing to accept assignment are called *Medicare-participating* doctors and suppliers. Their names and addresses are listed in a directory available at all Social Security offices and Area Agencies on Aging or from the insurance carrier responsible for Medicare locally.

The doctor who does not accept assignment can charge any amount. Your parent pays the physician directly, files a Medicare claim with the carrier, and then is reimbursed for 80 percent of the approved amount. If the doctor has charged more than what the carrier terms *reasonable,* your parent pays the difference.

As of this writing, doctors aren't required by law to accept assignment for Medicare patients except in Massachusetts.

Appealing Medicare Decisions

You have the right to appeal any Medicare decisions with which you disagree if you feel your parent has not been properly reimbursed or covered for services to which he or she is entitled.

There are different procedures for different situations. For example, you can appeal a hospital insurance decision by asking for a Peer Organization Review. If you remain unsatisfied, and more than $200 is involved, you can go higher and ask for a hearing by a judge for the Social Security Administration. If still dissatisfied, and $2,000 or more is involved, you can appeal to a federal court.

Other appeals, involving skilled nursing facilities, home health services, and hospice care, go a somewhat different route. Requests for review here are submitted through the Medicare intermediary for each provider or through your local Social Security office. If in doubt, call the Social Security office for more information until you clearly understand the procedure.

If your claims submitted to the Medicare insurance carrier under medical insurance are rejected, or allowed services are disputed, or the amount of money allowed is contrary to what you believe is justified under the regulations, then you can ask that the carrier review its decisions. There are definite procedures and time limits involved in this; be sure you check each "explanation of benefits" carefully and note the final date that appears on the explanation sheet for appeals. If you still disagree with the decision after the claim has been reviewed, request a hearing with the carrier. The decision of the carrier hearing officer is final—the law does not provide for federal court review. Small amounts of money (under $100) are not subject to review, but if you have a number of unsatisfactory claims totaling $100 within a six-month period, you can lump these together in one appeal.

If all this is too much for you, ask for help through the local Area Agency on Aging or a family service agency.

MEDICAID

Most middle- and upper-class people shudder at the thought of resorting to Medicaid, but many of those over 65 who are covered by Medicaid have never before accepted government aid. Responsible and productive people during their earlier years, their savings were consumed by the steep cost of living in their later years, especially medical costs and the cost of continuing care. They found that if their incomes fell low enough to meet eligibility requirements, Medicaid would cover almost all of their medical and health expenses.

One of Medicaid's purposes is to pay for a range of basic medical services for low-income older people. Medicaid can pay, in most cases, for everything Medicare pays for and more. All SSI recipients are eligible for Medicaid and so are the "medically needy" (those with slightly higher incomes but large medical expenses). Medicaid disbursements for the elderly go largely for that part of the population requiring long-term care.

Unlike Medicare, however, which is open to all people 65 or older and offers the same span of benefits all over the country, Medicaid eligibility requirements vary from state to state. In all states, Medicaid will pay for all or part of doctor, hospital, and nursing home bills. In some states it will also pay for prescription drugs, eyeglasses, appliances, laboratory and X-ray services, home health care, other medically related needs, and sometimes even housekeeping services if this will help keep the frail or handicapped elderly out of a nursing home. Medicare does not cover long-term nursing home costs; Medicaid can. Furthermore, benefits cover care and services furnished for three months before the application is made, so if your parent does qualify, Medicaid payments will be retroactive for this period.

The Older Women's League reports that "on average, an older person or their family would need $500,000 in assets producing about $40,000 a year to cover nursing home bills."[3] Medicaid often becomes the only alternative.

Medicaid Care at Home

Medicaid can pay for home health care and personal and housekeeping assistance in an older person's home if the person is eligible. If you think your parent can stay out of an institution with some help at home, which he or she cannot afford, inquire about Medicaid.

It's true that escalating medical costs and tightening state budgets are forcing cutbacks in some Medicaid services. You may be asked directly if you can help your parent financially, or you may be asked to provide the services yourself. You may feel a moral responsibility to help support parents whose income isn't sufficient to meet their needs, but there's no law that says you must. Whether or not your parent qualifies for Medicaid still depends essentially on your parent's income, not on yours, despite efforts of the Health Care Financing Administration to change this. If your Medicaid-eligible parent lives with you, it is still his or her income and assets that determine eligibility, not yours. Home health care ordered by the doctor, for example, can be paid for by Medicaid if your parent is eligible, regardless of your circumstances. If you contribute to your parent's support in his or her own home, however, how you do it can affect Medicaid eligibility. For example, it matters whether you give your parent the money to pay the rent or pay the rent directly yourself. You should inquire about this from the Medicaid office.

Medicaid income and assets eligibility requirements are similar to those for SSI but allow slightly higher maximum resources or income. Inquire in the state where your parent lives; if you live in a different state, check each state's eligibility requirements. People sometimes move to the most generous state, but you should investigate carefully before you decide to transplant your parent. It's true that there is no period of state residency required for Medicaid, but your parent may be asked for a statement of his or her intent in moving and should be prepared to explain, and document, that he or she moved for other reasons than to receive Medicaid. Your parent may have to offer some proof of residency (a lease or license) and proof that residency has been permanently given up in the other state. In cases where disputes occur between states, the mere physical presence of the person in a given state can determine the outcome, but your aged mother living in Florida can't maintain a residence there, come to New York for treatment and care, and then claim New York benefits.

Medicaid, Couples, and Long-Term Care

A spouse is financially responsible for another spouse, and the implications of this, in terms of Medicaid eligibility, can be very serious for your parents should one require long-term care. The interpretation of what can be retained to sustain the partner living at home and what must be given up to pay for the institutionalized partner is complicated by a variety of laws and regulations and is different in different states. Even where the rights of the *community spouse*—the one living at home—are legislated as a protection against total impoverishment, these laws have been so poorly publicized that potential benefactors have been pauperized nevertheless. Also, Medicaid officials have been known to issue illegal and unfair decisions. Imperiled individuals must then go to court to rectify these decisions and win their rights. The court cases dramatize the terrible plight of old couples in this situation. New legislation passed to correct this.

Older couples are sometimes advised to divorce so that the noninstitutionalized partner can be freed of legal financial responsibility and retain some of the family resources for his or her own living. While this is legal, it is a heartless process few older couples can bear to pursue.

To protect their resources and avoid destitution, some parents give away their hard-earned savings to their children so that they can meet the Medicaid standards. This practice is now limited by regulations that say such gifts have to be made at least two or three years before application for Medicaid (the time limit varies from state to state).

The practice of *spending down* raises personal and ethical issues. Some knowledgeable and wealthy elderly individuals do give away their resources within the legal time limits, usually to their children, with whom they have arranged that the funds be used for their own benefit until such time as they are institutionalized and their care is paid for by Medicaid. Some people with very modest assets who are informed about the legalities do likewise. But many older people balk at this procedure, fearful that by giving away their assets they are giving away their independence, which they cherish, and that they are making themselves hostage to a child's whims. Furthermore, giving away what they have worked hard to accumulate is an acknowledgment that the end has really come, an enormously difficult step to take for many if not most people.

"Why should my tax money be used to support a person whose family is wealthy and can afford to support its elderly parents?" many people would say. But the hard truth is that this is the case with relatively few. The majority of people faced with nursing home costs do not have large stores of capital secreted in legal hideaways. The majority have saved just enough to provide themselves with some dignity in their retirement; it is this small stake that is wiped out quickly by the costs of long-term care, leaving them at the mercy of public policy.

Being covered by Medicaid has undeniable frustrations. The process of being investigated and of supplying the required detailed information on income, rent, and bank accounts, for example, may be very time-consuming, and there are subsequent periodic reviews of eligibility, which may be as frequent as every month.

Medicaid patients are free to use the doctor, hospital, or nursing facility of their choice, or engage home health aides or other home help, provided that the doctor agrees and that the institution or personnel agency is participating in Medicaid. Some doctors won't accept Medicaid patients; some nursing homes won't, and others have a limited number of beds for Medicaid patients. Find this out in advance. One woman reported that her 100-year-old uncle, who had been living in a private nursing home in Florida, had used up all his assets to pay for his care. The nursing home where he had lived for many years did not accept Medicaid patients, so when he was the most frail, he had to move.

Most people do not know what course their old age will take, how long they will live, or what specific needs will arise. They plan according to their best knowledge and hope it all works out. If your family is trying to plan for long-term care for an institutionalized parent, it is best to consult the local Area Agency on Aging for applicable regulations on Medicaid in that state and to have the advice of a lawyer experienced in Medicaid actions. In trying to pursue the ins and outs of Medicaid, however, it is often more productive to work through a social worker and a social service agency.

FOOD STAMPS

The Food Stamp program is dramatically underused by people over 65 who can qualify for it. They equate it with welfare, or they're deterred by the bureaucratic processes they must endure to receive the stamps or the embarrassment of using them in front of others at the checkout line.

If your parent's income qualifies him or her for Food Stamps, you might review together the advantages and drawbacks. Your parent can qualify for Food Stamps with a higher income and resources than for SSI and beginning at age 60, or sometimes younger. Almost anyone living on Social Security income alone is eligible for at least the minimum of $10 a month in Food Stamps. Eligibility is calculated by a formula somewhat different from that for SSI. The minimum monthly allotment of $10 for one or two people rises, according to need, to $81 for an individual or $149 for two.

Application must be made in person at the Food Stamps office, but your parent can authorize you or any adult (a neighbor or friend) to appear instead. (An authorized person can even redeem the Food Stamps and shop for the elderly person.) In certain instances, the process can be handled by mail, especially if the person is already receiving SSI.

You can pick up an application at the Social Security office, but only a trip to the Food Stamps office will net you detailed information on personal eligibility and allotments. To apply, you need identification, proof of the Social Security number of each person in your parent's household, proof of earnings or other income (including Social Security and pensions) for each household member, and medical bills for those 60 or older for those receiving SSI, and for those who retired early on Social Security disability benefits.

Once your parent has been given an authorization to participate—ATP—he or she will have to convert the authorization card to coupons for food purchases. This procedure is different in different parts of the country: in some, the ATP must be taken to a specified bank for redemption; in others, there are check-casher services that redeem ATPs; elsewhere, some grocery stores are permitted to do this. When your parent finally has the Food Stamps in hand, he or she can use them at groceries and supermarkets for "nutritious" food only—no candy, beer, soda, alcohol, or tobacco and no soaps, powders, or other nonedibles. Food Stamps can also be used for Meals on Wheels and for meals in licensed communal or congregate eating centers such as those in senior centers (see chapter 2). Even the minimum $10 a month allowance will cover bread and milk for most people.

It isn't always so easy to find the Food Stamps program in your telephone book, but you can inquire at a department of social services in the community where your parent lives, at the Area Agency on Aging, or at the nearest Social Security office.

VETERANS' BENEFITS

By the end of this century, two out of every three men over 65 will be veterans, making veterans the largest single segment of the elderly male population in the country. In all, elderly veterans are expected to number 7.3 million by 1990 and 9 million by the end of the century, not too many years away.

The Veterans Administration (VA) administers all veterans' benefits. If you are the child of a veteran, you should know that various cash, medical, and burial benefits may be available for assistance. In any disputes about benefits, decisions by the Administrator are final and not subject to review by the courts. By the quirk of a special law reaching back to the end of the Civil War, veterans are not permitted to spend more than $10 for legal fees (to avoid being exploited) if they have problems with these benefits. As a result, many elderly veterans who are wrongfully deprived of their legal entitlements must depend on organizations that advocate on their behalf for no fee to secure what they desperately need and deserve.

If your parent is a veteran over 65 and has a low enough income, he or she will probably be able to get a small monthly pension from the Veterans Administration: for a single person it is $5,963 a year; for a couple, $7,811 (1987 figures). Sometimes pensions are paid on a sliding scale to veterans with slightly higher incomes. If your mother is a veteran's widow and has a low income, she should also be eligible for a pension. Widowers of female veterans have the same entitlements.

Veterans' hospitals and nursing homes will sometimes accept needy veterans even though they may not have a service-connected disability; but as numbers of veterans increase and facilities are limited, this is less likely to occur. In any event, doctors must provide affidavits documenting the medical need of the veteran for admission.

To find out if your parent can qualify for veterans' benefits, check the nearest Veterans Administration office. Telephone numbers are listed in the directory under U.S. Government: Veterans. You may be frustrated by endless busy signals on regional office telephones. Ask the Area Agency on Aging for the telephone number of a local office if it is not listed separately in the telephone book and you are more likely to get a quick response to your questions.

Counselors in the VA can answer questions about disability compensation; education benefits; dental care; death benefits; hospital, nursing home, and domiciliary care; and outpatient medical care at VA facilities. A spouse may also be eligible for these services. If you go for assistance, bring with you the veteran's service papers and marriage certificates. Find out whether your parent had a National Service Life Insurance policy while in service. For low-income assistance, you will need income information, including other retirement pensions, net worth, and verification for any other income-related items your parent may be asked to list.

For additional assistance, ask for help from the Veterans of Foreign Wars, Disabled American Veterans, and the American Legion (see Appendix under Veterans).

Dealing with Government Offices and Staff

Trying to deal with any bureaucratic agency can be time-consuming, frustrating, and sometimes infuriating. Offices are usually understaffed, have too few telephone lines, and face a rising number of daily inquiries about fairly complicated material. Ultimately you can get the information you want, but here are some tips to help you through the process:

- Always try to use the telephone first and get as much information as possible that way, or request that relevant pamphlets be mailed to you. If you must visit the office, learn beforehand what papers, documents, and information you need to bring with you to be spared a second trip.

- Make a list of your questions beforehand and keep it in front of you at the telephone or at the office you're visiting. Check off the questions as you go through the list to be sure you've asked everything. Write down answers, so you won't forget them. Ask for explanations of answers you don't understand. Don't be disconcerted if you don't know the meaning of jargon the staff members take for granted. Ask the counselor to translate it and apply it to your case.

- Learn the name of the person with whom you're dealing and try to talk to that person each time. This will make communication easier as you get to know and trust each other and save you the time and trouble of having to repeat your whole story to a new person.

- Mondays, the day after a holiday, and the first week of the month are particularly busy in these offices. Try to call or visit later in the week and later in the month.
- Even if you become frustrated or annoyed during your quest for information, it's best to remain courteous and calm.
- Keep all papers and correspondence that come from a government office or that relate to the subject you're negotiating. You'll need them for future reference. Always keep a copy of everything in your own files.
- Always ask about the appeal procedures so that you know what to do if you believe your parent has been denied benefits to which he or she is entitled. Be sure you know what time limits exist for appeal, what money limits may be involved in an appeal, and where and how appeals should be made.

MEDIGAP AND PRIVATE HEALTH INSURANCE

"Medigap" insurance is insurance that covers the difference between what Medicare pays and what your parent has to pay out of pocket. Many older people who buy Medigap insurance are not clear about what they are buying, buy policies that duplicate each other, and continue to remain uncovered for some essential health care situations. Some widely advertised health insurance schemes targeted to older people are misleading, costly, and may be considered fraudulent by some state insurance departments. Medigap policies vary greatly. Some pay the additional 20 percent Medicare deducts from its reimbursement for *allowed* services at *approved* fees but do not pay the difference between what is approved and what your parent owes a doctor who charges more or who performs other services. Other policies cover the differences completely and cover other essential health care needs as well. A good private insurance policy can help pay for all or part of the "Medigap."

Many states publish guides to the health insurance legally available for sale there and compare the premiums and benefits. Others publish guidelines to help consumers read policies and understand what is and is not covered. Inquire at the Area Agency on Aging or write to the state insurance department. The Health Care Financing Administration's *Guide to Health Insurance for People with Medicare* is available at your local Social Security office. The AARP publishes *Information on Medicare and Health Insurance for Older People* and *Policy Wise: The Practical Guide to Insurance Decisions for Older People* (see Appendix under Insurance). These are excellent publications to help your parent avoid mistaking flashy advertising for sound coverage.

Most policies for people over 65 don't cover home health care except perhaps for a registered nurse ordered by a doctor. They may, but generally don't, cover the costs of a homemaker, or unlicensed home health aide who helps with bathing, dressing, and housekeeping. Since Medicare pays only for limited home health services after hospitalization, and because people are sent home quicker and sicker now than ever before, it is wise to get insurance coverage for this kind of care, if at all possible. Inquire about this from your state insurance department and compare costs and benefits carefully. Look into policies offered by more than one company. All give benefits for hospital and posthospital nursing home stays, but not all will cover special nursing and out-of-hospital medications, and still fewer provide home health care coverage.

Most reliable insurance companies offer special Medigap policies to people over 65 that supplement Medicare benefits. Major medical insurance, with larger premiums, can relieve your parent of the serious financial burden of required medical care that is not covered by Medicare or Medigap policies. If federal catastrophic insurance legislation (limiting individual hospital and medical liability) has passed into law by the time

- Be familiar with Medicare benefits before buying a policy, and with benefits from any other policy your parent may hold. If a policy duplicates benefits your parents already have, they will be paying part of the premiums for something they don't need.

- Comprehensive coverage in one good policy is better than several policies with duplicate or overlapping coverage. This may be obtainable by continuing a group policy your parent already has from an employer, by purchasing a major medical policy, or by buying a Medigap policy.

- Your parent may be a good candidate for membership in an HMO, which offers comprehensive coverage, if there is a good HMO enlisting older people where your parent lives (see chapter 7).

- Check for limitations on benefits for pre-existing conditions. Find out exactly what the company's definition of a pre-existing condition is, and how far back it will inquire into your parent's medical history to determine if one exists. Compare policies and try to get one where coverage of pre-existing conditions begins as soon as possible after the effective date of the policy. This may be after six months, or a year or two. Be careful, even if the policy says "No physical or medical examination required," to read what it says about pre-existing conditions.

- Be careful about canceling an old policy and buying a new one, even though it may appear that the new one has better benefits. Remember that with a new policy the limitation on pre-existing conditions begins all over again. On the other hand, don't forego a new policy with excellent coverage if an old one is inadequate, especially in the light of new circumstances.

- Check the date when the policy becomes effective to be sure there isn't too long a waiting period.
- Check to see if there's a cancellation clause (a clause that allows the company to cancel the policy if certain conditions occur). Understand the renewal policy, and try to find a company that renews automatically.
- Deal with reputable insurance companies and agents licensed in the state where your parent lives. Some reputable national membership organizations offer good health insurance coverage to their members by mail, often for less money than individual policies. These are different from the numerous—not always trustworthy—commercial sales efforts to solicit new customers by direct mail and television advertising.
- Do not be taken in by a salesperson who claims to represent a government agency or government program selling Medicare supplemental insurance. The government does not solicit for or sell such insurance. Federal criminal penalties can be imposed in these cases.
- Once your parent decides on an appropriate policy, review the policy once again, fill out the application carefully, and keep copies of the application and all subsequent payments and correspondence. Don't pay bills by cash, and pay only to the insurance company, not to individuals.
- Take advantage of the "free look" provisions most companies offer. If you don't like what you see within the ten-day free period, send the policy back and ask for a refund. Don't be pressured by short enrollment periods.
- If you have problems with refunds or payment of benefits, get in touch with your state insurance department. It is actively concerned about protecting the

insurance-buying public; if you feel you've been victimized, waste no time in informing them.

- Federal criminal penalties can be imposed against any company or agent that knowingly sells a policy duplicating Medicare coverage or coverage by any private health insurance you already own, without paying duplicate benefits.

Long-Term Care Insurance

Medicare does not pay for long-term care in nursing homes. Most older people who require such care receive it from their families at home. Less than 1 percent of the total $38.1 billion nursing home bill in this country in 1986 was paid for by private insurance, according to the Department of Health and Human Services. About half (51 percent) was paid directly by patients and their relatives and most of the remainder (41 percent) by Medicaid.[6]

Long-term care insurance is an idea whose time has certainly come, and a number of private insurance companies are now offering it. The premiums are high, and while coverage is more extensive than anything previously available, it is still limited. Congressional and foundation studies are under way to help meet the challenge of long-term care insurance. For up-to-date information, check the Social Security office, your congressional representative, a representative of one of the major insurance companies, or the Health Insurance Association of America (see Appendix under Insurance).

According to the Senate Special Committee on Aging, in its 1986 report covering the dozen companies offering long-term care insurance at the time, indemnity benefits typically were for three years of care in a licensed nursing home and paid from $10 to $50 a day. Also:

> All policies are offered with either a deductible or a reduced benefit for some initial period of time. . . . In effect these policies protect against catastrophic costs and are more like casualty insurance than

traditional health insurance. Only individuals with extended stays are fully eligible for many plan benefits. . . . All policies are to some extent oriented to a stay in a skilled nursing facility, or care in a facility with a full-time nurse. By excluding home care benefits, it is easier for the insurer to define the insurable event and thereby to limit the insurer's liability. . . . Between 60 and 95 percent of home care is given by family and friends."[7]

Nursing homes vary in cost from about $12,000 to as much as $71,000 a year, well beyond the budgets of most Americans.

Follow Up

If your elderly parent has a good health insurance policy, it's wise to check regularly that the premiums are being paid, or take this task over yourself to be sure. One 90-year-old canceled a major medical policy she had carried for some years, without mentioning this to her son. When she was suddenly hospitalized and he inquired about the policy, she said, "Oh, it cost too much money, and I'm never sick. That Blue Cross/Blue Shield supplement is good enough, my neighbor told me. I canceled that other one three years ago." She had canceled a policy, no longer written, that would have covered all her private nursing care and many of the expenses she incurred in her week in the hospital that were not covered by Medicare. All her supplement did was pay 20 percent of what Medicare allowed.

TAXES

The tax laws are constantly changing, and you should keep abreast of the special rules that apply to the elderly and to you if you help support a parent. The tax reform of 1986 changed the old rules, eliminating some benefits and altering deductions. Some changes are being phased in over a period of years. Some changes may be changed again, depending on how present and future legislators assess their effects. The intent was to simplify the tax law and reduce taxes for most people. This may or may not be the result for your family. The following information can be a guide to particular areas of concern, but in every instance you should check with competent tax advisers to know what pertains for your family at any given time.

Help in Tax Preparation

Local offices of the Internal Revenue Service provide help to taxpayers. For seniors in particular, the IRS works with nonprofit organizations such as the AARP and Retired Senior Volunteer Program (RSVP), which train volunteers to help people 60 and older with their tax returns at no charge to the taxpayer. The AARP Tax Aide program uses older citizens as volunteers to counsel other older people in more than 8,000 communities around the country. Check the local IRS for a Tax Aide program in your parent's locale or write to AARP. The Area Agency on Aging can tell you when AARP or RSVP volunteers are available at different sites during tax season. Local communities may also sponsor such programs at senior centers.

You can get taped information on a variety of tax topics by telephoning the IRS Tele-Tax number (see Appendix under Taxes or look in the blue pages of your telephone directory under U.S. Government, Internal Revenue Service, for a local Tele-Tax number). You will need code numbers to access specific topics from your telephone. Listen carefully to the instructions and jot them down, or write to the IRS for a copy of *Guide to Free Tax Services*. Some tapes are also available in Spanish.

The IRS Volunteer Income Tax Assistance (VITA) program provides tax assistance to low-income people, the elderly, and non-English-speaking taxpayers at various community locations. Deaf people with access to TTY equipment can receive special tax assistance through this equipment from the IRS. The IRS will send publications free of charge to older taxpayers. The U.S. Senate Special Committee on Aging will also send you a list of tax tips for older Americans at no cost.

See the Appendix under Taxes.

To find a tax attorney, ask trusted friends to recommend one or ask your local bar association or county courthouse for a list of attorneys specializing in tax law. Your friends who operate businesses or your bank might be able to suggest a certified public accountant. Talk to several, and then make a choice.

The New Law: Tax Breaks for You

If you are providing more than half your parent's support, and your parent's gross income is less than a specified amount, you can claim your parent as a dependent on your federal income tax form under a particular formula. You will need to document all special expenses you claim on your parent's behalf, such as medical or dental expenses over what Medicare and other insurance pay. If you intend to claim a medical deduction for your parent, be sure it is you, not your parent, who writes the checks for the medical bills, and that you keep all receipted bills. To claim any medical deductions at all, the total of your unreimbursed medical expenses, including those of all your dependents, must exceed a percentage of your gross adjusted income. (In 1987 this was 7.5 percent.) The same tax rules apply if other elderly relatives such as grandparents, in-laws, or step-parents receive more than half their support from you. A nonrelative, such as an elderly friend, who lives with you the entire year and for whom you provide more than half the support, may also be claimed as a dependent.

If you and one or more of your siblings together are contributing more than half your parent's support—and your parent's gross income is no greater than the current regulations for that year stipulate—then one of you can claim your parent as a dependent, provided no one of you has contributed more than half the support. In this case, the child claiming the parent as a deduction must contribute more than 10 percent of the parent's support. You and your brothers or sisters can arrange to alternate or rotate the dependency claim from one year to the next so that you each get the tax benefit in turn. To do this, you must file a written statement—get the form from the IRS—signed by the others, saying that they are not claiming your parent as a dependent in that calendar year and that you may do so.

Note that a taxpayer's death does not necessarily mean that a federal income tax return is no longer required. Someone with legal responsibility for the decedent's affairs, such as an executor, must follow through, file the return, or file for a refund for tax witheld if a return is not required. In cases of joint returns in such situations, special rules apply. Check with the IRS.

The New Law: Tax Breaks for Your Parent

Under the Tax Reform Act of 1986, *personal exemptions* for each individual, spouse, and eligible dependent have been raised. In 1988 the personal exemption is $1,950 for each individual; in 1989 it will be $2,000. It is anticipated that after 1990 the amount will be adjusted for inflation. Other, more complicated rules about personal exemptions apply to those with high incomes. The *standard deductions* were also changed and vary according to whether or not the taxpayer is single, married, head of a household, a surviving spouse, or filing a separate or joint return. *Special exemptions* for the elderly and the blind have been eliminated. There is now an *additional standard deduction for the elderly and the blind*. Determine from the IRS which amounts apply to your parent.

People over 65 don't have to file at all if their gross income does not exceed specified amounts, from a low of $5,700 to a high of $10,100 (in 1988), depending on which category (single, married, survivor, filing separately, jointly, etc.) pertains. Tax liability should be checked for changes each year.

The New Law: Important Points

The following will give you some idea of important areas of change, but this list is not comprehensive, only illustrative:

- There are important new tax rules on pensions and annuities.

- Claims for contributions to charity must be itemized.
- Nonmortgage interest payments are no longer deductible, and mortgage interest is limited to first and second homes. Interest on credit cards or auto loans, for example, is no longer deductible.
- State and local sales tax is no longer deductible.
- Distinctions between short- and long-term capital gains are gone.
- If one of your parents is the beneficiary of a life insurance policy, and the death benefit is not paid immediately but is paid later and/or in installments and interest is involved, new rules have been made about the tax liability involved.
- Estimated tax for any year must be 90 percent paid up before the end of the taxable year or the taxpayer will suffer considerable penalties.
- Many new regulations relating to trusts, inheritance taxes, and gifts can seriously affect your family's financial planning. Get tax advice early in the tax year.

One important tax break that continues is that taxpayers who are 55 or older can still exclude the first $125,000 of profit from the sale of a principal residence, in which they have lived for at least three of the five years ending on the date of sale or exchange—once in a lifetime. The remainder of the profit, if there is any, can also be shielded from tax if it is used to purchase another principal residence which is occupied within two years.

As people live longer and become frail or handicapped, they sometimes need to modify their homes; for example, by installing ramps instead of steps and by widening doorways to accommodate wheelchairs. Medically necessary capital costs such as these can be deducted from income. Be sure to keep records and receipts for such expenditures.

State and Local Tax Breaks

Don't overlook state and local tax breaks for your parent. Special tax treatment may be accorded to retirement income or medical expenses for older people, over and beyond what is allowed on federal taxes.

Almost all states give older residents some property tax relief, often called circuit-breakers or homestead exemptions. Sometimes there's an outright exemption from property tax payments, sometimes a credit or partial refund. Generally, this help is allowed to people over 65; in some states it starts at 62; and in a few, not until 72. These property tax exemptions usually require a period of prior residence and usually apply only if income is below a specified level or the value of the property is below a specified amount.

If your retired parent has a second home in another state, it is useful to analyze which is the preferred state for a permanent residence, not only in terms of personal preferences, but in terms of tax consequences and insurance costs.

Tax relief provisions vary enormously from state to state and are frequently revised. Periodically check the situation with the state department of finance or taxation where your parent pays his or her taxes.

Don't forget that your parent's local city or county government may also offer special tax relief for older citizens. Check the local department of finance to see just what benefits apply to your parent.

ESTATES

You may know roughly the amount of your parent's estate and just what it consists of. You may be familiar with the terms of your parent's will. If you're informed at all, you're ahead. It's important that you know to what degree your parent's estate is protected from potential tax inroads. If you think your parent could arrange for better future protection, you might decide to talk about this together soon. But if you're ignorant of your parent's worth and plans, you should make some effort to suggest that your parent consult a good estate attorney in view of the complex new tax laws, even if your father or mother prefers not discussing this with you. There are perfectly legal ways to protect legacies from excessive tax bites.

The rules your parent may remember about estates and gift taxes were swept away by the Tax Reform Act of 1976. Previous exemptions were replaced with a unified system of tax credits, which lumps together both the gifts made during a lifetime and the inheritance passed on after death. (Excluded as taxable gifts are annual allowed gifts of up to $10,000 each, to any number of people, and direct payments made by your parent for medical or educational expenses for you, your children, or others as discussed below.) The total amount of these tax-free credits has been raised over the years to the 1987 level, which continues to prevail (unless further changed), and in effect exempts estates of $600,000 or less from federal tax. Remember that this amount includes any nonexempt gifts your parent may have made since 1976 on which tax has not already been paid.

All estates with a net value of more than $600,000, after allowed deductions (marital, charitable, and others), are now subject to federal estate taxes. Even though the marital deductions may seem to free your parents from any worry about passing their assets from one to the other, how and when they do this may have serious tax consequences. There are also various state death taxes to consider.

Talking with Parents

Many adult children don't want to confront a parent with questions about wills and estates. If you have a practical parent who wants to sit down and talk with you about his or her will or estate, don't brush the overture aside. Many adult children, feeling flustered and uncomfortable, answer with "Don't be silly. You're not going to die anytime soon," and repeatedly postpone such a discussion. This attitude can create great problems after the inevitable does, in fact, occur.

One way to deal with all this is to remove the discussion from the arena of age and health. Try telling your parent that you're making your will, that all your contemporaries have wills because otherwise large sums of money will go to lawyers working to settle their estates, and furthermore you want to decide how to bequeath your possessions and assets. This might suggest to your parent that making a will is really a practical matter and is a way of their carrying out their objectives. Making a will, as a matter of fact, is an act of love, and not making one is sometimes an act of hostility, bequeathing heirs years of time-consuming, energy-draining, and very costly dealings with the courts.

Despite the feminist revolution, many older women who become widows are still ignorant of how to manage their financial affairs on their own. If both your parents are alive and if your elderly mother is likely to have great difficulty managing finances on her own, it is not inappropriate for you to talk with your father about his estate and to ask to what degree he has protected her from possible legal and tax problems should he predecease her. Your father himself may not have the current knowledge to make the best estate decisions, so a well-timed word from you may be welcome. If your mother is a widow, she may be uncertain what steps to take, if any, to give both herself and you the greatest possible protection, and she may be relieved to have your interest and general advice.

A parent who is close-mouthed about assets and their disposal may be a little suspicious and hostile to begin with, and you will have to tread carefully. But sometimes, as a parent grows older, he or she will voluntarily bring up the subject of estates and wills and where you or other heirs can find papers, documents, and valuables after his or her death. If your parent does this, consider yourself fortunate and sit down and listen. If it involves, as it did with one grandmother who lived alone in an urban apartment, hiding jewelry in a bag of onions, cash in a can of mothballs, bankbooks in bookshelves, and documents tucked into drawers, take notes so you will remember it all. Some older people need to have peace of mind about what will happen to their goods and belongings after death, to know that their children and grandchildren will have everything that is coming to them. This knowledge may represent continuity and security to the older parent. Don't treat the subject lightly; pay attention.

If you really find it too uncomfortable to discuss wills and estates with your parent, you may find that an article or a book written by an outsider, with no emotional family ties or anything personal to be gained, can introduce this sensitive subject more successfully. This book, the AARP's *The Essential Guide to Wills, Estates, Trusts, and Death Taxes,* or numerous newspaper and magazine articles can all help your parent to confront the subject and deal with it sensibly.

In any event talking about wills and estates should take place while a parent is in good health. A sickbed, particularly at a time of terminal or catastrophic illness, is an unsuitable background for this kind of discussion and also limits severely what a parent can do to avoid estate taxes. The time to talk to your parent is now, and not during an illness or a crisis situation.

Does Your Parent Have an Estate?

Your parent doesn't have to be a J. Paul Getty or the president of a huge congolomerate to leave an estate. If your mother or father owns a house, a condominium, a car, some investments in stocks or bonds, one or more savings or money market accounts, an insurance policy, a pension fund, an annuity, or some IRAs or CDs, he or she probably has a taxable estate. Many of these assets are likely to have increased in value over the years. Just think what has happened to the price of real estate in the last decade—in some parts of the country, a house bought for $24,000 in the fifties is worth half a million or more now. Real estate may not have appreciated that much where your parent lives, but it surely has gone up considerably over its original price to your parent. Or perhaps your mother or father has been a sporadic collector of stamps, coins, or even lithographs or prints. The IRS can come in after your parent's death and value a collection at an amount that can astonish and pain you when the bill for estate tax deficiencies appears.

Estate taxes, like income taxes, are progressive; the greater the value of the estate, the higher the tax is proportionately. If you know the total value of your parent's taxable estate, you can figure out roughly what the federal taxes will be. If the assets are not in cash, you may have to sell something to pay the taxes.

States also levy taxes on death. These may be inheritance taxes—the taxes to be paid on each separate beneficiary's share of the estate—or taxes on the estate itself, or some combination of these. Death taxes exist in some form in almost every state, but the rates may differ. These state taxes are usually levied at much more modest rates than the federal estate tax and generally are credited against the federal tax liability. Estate expert Theodore Wagner points out that "many states, such as Florida, advertise that they have no estate taxes. This is incorrect, for they do. What they mean is that any amount of tax the estate must pay to the state is credited against, and thus reduces, the federal estate tax."

In addition, the estate will be docked for the lawyers' fees and administrative costs involved in settling it. These are generally calculated as a percentage of the gross estate and can add up considerably.

These general statements are made to caution you and your parent: do not assume that a small estate is not worth bothering about. Complex rules govern the transfer of property. It is best for your father and mother to sit down with an attorney and plan how best to satisfy their wishes for the disposal of their estate.

Factors in Estate Taxes

One approach that can cut down on potential estate taxes is making annual gifts during a lifetime. The law allows an individual to make untaxed gifts to any donee of $10,000 a year. If your parent is well-fixed financially, he or she can give up to this amount each year to any number of his or her children, grandchildren, and other relatives with no gift or estate tax liability. If you have two parents, they can give up to $20,000 annually untaxed to an unlimited number of people, or one can use both exclusions, without charge, providing the other consents.

In addition, your parent may wish to help pay for your

children's or grandchildren's tuition or medical expenses. If your parent pays the school or the medical bills directly, these gifts are not taxable. Bills should be addressed to the payer.

Overall tax savings may also be achieved if gifts are in the form of property, which may increase further in value over the years after the gifts are made. The increased value of the property is no longer part of your parent's estate and is not subject to estate taxes if transfer is made within the specified legal time.

Beyond these exemptions, gifts are now subject to the unified gift and estate tax. It is still possible for your parent to make gifts of greater amounts during his or her lifetime, free of taxes. However, this amount will count toward the total $600,000 allowed in the estate before federal taxes are imposed. Each parent is an individual in estate tax matters, and if both your parents are alive, the gifts, the marital deductions, and the transfer of assets from one to the other or to others in the family must be looked at to make the most favorable decisions. Wealthy people should be aware of the new tax regulations that govern generation-skipping transfers of property and gifts. Professor John Regan cautions lawyers giving estate planning advice to be careful about avoiding double tax on lifetime gifts. "Lifetime gifts to grandchildren must be approached with extreme caution."[8]

In any case, it is generally the person who leaves the estate who pays the taxes, because they are taken from the body of the estate before it is distributed. It is possible for the donor to pay the tax, thus reducing the amount of the taxable gift. Parents with potentially substantial taxable estates will have to decide whether taxes will be paid now, during their lifetime, or out of the estate after death.

Another factor to consider in this connection is that some states impose gift taxes. These may—in variance with the federal regulations—be lower than the state's inheritance or estate taxes. It is important for your parent to check this out in his or her own state. If your parent owns property in more than one state, there may be estate tax liabilities in more than one location. One woman, fifteen years after her husband's death, got a sizable bill from another state, for the small inheritance tax—plus large penalties—that tax officials said she owed on a small parcel of land her husband had owned with some other partners.

Finally there are ways of providing for other people through trusts, some irrevocable, others revocable. The donor of an irrevocable trust cannot change his or her mind to recapture the assets, though it may be possible to make amendments. Revocable trusts can be revoked by the donor at will and the assets recaptured, or they can be continued and used for the the donor's own benefit or for someone else's benefit. Living trusts are sometimes used in planning for incapacity: they can be revocable while the grantor is in good shape and become irrevocable if the person granting it becomes incompetent.

Setting up trusts to achieve favorable tax benefits is a route that must be pursued with extreme caution. The Tax Reform Act of 1986, for example, changed the rules for Clifford trusts and spousal remainder trusts, instruments your parent might have used earlier to reduce tax liabilities. Because the whole area of trusts is extremely complicated, it is best for your parent to explore it very carefully with an attorney familiar with federal and state law before committing any resources in this manner.

WILLS

Your parent should have a will, whether or not she or he has an estate, and the will should be drawn by a competent attorney. It should be up to date, based on the current laws and on the current ages, situations, and needs of the heirs. A 25-year-old will is almost certain to be out of date, and even a 10-year-old will might not reflect family relationships and requirements at the time a parent dies.

Wills should be revised periodically, and almost automatically after major family changes—births, deaths, marriages, divorces, remarriages. They should also be gone over when tax regulations and other applicable laws are changed and if your parent moves from one state to another. State laws differ, and often a will that complies with one state's requirements flouts those of another.

If either or both of your parents have substantial assets, careful consideration should be given to the ultimate tax effect the will of one parent may have on the will of a surviving parent, and on their adult children and other beneficiaries after both have died. Estate taxes crossing over surviving generations can be minimized through careful will and estate planning.

If your parent leaves no will, you may be subject to some nasty surprises:

- The estate may not go where your parent wanted it to go; intestacy statutes will decide its disposition.
- Estate taxes may be higher, and certain deductions may be lost.
- Administration costs and legal fees may be higher.
- Since your parent has no executor, a court will appoint an administrator, who will probably be required to file a surety bond. Not only may the surety company then supervise the administrator constantly, but he or she will have to go to the court for orders to act on many of the matters connected with the estate. An executor who is named in a will can serve without bond.
- Distribution of the estate will probably take longer, and family tempers will grow shorter. Brother and sister, parent and child with histories of harmonious relationships have been known to engage in sharp infighting when faced with the sour plum of an undirected estate.

If you can discuss no other aspect of money with your parent, you should at least ascertain whether or not he or she has an up-to-date will. Use the Tax Reform Act as a peg for the question, or once again talk about your own will. Mention why you are updating it and ask for advice based on what your parent has done. This will give your parents a chance to discuss their own situation and give you an opportunity to pass on any new information you may have or to suggest the wisdom of consulting a good estate planner.

PLANNING AHEAD FOR INCAPACITY

Do You Know Where Important Documents Are Kept?

There are some arrangements you can make now that will make life—and death—easier. You will be able to act expeditiously, if your parent suddenly becomes ill or is incapacitated, if you know:

- whether or not your parent has made a living will and what it says and have ready access to it
- whether or not your parent has made or purchased any funeral arrangements and left instructions
- where your parent keeps his or her will, bankbooks, insurance policies, stock certificates and bonds, business contracts, leases, mortgage, etc. Wills and documents relating to funerals (instructions or burial plot deeds) should *not* be kept in your parent's safe deposit box, which in most states is sealed upon his or her death and cannot be opened without a court order prior to the appointment of the executor. Of course, no executor can be appointed as long as the original will is in the box.
- your parent's Social Security and Medicare numbers
- the location and numbers of checking and savings accounts and safe deposit boxes. (Consult an attorney about the advisability of joint bank accounts.)
- the companies with which your parent has life, health, or other insurance policies and the numbers of the policies
- institutions responsible for your parent's pension plan, Keogh or IRA account, and other retirement plans or annuities

If your relationship with your parent makes it possible, you should go beyond this in sharing essential financial facts to insure easier action in emergency and crisis situations. This is also the time to have a real heart to heart talk about your parents' wishes should they become incapacitated and need someone else to act on their behalf.

Powers of Attorney

You or a sibling should have power of attorney, specifying how you can act for your parent in financial matters should the need arise. This can be a limited or durable power of attorney. For the *limited power of attorney,* buy a printed form in a stationery store; or for banking or stock purposes, obtain one from the bank or brokerage house where your parent has an account. Your best approach, however, is to ask a lawyer to draw up a form in which your parent designates exactly what powers he or she gives you. In many families, parent and child exchange such powers of attorney so that the parent can act for the child if the emergency situation is reversed. These powers of attorney expire if the donor becomes incompetent or dies.

Durable powers of attorney can survive the donor's becoming incompetent, can also be broad or specific, and can sometimes cover matters of health care as well as assets. If your parent grants you or some other trusted person a durable power of attorney, it will be valid for such time as he or she is incapable of making judgments and decisions; for example, because of a serious accident, a permanent loss of consciousness, or a degenerating illness that reduces mental capacity. Durable powers of attorney are now recognized in all the states, and the District of Columbia has bills pending to permit durable powers of attorney there.

These powers may be given to anyone, except in Florida where only certain family members may be appointed. In general, it is not considered desirable to give them to physicians or other people providing health care, or to the institutions or agencies providing health care, because of possible conflicts of interest or the appearance of impropriety.

There can be tangled legal problems if questions are raised about a person's competence at the time he or she granted durable powers of attorney. Only a few states have legislated specifically that durable powers are valid for health care decisions. And there are other unresolved issues about these powers. For these reasons, some lawyers recommend that living wills and living trusts also be executed (see below). The message, as always, is that nothing of such a serious nature should be undertaken without the advice of a competent attorney. Powers should never be given to anyone about whom there is the slightest suspicion, and the experience of using such powers in a particular locality should be considered when making advance plans for incapacity.

Assuming a Watchful Role

Suppose your father has not assigned powers of attorney and you see signs that his judgment isn't as keen as it was. Or suppose your mother has executed a durable power of attorney but is not willing to admit that it is time for you to begin using it. Then you must be vigilant without being overbearing.

You must see to it that your parent doesn't enter into any contract without having a lawyer go over it—a contract for sale, rental, or purchase of a home; for buying an automobile or other major item; for purchasing an insurance policy; for a course of instruction or recreation, from yoga lessons to a Caribbean cruise.

You must check on dates when payments are due—for utilities, rent, or mortgage—to be sure that they continue to be made on time. Inform the organizations involved that you are the third party to whom notices should be sent.

Be sure that Social Security and all other income checks are deposited in your parent's account as they arrive. (As noted earlier, Social Security checks can be sent directly to the bank.) Otherwise your parent may overlook the arriving checks or put them away and forget them. Alternatively, you can have yourself appointed *representative payee*—or recipient of your parent's Social Security checks. The local Social Security office can arrange this for you if you provide medical and other documentation testifying that your parent can no longer handle his or her own funds. The checks will then come to you and must be used only for your parent's expenses.

You must assume a watchful role, trying to keep a balance between protecting your parent and maintaining his or her independence. Perhaps he or she will only need some reminders as to dates for paying bills. Prepare a checklist for your parent and keep one for yourself. Perhaps you should offer to help by working with your parent to pay bills and keep the checking account in order

You should consult your parent's physician to evaluate the changes in behavior you observe. (See chapter 9.)

Living Trusts

If your parent becomes more forgetful and confused, problems will arise. There are some things you can do. You can use the power of attorney he or she has given you—assuming it is broad enough, and depending on what rights it allows you—to pay bills, deposit and withdraw money from bank accounts, perhaps to sell stock or other assets if your parent needs cash.

But the power of attorney doesn't deprive your parent of the power to handle money. And if your parent's judgment is impaired—for whatever reason—he or she may be doing unwise things with the money, draining funds that are needed for his or her continuing support. Or the older person, far from behaving aggressively and spending large amounts of money, may be too damaged mentally to manage money in any way. And remember that unless your power of attorney has been designated as durable, certain states will consider it invalid if your parent becomes mentally incompetent.

Perhaps the most flexible and useful device for handling the financial affairs of a parent who is beginning to show signs of abnormal behavior is a "living" trust. Even elderly parents who are functioning well might wish to establish this kind of trust because it relieves them from having to pay any attention to bills, checks, and bank accounts and removes any concern about handling money. Under this arrangement, your parent transfers his or her assets to a revocable trust (which can be changed at will). You and/or your siblings can be the trustees, or, if this is not feasible, a local bank or your parent's attorney can be trustee or cotrustee (usually for a fee). The trust agreement would authorize the trustee to use the trust income—and principal if necessary—to pay your parent's bills and otherwise provide for his or her care, maintenance, and support. It would contain the powers to handle property that are usually in a power of attorney, but unlike a limited power of attorney, will remain in force even if your parent subsequently becomes incapacitated.

In many states it's possible for your parent to specify in the trust agreement where the remaining trust property is to go after his or her death—in other words, to write a will into the trust document. If this is done, the remaining trust property will pass directly to the beneficiaries without the delays and administrative expenses of probate. The trust property will be included in your parent's total estate for tax purposes. Managing a trust with nonfamily trustees can be expensive. If your parent is already incompetent, it is too late to establish such a trust.

Protective Services

Protective services is the term applied to legal services for people who can no longer manage their own lives. Usually these services are given by a state agency or through the Area Agency on Aging to older people who are without family and relatives, first judging whether, in fact, the older person needs them and then deciding what the extent of the services will be. This is a simplified description of protective services, but it defines the kind of action you may have to initiate yourself.

How can you judge when you have to intervene for your parent? Intervention is a sensitive problem. Courts are more and more cautious in taking away the civil rights of any human being. And almost no child chooses willingly to strip a parent of self-determination and dignity.

Lawyers and social workers in protective services agencies have certain criteria for determining the need for protective services. Broad though they are, they might serve in your own situation. Your parent may be in need of protection if he or she:

- is unwilling or unable to take action to protect his or her interests
- is mentally confused
- shows mental, physical, or emotional incapacity that may lead to harming himself, herself, or others
- cannot do what is needed to maintain life
- is incapable of managing money

Geriatric evaluation services, to help you determine whether protective services should be sought and instituted, are offered through some state agencies and university medical centers. A team, consisting usually of a doctor, a psychiatrist, a neurologist, and perhaps a nurse or social worker, will examine your parent thoroughly, make an evaluation, and then recommend whether and to what degree he or she is able to take care of himself or herself. The Area Agency on Aging or the department of health or social services in your parent's locality should be able to tell you where such a service is available.

These diagnoses, whether they come from private physicians or from an evaluation team—preferably, perhaps, from both—will give you the expert's judgment. Then, depending on the circumstances, a court can appoint a temporary guardian or conservator or a permanent one. The terms *guardian* and *conservator* are sometimes used interchangeably, but they may have different meanings in different states. Laws governing them differ among the states, so be sure you know the law in the state where your parent lives and that the attorney you select is knowledgeable about such proceedings.

This is not a step to be taken lightly, and although state regulations differ, it always involves a legal procedure. If the court appoints a conservator, your parent will no longer have control over his or her own financial affairs. The conservator will manage them, supplying your parent with money to live on and making regular reports on your parent's finances. The conservator will be awarded a fee for these services. You might be appointed conservator yourself, in which case you will be responsible to the court that appointed you.

The common assumption is that a person who has been declared incompetent is doomed forever to incompetence. This is not necessarily true. Treatment and changed conditions can sometimes ameliorate a seemingly acute condition, and the need for a conservator, in those cases, may be temporary.

Going to court to ask for a conservator is an extreme step in trying to guard your parent from the financial consequences of his or her erratic behavior. Typically it is done when large sums of money are involved. If there is no other way to restrain your parent's abnormal behavior, or to give you access to funds for your parent's well-being, then this is a step you can take properly and in good conscience.

You can protect your parent in this way whether or not you live nearby. If your parents live at a distance and there's no compelling reason to change their residence to your vicinity, there may be a trusted relative who can be appointed conservator by the court. Or you can turn to a county, city, or philanthropic agency in your parent's area for advice and help in dealing with the legal process. The Area Agency on Aging has a legal services unit that can help.

SEVEN

DOCTORS, HOSPITALS, AND HMOs

One of the most encouraging advances in medicine in recent years is its increasing knowledge about old age. Good doctors are beginning to understand better the bodily changes that occur as we go through the life cycle. They are more able to retard or reverse some of the destructive processes that rob so many of a healthy old age. Many myths are being exploded that previously deterred people from seeking medical advice or doctors from attempting treatments. The deepening knowledge of the interaction of physical and mental status, the growing sophistication of diagnostic tools, surgery, and rehabilitation therapies, the extensive educational campaigns to help people help themselves—all have had significant and positive impact on the lives of older people.

Despite these advances in knowledge, countless older people continue to be sick and miserable, and countless families are dealing with the everyday consequences of the chronic or catastrophic illness of their parents. Together they are enmeshed in the "health care system," which determines who gives and gets care, what kind, and how much. To most patients, it is the doctor who is central to their confidence. It is the doctor to whom the patient turns first for care and comfort, for counsel and treatment, and in some cases, for miracles. The doctor and the hospital, clinic, or health maintenance organization, and all the people who staff the institutions to which a patient goes, will determine how well or poorly an individual patient will be treated.

Finding the right doctor at the right time can be a real problem. Protecting an elderly patient in a big hospital is a real responsibility. Talking to a doctor so that each of you is contributing to the success of your parent's medical care is a real talent. Not being overawed or cowed by the mystique of medicine is a real necessity. Finding out enough about your parent's illness so that you can be alert to danger signals is a wise precaution. The outstanding practitioners in the field of geriatric medicine are the first to tell you that things are not necessarily what they ought to be. It is essential in today's world to develop the art of being a successful patient. This is especially true for the aging.

The challenge, then, if you are the caring child of an ailing parent, is first to help find a good doctor who cares about what happens to your parent, then to inform yourself about the particulars of your parent's illness so that you can cooperate intelligently in the prescribed treatment or be an ombudsman if required.

FINDING THE RIGHT DOCTOR

"The secret of the care of the patient," said a respected teacher of medicine, a generation or so ago, "is in caring for the patient."[1]

Not too long ago, many older people were abandoned needlessly by unknowing families and even by their physicians who believed "old age" was responsible for their symptoms. Many doctors didn't even try to treat these symptoms. Doctors like that still exist. They patronize their older patients and don't attempt to improve their function by even small measures. Many chronic illnesses may not be curable, but slight improvements can make an enormous difference in a person's comfort and ability to function independently. A growing body of information is coming from university geriatric centers, medical schools, and the National Institute on Aging (NIA) intended to broaden the individual physician's knowledge for treatment of older patients. While many doctors, old and young, are eager to improve their practice with new knowledge for the benefit of their elderly patients, other physicians continue to hold their own prejudices about older people.

Witness the experience of one family whose 90-year-old, very deaf mother had continuing difficulty communicating with her physician, a well-recommended doctor who had assumed her care when the old woman's doctor retired. The patient could hardly hear the doctor, and the busy doctor became increasingly impatient with the often frustrating process of exchanging necessary information with the old woman. On one occasion, the exasperated doctor indicated to the family that she believed their mother was demented. While she twirled her forefinger near her temple to signal her opinion, she exclaimed, "Trying to talk to her is like trying to talk to an animal!" The family rose, took their mother, and left the office.

After a frantic search they made an appointment with a young physician in one of the new geriatric programs. The old woman gave her history and recounted to the new physician the events in the previous physician's office, also describing the hand signals the family were not sure she had observed. The new doctor listened attentively, asked questions, made sure they were understood, and listened patiently for the answers. He continues as her physician. The old woman is forthcoming and cooperative. She is frail and deaf, but not demented. She lives alone, with the daily help of a companion. She is responsible about her own medication and cooks her own meals. The whole family has been refreshed and relieved by the experience with the new doctor; all are doing the best they can.

Other factors than attitude intrude on the quality of patient care a doctor provides. One is the Medicare system, which pays for acute care, tests, and surgery but not chronic care, which is the primary need of older people. (New payment schedules were under consideration in 1988 to alter this.) Another is the overwhelming presence of the third party—the insurance carrier—which determines what is and isn't covered and therefore influences what is and isn't done. The government and the insurance companies, through their reimbursement policies, significantly influence what happens in the doctor's office. Doctors who want to give older patients with chronic ailments the time and interest that they require are often penalized financially, because the set fee structures reimburse for tests, procedures, and surgery for acute illness, not for listening, talking, and advising.

Consider also the escalating malpractice premiums and rent the doctor is paying and the rising office overhead, which now includes salaries for numbers of people just filling out the required insurance forms. The best-intentioned doctor is now pressed between trying to spend the longer time an elderly patient often requires and seeing enough patients to meet rising expenses. If your mother or father gets too much attention in the way of tests and procedures and too little attention in the way of listening, if the doctor doesn't take the time to understand all the ramifications of your parent's life that affect emotional as well as physical health—these are common responses to the pressures on today's doctors.

Seriously ill, handicapped, or frail people have special needs, and their families have special problems. You should make every effort to choose a doctor who will give the time and have the patience to treat your parent with respect and compassion. You will have no trouble giving this doctor the respect and appreciation he or she deserves.

Where to Look

While there are many good doctors, some of them are not necessarily suitable for elderly people. You will want to find someone who is professionally competent, personally compatible, and preferably attached to a good hospital. Here are some ways to go about the search.

- A good doctor can usually recommend another good doctor. Ask your own, your children's, or a friend's physician for a recommendation for your parent. If your parent lives in a different community or state, geography is not a problem.

Doctors have medical school colleagues, professional society colleagues, and detailed directories to consult for references in other parts of the country. Be careful about asking casual friends and neighbors to recommend a doctor; ask only people whose judgment you respect. Gossipy tales won't help much, although they may alert you to potential problems or personality conflicts.

- A university medical school or any large public or voluntary hospital is an excellent source of referrals. Usually you're given several names from which to choose.
- The Department of Geriatrics at Mount Sinai Medical Center in New York City now furnishes a national listing of physicians who see geriatric patients in all states except Hawaii and Alaska. There is a small fee for the list (see Appendix under Geriatric Physicians).
- Double-check with the national health organizations for medical specialists; for example, the Heart Association for cardiologists, the American Cancer Society for oncologists, the Arthritis Foundation for rheumatologists.
- When you're choosing a surgeon, it's wise to find one who is board certified—one who has had a number of years of training and passed an examination in a specialty such as orthopedics, or colon and rectal surgery, or neurological surgery. Some surgeons are also Fellows of the American College of Surgeons and carry the initials FACS after the MD. This is another indication of special skill. You can ask the physician directly about certification, or the local or state medical society can verify the specialist's qualifications. Try to choose an experienced surgeon who operates on a regular basis (several times a week).
- Inquire of a county medical society or privately owned hospital, although recommendations from these sources are normally limited to their own membership.
- The state medical directory in the library lists each licensed physician in the state, but it isn't a good idea to go by the book alone. A good education and hospital affiliation are usually assurances of technical competence but give you no

clue to personality or current professional development and experience.

- Be especially careful about hospital affiliation. When you check a doctor, check the hospital with which he or she is affiliated. You can ask highly respected physicians in a community how they regard that particular hospital. In general, affiliations with university and large voluntary hospitals signify a high standard of performance, but there are many first-rate smaller community institutions. Relatively new to the scene are the hospitals being run by large private corporations. Information about these may be more difficult to find. In some instances these have merely been converted from freestanding community hospitals to membership in a national for-profit chain. You'll have to rely on good local informants to evaluate them. Doctors previously affiliated with the local hospital may or may not continue with the new administration. In general, if you visit a hospital you can observe how elderly patients are treated.

It's not a good idea to go searching for a specialist before you find a good internist to be in general charge of your parent's medical care. The internist today is the closest counterpart of yesterday's family doctor. (Note that family medicine is returning as a specialty in its own right, in some medical schools.) Most good internists are equipped to deal with the chronic illnesses of the elderly and know when to call on specialists for additional consultation or treatment. In these days of many specialties, it's wise to have one doctor who is in a position to keep track of what other doctors are doing with the patient and to help resolve conflicting advice. Someone needs to be the manager in multiproblem cases, and the internist is often the best such person.

Evaluating a Doctor

If your parent has selected a doctor with good hospital connections, who is well recommended and pleasant, what next?

The first appointment will give you a great deal of information. It is a good idea for a family member to accompany your parent on the first visit. Your parent and you can then decide whether your choice is suitable. Ask yourselves these questions:

- *Was sufficient time made available for this initial visit?* An hour is reasonable. Elderly people need time and compassion from their physicians, as well as technical competence. During the first visit, the doctor should take a comprehensive medical history; learn if there are any family medical idiosycrasies, unusual incidents, allergies, or common complaints; and perform standard tests. The doctor should inquire about the medications the patient is taking, including over-the-counter-drugs: what are they, how long has your parent been taking them, and who prescribed them. The doctor should take the time to chat with your parent, get a real feel for his or her personality and anxieties, and allow time for questions. The doctor should know about your parent's social and economic circumstances and should be interested in talking with you, as well, to get your perspective. It is up to the doctor to put the pieces together; often the medical problem is not what the patient thinks it is. If the visit is too brief and impersonal, then this doctor is not desirable for your elderly parent. These cautions apply, of course, to the physician in overall charge of your parent's medical care and are less relevant to a visit to a specialist or surgeon for a particular situation—though it is always less stressful to deal with a doctor who is compatible as well as expert. If your parent or you are unhappy with the initial visit to a new doctor, it's preferable to find a different one than to start a relationship of frustration and unhappiness.
- *During subsequent visits, does the doctor continue to give your parent the attention his or her condition requires?* After the initial evaluation and diagnosis, a doctor should be reasonable about answering questions and explaining procedures so that your parent and you continue to understand clearly what is happening, what to do, and what to expect.
- *Are you confident that the doctor is sensitive to the limits of his or her knowledge?* A good doctor should know when to call

another doctor for consultation or for help in diagnosis of an unusual case. Lay people are sometimes shaken when a physician suggests calling another doctor. It is good, not bad, when doctors are willing to admit they don't know or are unsure and are willing to ask for help.

- *Does this doctor object if your parent or you want another opinion?* Second opinions are now required by insurance carriers and many health plans before surgery or other special procedures are undertaken, and they are desirable from the patient's point of view as well. But even under other circumstances, if you wish to have another opinion you should feel free to request this without impairing your relationship with a doctor.
- *Has the doctor told you how to reach him or her in emergencies, late at night, or over weekends and holidays?* Your parents and you should know what alternative arrangements are available in these circumstances, including the name of the physician(s) covering for your doctor and the names and locations of emergency facilities.

A case in point will illustrate how a physician can affect a patient's status: About twenty-five years ago, a doctor told an over-65-year-old patient suffering with severe viral pneumonia that her heart had been damaged. He ordered her to take digitalis and put her on a salt-free diet. This would be a permanent regimen, he said. Following this diagnosis and prescription, the patient seemed to age ten years overnight. Concerned abut the dramatic change in her mother's appearance and behavior, her daughter insisted she see another physician. The second doctor explained that unusually rapid heart action sometimes does accompany a pneumonia but that she had now recovered completely and there was no residual permanent effect. "I hope I look as good as you when I'm your age," said this new doctor. The patient left the office smiling, a new spring in her step, the extra ten years shed. When last heard from she was 92 years old, vigorous and healthy—no heart problems.

So pay attention to this most important person in your parent's life. A good doctor can make all the difference.

INSURING THE BEST RESULTS

Be Open There should be no hesitancy on your parent's part, or on yours, about mentioning anything unusual regarding health, anxieties, living circumstances, or behavior. The doctor may see you separately for part of a visit to get your side of the story. Since the doctor must know everything in order to help, he or she should encourage this and give you confidence that the privacy of the information divulged will be respected. It is important to establish an open relationship.

Appoint a Family Spokesperson In times of chronic as well as acute illness, appoint one member of the family to be in touch with the doctor. Preferably this person should be comfortable about talking to doctors and not shy about asking questions or about telephoning between appointments if something unusual arises. You cannot expect a doctor to repeat over and over again to different people what is happening with the patient.

Cooperate with the Doctor Just as you expect the doctor to be responsible and responsive, so must you be cooperative. The doctor has many patients and families who are owed time, skill, patience, compassion, understanding, and information. Be aware of the time you take. Don't be a pest, calling needlessly to prove you are attentive to your parent, more responsible than your sister, more caring than your brother. Don't telephone without a specific question to ask, or information to give. If you wish to have a long discussion, make an appointment and inform the doctor ahead of time of your purpose. It is reasonable to be charged for this visit. If you want advice on how to handle a problem, let the doctor know that. If you don't understand a technicality of language, say so and ask for an explanation; don't wander in a blizzard of confusion and blame it on the physician. And help your parent to understand and carry out the doctor's directions.

Be Vigilant If you notice something unusual and inform the doctor, this should not be regarded as interference. Don't wait for the next scheduled appointment to report bad side effects of medication, or extreme pain. If your timid parent doesn't want to "bother the doctor," the doctor will not be aware of undesirable events. Some physicians insist that elderly patients call them at a specified time and if they don't hear from the patient, they call instead, but don't expect that. Good doctors are not offended by the questions or intercessions of a concerned family. They appreciate information from a responsible person, which would not otherwise be available, so that appropriate action can be taken.

Be Realistic Doctors are people. They are subject to the same drives and ego needs as everyone else. They like approval and try to avoid pain. They like success and don't like failure. That is why some doctors avoid taking on the care of old people; people likely to die fairly soon don't make good records. Some doctors have emotional problems about death and dying themselves, and see the elderly patient as a constant reminder of unpleasant things to come. Other doctors are prima donnas, expecting patients to put up with really rude or unconscionable behavior in exchange for their medical knowledge or skill. A few doctors are simply unpleasant, and neither your parents nor you should feel so overawed that you tolerate behavior in a doctor you would not find acceptable in anyone else. But suppose the doctor is a really nice person, dedicated, attentive, and obviously doing the best that can be done? Then don't invest that physician with superhuman qualities. It is best to be comfortable in the doctor-patient relationship. Have confidence. Ask questions. Appreciate the truly skilled hands to which you entrust your parent's life. But don't expect miracles.

Stay in Touch—Long Distance Here you are at home. Your mother is across the country, hospitalized. An aunt has seen to the emergency and tells you there's no need to travel now; come later when your mother will need you at home.

But you're unsure, restless. Should you talk to the doctor yourself? Of course you should. But use your common sense. When you telephone, call person-to-person. Introduce yourself and quickly explain your relationship to the patient. Unless there is an emergency, don't insist on speaking with the doctor at that precise time. You may be interfering with office hours or hospital rounds. Ask that the call be returned, collect, at the doctor's convenience, during a time period when you're also available. If there *is* an emergency, explain what it is so that the nurse or answering service can take appropriate action. You can suggest that the doctor telephone you directly, collect, at any time if he or she thinks you should be informed of a new development or your presence is required.

Be Reasonable Elderly people, frequently lonely, often worried about their symptoms, and sometimes forgetful, can take up a great deal of a doctor's time without realizing that time does cost money. It is this aspect of geriatric care that concerns so many physicians who would like to meet their older patients' needs but cannot devote the time to do so without compensation. It takes a diplomatic and caring physician to offer advice or comfort quickly, without seeming too abrupt. Know your parent's habits and failings before you make harsh judgments about the doctor's attitude. There is no absolute definition of "reasonable" attention. Just take a little time and think about it before you decide what is or isn't reasonable.

Older people tend to compare current fees with those they remember from their younger days and to complain. This is no different from remarks about the price of meat or tomatoes or the price of a movie. When one patient complained to the dentist about a new crown for which he charged several hundred dollars, he replied, "Two crowns a month paid a dentist's rent fifty years ago, and two crowns pay my rent now. Is that reasonable?" She grudgingly agreed that it was.

Another aspect of this problem is the unseen components of physician's bills. The doctor who looks in on a patient in a hospital room, says "Good morning, how are you?" from the doorway, and then sends a bill for a visit properly draws the patient's ire. But before you get angry, be sure the doctor has not been consulting the radiologist who has studied your parent's X rays or the pathologist who studied the slides—people you never see, but with whom the doctor has spent considerable time on your parent's behalf.

IF YOUR PARENT MUST BE HOSPITALIZED

The AARP has distributed hundreds of thousands of copies of *Medicare's Prospective Payment System: Knowing Your Rights.*[2] It clearly outlines Medicare patients' rights in hospitals and describes Medicare's prospective payment system using diagnosis-related groups (DRGs). The following checklist is adapted from this publication.

Before Admission

- Ask the doctor if the prescribed treatment could be safely and effectively administered on an outpatient basis.
- Calculate what you estimate the out-of-pocket expenses will be, after Medicare and/or other insurance.
- Ask the physician to explain the prospective payment system and DRGs.
- Make initial plans for posthospital health care. Inquire from the doctor what kind of home care will be necessary; determine what it will cost and whether it will be covered by Medicare or your private insurance; and make arrangements for the service to be provided.

In the Hospital

- Never sign documents you haven't read and understood. Read informed consent and financial documents especially carefully.
- Find out who in the hospital handles discharge planning and get the telephone number and office where that person can be reached.
- Keep handy the address and telephone number of the area PRO (review board).

- Be available to ask questions for your parent in the hospital—anything that concerns him or her about treatment or comfort.
- For questions about medical treatment, contact the physician.
- For questions about nursing or other hospital services, contact the registered nurse responsible for the patient's care, the nursing director, the social services director, the patient representative, or the patient ombudsman.
- Find out precisely what the current rules are if the hospital decides your parent no longer requires inpatient care. You are entitled to receive written notice of their intentions and to be informed of the appeals procedures. It is essential that you understand these or your parent will be liable for charges beginning the third day after receipt of the notice, unless he or she or you follow these procedures exactly.
- Keep copies of all documents and bills.

Questions You May Forget to Ask

- *How much will this cost?* It is not unusual for people worried about the immediate medical emergency to forget to ask how much the treatment, surgery, or hospitalization will cost, and then be upset when the bill arrives.
- *If surgery is planned, is special nursing necessary and available?* This should be arranged ahead of time, if possible, to assure the patient's comfort and security, and is especially valuable the first night or first few days after surgery unless the patient is in the intensive care or special recovery unit. If you call at the last minute and there is a shortage of private nurses, you may be the one to sit up all night. Private nursing can be expensive. If you order it for your parent's comfort or your peace of mind, be sure to determine the fees in advance.
- *Does the doctor expect that a visiting nurse, home care, or a companion will be necessary at home, following surgery or any other hospitalization?* The discharge staff in the hospital, including a social worker, normally plans this with a family, but it's better

to prepare for it in good time, not during the last days of a hospital stay.

Being Your Parent's Ombudsman

Once upon a time, when the doctor and the nurse were among the few educated members of the community, their authority was unquestioned and their practice assumed to be correct. Nowadays, other people are also educated and able to comprehend information provided by professionals. Indeed, it's a good idea to learn from a doctor what will happen in the hospital, what medication is prescribed, and how often it should be taken. The problem now is that the staff in charge is frequently hard-pressed to cover the patient load assigned; some are poorly or insufficiently trained and/or supervised; some do not speak English fluently or clearly. Mistakes are made, even in the so-called best hospitals. One woman, who unfortunately is a frequent patient at a major New York hospital, routinely asks the nurse each time medication is delivered, "What is that? For whom is it prescribed?" Too often she has been offered someone else's medication, or her own too frequently or not frequently enough. The assumption that one is in good hands in a hospital is not necessarily supported by experience.

"The last place to be if you're sick is a hospital," is a common cliché. In the intensive care or recovery units, you are likely to have the best professional care the hospital has to offer. But once back on the floor, patients may not receive the tender, loving care once associated with a hospital stay. Light or call buttons may remain unanswered for long periods; requests for bedpans ignored beyond comfort. Those with hearing impairments may find it difficult to communicate through the intercom systems designed to save the staff time and use their services more efficiently. Patients may or may not get help with washing or meals or be taken for a walk. Rooms may be dirty, and infection rates may be high because of poor hygiene and sloppy supervision.

Hospitals now have patient representatives to deal with problems. Don't hesitate to use their services on your parent's

WHAT TO LOOK FOR IN A HOSPITAL

- *a clean, well-ventilated, and well-heated room, clean water pitchers, clean glasses, and a drinking tube*
- *a way to call for help*—an easily reachable button or light that gets a prompt response
- *professional attention on a regular basis*—The nurse, doctor, intern, resident, aide—someone should be checking vital signs at regular intervals each day. The effect of medication, progress or regression, bowel movements and urinary function must all be monitored. There should be a timely response to unusual symptoms. It is possible for a patient to get lost between the cracks of specialized care, so one physician should be in overall charge of the patient's condition and progress, not just the specific condition for which the patient may have been brought into the hospital.

The director of one large city hospital said, "Don't assume excellent care, or that attention is being given to all the important details. It's a good idea for a family to keep track of urine, bowels, drinking enough fluids, eating, and sleep—someone really has to check on this. Neglect can be dangerous, and serious secondary complications can arise because of this neglect."

- *correct diet trays*—If your parent is on a salt-free, sugar-free, low-cholesterol, or other specially prescribed diet, is that what is delivered? Check the trays, especially at the beginning of a hospital stay. Not everyone in the kitchen is literate or careful. Supervision may be lax, and it may be your diabetic parent who is getting nondietetic ice cream for dessert, sauerbraten the day after an intestinal operation, or prunes the day after a bout of diarrhea. It happens.
- *correct medication*—Is the pill the right one, for the right

patient, at the right time? If the medication is making your parent feel rotten instead of better, causing vomiting, sleeplessness, dizziness or palpitations, depression, anxiety, headaches, or manic exaltation, don't ignore it. Call it to the doctor's attention. No one else may do so.

- *follow-up on new orders*—Perhap the doctor makes a change in medication or diet. Days pass. Nothing is different. Or the doctor has asked for a new test. Nothing happens. You'd better start asking questions.

- *good treatment*—Old people are vulnerable to abuse. Some staff members think the elderly are cute, like babies, and treat them carefully, even if they sometimes patronize them. Others are repelled by gnarled fingers, lax muscles, untidy habits. They may neglect or intimidate older patients who are forgetful, or vent personal anger and frustration on those who cannot defend themselves. Abuse is not limited to low-level employees. Professional staff can also be cruel, rough, intimidating, and insulting. If your mother or father complains to you and is afraid to speak up to responsible hospital staff, don't ignore the complaint or dismiss it as paranoia without investigating and assuring yourself that everything is as it should be. Be sure to inform the patient representative as well as the doctor if you find the complaints justified.

A word of practical advice: It never hurts to bring some small token of your appreciation to the nursing staff or aides taking care of your mother or father; some cookies or fruit or one of your specialties are always appreciated. Doctors are known to respond favorably to this kind of attention as well. They will all appreciate your attention to them as individuals, and in turn, your parent may emerge from the crowd as an individual, not just a case on the chart.

behalf. Even with their intevention, you'll find it a good idea to stick around when your elderly parent is hospitalized. Is someone paying attention? Maybe it should be you. Don't assume anything.

The Patient's Bill of Rights

The American Hospital Association–approved statement of the Patient's Bill of Rights can be read in full in the Appendix. These rights have been incorporated into some state health codes. In general, the patient is to be assured of considerate and respectful care; the confidentiality of his or her case; the right to information about the case, including possible risks—information necessary in order to give informed consent; the right to refuse treatment to the extent permitted by law; protection from unwanted experimentation; the right to information about the professional people assigned to his or her care and about alternate facilities to which he or she might be transferred, including the relationship between the hospital and proposed new facility; the right to know the rules of the hospital; the right to continuity of care; and the right to examine and receive explanations of his or her bill, regardless of the source of payment.

Discharge Planning

Discharge planning is now a recognized hospital responsibility. Because new regulations give hospitals the incentive to discharge patients as quickly as possible, it is of the utmost importance to pay close attention to the discharge plans a hospital has for your mother or father. Check with the physician on a regular basis to determine when he or she expects to discharge your parent. If you feel strongly that the plan is inappropriate, ask the physician to reconsider the situation in light of your parent's condition. Some doctors will make every effort to keep patients hospitalized as long as they believe it is medically necessary. Others will not.

If the hospital decides that inpatient care is no longer

needed, remember that your parent has the right to receive written notice that he or she no longer requires such care (and why not), that he or she will be liable for charges beginning the third day after receipt of the notice, and that your parent (or you) has the right to appeal this decision immediately to the PRO. If the notice is given verbally, ask for it in writing. If you or your parent disagree that your parent should leave the hospital, you must appeal immediately. The PRO decides whether or not Medicare will pay for any additional hospital days after the notice is given. Much depends on how quickly you enter the appeal and whether or not the doctor agrees with the hospital's decision. Hospitals can go directly to the PRO when the doctor disagrees and get a decision. The PRO must contact you before making this decision, but even if they agree with the hospital and your parent is given a notice of noncoverage, you still have the right to appeal to them to reverse the decision. You can do this by telephone. You should record the time when you first were notified, because if your parent stays on in the hospital, personal financial liability for the charges will begin unless you have appealed within the specified time and win the appeal. This is very complex and it is essential that you understand the precise current rules. The AARP pamphlet *Medicare's Prospective Payment System: Knowing Your Rights* spells them out very clearly.

Discharge planning is supposed to protect the continuing high quality of patient care after hospitalization. It is supposed to help patients and families make their decisions about how care will be provided after hospitalization. The hospital staff, usually through a social worker who coordinates the process, should organize a feasible plan for your elder's posthospital care. In complex cases, this can be quite extensive and includes knowing how your mother or father normally lives; whether or not someone will be at home to care for them; whether additional home care is required for medical, nursing, therapeutic or other purposes; what community services are necessary and available; and what financial arrangements are necessary (including Medicare or Medicaid reimbursements) to accomplish the appropriate supportive services. While some hospital staffs are enormously helpful in carrying out these responsibilities, others are less so.

Home care in all its ramifications is discussed in chapter 2.

Emergency Rooms, Emergicenters, Walk-In Clinics, Outpatient or Ambulatory Care

These are all different and should be used differently.

Emergency rooms are exactly what the name implies: a place to go for anything that demands immediate medical attention and for which your parent is unable to see his or her own physician promptly: sudden chest pains, severe accidents, uncontrolled bleeding or vomiting, severe abdominal pain or allergic reactions, inability to breathe, abrupt dizziness, fainting. Your parent's doctor may send your parent to the emergency room for immediate care, but this is not the place for ongoing care. Medicare reimburses for emergency treatment, not routine treatment in emergency rooms. Emergency room care can be very expensive.

Less expensive health care centers have sprung up in recent years for emergency or ongoing care which might be appropriate for your parent's situation, but not necessarily.

Emergicenters are described as clinics offering medical services that fall between those provided by a hospital emergency room and by a doctor's office. These clinics can handle lesser emergencies than life-threatening ones and cost less money than emergency rooms but, if you aren't sure your parent can evaluate his or her symptoms properly, better go to a hospital emergency room. The County Medical Society or the National Association for Ambulatory Care should have information on local emergicenters. (See Appendix under National Health Organizations.)

Walk-in clinics may be free-standing or associated with a hospital and may not have the usual array of specialists or the sophisticated equipment of hospitals, or the same level of attention as a private physician. However, they make health care available to those who would not otherwise have access to it either because of finances or transportation problems.

Outpatient or *ambulatory care* (or some variation on these words) is the name used to cover the broad range of services provided by hospitals to those who are not admitted as overnight patients. Some hospitals thus offer regular medical care to patients in the community for fees considerably less than those of a private doctor, but the patient can't expect the traditional doctor-patient relationship since it's unlikely that the same doctor will provide treatment at each visit. Some outpatient hospital services are not covered by Medicare. Check. These services are different from the surgery or procedures, also called outpatient or ambulatory, that are performed in hospitals for patients who are treated by their own physicians or surgeons for conditions that do not require overnight admission. Medicare covers these under their usual formula.

HMOs, CMPs, IPAs, and PPOs

HMO (health maintenance organization)—may be group practice in central HMO offices, or individual practice through IPA

IPA (independent practice association)—independent physicians see patients in their own offices under contract to an HMO

CMP (competitive medical plan)—have contracts with Medicare to provide patient services covered by hospital or medical insurance

PPO (preferred provider organization)—physicians and hospitals that have contracts with employers or insurers to provide care at prenegotiated fees

There is growing pressure to change how people receive medical care and how they pay for it. Most of the pressure comes from the government trying to contain a burgeoning Medicare bill. Some of it comes from physicians dissatisfied with the fact that Medicare reimburses specialists and surgeons and those who provide acute care or perform special tests and procedures but doesn't reimburse sufficiently for ongoing medical care of the patient with chronic illness. While others debate what to do about all this, the consumers of health care—the patients—must wind their way through a complicated maze of choices and hope the decisions they make will give them what they want: a good doctor at the right time at a fee they can afford.

HMOs are designed to provide comprehensive medical care for a flat fee. Medicare covers participation in an HMO if the HMO is Medicare-certified. In that case, a modest monthly premium, in addition to that required to maintain Medicare Part B, covers the individual's total health care costs. The HMO premium may be about $30 a month, for which the HMO provides professional services, hospital, and other health care costs. These services include but are usually not limited to those allowed by Medicare and may also include dental care; eye and hearing examinations; eyeglasses, hearing aids, and medications at discount; podiatry; and chronic care. In addition, preventive medicine is usually a feature of HMOs.

However, members must use the physicians and hospitals associated with the HMO. These may be physicians engaged in a group practice in the offices of the HMO or doctors who are members of an IPA. Within these groups, patients can usually select their own physician, although in some HMOs they are assigned. Patients may use physicians not belonging to the HMO without additional charge only under emergency conditions or when they're referred to a specialist outside the group by agreement of physicians within the group.

Cost, quality of service, convenience, accessibility, and restrictions on service are among the factors your parent should consider when deciding whether to give up a private physician and join an HMO. Anyone who feels a particular bond with his or her physician should think twice about abandoning that relationship. It may be hard to replace.

Prepayment plans other than HMOs also restrict individual options about selecting doctors. Some private insurance policies bought by older people tie reimbursement to using specified PPOs. Some corporate employee health plans to which retired people continue to belong specify a list of doctors from which the patient must choose. Some plans don't restrict choice of physicians but provide only for restricted services, and these are generally the CMPs.

CMPs are defined in specific legislation—TEFRA (Tax Equity and Financial Responsibility Act)—and include any organization which provides "a minimum range of Medicare services through physicians who are employers, partners, or contractors."[3] CMPs contract with Medicare to receive direct payment from them for *Medicare-insured* health services (hospitals or doctors) delivered to older people, and often include the arrangements made under employee health plans for Medicare-eligible participants. This is another way the government hopes to reduce health care costs.

Because the government is so deeply commited to containing health care costs, and care for the elderly makes up such a large part of the federal bill, Medicare encourages individuals to enroll in HMOs. Some analysts believe that Medicare may one day soon mandate use of HMOs for its recipients. But others, such as the House Select Committee on Aging, are deeply concerned about the imperfect implementation of the HMO idea in many instances and believe careful standards are needed to protect health care for enrollees. Many believe the private system is too deeply ingrained in American attitudes to permit such extensive government control over individual health care decisions.

HMOs are required to open their admissions to new members for thirty days during an annual period. Because older people require more services than younger ones, some HMOs limit the number of elderly members in order to balance their budgets. Gaining admission, even if you want to join, can then become questionable. AARP reports that participants have saved from 10 to 40 percent over using private physicians. Nevertheless, the AARP, along with other advocates for older people, points out that HMOs are not for everyone. Write for their guide *More Health for Your Dollar* (see Appendix under HMOs).

Questions to Ask about HMOs

The Washington, D.C., United Seniors Health Cooperative suggests asking the following questions about HMOs[4]:

- Are the offices convenient? This applies both to doctor's offices and to the place where you would be hospitalized. How much choice is there?
- What specialists do you see regularly, and are these specialties represented on the staff of the HMO?
- How quickly can you get an appointment to see a doctor for an emergency visit? a routine visit? Will you be able to see an MD or will treatment be given by a nurse or physician's assistant?
- Will you be covered for emergency services if you are out of town? What if you need routine care away from home?
- Should you feel you need an additional medical opinion, or feel you need to go to a specialist outside of the HMO, will any of the cost be paid for by the HMO or by Medicare?
- Are there doctors available to you who are experienced in geriatrics? What services are provided for older people, such as podiatry? Should you need home care, what services does the HMO pay for?
- What coverage is there for mental health visits outside of a hospital?
- How difficult would it be to leave the HMO? (When you join an HMO, your eligibility for Medicare benefits is transferred to the HMO; if you terminate your membership, you cannot go to a private doctor and be reimbursed by Medicare until the HMO has closed out your record, a process that may take several months.)

Older persons who join HMOs are also urged to review their Medigap insurance policies (see chapter 6 on health insurance) and determine whether to retain this coverage while belonging to an HMO. The important thing is not to take any irrevocable decisions about other protections until your parent is convinced that the HMO is a satisfactory solution to his or her health care needs. Apparently a great many people are not convinced. Some HMOs are sponsored by large profit-making organizations, and their goals are at least as much to make money as to provide good medical care. Others are sponsored by nonprofit groups whose primary interest is the welfare of the membership, but obviously these cannot continue if they lose money. Balancing the organizational need and the individual's need is a tricky operation. Analysts believe it will take a few years to work out the kinks and that some presently constituted HMOs may not survive the endurance test.

SHMOs

Among the HMOs created for the sole benefit of seniors is Elderplan, organized in Brooklyn, New York, by the Metropolitan Jewish Geriatric Center. Elderplan is among four demonstration models in the nation offering extensive on-site health care and health insurance. It provides whatever Medicare allows plus additional benefits and offers some limited assistance for home care and long-term care. The plan was developed in cooperation with Medicare, under contract with the Health Care Financing Administration. Elderplan is a Social Health Maintenance Organization—SHMO, an acronym that has elicited lots of jokes. Nevertheless, among its innovative contributions is the promotion of volunteer work among its members for health care of other members. By building up credits in caring for others, individuals earn extra care for themselves. The volunteer efforts keep costs down, add a social dimension to the HMO, and help people take more responsibility for their own well-being.

Dennis Kodner, executive director of Elderplan, says:

> The SHMOs have demonstrated that health care needs of older people can be met, including both acute and long-term care, within a managed organizational budget, if the membership is large enough. We can provide reasonable continuity and quality that meets or exceeds past levels of experience. Families who want to care for elders

at home and don't want Medicaid can maintain their parents at home with proper care this way. Our focus on prevention protects people from having more serious problems. . . . But we have also learned that it is very difficult to market this idea to older people who are not familiar with our concept and have long-standing emotive ties to their personal physicians. They are reluctant to switch. People don't understand what Medicare and other supplements cover and what further benefits a SHMO can supply.

Are HMOs or SHMOs the wave of the future? It's too soon to tell.

EIGHT

DISEASES AND DISORDERS OF THE ELDERLY

Doctors and researchers are working hard to distinguish the disease process from the aging process so as to understand how better to treat their older patients. Some functions change with age, but not uniformly for all people. One feisty 90-year-old was told by her doctor, "You have the heart of a 20-year-old." A 60-year-smoker was told, "Your body is older than your chronological age." What changes and the rate of change with age are very individual matters. The body and the brain do slow down—some more, some less—some processes that regulate the various functions alter, tissues change, cells change and die, muscles weaken. And as we come to the end of our natural life cycle, we become more vulnerable to the stress of disease, the breakdown of systems, and the accident that kills.

If people don't die of old age per se, why do they die? Heart disease, cancer, stroke, diabetes, and accidents are the most common causes of death in people over 65.[1] Alzheimer's disease is often cited as the fourth leading cause of death in this country, but patients with dementia usually die of some other cause.[2] What doesn't kill old people can disable them or put them in pain and misery. Arthritis and rheumatism are high on this list of offenders. Pulmonary disease, with resultant difficulties in breathing, various circulatory diseases, and gastrointestinal disorders can limit the activity of chronic sufferers. Older men are especially vulnerable to diseases of the urinary tract. Incontinence can become a problem to both sexes.

There is a close correlation between physical impairment and mental disorder. Depression is a frequent companion of the elderly who are ill. But depression also appears without physical cause, with sudden bereavement, retirement, loss of income or social status, or without any apparent cause at all.

The elderly are frequently victims of several diseases simultaneously, and treatment depends on carefully orchestrating the routines and medications so that these do not interfere with one another.

Much is now known about the diseases that afflict the elderly; much is known about the possibilities of treatment, cure, and rehabilitation when handicaps appear. Much is known about medication, surgery, and psychiatry, and how aging affects one's responses to these interventions. If you know about these you can help your older parent live a longer, more comfortable life.

In this chapter you will find information about the major diseases and disorders that influence the lives of older people. Chapter 9 has information about behavioral changes, including Alzheimer's. This information is not intended to make you a physician but to help you deal better with your parent's medical problems.

HEART DISEASE

Despite all the good news about the remarkable improvement in survival rates from heart attack, heart disease still remains the number one killer disease in this country. Newly introduced drugs and, according to dramatic evidence, aspirin prescribed by a physician to be used alone or in combination with some of these drugs are clearly altering the statistics about heart fatalities. The hope is that healthier lifestyles and continued medical advances will further reduce the occurrence and impact of heart disease. Nevertheless, the presence of heart disease in any individual remains a serious matter that requires regular medical attention, and no medication, including aspirin, should be taken without a doctor's advice.

Heart disease is a loose description of various kinds of heart ailments. You need to know the characteristics of the particular kind of heart disease afflicting your parent if you're to deal intelligently and sympathetically with it. Diets, exercise, medication, and routines differ accordingly. A supervised, reasonably intensive exercise program may be just what the doctor orders for a person with a good recovery from a heart attack. A similar program could harm a patient with a poor recovery or with congestive heart failure. So before you give your own advice about what is or isn't a good idea, discuss with the doctor the precise nature of your parent's cardiac problem.

Most heart disease in older people results from hypertension (high blood pressure) or from arteriosclerosis, also called atherosclerosis (hardening of the arteries). Narrowing and thickening of the walls of the arteries can cause closure, clots, blockage, and heart attacks. A heart attack is a sudden disruption in flow of blood to the heart, causing death of tissue. Diseases of the heart and blood vessels are known as cardiovascular diseases. Congestive heart failure is usually associated with deterioration of the heart muscle and usually results in shortness of breath, swelling, and reduced tolerance of exercise. People may be born with (have congenital) heart disease, or malformation. People in acute heart failure may be drowning in the fluid accumulated in their lungs as a result of the heart's faulty pumping action. They require quick relief. Hearts may be enlarged, have a great deal of dead muscle (necrosis) or scar tissue as a result of heart attack, have damaged valves, or a variety of other pathological conditions. All affect the heart's function, which is to pump blood through the arteries and nourish the systems.

Cardiac arrest—in which the heart stops pumping—can result from any of these causes. If emergency treatment is undertaken quickly, the heart can sometimes be made to function again. If too long a time has elapsed before heart action is started again, brain damage occurs. If function is not restored, of course, the patient dies.

Red Cross chapters, local hospitals, and other organizations sponsor CPR (cardiopulmonary resuscitation) classes, which teach people how to treat acute heart problems immediately, before other help arrives. Most cardiac deaths take place outside of hospitals, and it is estimated that many thousands could have been prevented if basic first aid had been given in the first few seconds after cardiac arrest. CPR provides artificial circulation and breathing to the person whose heart and lungs have ceased functioning.

Many cardiac patients are in the sole care of their family physicians or internists and do very well. However, it is worthwhile to have a review by an experienced cardiologist occasionally, because some subtleties of diagnosis and treatment may be better known to the specialist. Computers with telephone hookups now make it possible to transmit such data as cardiograms to a specialist as the test is actually taking place and to get instant diagnostic consultation no matter where you live.

Your parent's doctor needs to understand personality and attitudes as well as physical state to prescribe a beneficial course of action. Some patients with minor heart damage are so frightened by heart disease they resist the physical exercise they can and should do. Others, even with enormous damage, so deny their disease that they overperform at real peril to their lives. Some patients after a good recovery from a heart attack believe they are good as new and ignore the need for careful diet and regular exercise, little realizing that they continue to suffer from the disease of arteriosclerosis with its continuing risks.

Risk Factors

You can help your parent prevent or postpone the most serious consequences of heart disease by understanding the risk factors and seeking early diagnosis and treatment. High risk factors for coronary artery disease are:

- high blood pressure
- high cholesterol or triglyceride levels

- diabetes
- genetics (family history of heart disease)
- smoking
- obesity
- poor diet
- insufficient or poor quality exercise

Sudden death is a real danger for people who deny their symptoms, says cardiologist Dr. Ira Gelb, for those who fail to take advantage of good advice and all those who are unaware of their problems and have "silent" heart attacks. "These are the people," says Dr. Gelb, "who 'drop dead.' " Diabetics are at special risk because some patients suffer nerve damage (neuropathy) and don't feel the pain while a heart attack is in progress. All older people should have regular medical check-ups, which include heart evaluation. The more precise diagnostic and treatment techniques presently available have greatly improved people's chances of successful treatment and longer life.

Emergency: Call the Doctor

The best general rule to follow is this: If you note a dramatic difference in behavior, appearance, eating habits, bowel habits, sleeping habits, or if you note increasing fatigue, shortness of breath, intensity or frequency of pain, coughing, or cold sweat, *call the doctor.*

- *chest pains.* If your parent seems unusually quiet, has chest pain that radiates out to the arms, and is breaking out in a cold sweat, waste no time—*call the doctor*. Anything unusual is significant. Pay particular attention if your parent suffers from angina pectoris and has "learned to live with pain." If there are changes in the character or increases in the frequency and duration of this pain, *call the doctor*.
- *suffocation sensation, shortness of breath.* These symptoms, which may awaken people from sleep with the feeling that they can't breathe, may be signs of acute heart failure. An open window or door may seem to give temporary relief, but

watch out for coughing, a cold sweat, or foam at the mouth. *Call the doctor.*

- *indigestion, nausea, cold sweat.* These symptoms, also accompanied by diffuse pain, frequently disguise the presence of an ongoing heart attack. Sometimes people think they're having gas pains or a gall bladder attack. *Call the doctor.*
- *loss of appetite, nausea, dizziness, diarrhea, profound weakness, palpitations, ringing in the ears, headaches, seeing spots, blurred vision, depression.* These symptoms may signify drug toxicity from too high a dose, drug interactions, or individual sensitivities. If your parent takes diuretics, digitalis, quinidine, beta blockers, or other medication that must be carefully monitored, be observant. If there are changes in habits or feelings, *call the doctor.*
- *swelling of feet, abdomen, unaccountable weight increase, lightheadedness, shortness of breath.* These signs of congestive heart failure in a known cardiac patient signify that the patient needs treatment. These symptoms accompanied by a cold sweat and difficulty in breathing can mean the patient is in acute heart failure. *Call the doctor.*
- *change in heart action—rapid or slow or irregular.* It is an emergency if the pulse suddenly rises or falls. If your parent reports that his or her heart is "racing" or "bumping," or going very slowly, or that he or she feels faint, remember that sudden changes in pulse rate can reflect heart damage or drug intoxication. *Call the doctor.*

Living with Heart Disease

Routine use of nitroglycerine can relieve the temporary pain of angina pectoris, a suffocating pain in the chest that results when the heart muscle is not getting enough oxygen because the blood supply is impaired. Heart patients are usually told to carry nitros with them for emergency use. Some use the new salve. Treating angina with nitros may cause headaches initially, but these usually go away. There's no reason for persons with angina not to live normally, provided they're not having unusually long-lasting symptoms and take reasonable precautions to avoid physical or emotional stress.

Sufferers cannot afford the luxury of violent emotions, and families are cautioned to this effect.

Some patients use the recurrent pain of angina to manipulate those around them. If your parent complains of chest pains every time you go out for the evening, or when you are planning a vacation, or when your daughter dates someone your parent doesn't like, ask the doctor to evaluate such behavior for you and advise you how to respond. Knowing the emergency signs listed above should help. When in doubt, call the doctor.

It is very important for your parent and you to understand the importance of pain as a signal or symptom, of medication, diet, and prescribed routines. Dr. Robert Stivelman, a noted California cardiologist, says, "The hardest part of taking care of patients with heart disease is getting them to follow diets and live emotionally with their disease." Those who are disabled emotionally by their disease are frequently very difficult to treat. Some benefit from psychiatric counseling. Some hospitals include psychiatric teams in cardiac care from the beginning. Community self-help groups also help patients deal realistically with their situations. Depression can become serious enough for the cardiac patient to seek further psychiatric therapy for a while; medication can cause depression and should be reviewed by the cardiologist. The new calcium channel-blockers, says Dr. Stivelman, are less likely to cause depression than drugs like Inderal, which have caused some patients mood problems.

Families sometimes counter the doctor's advice. "It won't hurt," you might say, "to have a rich dessert, or an omelet, or a little salt now and then." An occasional high-cholesterol goody may not have serious consequences for those on a low-cholesterol diet, but for patients on low-sodium diets and those with pulmonary edema, hypertension, or congestive heart failure, it is essential to be rigorous. It is not true that a little bit won't hurt, although new drugs may hold promise for a less restricted life in the future.

Some patients, particularly those in congestive heart failure who cannot take any exercise, may become very isolated and depressed. Some decide to take their chances and "live a little," mindful of the risks and no longer caring to prolong so restricted a life. Some widows, angry at this seemingly careless behavior on the part of their husbands, carry angry grudges for long periods after the husband's death, because "he should have thought of me and taken care of himself." Whether love demands that a partner hang on to life by becoming an invalid or let go by living the imprudent life is one of those eternal questions, always to be debated. The families of elderly parents who must live a restricted life have an extra responsibility to bring the world to them, to relieve the tedium, and to provide some of the small pleasures that make it worthwhile to get up in the morning.

Should Cardiacs Live Alone?

No one can predict a sudden emergency. But in general, unless a patient has become too weak to take care of his or her daily needs, or is too terrified, a patient with heart damage can live alone, work, shop, socialize, and take exercise according to the physician's directions. For peace of mind, install a communication alert system that brings quick help (see chapter 2).

You may recall a grandmother tucked away from life's ongoing activities because she had a "heart condition." Today's physicians believe that as nearly a normal a life as possible may be more beneficial. One says, "Social intercourse and participation often benefit more than digitalis."

But be observant. When your mother begins to have palpitations after carrying heavy groceries, when you notice that your father has added another pillow or two to his bed and says he breathes better that way at night, or regularly returns from some exercise with a gray complexion or blue lips, it is time to reevaluate the situation, consult the doctor, and make new living arrangements that will provide the attention and security required.

Pacemakers, New Technologies, Surgery

Longer life for many cardiac patients has resulted from advances in technology and surgical techniques.

Pacemakers in many cases effectively control heart rate and avert the faintness and even sudden death that can come with irregular heart action. Pacemakers need to be checked on a regular basis and usually are replaced periodically. The procedure for checking and replacement is benign. Keep track of the schedule and remind an elderly parent when it is time for the appointment. Pacemakers are often checked by telephone at home; other times a visit to the physician or clinic is required.

Carefully monitored stress tests provide the physician with information about heart function. They are especially important in determining a plan of exercise for the cardiac patient or in uncovering hidden heart problems. Sophisticated new diagnostic techniques improve the cardiologists' ability to pinpoint the exact cause of a patient's cardiac problems and improve the possibilities for successful treatment. New aggressive techniques, including angioplasty (inserting a balloon to open up a blocked artery) and new medications can sometimes alter the course and effects of a heart attack if undertaken within the first few hours of an attack.

Open heart surgery, valve replacement, bypass surgery, laser surgery, and vascular surgery are available options for many people, including the elderly. The general medical and mental condition, not the age, of the patient are the criteria for deciding what is suitable. Your parent's doctor should spell out the advantages and dangers for any given surgery. Don't be embarrassed to get another opinion. The final decision has to be made by your parent, not you. You should be supportive of whatever that is.

Should You Tell a Person with Heart Trouble Bad News?

"Families take a big chance," says one cardiologist, "when they keep things from their ailing parents." The right to grieve for a departed relative or to visit a fatally ill child or grandchild is a right that should not be taken away without considerable thought. Find a way to lessen the shock of bad news, to introduce the problem gently, in protected circumstances, with the doctor or someone else close to your parent. Follow the doctor's advice as to whether the news is too stressful and dangerous for a very ill person to hear. As one study demonstrated, "mental stress can cause episodes of potentially serious blood shortage to the heart muscle in some patients who already have diseased coronary arteries."[3] You may be advised to delay this news for a time, but most doctors believe there are ways to present bad news, sooner rather than later, to avoid problems. By sheer coincidence a stranger may inform your parent or assume he or she already knows and offer condolences. This emotional shock may be worse than the one you were trying to avoid.

HYPERTENSION (HIGH BLOOD PRESSURE)

High blood pressure—the silent killer—is the most prevalent chronic disease in America. It can exist without apparent symptoms. Its effects can cause sudden damage to the heart and/or brain. Doctors refer to it as hypertension. It is a result of hypertensive disease which impairs the system that regulates blood pressure while blood is being pumped through the circulatory system. If blood pressure increases beyond normal limits, the heart has to work harder. Overworked, it enlarges. Overtaxed, its pumping action falters. Congestive heart failure or coronary thrombosis can result. Improper flow of blood to the brain can cause stroke. High blood pressure can also damage the kidneys, with subsequent kidney failure and a buildup of waste, causing uremic poisoning. Death can be the result of any of these effects of high blood pressure.

It is essential to have blood pressure checked regularly, at least once a year. Doctors do this routinely with each patient visit, but it's easy to have blood pressure checks at other places: the nearest public health station, at a senior citizens' center, even from a mobile van. Any abnormality requires evaluation so that prompt and appropriate treatment can begin. The average normal adult reading is 120/80, but this can vary for older people. The physician should determine what is safe for any individual.

Those who are overweight or indulge in high-salt diets are candidates for hypertension, but other factors may also be responsible. Hypertension is more prevalent among the black than the white population and is a major factor in the shorter life spans of blacks. Hypertension seems to run in families. Even among those who have had normal or low blood pressure through much of their lives, high blood pressure commonly appears in later life. Sometimes blood pressure becomes elevated as a secondary effect of other diseases; when the other disease is treated the high blood pressure is cured. Primary hypertension—the disease which afflicts the majority of hypertensive patients—cannot be cured as yet.

"Hypertension is so prevalent in the aged that many physicians consider it a normal, even inevitable aspect of aging that does not require treatment. This view is untrue."[4] The National Institute on Aging recommends that even those with mild hypertension consult the doctor again to determine whether some form of treatment might be suitable.

Hypertension, once diagnosed, is a lifetime disease that must be monitored regularly. Low-salt diets and exercise, in combination with medication, will usually keep blood pressure in reasonably good control. Most people taking hypertensive drugs are cautioned to eat foods high in potassium, such as bananas and oranges, to make up for the potassium lost through use of diuretics. Some people need a potassium supplement to maintain required levels. Whatever regimen has been prescribed should be rigorously followed. Remind your parent not to "double up" if he or she has forgotten to take medication one day. Instead, call the doctor for advice. The best way for anyone to take medicine is to take it at the same time each day so that it becomes routine.

Report any side effects (faintness, nausea, dizziness, headache, etc.) immediately to the physician. Dosages of anti-hypertensive medication for elderly patients must be very closely monitored so that required changes can be instituted quickly if necessary. The low-salt diets, diuretics, and medication are designed to remove the salt and excess fluids that accumulate in lungs and limbs and to reduce the pressure that causes this and other effects. But the chemical balance is so critical and elderly patients are so sensitive to certain drugs that it is not good enough to get a prescription and then merely take it. The doctor may try a variety of combinations of drugs and therapy to find the one most appropriate for the individual at any given time, then keep tabs for ongoing changes.

Emotional stress can elevate blood pressure, and for the person with hypertensive disease, this can be quite serious. The prudent course for the family of an elderly person with high blood pressure is to avoid confrontations and highly charged emotional scenes.

Hypertension Danger Signals

- light-headedness
- dizziness
- sleeplessness
- shortness of breath
- vision problems
- palpitations of the heart
- swelling of the ankles

STROKE

The majority of stroke victims are among the male elderly. Stroke, the third leading cause of death, is a major cause of long-term disability and nursing home placement. But despite the fact that 400,000 Americans suffer stroke each year and that about two million survivors are currently disabled by stroke,[5] this leading neurological disorder can often be prevented.

The risk factors or conditions that lead to stroke include:

- TIAs (transient ischemic attacks), temporary insufficient blood flow to the brain
- high blood pressure
- atherosclerosis
- heart disease
- diabetes
- smoking
- obesity
- continued high levels of stress
- lack of exercise
- hereditary disorders that lead to accumulation of fat or cholesterol in blood

It is currently believed that the stroke that "comes out of the blue" has in reality been building over time. By paying attention to the warning signs and reporting these to a doctor, and by following his or her advice to alter or control the causes, many potential victims can be saved the devastating effects of stroke.

A stroke is a sudden disruption in the flow of blood to an area of the brain. The results vary according to which part of the brain has been affected. Brain cells are either damaged or die, and this damage often results in disability. New evidence indicates that, while dead brain cells are never regenerated, the brain can generate growth of new nerve tissue to facilitate new connections and overcome some of the stroke-caused deficits. Nevertheless, the disabling effects of brain cell death and damage can thwart the ability of many stroke victims to regain an independent life. Aside from the familiar and disabling handicaps that can follow stroke, neurologists now report that when stroke results from hypertensive atherosclerosis, about 20 percent of the survivors are left with varying degrees of dementia, or loss of mental skills and intellectual function.[6]

There are three kinds of stroke. The most common, the *thrombotic* stroke, is related to atherosclerosis. The buildup of fatty deposits on the walls of the arteries results in narrowing the blood vessels that feed blood to the brain and severely reducing the blood flow until eventually a blood clot (called a thrombus) in an artery entirely blocks the path of blood. The *embolic* stroke occurs when undissolved matter, usually a blood clot (an embolus), formed elsewhere in the body, is detached and travels through the circulatory system to the brain, where it blocks the blood flow. The most severe type of stroke occurs when a blood vessel in the brain bursts, causing a hemorrhage. This is called a *hemorrhagic* stroke.

Sometimes doctors describe a stroke as an *infarct*. An infarct means that an area of tissue has died following interference with the blood supply to it. Two-thirds of all strokes are due to infarct.

Any stroke is an emergency and demands immediate treatment to help insure that no further damage to brain cells occurs. Neurologists are the doctors who specialize in diagnosing and treating stroke victims. Your parent's doctor will probably call on a neurologist if stroke is suspected or known to be the cause of your parent's symptoms. Anticoagulants may be used to prevent new blood clots from forming. These drugs will not be used if hemorrhage is the cause of the stroke, in which case if clots are present they might be preserved for a time to help plug up the injury to the blood vessel, while drugs to reduce brain swelling or high blood pressure might be used.

In order to determine what is actually happening in the brain and what treatment to institute, physicians now have an elaborate array of new equipment and techniques. These include the CAT scan, a painless technique that presents computerized images of the brain and can differentiate between healthy and damaged tissue; arteriography, a technique with some risk for other damage, which permits the doctor to study the entire arterial system; DIVA (digitized intravenous arteriography), another technique for X-raying the brain that is described as convenient, fast and safe but not as detailed as arteriograms and is generally preferred for patients too ill for arteriography, or to determine whether arteriography is needed; and ultrasonography, a painless procedure that uses ultrasound equipment to inspect the arteries of the neck for defects.

While sophisticated procedures and surgery in combination with powerful drugs have improved treatment for stroke, the priorities for any family are to prevent stroke, if possible; to recognize the warning signals that stroke may be imminent; to inform the doctor so that preventive measures can be taken; to treat stroke immediately if it occurs; and to take advantage of all the rehabilitation therapy possible to restore function to the stroke victim.

Helping to Prevent Stroke

The death rate from stroke fell 45 percent between 1970 and 1986[7] partly because of new diagnostic tests and treatments, partly because people have adopted more sensible health habits. Encourage your parent to take the following steps:

- Control blood pressure. Have periodic checkups and follow the doctor's advice.
- Eat a healthy diet, low in cholesterol, and be careful about salt.
- Exercise regularly to strengthen the heart, improve circulation, and control weight. Check with a physician.
- Control diabetes, which untreated can cause destructive changes in blood vessels throughout the body.
- Learn to manage stress better, and try to avoid continued high levels of stress.
- Promptly report warning signs of stroke to the doctor.

Other risk factors that should be considered for the older patient trying to avoid stroke are the presence of heart disease, hereditary disorders that predispose toward accumulation of fat or cholesterol in blood, and sickle cell anemia or other blood disorders. Patients with these conditions should always be carefully monitored by physicians. In some cases arteries are "reamed" and obstructions removed. For some, daily doses of aspirin or other drugs are prescribed.

Warning Signs of Stroke

The four most common warnings of stroke, *which should never be ignored*, are:

- transient numbness, tingling, or weakness in an arm or leg or on one side of the face
- temporary blindness in one or both eyes
- temporary difficulty with speech
- loss of strength in a limb

These are the clearest symptoms that a stroke may occur. They usually stem from TIAs—transient ischemic attacks—or temporary lack of sufficient blood to the brain. Untreated they can lead to a major stroke. They may also produce other strokelike symptoms, such as:

- unexplained headaches
- dizziness or light-headedness
- drowsiness
- nausea or vomiting
- impaired judgment, abrupt personality changes, forgetfulness

These warning signs may be of brief duration—only a few seconds—or last several minutes or longer. Even if the symptoms pass quickly, a physician should be seen immediately, either in the office or in the emergency room, to determine whether a stroke has occurred or is imminent. A stroke can last from minutes to hours or, on rare occasions, for days.

The Acute Stage During the early period immediately following a stroke, the patient's condition may be generally unstable and symptoms may emerge rapidly but fluctuate. For reasons as yet not understood, the brain swells a few days after a severe stroke, which may cause further damage. Some patients soon start to improve; others seem to get worse and then improve; some do not improve. Symptoms may come and go, including impaired speech, paralysis, and unconsciousness. If this is happening to your parent you will want to know what to expect, but the doctor may not be able to answer your questions as quickly as you might like.

Watching, waiting, and prompt intervention are the order of business during the acute stage. Once your parent is stabilized and out of danger and once tests establish what loss of function has occurred, current expert advice is to start rehabilitation.

Rehabilitation

Families are cautioned that "sometimes stroke survivors lose the benefits of rehabilitative treatment because they don't realize they should have it, they don't know where to find it, or they don't continue treatment long enough to see lasting improvement."[8]

Rehabilitation involves a team of professionals working with the patient and the family to achieve maximum recovery from stroke. The team includes the physician and various therapists and specialists:

- *Physical therapists* help patients strengthen muscles, improve balance and coordination, and relearn the movement necessary for sitting, standing, and walking. They teach patients how to use such mechanical aids as a walker, crutches, a cane, or braces.
- *Speech and language therapists* help those whose communication skills have been damaged. Patients who cannot speak but can still read can use alphabet charts to communicate their needs and wants as they work with the therapists to regain their communication functions.
- *Occupational therapists* work to improve eye-hand coordination and strengthen the skills individuals require for bathing, dressing, preparing food, writing, and using tools.
- *Social workers* help patients and families make the transition from previous lifestyles to what may be required

after a stroke. They can coordinate activities and advise you how to alter a stroke victim's home environment for maximum independence.

Rehabilitation usually begins in the hospital and may be continued at a rehabilitation center and at home. Medicare will pay for this if it is determined that the patient will benefit by it. The period of reimbursed care depends on the doctor's evaluation of need and the interpretation of the regulations by the third party paying for the therapy. One caution: Medicare reimbursement for rehabilitation is often narrowly interpreted and even denied retroactively. To avoid costly errors, be vigilant in seeking expert advice. You may well wish to proceed on your own or your parent's financial resources, but you should know ahead of time what to expect.

Many patients recover quickly; others take months or years. Older people who suffer from other conditions as well as multiple handicaps from stroke may be less responsive to rehabilitation therapies. Great patience and sensitivity from the professionals as well as from a supportive and encouraging family appear to pay off in greater survival rates, however. Don't give up too quickly.

Be cautioned that poststroke depression, mostly likely to occur between six months and two years after a stroke, is not uncommon. This depression is attributed partially to the brain's reaction to the stroke and partially to psychological reaction. Medication and psychiatric therapy may help.

Where to Go for Help

There is a great deal of help available for stroke patients and their families. Rehabilitation centers can be found in all fifty states. Stroke units can be found in major research and teaching hospitals and smaller community hospitals. You can even seek treatment at one of the cerebrovascular clinical research centers operated by the National Institute of Neurological and Communicable Diseases and Stroke. National health organizations such as the American Heart Association publish excellent guides on stroke and there are many government publications as well. The National Easter Seal Society or its local chapters, the Will Rogers Institute, and the Association of Rehabilitation Facilities can also direct you to local sources of help. Among the best-known centers are Rusk Rehabilitation Institute of New York University; Rancho Los Amigos in Downey, California; Texas Institute of Rehabilitation and Research of Baylor University; the Rehabilitation Institute of Chicago; and Cornell University's Burke Rehabilitation Center in White Plains, New York.

See Appendix under National Health Organizations.

CANCER

Cancer takes more lives than any other disease except those of the heart and vascular system. People dread it because most have been witness to the devastation it can cause. Some cancers, caught early, are curable. Some cancers, treated with chemotherapy or radiation, can be arrested. Some cancers can be excised by surgery. Others resist all treatment and kill.

Cancers are of enormous variety and range. Indeed, cancer is a general term for more than a hundred diseases characterized by uncontrolled, abnormal growth of cells that can invade and destroy healthy tissues. Any tissue of the body is susceptible to cancer. *Metastasis* means that cancer cells have traveled through the lymph channels and bloodstream and settled in new places, causing new tumors to grow. When this happens, the prognosis is usually not favorable. When the cancer is contained in a particular place where treatment can be focused or surgery used to eliminate it, there is greater chance of successful treatment.

Physicians who specialize in the treatment of tumors, especially cancers, are called *oncologists*. The important thing is to have regular medical checkups and ongoing care by reputable physicians, to report without delay any unusual symptoms, and to take advantage of the numerous support groups that are available to patients and families to help you cope not only with the disease but its emotional impact.

The greatest contribution you can make to your parent's bout with cancer is to be alert to its early signs. Any of the following signals should send a person to the doctor for examination and treatment.

Cancer Warning Signals

- change in bowel or bladder habits
- a sore that does not heal
- unusual bleeding or discharge
- unexplained weight loss
- thickening or lump in the breast or elsewhere
- indigestion or difficulty in swallowing
- obvious change in a wart, mole, or freckle
- nagging cough or hoarseness

Prognosis and Treatment

Cancer treatment is costly. Many thousands of dollars are involved for surgery, radiation therapy, chemotherapy, nursing care, and home care. It is important to understand the financial arrangements at each step and to use whatever entitlements and insurance are available. Check the Medicare entitlements new in 1989. All the financial considerations involved in other long-term care apply here (see chapter 5).

Sometimes medical advice is clearcut and there are no real differences of opinion among doctors, but not always. One may say surgery is best, another radiation. Many patients are given statistics about cure rates and life expectancy for this or that course of treatment and asked to choose for themselves from among several options the course they will follow. What if you ask a doctor "What would you choose?" and the reply is "I'm not sure." The answer for many lies in asking advice from yet another specialist till some consensus forms. If the patient's personal physician goes through this process with the conflicted patient, then together they can talk out the advice of others and come to some decision on how to proceed.

Facing up to the knowledge that there are often no sure answers to this disease is one of the first challenges presented to the cancer patient. It is a challenge to overcome the initial fear and dread that a cancer diagnosis provokes. In fact, real progress continues to be made in improving the survival rate among cancer patients. Dr. Arthur Holleb writes in a book he edited for the American Cancer Society: "More than five million Americans have a history of cancer. Three million of them developed the disease more than five years ago, and many are now considered cured, meaning there is no longer any sign of cancer and the person can expect to live as long as someone who has never had cancer." In the early thirties, only out of five cancer patients survived more than five years. Today 50,000 more people are saved each year than two decades ago.[9]

Indeed, so many people have survived over long years with modern treatments that one young woman's advice to her father is especially relevant: "The trick," she said, "is to learn to live with your cancer, not to dwell on dying of it." Many cancer patients die of other diseases before they die of cancer.

Improving one's chances against cancer depends strongly on avoiding cancer risk habits such as smoking, obesity, and poor diet and on regular monitoring, early detection, and prompt treatment. You may be of great help in your mother's and father's understanding this.

Families can help an elderly cancer patient to lead as normal a life as possible and not limit the patient who is prepared to do this. There is still a stigma attached to cancer. People who have been successfully treated and return to work often find difficulties in being accepted as before; it is as though others were waiting for the other shoe to drop. Prospects for promotion dim. Social engagements fall off. Friends and acquaintances may admire your parent's brave fight with the dread disease but from a distance. People taking care of their cancer-stricken loved ones may also find themselves increasingly isolated. To overcome this, don't wait for others to make the first move: invite friends to visit your parent or you, or to help you through a rough period.

Age and Cancer

As people survive other diseases that once would have killed them, they become candidates for cancer as they age. Approximately half the incidence of cancer is among the population more than 65 years of age. Certain cancers are diagnosed more frequently among the old: cancers of the stomach, colon, rectum, and prostate among men, and cancer of the breast among women. The incidence of breast cancer increases with age. Older men commonly suffer from lung cancer, a condition now being diagnosed in women as well—smoking is regarded as the culprit. Certain gynecological cancers are becoming more common among elderly women, which indicates that women should continue to visit a gynecologist for regular checkups.

Older cancer patients will usually be treated by the same therapies as younger ones except that the physician may have to evaluate treatment in relation to the presence of other conditions. Thus surgery might or might not be a good risk for certain elderly patients, or extensive chemotherapy might be questioned. Current expert opinion is that "the great majority of elderly patients . . . will profit from comprehensive management, including specific efforts to treat the cancer. . . . As long as surgical procedures are well planned and patients are carefully selected, major cancer surgery in the elderly is justified."[10]

What you must consider is how your parent regards the quality of his or her life at the time treatments are undertaken, what the side effects of these treatments may be, and what the prognosis is after the treatment. Some treatments have few side effects, and most people are willing to endure the pain or nausea some treatments create for a period when the results can reasonably be expected to be positive. Many are less willing to be kept alive by invasive therapies and aggressive treatments if the result is only prolongation of life without quality. How any patient and family responds to these dilemmas is a private and individual matter.

The hospice movement has made an enormous contribution

to cancer patients and their families who are facing the terminal period of the illness, and especially those who are in pain. Hospice teams work with families as well as patients to deal with the physical, emotional, and spiritual factors involved in the process of dying and make the period as pain-free, graceful, and dignified as possible. For example, hospice patients who are terminally ill and need to be readmitted to a hospital two or three times for round-the-clock nursing or other care are spared the repeated evaluation, testing, and aggressive treatments that normally go with hospital admission. They are also spared the expense of these procedures. Hospice is now a Medicare option if a physician certifies that the patient is terminally ill and will probably die within six months. See chapter 11 for more on this.

Where to Go for Help

As always, the more information you have, the better off you are. The Cancer Information Service, an arm of the National Cancer Institute, helps physicians quickly with the latest treatment information and also responds to inquiries from patients themselves. Experts take your calls, will provide some information immediately, and are very helpful in sending additional information. This resource will augment what your parent's doctor tells you. The American Cancer Society, the American Red Cross, and other more specialized organizations will also guide you to local resources and may be able to help you with transportation, special care at home, financial planning, local support groups, or whatever special needs develop.

See Appendix under Cancer.

DIABETES

Diabetes, with its complications, is a major American health problem and a leading cause of death. It is expected to escalate in coming decades. Nevertheless, early diagnosis and treatment can reduce its impact.

In diabetes, the mechanism that controls the amount of glucose in the blood breaks down. The body then cannot convert foods properly into the energy needed for daily activity. When you eat sugars and starches, your body normally converts these to glucose, which then circulates in the bloodstream for immediate use or is stored in the liver for future use in the form of glycogen. When the mechanism that controls this process is flawed, dangerous levels of glucose can build up, which can damage body organs. Glucose buildup can occur because the body has insufficient insulin (the hormone that regulates glucose level) or because the insulin is not doing its job effectively on body tissues. Sometimes glucose levels are too low, and this too can cause a medical emergency.

What some people call "sugar diabetes" is known medically as *diabetes mellitus.* It appears in two main forms. Type I, the most severe form, can appear at any age, though it more commonly occurs in childhood or early adolescence. It requires lifelong treatment with insulin, as well as planned exercise and a controlled diet. Type II diabetes more commonly appears in the adult years. It was previously described as *adult-onset diabetes* and is not as dependent on insulin for control. More than 85 percent of people with diabetes have Type II, and most do not require insulin injections. By rigorously reducing and controlling their weight, watching their diets, and following an exercise program, such people can usually keep their blood sugar levels near normal. Orally administered drugs are also used to control Type II diabetes, and insulin therapy is used whenever necessary.

The genetic links in this disease are strong. Also, as the life span increases, those without knowledge of previous family history are showing diabetic symptoms in middle and old age. There is evidence that the older body does not process carbohydrates (sugars and starches) as efficiently as before. Therefore, eating too much, in combination with insufficient exercise, raises the risk of acquiring diabetes in the years after 40. Blacks and Hispanics also have a significantly higher incidence of noninsulin-dependent diabetes than the general population.

Symptoms of Diabetes

- increased thirst
- frequent urination, especially at night
- unexplained weight loss
- fatigue and irritability
- blurred vision
- skin infections
- itching
- slow-healing cuts and bruises
- tingling and numbness in legs, feet, or fingers
- extreme hunger
- nausea and vomiting

Insulin-dependent diabetes usually has a sudden onset; noninsulin-dependent diabetes usually appears more gradually. Sometimes the individual only feels run down and ignores these telling symptoms. Sometimes, the disorder is first discovered by the doctor in a routine physical examination, when sugar is detected in the urine, or too much sugar is in the blood. The doctor may order a glucose tolerance test to confirm or eliminate a diagnosis of diabetes. This test usually takes several hours, is done in the doctor's office, and involves measuring the glucose level in the blood at timed intervals before and after the patient drinks a special glucose liquid.

Recent research has shown that blood glucose levels may rise as a natural function of aging. As a result, the National Institute on Aging encourages physicians to match older people's glucose levels against those of other older people rather than against younger people's performance on the glucose test as a means of avoiding incorrect diagnosis. Nevertheless, of the 11 million Americans who had diabetes in 1985, the American Diabetes Association estimates that 5 million didn't know it.[11] Typically, it is older people who fail to report legitimate symptoms of serious but treatable disease.

Dr. Harold Rifkin, a diabetes expert and recent president of the American Diabetes Association, reminds families:

Diabetes in older people may manifest itself in ways that are similar to symptoms in younger people, but not always. Older people may show very different symptoms: a sudden increase in weight, for example. They commonly report itching skin, particularly in the genital area, because of the increasing presence of sugar in the urine. But frequently, mature diabetes is picked up only by the complications it presents: cataracts, glaucoma, high blood pressure, kidney disease, retinal pathology, or neurological disease. It may appear suddenly after an acute emotional upset or a catastrophic illness, such as a stroke or coronary attack, or with the onset of gangrene of the legs. . . .

Sometimes the very first manifestation of diabetes in old people is coma brought on by dehydration. We are seeing this more frequently with people who never knew they had diabetes. Such situations are often mistakenly diagnosed as massive stroke. If this happens, it becomes a real medical emergency. Perhaps they've had diarrhea or vomiting, or a small infection, and they haven't been drinking water to compensate for the fluid they've lost. These people with *latent diabetes* can go quickly into coma, a condition which is reversible with appropriate fluids. But quick diagnosis and treatment is of the utmost importance.

Diabetic people may go into coma when their blood sugar gets very high or, as a result of insulin shock, when their blood sugar levels are too low. Learn from the doctor what emergency procedures to use if this occurs. People with diabetes should wear a medical identification bracelet or necklace at all times indicating that they have the disease and specifying the type of treatment they require in emergencies. The American Diabetes Association (ADA) can refer you to a local source for this identification.

Treatment

Diabetes cannot be cured but it can be controlled. Most experts believe that vigilant care and control will either prevent or lessen the long-term complications of this disease, which include stroke, blindness, heart disease, kidney failure, gangrene, and nerve damage.

All those with diabetes should be under a doctor's care, be regularly monitored, and follow the planned regimen rigorously. The more serious the condition, the more necessary not to deviate from the doctor's orders. Less serious cases can become serious if patients become too casual in following the doctor's advice. It is particularly important for the person with diabetes to be careful at times of great stress or during other illnesses, when diabetes can go out of control.

Control is usually achieved by diet, medication, and/or injection of insulin. New problems may arise, however, if previously active people become sedentary as they grow older, or if they don't have the money to pay for the diet they require, or if their digestion becomes impaired. They may complain of diarrhea or bellyache, have no appetite, and avoid eating at all. Any of these factors can contribute to destabilizing the management of their diabetes. Further complications result, even for those long accustomed to injecting insulin, if they can no longer administer the lifesaving drug properly because of failing eyesight or trembling hands.

If your parent has had diabetes for a long time, you may be taking the treatment for granted. Check with the doctor to be sure your parent's diet and medication are current and the regimen being followed is correct. Don't assume that emerging symptoms of deterioration can't be reversed. You, or someone else, may need to assist your parent with the insulin injection or monitor his or her diet more carefully.

A leading diabetes researcher at the National Institutes of Health, Dr. Simeon Taylor, underlines the necessity for yearly examinations by an ophthalmologist for those with diabetes: "Laser surgery has made it possible for us to prevent loss of vision among diabetic people, *if* retinopathy is diagnosed early. There are many things doctors cannot do—this is something we can do. We are trying to understand better the causes of diabetes, to develop new drugs to prevent the complications, and we have made real progress in our work, but nothing is so presently possible to prevent blindness as laser surgery for early retinopathy."

Fear of amputation also haunts those with diabetes. With

newer surgical techniques for bypass vascular surgery, there is now greater hope that diabetics can be spared amputation. If your parent can't avoid amputation, however, you can be reassuring about future mobility because of improvements in prosthetic devices and help your parent to understand that surgery of any kind is not the menace it once was. Some believe that diabetic people can't handle infection, that they can't heal after surgery. "Not true," says Dr. Rifkin. "They can handle infection quite well with quick action by the doctor, and they can heal with proper care."

And finally, be sensitive to the psychological stress the disease imposes. Because of poor eyesight, pains in the limbs, or rigid meal schedules, some people with diabetes find it difficult to socialize, sit through a movie, eat in a restaurant, or enjoy a party. They then are additionally vulnerable to the deterioration that comes with loss of social stimulation. Then there is the guilt that older people feel when their children or their grandchildren show diabetic symptoms. Says Dr. Rifkin, "They blame themselves for transmitting the disease and get renewed flare-ups of their own symptoms. Because people are more familiar with the tendency in families to develop diabetes than the tendency to acquire cancer or heart disease, there seems to be a greater guilt syndrome attached to diabetes, which interferes with conventional treatment. These people require a great deal of tender loving care and reassurance that they are not to blame."

The local chapter of the American Diabetes Association is a good source of information about local physicians who are specialists in the treatment of diabetes and about such programs as counseling services and self-help groups.

See the Appendix under National Health Organizations.

BREATHING AND RESPIRATORY PROBLEMS

Pneumonia used to be known as the old man's friend —when everything else in his life was falling apart, pneumonia came and carried him off. Now many pneumonias succumb to antibiotics, leaving the elderly to wrestle with other diseases. Lung cancer and emphysema (both linked to smoking and pollutants) are the major respiratory killers these days, but pneumonia can still cause trouble for an elderly person, particularly the viral pneumonias that antibiotics can't help.

To avoid pneumonia after surgery, older people, who for other reasons may be collecting fluid in their lungs or bronchia, are soon encouraged to get out of bed, even if it's painful; to move around in bed rather than stay still; and to cough up phlegm, to break up pockets of congestion and thwart the development of infection, which can start a pneumonia. Pneumonia is the fifth leading cause of death among persons over 65.

Lung cancer, pneumonia, emphysema, bronchial disorders, and asthma are among the diseases that attack breathing capacity. Breathing involves inhaling air to be processed by the lungs to provide oxygen to the blood and exhaling to eliminate the waste product of the blood—carbon dioxide. When a person cannot breathe, death follows.

Everyone who ages, even without obvious pathology and disease, loses some breathing capacity. As muscle strength diminishes, the act of breathing becomes more difficult. This loss of muscle strength and breathing capacity combine to reduce the ability to work and exercise. It is a process that begins quite early in life—note the champion athletes who retire in their thirties because they can no longer compete with prime athletes in their twenties. Exercise and weight control are the necessary ingredients to maintain optimum breathing capacity at each stage of life.

This slowly diminishing breathing capacity should not be confused with chronic symptoms that require treatment. Shortness of breath, wheezing and coughing, and recurring repiratory infections among the elderly are not just chronic conditions to be tolerated but medical conditions to be investigated. Medication, inhalants, and home use of oxygen are among the treatments that make people more comfortable and enable them to function.

Smoking and polluted air worsen almost any breathing

problem. In times of pollution alerts, deaths among the elderly rise. Deaths among the elderly also rise during flu epidemics. Doctors recommend that elderly people take flu shots each year as a precaution. It is not that flu in itself is usually fatal, but its complications may be life-threatening. Those with chronic diseases, such as heart disease, kidney disease, emphysema, asthma, bronchitis, and diabetes, are at greatest risk of developing secondary infections with flu, the most serious of which is pneumonia.

Some people with reduced lung capacity are taught how to improve their breathing function or how to live more comfortably with what function they retain through programs sponsored by rehabilitation centers. One woman with obstructive pulmonary lung disease had deteriorated in seven years from an active, outgoing community leader to a sedentary invalid, no longer able to walk to the second floor of her home without stopping along the way. She found cooking too taxing most of the time, and her husband had become the shopper and family cook. Depressed and desperate, this woman enrolled in a four-week live-in program at the Burke Rehabilitation Center, in New York, where she learned to make the most of her diminished capacities, to exercise and eat appropriately, and to sit, stand, and walk in ways that enhanced rather than retarded her capacity to function. She emerged from the program glowing and positive. She knows her limitations, but is no longer reclusive; she entertains again, goes out more frequently. She goes south in the winter because she cannot tolerate the cold and has moved to a one-floor house to use her strength to better purpose than walking up stairs. Your parent's physician can tell you whether a rehabilitation program is appropriate for your mother or father.

HYPOTHERMIA

Older people are not being hypochondriacs when they complain that they are chilly when others are warm, or that they feel drafts and are afraid to "take cold." They feel colder and are more sensitive to drafts and chills because they tend to be less well insulated. The loss of some of their subcutaneous fat makes them more acutely aware of temperature changes. Grandma may really need a shawl and Grandpa a lap robe to keep comfortable while others are sitting around in their shirt-sleeves.

It sometimes takes a terrible tragedy, like finding an old person frozen to death in an unheated apartment during a winter blizzard, to dramatize the real dangers older people face from excessive exposure to extremes of heat and cold. As we age, our bodies are less responsive to the challenges these temperature extremes pose. Sometimes the mechanism that controls body temperature becomes impaired. The chronically ill, those saving money by reducing room temperature, and those whose internal body thermostats are defective are all candidates for hypothermia—subnormal body temperature—which can be fatal if not promptly treated.

If you find any of these signs of hypothermia, get emergency medical help:

- unusual change in appearance or behavior during cold weather
- slow and sometimes irregular heartbeat
- slurred speech
- shallow, very slow breathing
- sluggishness
- confusion
- a body temperature of 95 degrees or below

The treatment for hypothermia is to rewarm the person under a doctor's supervision.

To protect against hypothermia:

- Keep living and sleeping quarters warm enough for elderly people. Although 65 degrees is safe for most people except the sick, some experts suggest that 68 degrees is a better level. Many chronically ill older people with heart and circulatory problems, and those who complain of the cold, are more comfortable at 70 degrees.

- Dress warmly, in layers, eat enough food, and stay active.
- Keep warm in bed by wearing warm nightclothes and using enough blankets. A large portion of body heat is lost through the uncovered head. Old-fashioned nightcaps had their function. Get one for your parent.
- Talk to the doctor about your parent's medication: drugs used to treat anxiety, depression, nervousness, or nausea can affect control of body temperature.
- If your parent lives alone, ask friends or neighbors, or arrange for a friendly visitor, to check your mother or father during cold weather.
- If money is a problem, arrange through your parents' Area Agency on Aging for help in paying high energy bills, weatherizing and insulating their home, and getting emergency repairs.

HEAT STROKE, EXHAUSTION, PROSTRATION

Excessive heat can also be a hazard to elderly people, especially during hot and humid weather, when body heat can build up and cause heat stroke (sometimes called prostration) or heat exhaustion. Those with heart and circulatory diseases, stroke, or diabetes are particularly vulnerable.

Heat stroke is a medical emergency and requires immediate medical attention. Warning signs of heat stroke are:

- faintness
- headache
- loss of consciousness
- dizziness
- nausea
- a body temperature of 104 degrees or higher

Heat exhaustion results from the loss of body water and salt. It develops over a longer period of time and is treated by resting in a cool place and drinking cool liquids. Warning signs of heat exhaustion are:

- weakness
- heavy sweating
- fatigue
- nausea
- giddiness

To protect against heat-related illnesses, remind your parents to take the following precautions during hot weather:

- Remain indoors in an air-conditioned room, use a fan, or go to a cool public place during peak hot hours.
- Cool off by taking a cool (not cold) bath or shower.
- Wear loose-fitting, lightweight clothes so sweat can evaporate.
- Avoid strenous activity
- Drink plenty of water, juice, or iced tea to replace fluids lost through sweating; check with a doctor about alcoholic or carbonated beverages containing salt.
- Take salt tablets only under a doctor's direction

ARTHRITIS

Arthritis is the most prevalent chronic condition causing limitation of activity for older people. The likelihood of suffering from arthritis is 80 percent higher for those 65 and older than for the middle aged.[12] Arthritis accounts for a great deal of pain and misery and leaves its victims particularly vulnerable to the appeals of quack cures. It is not a life-threatening disease but can certainly diminish its victims' independence and zest for living. Arthritis is in fact a general name for a group of more than a hundred different diseases, generally known as rheumatic diseases. *Rheumatologists* are physicians who specialize in the treatment of arthritis.

The symptoms of arthritis are:

- persistent pain and stiffness on arising
- pain, swelling, or tenderness in one or more joints
- recurrence of these symptoms, especially when they involve more than one joint

- pain and stiffness in the neck, lower back, knees, and other joints
- tingling sensation in the fingertips, hands, and feet
- unexplained weight loss, fever, weakness, or fatigue combined with joint pain
- symptoms such as these that last for more than two weeks

Forms of Arthritis

Arthritis appears in several forms, the most common of which is osteoarthritis. According to the Arthritis Foundation, most people over 60 have osteoarthritis to some degree, but only a few have it badly enough to notice symptoms, and people who expect to feel aches and pains as they age may dismiss these symptoms. The disease is often mild, but it can be severe.

Excessive use of an arthritic joint sometimes speeds the arthritic process, as can an accidental injury or excessive weight. When an enlarged joint presses on nearby nerves in the neck, spine, or ribs, pain radiates out to other places beyond the point of origin. Osteoarthritis is usually limited to one or two joints but can nevertheless cause serious disability and substantial pain and discomfort. The knee joints are often sites for osteoarthritis. Bony nodes on fingers are common sights among the elderly, who may be self-conscious about such deformities. The hip is the most disabling site of the disease. When ribs are affected, arthritis can cause pain in the chest wall or upper abdomen, causing some to believe they're having a heart attack.

Most feared is the less common rheumatoid arthritis, which inflames joints; they swell, are tender, ache, and become stiff. This disease is systemic. Its cause is still unknown, but it is chronic and progressive. It can cause great deformity if not treated early and can make people feel "sick all over." Rest and appropriate medication balanced with prescribed exercise are important factors in treating this form of arthritis.

Gout is a form of arthritis. It is very painful, occurs more frequently among men, and is associated with a buildup of uric acid in the body. Red meats and alcohol can aggravate the buildup of uric acid. Gout usually, but not necessarily, only affects the big toe. Psoriatic arthritis is a potential danger for people suffering from psoriasis and most typically affects fingers and toes.

Treatment

It is true that arthritics can feel a change in the weather, but not necessarily true that a change of climate will provide relief. People have arthritis in warm, dry climates as well as in damp and chilly climates. So try to persuade your arthritic parent to try out a new climate before making a permanent move.

Arthritis hurts. Be vigilant and try to protect your parent from the quack or radical "cures" so many are willing to try. There are no miracle cures for arthritis. The best help comes from early and continuing treatment by the doctor and a good exercise program designed by a physical therapist or *physiatrist,* a doctor specializing in physical medicine. Stiffness and discomfort can usually be eased with heat or a warm bath, but extreme inflammation is sometimes treated with cold. Gentle motion or massage sometimes helps. Better posture to prevent further irritation of joints, better diets to reduce weight, rest when pain is acute, bed-boards for too-soft beds, shoes that fit and provide adequate support and balance, and prescribed exercise to avoid jelling and atrophy of cartilage, joint, or muscle can provide some relief. Aspirin, for those not sensitive to it, is still regarded as the drug with the most benefit and fewest complications for treatment of arthritis. A new battery of nonsteroidal, anti-inflammatory drugs, more expensive than aspirin, is also being prescribed with good result, and other medications are used for special situations.

In the most severe cases of damage or pain from arthritis, surgery is sometimes employed. Modern technology can provide new hip joints, new knee joints, even new finger joints to replace these moving parts if they become immobilized. The artificial hip has had the most success. One 75-year-old woman with two hip replacements was dancing at a ball the year after her surgery.

Pain is a miserable companion. As it comes and goes, your parent may be limber one part of the day and unable to move the next. Arthritis acts that way, so don't think you're being manipulated. Families are reminded: "Some people think the arthritis patient gets cantankerous and uses his disease to gain sympathy. Sympathy he needs, but not the overbearing kind. He needs quiet and understanding and help in 'getting out of himself.' Don't exclude him from your affairs. His knees may be stiff, his fingers crooked, but his mind and emotions are active and sensitive. Help him use them—and it will help his arthritis."[13]

The Arthritis Foundation, through its local chapters, actively helps patients and their families cope with this disease. See Appendix under National Health Organizations.

OSTEOPOROSIS AND FRACTURES

Fractures often result from accidents, but they are also the frequent consequence of degeneration of the bone tissue, a condition called osteoporosis. With this condition, even minor stress can break a bone.

Women seem to be more prone than men to osteoporosis as they age, but both sexes can be prey to the process, which usually first affects the spine and pelvis. Sometimes it signals its arrival with chronic midback pain. Sometimes it progresses without discomfort but can be observed as the back starts to curve and seems to hump (also known as dowager's hump or the Duchess's hump). Stricken individuals seem to shrink, are measurably shorter, and physical activity can become more and more burdensome. Sometimes a spontaneous fracture occurring in the spine or hip is the first sign of the damage already done. Sometimes a minor mishap results in a broken bone. Osteoporosis can be diagnosed by X ray and sophisticated new medical devices, which can detect bone loss.

Hormones seem to have a great influence on the bone-making functions of the body—osteoporosis appears in the majority of women after menopause. Other culprits include poor nutrition, sedentary habits, cigarette smoking, and alcohol consumption. Continued use of certain steroid medications is also suspect in bringing on osteoporosis. The highest incidence of osteoporosis occurs among very thin, slight, white, postmenopausal females.[14] So there is some advantage in being slightly plump after all!

Walking and simple exercise that does not overly stress the spine and long bones of the body are considered good preventive measures, and continuing appropriate exercise is prescribed for some osteoporosis patients, since there is evidence that exercise can help even elderly women regain healthier bone tissue. Braces and bed rest may be required by others. Fractures may be more severe in people who have osteoporosis, but the healing process and treatment usually follow the normal course.

These days it is hard to avoid the televised warnings about osteoporosis and the adjurations to increase calcium intake. There is some dispute about the value of additional calcium supplements "after the fact." Some researchers believe that the mineral is successfully absorbed only in conjunction with hormone (estrogen) therapy. Others believe extra calcium can't hurt, especially among the elderly or those who refuse to eat or can't digest calcium-rich foods. Some believe it can hurt, especially among those prone to form kidney stones. Most seem to agree that good calcium and protein intake in the growing years is the best insurance against osteoporosis. But if your parent is already a victim, you'll want to consult his or her physician to determine what should be done now to protect against further damage. Research continues in this field as the increasing number of people, especially women, surviving into old age has turned the bone loss of osteoporosis into an epidemic.

DIGESTIVE COMPLAINTS—FROM THE ANNOYING TO THE SERIOUS

Digesting food, an essential life process, is vulnerable to some of the changes that naturally occur with aging. It need not cause serious problems for most older people who follow good dietary habits, exercise, avoid large amounts of caffeine or alcohol, and are cautious about taking over-the-counter drugs. Nevertheless, digestive disorders do erupt.

Typically annoying and uncomfortable are gas, constipation, diarrhea, heartburn, indigestion, hemorrhoids, and intolerance to milk. Some of these are related to the slower muscle and reduced acid production associated with aging. Individuals vary greatly; each older person needs to fine-tune his or her eating habits to avoid the foods or habits that cause unwanted symptoms. In some instances remedial action is important. For example, because diarrhea dehydrates the body, it is essential to replace lost fluids or risk dizziness and a fainting episode. Hemorrhoids, which are aggravated by constipation, obesity, or other conditions, can be relieved by warm baths, creams, or suppositories. If these don't bring relief, injections or surgery may be indicated.

The gastrointestinal system is particularly sensitive to emotional stress. Elderly people often complain of discomfort for which doctors cannot find an organic cause, and families are never sure whether poor eating habits, insufficient exercise, self-preoccupation, and worry are the root causes of the distress, or whether more serious conditions are at fault.

Examination by a good internist is the first step to rule out the presence of organic disease. As people age, colon and rectal cancers occur more frequently. For this reason, older people with or without direct symptoms are urged to have periodic checkups, annual digital rectal examinations, stool analysis, and periodic proctosigmoidoscopy examinations, so that if cancer is present it can be more readily detected and prompt treatment can begin. Examination can detect or rule out the presence of other gastrointestinal disease, such as ulcers, gall stones, diverticulitis, hiatal hernia, or ulcerative colitis. Treatment for these may include special diet, medication, and/or surgery. The problem can be managed so long as it is not ignored.

The presence of other diseases—arteriosclerosis, heart disease, liver or kidney disease, diabetes, depression—can also interfere with proper digestive function. If your father has lost his teeth and sticks to a soft diet, avoiding hard-to-chew foods, constipation may result. If your mother is tense or depressed, she may also become constipated or have an attack of colitis. The body's various systems are interdependent.

A physician may suggest that your parent's complaints are psychosomatic, that the bodily discomfort has its roots in psychological factors. Many elderly people are not conversant with or satisfied by psychosomatic explanations of physical discomfort. When their digestive systems go awry because they're grieving or lonely, sexually frustrated, feeling useless, poor, or worried, are afraid of cancer or of death, they frequently disbelieve the doctor who tells them there is nothing "organically" wrong with them. The fact is that they have physical pain, and many signs mimic the symptoms of organic diseases. Doctors and families alike need to deal with the symptoms and provide continuing support to overcome whatever triggers the whole syndrome. Psychotherapy, mild sedation, a bland diet, reasonable exercise, and new interests often help a patient gain better control of bodily functions.

Having accepted a possible psychosomatic explanation, however, don't go overboard. Acute gastrointestinal symptoms, for example, are frequently a sign of heart attack and call for prompt medical attention. New organic causes or those that escaped earlier observation may require treatment.

Constipation

Among the nagging problems that plague older people is constipation, which is not a disease but, in the the words of the National Institute on Aging, "is frequently an overemphasized ailment."[15] Misuse of laxatives can cause or aggravate the problem. Laxatives account for $250 million of consumer expenditure in this country each year; they are heavily advertised, bought over the counter, and are regarded by the experts as largely unnecessary. They can, in fact, be habit-forming and counterproductive if the body begins to rely on them.

If your mother or father has been ill and bedridden, this may result in temporary constipation for which the physician may prescribe drugs. Anatomical obstructions may exist, or a tumor or polyp may interfere with normal function. But in general, regularity means what is normally regular for the individual, whether that is a bowel movement every day, or twice a day, or three or four times a week. Changes in pattern, or the presence of pain, are what need to be investigated. In most instances, a less anxious attitude, exercise, a balanced diet, one or two quarts of liquid a day (except for those with heart, circulatory, or kidney problems, whose liquid intake is carefully prescribed), and for some individuals the addition of small amounts of unprocessed bran will help return your parent to "regularity."

When to See the Doctor

Children of parents who complain frequently about various stomach discomforts may tend to ignore signs of trouble that require prompt medical attention. The National Digestive Diseases Education and Information Clearinghouse lists these important warning signs of serious concern:

- stomach pains that are severe, last a long time, are recurring, or come with shaking chills and cold, clammy skin
- blood in vomit or recurrent vomiting
- a sudden change in bowel habits or change in the consistency of stools lasting more than a few days—for example, diarrhea for more than three days or the sudden onset of constipation
- jaundice—a yellowing of the skin and the whites of the eyes—or dark, tea-colored urine
- pain or difficulty swallowing food

- continuing loss of appetite or unexplained weight loss
- diarrhea that wakes one up at night.

Disorders of the digestive tract cause more hospital admissions than any other group of diseases and occur most frequently among the middle-aged or older population. Progress has been made in diagnosing and treating many digestive diseases, though the causes of some remain unknown. New noninvasive techniques such as ultra sound, CAT scans, and MRI (magnetic resonance imaging) make it possible to study internal organs in detail, often eliminating the need for exploratory surgery. The endoscope can be used to see inside the esophagus, stomach, duodenum, and colon, to perform biopsies and some forms of minisurgery. All of these advances add up to better diagnosis and treatment and reduced fatalities. Encourage your parent to overcome the fear "that they'll find something terrible" and take advantage of the progress modern medicine has made.

PARKINSON'S DISEASE

The average age of an individual with Parkinson's disease is 65; rarely is it discovered in those under 40. The dramatic increase in numbers of older people in the population may foreshadow a dramatic increase in the number of Parkinson's sufferers. American doctors are reported to be disillusioned about the claimed successes of experimental surgery in Mexico to reverse the deterioration that typically occurs with Parkinson's.[16] Whether or not we are on the brink of eradicating this disease remains to be seen.

Parkinson's is a progressive disease. It appears at first in the form of slight *tremor* and difficulty in arising from a deep chair. The tremors in time interfere with ordinary activities—eating or reading—and perversely may worsen when the victim is the most relaxed. A condition called *bradykinesis* affects the person's ability to move spontaneously—to walk, or shift position, or even to move the facial muscles appropriately. The voice is also affected, so that the patient may have difficulty speaking distinctly or loudly enough for others to understand. The third characteristic of this disease is *rigidity* which results in short jerky motions. Posture problems can also appear. Depression is common; it is not clear whether this is a reaction or a natural companion to the disease.

Patients in the very advanced stages can lose intellectual function and behave similarly to those with Alzheimer's. Slurred speech or difficulty communicating is not in itself a sign of this kind of deterioration; more significant is becoming forgetful, having trouble with numbers or money, becoming confused, and getting lost.

Parkinson's can be treated and some of the symptoms lessened or eliminated for short or longer periods of time, but without treatment it becomes progressively severe and disabling, making it virtually impossible for the patient to live without significant assistance. The experts say, however, that with currently available treatment, patients can live out a normal life span.

If the doctor prescribes L-dopa and other drugs, these must be expertly monitored so that early gains are not wiped out and positive effects are extended for longer periods. Drug-free periods are one way some doctors have improved the benefits of L-dopa therapy and overcome some of the problems associated with its use.

Physical therapy is an important adjunct to drug treatments. Exercise to strengthen muscles can improve a patient's ability to function but it does not change the course of the disease.

Community support groups to help individuals with Parkinson's and their families exist all over the country. These can help learn better how to cope with the disabling aspects of this disease and help patients make optimum use of their ability to function.

FALLING

Falling is such a common occurrence among older people that many believe falls are a natural result of the aging process. "Not so," says Dr. Rein Tideiksaar, codirector of the

Falls and Immobility Program at Mount Sinai Medical Center in New York. Some falls can be attributed to the effects of aging on vision, gait, or stride; some are a result of inappropriate or careless choice and arrangement of furnishings or lighting; but many are medically based. All falls should be investigated.

Falling is the leading cause of accidents in the over-65 population, and the largest single cause of death. Hip fracture is the most common result of falling injuries. A 15 to 20 percent mortality rate within the first three months of a fracture and 50 percent mortality rate after six months are among the statistics that should spur you to do what you can to avoid such a result for your parent.[17]

You can remedy the factors that encourage accidents, and treat the medical conditions that produce dizziness, imbalance, or blackouts. Falls can be prevented, avoided, or reduced when you know why they occur. People with a history of falling episodes can be helped to avoid future mishaps, and other older people can be taught how to change their habits to avoid becoming victims (see chapter 3).

Denial of aging, says Dr. Tideiksaar, is one of the reasons older people resist changing their habits to avoid the accidents that can seriously change their lives. The solution may lie simply in a new pair of glasses.

Dr. Tideiksaar feels that falls are underreported by older people because they fear the results: a restricted life. First "Don't take the bus; you may trip on the step." Then "Don't go for a walk; you may fall on the street." After a few such falls, the child may accept their inevitability and bring care into the parent's home or start applying for nursing home admission.

He cautions families—and physicians—to remember that falling is a symptom. "The body is trying to tell us something. It is important to find out what that is."

The medical causes of falling usually involve the cardiovascular system, the skeletal system, the metabolic system, or neurological damage. Transient ischemic attacks (TIAs) cause falls as do low blood pressure, high blood pressure, side effects of medication, and not taking prescribed medication. Dizziness and imbalance can come from stretching too high, bending too low, or bending the neck back in such as way as to interfere with proper blood flow to the brain. Remind your elderly parent to change positions slowly to avoid a tumble. Falls can also be "the first clue to heart attack, stroke, or gastrointestinal bleeding. . . the first sign of urinary tract, respiratory, or gall bladder infection."[18]

Mount Sinai will help patients outside its local area find specialized medical advice on falls where they live.

VISION

Poor eyesight is not an inevitable accompaniment to age, and many very old people with other decrements have sharp vision till the end of their days. Nevertheless, half the population of blind people in this country are 65 or older, and certain eye disorders and diseases occur more frequently as people age.[19] Some can be prevented, some can be treated or corrected, some result in blindness. Regular checkups by qualified eye doctors are the best way to detect incipient trouble and assure prompt treatment.

An *ophthalmologist* is a medical doctor who specializes in diseases of the eye. An *optometrist* is qualified to examine the eye for defects and prescribe corrective lenses or other treatment and is called a doctor but may not carry out treatments, which may only be carried out by a licensed physician. States differ in defining the scope of an optometrist's license. An *optician* is a technician who makes and fits eyeglasses, lenses, or other optical equipment.

Focusing becomes a problem for close reading or distant detail *(presbyopia)* usually between the ages of 40 and 60 and then begins to level off. Glasses or contact lenses usually compensate for the difficulties encountered. "My arms aren't long enough" is the common refrain when middle-aged people suddenly have focusing problems and have to hold reading matter as far away as possible. Another common complaint is seeing tiny specks or spots that float across the field of vision (floaters). These are normal and usually harmless, unless they appear with light flashes, in which case a doctor should be consulted. Also annoying, causing itching, burning, even reduced vision, are "dry eyes," which occurs when the tear glands produce too few tears. Special eyedrops can be prescribed to correct the problem. Too many tears, if they are caused by increased sensitivity to light, wind, or temperature change, can be helped by protecting the eyes under these conditions. Tearing that results from an eye infection or blocked tear duct can be treated.

Cataract, glaucoma, and retinal disorders resulting from macular disease or diabetes are the most common threats to the elderly eye. Diabetes, hypertension, arteriosclerosis, kidney disease, and neurological pathlogy often present themselves first as eye problems. An internist examining the eye in routine medical checkups may find the first clues to these problems.

Warning Signs

- hazy or blurred vision
- recurrent pain in or around the eye
- flashes of light or halos around lights
- a change in color of the pupil
- sensitivity to light and glare
- double vision
- hemorrhage in the eye

The National Institute on Aging recommends that older people have a complete eye examination every two or three years, including a vision evaluation, recheck of glasses, an eye muscle check, check for glaucoma, and thorough internal and external eye health exams. Those with diabetes or a family history of eye disease are urged to have more frequent examinations and to seek immediate attention if they experience any loss or dimness of vision, eye pain, excessive discharge from the eye, double vision, redness, or swelling of the eye or eyelid. If your parent requires a frequent change of glasses, it may be a cataract developing, but it may also be a sign of diabetes.

Until diabetes is stabilized or the cataract removed, your parent may continue to complain that his or her glasses are never right.

Cataract

This clouding of the eye's lens occurs in about 30 percent of those 65 or older. It usually develops gradually, painlessly, and without redness or tearing in the eye. When a cataract forms, light cannot pass properly through the lens as it does normally, and vision is impaired slightly or severely—even to the point of blindness—according to the size and density of the cataract.

In most cases, troublesome cataracts can be removed successfully by surgery. Age is not a factor in cataract surgery, and more than 90 percent of the patients regain useful vision. The ophthalmologist monitors the development of the cataract and recommends surgery at the appropriate time. According to the National Institute on Aging, cataract surgery is a safe procedure that is almost always successful, but your parent should discuss its risks and benefits with the doctor. Ophthalmologists warn that surgery is the only successful treatment, not eye drops, ointments, special diets, or eye exercises. Following removal of the cloudy lens, a plastic substitute may be implanted *(intraocular lens implant)* during surgery, or vision may be restored by use of special glasses or contact lenses.

Cataracts are *not* related to cancer, are *not* a new growth of skin over the eye, and do *not* spread from eye to eye, although they can develop in both eyes at the same time. They are *not* caused or aggravated by overuse of the eyes. You can help erase any such misconceptions from your parent's mind.

Be sympathetic to your parent's fears if surgery is recommended. Eyesight is so precious, blindness so feared, that statistics do not always overcome the dread that something may go wrong during surgery. The doctor will undoubtedly be persuasive in getting your parent's permission for surgery, and your parent will go through with the procedure. But do not be surprised if this is a tense and anxious time. The joy of bright new vision will quickly erase the bad moments.

Glaucoma

Acute glaucoma usually comes on suddenly and unmistakably with great pain, but chronic glaucoma can rob a patient of sight quite painlessly over a long period of time. Glaucoma is the leading single cause of blindness in the United States.

Chronic glaucoma is characterized by a buildup of fluid pressure in the eye, causing internal damage and eventually destroying the optic nerve. Although it presents no obvious symptoms to the patient during its early stages, its presence can be detected by a test, which should be conducted for all those over 35 during routine eye examinations. Those over 65 are urged to have this checkup every two years. Early diagnosis and treatment can usually prevent blindness but cannot restore sight already lost. Treatment does not eradicate the disease but can keep it from getting worse. Medication usually consists of eye drops three times a day. When medication is ineffective, some patients obtain relief through laser and conventional surgery, which opens new drainage canals for the liquid that normally flows through the inner eye.

At high risk for glaucoma are patients with a family history of glaucoma. Those suffering from other systemic diseases, especially diabetes, should be regularly checked for glaucoma.

Retinal Disorders

Of particular concern to older people are senile macular degeneration, diabetic retinopathy, and retinal detachment. The retina is the thin lining on the back of the eye made up of nerves that receive visual images and pass them on to the brain.

Macular degeneration signifies the progressive deterioration of the macula—the tiny part of the retina that provides sharp, straight-ahead vision and makes it possible to read and do close work comfortably. This deterioration is a common cause of visual loss among people over 65. It may come on gradually or suddenly and strike one or both eyes. While it causes considerable loss of clear central vision, macular disease does not cause total blindness and does not affect side vision. The first signs may include blurring of reading material, a dark spot in the center of a field of vision, and distortion of vertical lines. While lost sight cannot be regained, early diagnosis and treatment can sometimes halt further loss. Some cases, caught early, can be successfully treated with laser, but for the majority there is no effective treatment.

Macular degeneration is a major cause of what is known as *low vision*. Some people who are legally blind retain some visual function, and they can be helped by the use of low-vision aids. These include magnifying glasses, telescopic lenses, high-intensity lamps, and devices to hold a book close to the eyes. Low vision is the greatest handicap affecting older Americans next to heart disease and arthritis.[20]

Retinal detachment is a separation between the inner and outer layers of the retina. Retinas can usually be reattached surgically, and good or partial vision is restored. Increasing success is reported with use of new techniques.

Diabetic retinopathy is one of the possible complications of diabetes. It occurs when the small blood vessels that nourish the retina fail to function properly. At first the blood vessels may leak fluid, which distorts vision. In later stages new blood vessels may grow and release blood into the center of the eye, resulting in serious vision loss. Diabetes is the leading cause of new blindness in the United States. The longer a person has diabetes, the more likely retinopathy will develop. Lasers can be used to seal leaking blood vessels and, with other prompt treatment, can reduce the risk of severe visual loss.

The Eyeglasses Rule

Some states allow consumers to buy glasses "off the shelf" instead of by prescription only. This may make sense for the older person without serious impairment, not the patient who must be closely monitored by the ophthalmologist. In any case, the Federal Trade Commission urges consumers to be aware of "the eyeglasses rule," which requires eye doctors to make prescriptions for eyeglasses available to patients at no extra cost, immediately after an eye exam. You have a legal right to your prescription, so request it if it is not provided. (This rule does not apply to contact lenses.) With prescription in hand, you can shop for eyeglasses just as you would for any other product, looking for the best quality at the best price. Glasses have become a high-fashion item; prices have escalated enormously. Medicare does not cover eyeglass costs, so shop carefully.

Where to Go for Help

Poor vision need no longer be so restricting if you help your partially sighted parent to take advantage of the numerous special devices and publications currently available for people with vision impairment. Large-print newspapers, magazines, and books are available through your parent's library, as are recordings for the blind. Many organizations have information and programs for the near or legally blind. They include the National Eye Institute, the National Society to Prevent Blindness, the American Foundation for the Blind, the Lighthouse Center for Vision and Aging, the Vision Foundation, The American Academy of Ophthalmology, the American Optometric Association, and others. Ophthalmologists through their state societies and the American Academy of Ophthalmology sponsor a National Eye Care Project, which offers free ophthalmological care to U.S. citizens and legal residents 65 and over, unable to afford proper medical eye care. They also operate a toll-free Eye Care Helpline.

See the Appendix under Vision.

HEARING

Almost half of all adults over 65 suffer some hearing loss that interferes with their ability to communicate normally. The changes that occur in the inner ear and brain, and the conductive impairments that sometimes develop as a result of aging, are known as *presbycusis* (literally *old hearing*). The eardrum may thicken, the middle ear bones grow stiff, possibly as a result of impaired blood supply caused by heart disease, high blood pressure, or other circulatory problems. Excess wax buildup, anatomical abnormalities, or a perforated eardrum may block the normal conduction of sound.

Early signs of hearing loss are so gradual, you may not have noticed that in the last year or two you've been talking more and more loudly to your parent. You don't realize it until your own children tell you to stop talking so loudly or your friends wonder why you are so emphatic making your points with them. Whenever you become aware of your parent's increasing hearing problem, a trip to a physician who specializes in hearing and diseases of the ear is in order.

People with hearing loss may hear low-pitched voices better than high ones, or vice versa, which will account for their understanding some people better than others. It's not a matter of "hearing what they want to hear." Speaking slowly and enunciating clearly while looking directly at the person when you speak may help some but not others. You need to find out just what is causing your parent's hearing loss and direct your attention to that. The earlier a hearing problem is diagnosed, the greater the chances for successfully managing it, say the experts. Doctors who specialize in hearing problems are called *otologists* or *otolaryngologists*. They may refer your parent to an *audiologist*, who does not give medical treatment but does identify, help prevent, and manage hearing problems. They can recommend and sometimes supply hearing devices.

While hearing aids help, they often do not provide the same kind of positive help that glasses do, and many elderly people shun them for a variety of reasons, a major one of which is the annoyance of hearing all background noises amplified, not just what they want to hear. Some people retain "islands of hearing," which are unduly amplified by a nondiscriminating instrument and cause discomfort. Some people grow impatient with the frequent adjustments sometimes required to tune in properly, or the effort required to maintain the device properly for maximum benefit. For some reason, vanity seems to be more involved with hearing aids than with eyeglasses. Eyeglasses have become fashion adjuncts to enhance sex appeal. No one has done as much for hearing aids. Hearing problems are firmly associated in the public mind with aging. But without any assistance, hearing-impaired older people are in great danger of becoming isolated, withdrawn, depressed, frequently angry, and deprived of an otherwise normal existence.

Encourage your parent to try a hearing aid and to be patient during the period of adjustment. Discouraged, he or she may put the device in the drawer and forget about it. Perhaps a different kind of device will be more comfortable and more acceptable. Only a reputable supplier can provide the device that is best for your parent's particular problem. This is not an item to buy casually off the shelf, from a salesman at the door, or from a high-pressure, possibly fly-by-night hearing aid service. Some instruments work better for some people than others. Individual compatibility is essential, but don't expect the precise correction eyeglasses provide for visual impairment. Your parent will have to decide whether it is better to hear "funny" than not to hear at all.

Hearing aids can relieve serious hearing disabilities. Newly developed surgical techniques are also effective for some cases. If a disease, such as arteriosclerosis, is causing the loss, controlling the disease may help. Whatever the cause of diminished hearing, it is important to check with a reputable specialist for diagnosis and treatment. Don't assume that nothing will help.

The telephone company can make special arrangements for people with hearing problems. Check your local TV stations for "close captioned" equipment.

The National Information Center on Deafness and the American Speech-Language-Hearing Association are among the useful resources for help and information (see Appendix). The Area Agencies on Aging and local senior centers can also be good sources for information on local hearing aid suppliers.

See the Appendix under Hearing.

DENTAL PROBLEMS

The current generation of older Americans grew up before fluorides, but in the last thirty or forty years fluorides, improved knowledge, and modern dental techniques have dramatically improved protection against cavities, tooth loss, and gum disease. Nevertheless, a significant number of older people leave dental care at the bottom of their health priorities list. When they avoid dental checkups and substitute a soft diet for proper care and treatment, they are candidates for what geriatric dental expert Dr. Saul Kamen calls the domino effect: "They eat the easy, soft, starchy foods and risk nutritional defects, metabolic malfunctions. Among the other results of poor dental status is poor appearance, which negatively affects their mental status." In other words, by neglecting their dental health, older people also compromise their general health.

Your concern about your parent's general well-being should extend to good dental care. Modern dental techniques are much less painful than those people may remember from their younger years. And just as the elderly lose some of their acute sense of taste or smell, they also lose some sensitivity to pain originating in the teeth, so that treatment is less uncomfortable. Unfortunately, this also means that they can harbor infections, decay, or disease without the sharp discomforts that would send a younger person for immediate relief.

Typical problems in the later years, according to the American Dental Association, include new decay around old fillings and decay around the roots of teeth as roots become exposed by receding gums. Receding gums in turn result from periodontal (gum) disease.

Periodontal disease is the major cause of tooth loss in adults. It is wise to pay attention to the following signs of trouble, since in the early stages good treatment can reverse the devastating effects:

- gums that bleed when teeth are brushed
- red, swollen, or tender gums
- pus between teeth and gums that appears when gums are pressed
- teeth that are becoming loose or moving apart
- bad breath or bad taste

- change in the way teeth fit together (occlusion, or bite) or in the way dentures fit.

Tooth decay is also caused by *dry mouth*, which occurs when the saliva supply is reduced. This condition is a frequent side effect of certain medications, such as tranquilizers, barbiturates, antihistamines, and drugs for muscle control, and of radiation treatment to the head or neck. Treatment includes use of artificial saliva and a fluoride mouth rinse to prevent tooth decay.

Signs of dry mouth, which should send your parent to the dentist as well as to the telephone to inform the physician who has prescribed a medication that may be aggravating the condition, are

- a constant sore throat or uncomfortable burning sensation in the throat
- difficulty in speaking because of soreness in the mouth
- cracked or bleeding lips and mouth corners
- loss of taste or distortions of taste
- difficulty in swallowing food
- increasing discomfort wearing dentures
- frequently awakening from sleep with a hoarse throat and dry nasal passages.

Oral cancer is another threat that requires immediate attention. Smokers are five times more likely to develop this disease than nonsmokers.[21] If your mother or father has been a habitual smoker you should be especially sure that she or he has regular dental checkups, *even if your parent is wearing dentures.* Warning signs are

- a sore on lips, gums, or inside the mouth that does not heal within two or three weeks
- white scaly patches inside mouth or lips
- swelling or lumps in mouth, neck, lips, or tongue
- numbness or pain in mouth or throat without any apparent cause
- Repeated bleeding in mouth without any apparent cause

Unexplained pain in the head and neck can sometimes be traced to dental infection, poor bite, or problems in the muscles or nerves of the face or jaw. Do not overlook these possibilities. It is not inappropriate to raise the question with a physician who has not succeeded in finding the cause of certain kinds of pain.

Medicare does not cover routine dental care, and as a result many older people forego dental care because of the costs, unless they are covered by private insurance. Medicare does cover the hospitalization costs for certain dental procedures that require hospitalization, such as complex surgery, but not the cost of the procedures themselves. Medicare rules permit reimbursement for dental treatment of many soft-tissue problems, such as canker sores, which can be treated by a dentist, if the dentist is registered as a Medicare provider. Carriers who refuse such payments out of ignorance of this rule will reimburse on appeal.

See the Appendix under Dental Health.

FOOT PROBLEMS

Aching feet are common among the elderly. A lifetime in high heels and pointy narrow shoes may reap an unhappy harvest of pain in your mother's later years. But problems can occur even when people have not abused their feet. Circulatory problems causing poor blood supply can create serious foot problems; for those with diabetes this is especially dangerous. Corns, bunions, plantar warts, ulcers, and eroded or dry skin are not uncommon foot problems among the elderly. Arthritis can cause toe deformities as joints stiffen. None of these add up to comfort.

Improving your parent's comfort may depend on orthopedic shoes, special protective pads, arch support, or other mechanical corrections. Some foot problems can be treated with minor surgery, but this may not be the solution for those with circulatory problems. Inadvisable surgery can cause additional problems or complicate current ones.

Don't ignore foot problems. Encourage your parent to consult a doctor and the orthopedist or podiatrist he or she recommends. Once diseases or disorders that require a specialist's attention are ruled out, many foot problems of the elderly can be managed and helped by *podiatrists* (professionals trained in the care of the feet). They can treat chronic conditions, provide the necessary corrective devices and physical therapy, and even perform some surgical procedures. They work in private offices, hospitals, nursing homes, and other health care settings.

Medicare can help pay for any covered service of a licensed doctor of podiatry, including removal of plantar warts, but does not cover routine foot care (removal of corns, calluses, most warts) unless such care is required as a result of a medical condition affecting the lower limbs, such as severe diabetes.

Many foot problems can be prevented by proper care. If your parent is in a nursing home, check to see that proper foot care is being given, since bedridden patients are particularly vulnerable to problems. To keep feet healthy, remind your parent of these tips from the American Podiatric Medical Association:[22]

- Walking is the best exercise for your feet.
- A shoe with a firm sole and soft upper is best for daily activities.
- Do not wear restrictive garters or knot your stockings to keep them up.
- Socks or stockings should be of the correct size and preferably free of seams.
- Never cut corns and calluses with a razor, pocket knife, or any other instrument.
- Bathe your feet daily in lukewarm, not hot, water, using a mild soap.
- Trim or file your toenails straight across (helps to prevent ingrown toenails).
- Inspect your feet every day or have someone do this for you. If you notice any redness, swelling, cracks in the skin, or sores, consult a physician.

SLEEPING PROBLEMS

Older people who may deny or hide other problems in their lives are usually not shy about reporting how few hours they sleep. Many a child's glazed eye and deaf ear are the result. Therefore many take it for granted that older people don't sleep well.

"It is a myth that older people require less sleep," says Dr. Charles Herrera, medical director of the Sleep Disorders Center of City College in New York. "Unfortunately this myth continues to be propagated even in our medical and nursing schools and among the helping professions who work with older people. The reasons given for this lack of need for sleep are that older people are more sedentary and use less energy. This is not true."

What is true, he explains, is that the nature of sleep changes physiologically with age. Deep sleep is what is restorative and it is this kind of sleep that occurs for fewer hours after about the age of 45. As we grow older, we spend more hours in the lighter stages of sleep, which are less efficient and restorative. Older people awaken more frequently during the night, sometimes so briefly they are unaware of the interruption, but researchers have observed that it takes about 45 minutes to achieve deep sleep, and the interruptions make this difficult to achieve. Women after menopause, and men at slightly younger ages, begin to be aware of less satisfaction with the restorative quality of their sleep.

Not everyone needs 8 hours of sleep. It is said that Ben Franklin functioned on 3, while Einstein required 12. Churchill took little catnaps to keep him going seemingly endless hours during World War II. People's needs are different, and these needs change over the years.

Young adults with 8 hours' sleep are usually able to go through their normal activities without any loss of cognitive function, without fatigue or irritability. Older people complain of insomnia, even if they have had 8 hours' total sleep out of 24. "This may be a problem, but it is not a sleep disorder, which is medically diagnosable and treatable," says Dr. Herrera.

Sleep Disorders

Insomnia is a disorder characterized by the inability to sleep. This can be caused by depression, which can be treated; by worry and anxiety over a stressful situation, which may be temporary; by boredom or even insufficient social stimulus, which can be relieved.

"In time, an insomnia triggered by an event becomes autonomous. This causes anxiety, which in turn creates the self-fulfilling prohecy of 'I can't sleep'," says Dr. Herrera. He describes three kinds of insomnia: transient insomnia, such as that which may precede surgery; insomnia that is triggered by a stressful event, which may last up to about 3 weeks; and chronic insomnia, which may last for years.

Sleeplessness is sometimes the side effect of certain medications taken for other problems. Decongestants can trigger insomnia, as can certain antidepressants. Some drugs taken for high blood pressure can cause sleep problems. Some beta blockers used by cardiac patients can cause nightmares or hallucinations, as can some steroid drugs. Your parent should always report any side effects such as these to the physician.

Medical condition will also influence sleep, especially painful conditions such as arthritis, or urinary dysfunctions that cause frequent trips to the bathroom. Some diseases are worse at night, including asthma, ulcers, and migraine headaches. Older people are also subject to involuntary leg movements that interrupt good sleep. Even though the individual may be unaware of this "restless leg syndrome," a disturbed partner may be well aware of it.

While sleeping pills are sometimes prescribed by physicians, most experts agree that *no pill produces normal sleep.* In addition, many pills are dangerous for older people to use. Dr. Herrera warns: "They may compromise breathing or interact dangerously with other drugs being used for other conditions. They also tend to linger in the body, having a longer-term effect than one night's sleep." Many over-the-counter sedatives and antihistamines make people sleepy and may prove psychologically addictive, as may tranquilizers or sleeping pills prescribed for short-term use before or after a stressful event.

Many family physicians are not familiar with the new work on sleep disorders and may not be able to help your sleepless parent with the best new techniques. You can write to the Association of Sleep Disorders for referral to one of the sleep disorder centers throughout the country (see Appendix under National Health Organizations). In general the specialists' approach to insomnia problems (after medical causes have been ruled out or treatment begun) is to make a positive plan. The patient is given a prescribed sleep schedule: get into and out of bed at the same time each day and night. No naps are allowed. No exercise is taken in the late evening or before bedtime, and no alcohol, since it can interrupt the natural sleep stages. People are told that if they don't fall asleep in 10 minutes they should get out of bed and read a book, bake a cake, write a letter. When they become tired they can return to bed, but they must repeat the procedure if they aren't shortly asleep. The total time in bed in a 24-hour period is restricted. Says Dr. Herrera, "Bed is for sleeping and for sex. No lolling about."

Problem sleepers should make sure sleeping conditions are as comfortable as possible. This means a good bed, loose-fitting night clothes, and a darkened, quiet room. A restless or snoring partner can interfere with an insomniac's ability to establish a good sleep pattern; therefore separate sleeping quarters are recommended until a satisfactory sleep pattern is established. Light reading or a relaxing TV show are better than overstimulating activity before bedtime, and caffeine should be avoided at any time after lunch.[23]

Obstructive sleep apnea is a sleep disorder that can be fatal without treatment. It is associated with heavy snoring, obesity, and hypertension. Appropriate drug therapy, weight loss, and in some cases surgery can relieve the problem. Failure to seek treatment can lead to stroke, heart failure, heart attack, or cardiac arrest.

Tell your mother or father that if the other is snoring and gasping or if breathing seems to stop, to awaken the sleeper. This will generally stop the episode. But this kind of sleeping should be called to the doctor's attention for diagnosis and treatment. Dr. Herrera says, "Even if your parent lives alone and complains about feeling very tired after a night's sleep, morning headaches, and falling asleep unaccountably during the day, then get your parent to the doctor. You can place a tape recorder beside your parent's bed (to check on snoring) and let it run its course. Bring this to the physician for evaluation."

URINARY INCONTINENCE

Incontinence is a problem most individuals and families would prefer not to acknowledge or be forced to encounter. But incontinence is a growing problem in an ever-increasing number of aging persons. It is a major reason why families, unable or unwilling to cope at home, finally decide a nursing home is the only place for the offender. It is the reason why families are advised to pay attention to the smells of a nursing home or adult day care center; these are clues to how incontinence is handled in the institution.

Incontinence may appear to be mainly a female problem because more females than males survive to old age, but older men with prostate problems may also suffer the embarrassment of incontinence. The increasing number of advertisements for adult diapers is a tip-off that incontinence is coming "out of the closet" like so many other previously off-limits subjects. If this is a problem in your family, you know very well that it is difficult for all involved.

According to Dr. Perry Starer, of the incontinence program at Mt. Sinai Medical Center in New York, there are three common diagnoses for involuntary loss of urine: stress incontinence, urinary retention, and functional incontinence.

The bladder stores and empties the body's liquid waste products through urine. A malfunction in the storage system can cause the involuntary release of urine. When the condition is diagnosed as *stress incontinence,* the sphincter system is involved—the muscles that permit us to withold or release urine. When these muscles are weakened, accidental release of urine can occur with such small jolts to the body as sneezing or coughing. Medication and/or surgery can successfully treat this problem. Older women, with reduced estrogen after menopause, are more likely to suffer from stress incontinence. If they simply revert to using sanitary napkins, as many do, to take care of any "accident" and never mention the problem to a physician, they are doomed to continue having the problem, not solve it.

Urinary retention can result from weakened muscles or a blockage that interferes with appropriate and controlled emptying of the bladder. Older men often have blockage problems as a result of enlarged prostate glands. Pressure wthin the bladder then builds up excessively, causing involuntary leakage. Left untreated, blockage can lead to infection and death. Surgery can remove the blockage. Radical prostatectomy for males suffering prostate cancer can sometimes produce permanent incontinence, though new procedures for this operation are said to have somewhat reduced this danger.

Even when the bladder is normal, incontinence can result from other physical or mental circumstances that can influence a person's ability to retain urinary control. This is defined as *functional incontinence.* Thus, some medication, such as antidepressants, can cause involuntary release of urine. Older patients, particularly those in nursing homes who are restrained in a wheelchair or bed, can become incontinent when the pressure for release becomes excessive. Those with poor mobility, such as stroke victims or Parkinson's sufferers, are often victims of incontinence. Those with impaired cognition, such as Alzheimer's patients, become incontinent because they lose their ability to find their way to the bathroom or eventually lose the brain function that controls the muscles involved.

Treatment

"The simplest solutions are the best way to begin," says Dr. Starer. Consult the internist when a urinary problem first surfaces. The simple treatments can resolve problems for many people; sometimes these depend on changing medication that aggravates the problem; sometimes they involve paying attention to the environment in which the older person lives. By making it easier for your mother or father to use bathroom facilities, by lighting the way, marking the place, bringing a commode to the bedside, by providing a quick response to signals for help, the problem can be lessened, if not entirely eliminated. Surgery may be indicated when other solutions are inadequate.

"Diapers are not a solution," says Dr. Starer. "They are a deterrent to the restoration of normal function." By encouraging their use, you are telling your parent it is okay not to use normal toileting facilities. Diapers are really a last resort for those for whom there is no alternative.

The long-term use of indwelling catheters, which may make life easier for nursing home staffs, is a source of infection and trouble for the patient, says this geriatrics expert. If catheters are being used on your parent, it is not inappropriate to question their use with your parent's personal physician, the nursing home doctor, and the floor staff. Do not be satisfied with such answers as. "You brought your parent here because you couldn't deal with this at home; why should you expect us to deal with it except in the most efficient way?" A caring physician can review your parent's status with you and monitor the results, especially if catheters are prescribed. Just be sure to stay on top of the situation.

No one has said this is an easy problem to deal with. But new attention is being given to this growing problem. It is important to realize that incontinence occurs for reasons other than age alone. The causes should be examined and treatment given.

CHRONIC PAIN

Families are sympathetic to the pain that comes with cancer, but often seem to find it difficult to understand and sympathize with other chronic pain.

The most common chronic pain conditions affecting older adults are arthritis, cancer, and angina. Tic douloureux, a recurrent stabbing facial pain, is also a pain of the aging. Headaches in the elderly may be signals of an underlying and serious medical problem. All pain should be reported and investigated.

New research into the nature of pain makes it possible for people with chronic pain to get relief when little was available before. Instead of relying exclusively on potentially addictive painkillers, they can often be helped by a whole new arsenal of therapies. These many range from biofeedback (successful with migraine headache sufferers) to local electrical stimulation of nerve endings under the skin near where the pain is felt. Electrodes surgically implanted in the brain have relieved advanced cancer sufferers. Many of the new therapies depend on the growing body of information about endorphins, the pain-suppressing chemicals produced in the brain itself. Even acupuncture, the 2,000-year-old Chinese technique of inserting needles at designated spots, has received new credence among some investigators.

Plain aspirin helps pain. Excessive use interferes with the blood-clotting mechanism, so a physician should know if your parent is using large amounts of aspirin regularly. Some of the new drugs on the market are more effective than aspirin but may have more serious side effects or potential for abuse.

The answer to your parent's pain problem may lie in medical treatment to control or eliminate an underlying disease, surgery to relieve lower back problems, or simple bed rest. Psychological treatment for pain, in addition to biofeedback, may include psychotherapy, meditation and relaxation techniques, and various behavior modification programs.

Whatever the problem, start by consulting the family physician and the specialists he or she may recommend: neurologists, orthopedists, neurosurgeons. But if you find the physicians unsympathetic to your parent's problems, remember that there are more than 900 pain clinics in this country. In some instances chronic pain sufferers are admitted for several weeks for diagnosis and treatment; subsequent follow-up is an essential part of the program. If your parent is in pain, feeling hopeless or desperate, investigate a pain clinic. You can also receive help and information from active national health organizations or from a nearby university medical center, and from the National Institute of Neurological and Communicative Disorders and Stroke. Physicians can write to the American Society of Anesthesiologists for a worldwide directory of pain clinics.

See the Appendix under National Health Organizations.

NINE

BEHAVIORAL CHANGES

When a parent's behavior begins to change, families are understandably worried. It can be a time of great stress and fear, a time when many jump to the conclusion that the parent is becoming senile—losing the ability to lead an independent life. But the symptoms that worry them may result from many different causes, some common and benign, some serious but reversible, some indeed a sign of impending deterioration and dependence. It's important to know what is causing any gradual or dramatic change you observe and to treat what can be improved.

Alzheimer's disease is at the top of most people's list of fears, but it is not the fate of the majority. It is not a normal part of aging. It is estimated that one and a half million Americans currently suffer from severe dementia and must continually depend on others for care. An additional one million to five million have mild or moderate dementia. No precise figures on its prevalence are available, but about 5 to 7 percent of those over 65 are severely demented.[1] Most dementia is caused by Alzheimer's disease. Its highest incidence is among those in their 80s, but even among this fast-growing segment of the population, the majority are spared: about one-fourth are estimated to have severe dementia. Improved medical care has kept more Alzheimer's patients alive for a longer period, resulting in a marked presence in our population today of millions more Alzheimer's victims than ever before. But despite this apparent epidemic, most elderly people can look forward to many years of relatively independent life with their intellectual faculties intact.

The changes in behavior you observe in your parent may well have a different cause than Alzheimer's and a different outcome. With proper medical attention, your parent may be helped to regain cognitive and emotional well-being. Or you may have to prepare for the serious consequences of a debilitating disease.

BENIGN FORGETFULNESS

When you find you're frequently searching for a name or a word that pops up moments or days later, you may begin to joke about it, but underneath you're irritated, sometimes embarrassed, and even a little worried. When your older relatives forget the names of people or objects, or where they put their glasses, or repeat a story they've already told you several times, the worry flags also go up. Are you or they becoming senile? In most cases, no. You are probably the unwilling victims of something called benign forgetfulness. This is quite common. Why and how it happens are the subject of continuing research into memory.

Mildly forgetful, we can function as independent adults till the ends of our days. But forgetfulness should not be ignored as a symptom. If other changes in habits or behavior are evident, a doctor should evaluate its significance. Your parent can cope with the annoyances of benign forgetfulness by using some memory aids, such as making lists, keeping pads near the phone, using an engagement calendar, and using an alarm wrist watch to signal when it is time to go somewhere or take a pill. Memory aids can help. Quack remedies cannot. Drugs are being used in research studies to enhance memory but are not as yet in general use. Health store remedies like megavitamins and lecithin are not considered useful or effective routes to improved memory function.

Learning New Things

Recent experiments conducted under the auspices of the National Institute of Mental Health have shown that most older people can continue to learn and that some may even be better at solving complex problems and making decisions than younger people of similar intelligence. Wisdom and life experience offset the younger people's quickness. Reaction time does seem to slow with age, but even that can be partially regained with training. A growing body of evidence also shows that older people not suffering a dementing illness who make the effort to learn new things are more likely to preserve their intellectual competence. New research shows physical, photographable evidence of dendrite (nerve cell) growth in the brain when new learning occurs.

There's an enormous range of difference among old people so don't expect the same from each. In general, we expect an adult of normal intelligence and in reasonably good mental health to be in touch with reality, exercise good judgment, and be able to take care of himself or herself. As we age we lose some muscle strength and walk or talk more slowly, physical changes we can observe and even expect. The brain, which controls all our physical and mental functions, also changes, but in ways only now beginning to be understood. Some changes seem to be common to most persons who age—we all lose some of our eight to ten billion neurons, but not so many we can't function independently. Very bright people, not otherwise diminished by disease, continue to be very bright till the end of their days, even if they have lost some neurons and it takes them longer to think through a problem. "With a person of lower intelligence, loss of function may become more pronounced and happen sooner," explains one researcher.

Use It or Lose It

If your parents turn to you for help consider the reality of your mother or father's situation. One man decided, "Some physical chores are too hard for an old woman to perform, so

I do my mother-in-law's heavy chores for her, but I won't do her taxes. She's quite capable of doing them herself and has more time than I do to get the materials together." Not too many families refuse a direct request from an older person for help with taxes or filling out forms, even when they are intellectually able to help themselves. One privilege of old age, say the experts, is to give up some onerous tasks. Good judgment will tell you which activity is agreeably stimulating and which is more than you should reasonably expect your parent to perform.

"Use it or lose it" is the slogan. Withdrawal from life and ensuing isolation is a recipe for trouble. Any activity that stimulates your parent and maintains his or her social contact is desirable. One lonely 78-year-old widow had become listless, forgetful, unable to do anything for herself, and was described as becoming senile by her family. A niece found a residential hotel where her aunt could live without any housekeeping responsibilities. Not too many months later, the aunt recovered her energy, interest, and ability to take care of herself; she had met a man with whom romance flourished. All signs of senility disappeared.

Margaret Carlson, director of a senior center in Kansas, tells of another grieving widow who shunned most efforts to get her out of the house. A persistent neighbor finally persuaded her to attend a morning program at the local senior center. After a few such visits, the widow became an active member, recruiting others to join her in starting new programs and raising money to improve the center. "It really worked," says Ms. Carlson, "and is a good example of how people can be helped back to an active life."

MORE SERIOUS CHANGES

The relatively benign aspects of old age may demand your attention, but more serious behavioral changes demand evaluation and treatment. Of special concern to you should be differentiating among conditions that are treatable, such as depression or overmedication; those that may be misdiagnosed as irreversible and mimic senility but are not; and those progressive, deteriorating diseases that are irreversible.

Little more than a decade or two ago *senility* was the word most often used to describe confused or forgetful behavior in older people. "Hardening of the arteries" was the common explanation offered by physicians to families concerned about a parent's deteriorating condition. Often the doctor added, "What do you expect, it's old age." Becoming old does not make one demented. Disease does.

Names used in diagnosis of dementia (loss of intellectual function) have changed over the years. For a period physicians used the terms *reversible brain syndrome* and *chronic brain syndrome* to distinguish between reversible and irreversible conditions. Currently in use are the terms *reversible senile dementias* and *irreversible senile dementias*. The most recent American Psychiatric Association Manual denotes senile dementia of the Alzheimer's type as *primary degenerative dementia* (PDD). A physician treating your elder may use any of these terms.

Senile dementia is the current terminology for those who, in old age, clearly suffer impairment of intellecutal function—a complex of symptoms that can be caused by many underlying diseases. It is characterized by a loss of intellectual abilities and memory and one or more of the following: an impairment of abstract thinking or judgment; other disturbances involving language (*aphasia*); inability to make the body carry out a motor function (*apraxia*); failure to recognize or identify objects despite intact sensory function (*agnosia*); and constructional difficulties such as inability to draw a square inside a circle or build with blocks. There may also be a clouded state of consciousness.

Many people are confused by the word *dementia* and mistakenly believe it means the same thing as *psychosis*. It does not. Psychosis involves loss of contact with reality, but no substantial intellectual impairment or loss. Dementia involves loss of intellectual function.

Reversible dementias are those that can be eliminated if they are diagnosed quickly and treatment is instituted to deal with the precipitating causes of the behavior. Dr. Robert Butler describes them this way: "They are characterized by fluctuating levels of awareness, which may vary from mild confusion to stupor or active delirium. Hallucinations may be present, usually of the visual rather than the auditory type. The patient is typically disoriented, mistaking one person for another, and other intellectual functions can be impaired. Memory may be lost for recent as well as remote events. Restlessness, unusual aggressiveness, anxiety, fear, or a dazed expression may be noticed"[2] The patient may also be depressed.

Among the possible causes of this behavior are malnutrition, certain vitamin deficiencies, medication, surgical or emotional trauma, social isolation, a treatable mental illness (including depression), a serious viral infection, congestive heart failure, transient or small strokes, coma from diabetes, malfunctioning kidneys, alcoholism, and dehydration from diarrhea, vomiting, or diuretics.

Irreversible dementias are just that: no treatment will stop the progress of the disease, although appropriate medication may soften some of the behavioral effects. In addition to all of the above symptoms, the patient may be incontinent, delusional, extremely agitated, and physically and verbally abusive. These symptoms may come and go for a time, interspersed with normal or rational behavior, but increasingly as the disease progresses, irrational and uncontrolled behavior predominate.

Alzheimer's disease accounts for somewhat more than half the cases of irreversible senile dementia. Multifarct dementia (the accumulated result of numbers of small strokes or closing off of the smaller vessels of the brain) is responsible for about one-quarter of the cases. The remainder are attributed to a variety of other diseases including Parkinson's, Huntington's, or Pick's diseases, those resulting from a slow virus such as Kreutzfeld-Jakobs disease, or those of undetermined origin. In each case, damage to the brain has occurred. In some cases—stroke, for example—the damage is detectable through use of a variety of highly sophisticated scanning devices. The brain damage unique to Alzheimer's is not yet visible through noninvasive techniques and at present is verified in the United States only by autopsy.

Neuroses are quite common. They do not result in gross distortions of reality or profound personality disorganization, but may emerge in anxiety, pessimism, or other signs of unresolved emotional conflict.

Mental illness is a general term that covers a broad spectrum of disorders or disturbances, which can be mild or severe, interfering with an individual's feelings of well-being and ability to function at optimum capacity. Treatment for mental illness is as appropriate as treatment for physical illness and should not be shunned out of shame.

GERIATRIC EVALUATION

Serious behavioral symptoms, whatever they may be, can be misleading and may be misdiagnosed. Effective treatment depends on detecting the causes. Neither you nor your parent's physician should maintain any preconceived idea of what is wrong with your elderly parent. Your parent's doctor may suggest that it's time for a geriatric evaluation. This generally involves the participation of several specialists working together to investigate all the possible organic, psychological, or psychiatric causes for your parent's symptoms. Or you can seek out such teams yourself. They're generally to be found at major university hospitals or geriatric centers. You can help the physicians by being able to provide information about your parent's history that your mother or father may neglect to mention, for example, about a previous head injury from a fall or an automobile accident. Sometimes an individual may suffer from reversible and irreversible brain disorders at the same time, which makes diagnosis even more difficult.

Expect the geriatric evaluation to include

- examination for organic illness, including all basic laboratory tests

- a neurological assessment using state-of-the-art diagnostic tools
- a mental status exam
- a thorough examination of the patient's drug history
- a psychiatric evaluation
- a neuropsychological assessment
- an effort to determine whether or not the patient is suicidal
- a full background history of the patient's family and environment

It is only after this comprehensive examination is completed and evaluated that experienced physicians can help your parent effectively. Your parent may have to be seen two or three times for the evaluation. Precision in diagnosis is constantly improving but is not always perfect, so continuing follow-up may be necessary. Early dementias or brain tumors are sometimes seen only as depression; they may in fact exist together. But if, for example, it is a brain tumor that is causing the erratic behavior, then removing the tumor surgically may restore a patient to normal function.

DEPRESSION

It is estimated that between 15 and 20 percent of the population over 65 are afflicted with severe symptoms of depression, and that 85 percent of these neglect treatment. Many people, including the aging themselves, regard depression as a normal part of old age and don't know that treatment can alleviate their suffering. Others attach a great stigma to consulting a psychologist or psychiatrist. Some try treatment and stop because they don't enjoy immediate positive results. Treatment for depression takes time, but except in the most intractable cases, patients can be relieved of their symptoms.

Good diagnosis is the key to successful treatment. Sometimes depressed behavior accompanies other underlying, undetected disease. Sometimes it exists on its own or as part of a personality disorder. More often it is a reaction to a series of disturbing or traumatic life events.

Depression as a mental illness is defined by its characteristic symptoms. When a person is just sad, therapists may describe him or her as having a "depressive affect." Such behavior can be expected after loss of a spouse or other loved person and is part of normal bereavement and a way of expressing grief. This behavior recedes with time. Mourning patterns differ among different ethnic groups. The normal period of mourning in your family or ethnic group is a good rough measure of what you might consider a normal pattern for expressing grief over a loss. It is endless mourning, or inability to cope with losses or traumatic life events, that signals trouble.

A full-blown *depressive syndrome*, signifying mental illness, is described this way: The patient will have feelings of helplessness and hopelessness and lose humor and mirth—the ability to enjoy a happy event or engage in any merrymaking. A loss of appetite leads to noticeable weight loss. The depressed person may become constipated. Unusual sleep patterns develop. He or she may fall asleep easily but awaken many times during the night, and by three or four in the morning not return to sleep at all. The depressed person can be truly sleep-deprived and therefore may be fatigued in the early part of the day and then, perhaps, get a lift at the end of the day. Usually, this is just the reverse in *anxiety*. The two disorders require different treatment or medication.

The person who becomes depressed as a reaction to external events such as widowhood or retirement is considered to be suffering a *reactive depression* (one with outside causes). Moods go up and down according to the course of these external events. Psychotherapy is usually effective, but medication may occasionally be needed.

An *endogenous depression*, on the other hand, is usually triggered by internal events, such as a chemical or hormonal imbalance. If the imbalance is caused by inappropriate medication, removing the medication may relieve the depression. If the imbalance is the result of an individual's own chemical or hormonal system, then drug therapies can often help. Failing this, good results have been reported for electroconvulsive shock therapy (ECT). Endogenous depressions may also have psychotic components. No external event is necessary to bring on a psychotic depression. It follows its own course. Drug therapy and ECT are treatments of choice for such depressions, say the experts. People who are depressed may say "I feel empty." Psychotic depressives may believe they actually are empty, have no internal organs. The delusional aspects are one clue to diagnosing such patients.

What You Can Do

At what point, you may ask, do caring children change from understanding that life is really tough for their parents to knowing that something is wrong that needs attention? Many older persons suffer significant losses: They become ill or handicapped. A spouse may die, friends move away. Finances become difficult. They lose status. One senior comments, "Old age ain't for sissies!"

"It is time to go into action," says Dr. Steven Mattis, "when you notice characteristic physical changes in daily habits and/or when you notice a real withdrawal from social contact, even with what at first may appear rational excuses: 'I don't feel like seeing anybody; I'm not in the mood for company. So and so annoys me.' A loner may go unnoticed for a long time before a child becomes aware that this parent is never cheerful, that he or she never calls any friends and rebuffs the ones who call him or her."

You may succeed in persuading such a parent to see the family doctor on the basis that there may be some physical cause for their not feeling well. Once again, the quality of the physician you consult is paramount. If there is no physical cause for the depression, it won't help for the doctor to say, "You're okay—stop worrying." A really depressed person needs more than that, and many well-trained and experienced internists are prepared to offer more than that. But if your parent's doctor does not take the next step to help with treatment, then perhaps you will want to consult a psychiatrist, especially if you begin to hear, "What is life all about? It isn't worth living."

Suppose your parent says, "It's not your business, leave me alone. You don't know what it's like to be my age, or to live like this, or to lose someone you love." You are concerned, want to help, and you're frustrated.

Dr. Charles Shamoian, a psychiatrist and director of Geriatric Services at New York Hospital/Cornell Medical Center, White Plains, describes what happens next: "After a while you're likely to become irritable, then angry, feel like abandoning this person who refuses to be helped. You may think 'Get out of my life!' and if you do, then of course you'll feel guilty. After that you'll be ready to start your support system. If this is happening to you as a result of your concern for a troubled but recalcitrant parent, at this point you are likely to go to the doctor and ask for help: 'Do something for me, how can I get help for my mother or father?' "

The decision to intervene in a parent's life at such junctures means taking on the responsibility to obtain treatment for an illness less tangible, perhaps, than appendicitis, but just as real in how it affects your parent. Either the experienced family doctor or the psychiatrist can suggest some treatment and help your elder to understand that it will take some time to get good results. The doctor should schedule appointments from one time to the next so that the medication and dosages can be monitored carefully, not wait for your parent to take the initiative. A physician familiar with depression among older people should be knowledgeable about antidepressant medications and the ways older people react to them and should take the time required to help make the treatment effective.

Encourage your parent to stay the course. Be there, if you possibly can, to make sure that medication is taken and appointments are kept. Antidepressant drugs sometimes have undesirable side effects, which include dry mouth, blurred vision, constipation, sleeplessness, and memory problems. If these or any other unpleasant side effects occur, always inform the physician promptly. Other medications can be substituted. "Don't wait until the side effects are severe. Even mild light-headedness or dizziness as a result of medication should get you to the phone," says Dr. Shamoian. "Geriatric patients need extra attention from their doctors at such times. I hope physicians will say, 'I want to hear from you. If I don't hear from you, I'll call you.' "

Once the medication takes hold and appears to be effective it still needs to be monitored. Don't assume that once the depression disappears, medication can be immediately stopped. If medication is stopped, the depression may return. After six months or a year, the drug treatment may no longer be necessary, depending on the individual. The doctor should be the one who determines that. Older persons with a chronic history of depression, or recurring episodes, may be maintained on medication for the rest of their lives.

Sometimes more is required. If the doctor suggests shock therapy, you should not turn tail and run without understanding why or when it's used. According to Dr. Shamoian,

> People are terrified of electroconvulsive therapy, but if a patient is psychotically depressed, delusional, feels trapped, is losing weight, and is suicidal, the safest, quickest, most effective treatment is with ECT. This treatment is now given with anesthesia. It is not scary as it was in the old days or the way it was depicted in *One Flew Over the Cuckoo's Nest.* Now the patient is asleep, has no memory of the experience. It is really a painless experience. After three or four such treatments, the patient starts coming out of the depression. Six or eight treatments will usually complete the process. There may be a temporary period of confusion and disorientation for several weeks after ECT. Continuing memory deficits or other symptoms are virtually nonexistent if ECT is appropriately administered and medication is used. If you have an elder with severe depressions and severe medical problems which preclude using antidepressant drugs, a good physician might consider use of ECT.

Your parent's mood may not require medication at all. He or she may be an eternal pessimist, always gloomy or tired, who reports numerous physical complaints to the internist. These are signs of *dysthmic disorder,* a depressive neurosis. "We do not treat such personality disorders with medication," says Dr. Shamoian." It is possible that in addition to the personality disorder, a patient may have a major depression, which we do treat with medication. But by eradicating the depression, we do not influence social behavior or interactive skills. This is where psychotherapy comes in, to help the individual cope with his or her isolation, learn how his or her thinking has brought on a negative approach."

Sometimes other organic disease precipitates or aggravates depression—a hypothyroid condition, cancer of the pancreas, or rheumatoid arthritis. Or a depression can aggravate other chronic illnesses, which worsen because the depressed person doesn't care about himself or herself and neglects the regimen that controls the illness. Dr. Shamoian cites the person who becomes depressed because she has diabetes, neglects medication and diet, and the diabetes goes out of control. If the depression is treated, the diabetes may improve. Sometimes "drug intoxication" causes depression, and eliminating, changing, or reducing the medication will end the erratic or depressed behavior. Some antidepressants can aggravate a cardiovascular problem; some drugs used to treat cardiovascular problems can precipitate a depression. It's important not to make snap judgments but to determine why your parent is behaving in any unusual way.

Is Your Parent Suicidal?

The rate of suicide is highest among elderly males. Among men between 80 and 90, suicide occurs at the rate of 150 per 100,000. Among females the highest period of incidence is between ages 55 and 65, but only at the rate of 15 per 100,000. In all, 25 percent of the suicides in the United States are committed by the elderly. They make fewer attempts, but they are more successful.

There are no good predictors of who will be suicidal. But, says Dr. Shamoian, "We do have some prime candidates, particularly those who have made a concrete plan and will tell you they've saved up their medications and know the time of the day or week they're least likely to be interrupted. You'd better be concerned if your mother or father tells you something of this sort. Or if your parent is living alone, has just lost a spouse, has a history of chronic debilitating illness, drug or alcohol abuse, or a history of prior attempts, then you should be in touch with a physician."

There is growing debate among physicians, clerics, philosophers, and lay people about important issues of life and death. This discussion usually pertains to prolonging life without meaning, the use of high technology to sustain life when death is imminent, or the more complex issues of providing food and water to a person who has clearly stated in person or through a proxy that he or she does not wish to be sustained by artificial means. (See chapter 11.)

Suicide, however, is usually discussed in a different context. There are those who passionately believe that any individual should be in charge of his or her own life—and death—however that may occur. Religious precepts teach that life is a gift, not to be taken by any individual. Within these two boundaries are the values of great numbers of people who are sometimes ambivalent in their feelings, particularly if someone they love is suffering great pain or has become comatose or so intellectually deprived that his or her life is "no longer worth living." You have often heard people say that death has come to such an older person "as a blessing." When children are faced with suicidal parents they too may have unexpressed feelings that death may be a blessing. Rarely do children knowingly participate in such an event. The law is not on their side if they do. A recent book depicts the occasion when a daughter did help her mother to die with dignity. A hospice worker commented that a good hospice program could have helped this patient control pain and might have altered this family's decisions.

Not all patients with terrible illnesses or physical pain wish to die or choose suicide. What is different about the depressed person who is suicidal is that the feelings that propel a depressed person to take his or her own life are not necessarily generated by terrible physical pain or terminal illness but by psychic pain generated and nourished by the depression itself. If the depression can be controlled, the self-destructive impulses can be subdued in some, if not all, cases. Quick response from a family or physician can sometimes make the difference between life and death. There are also crisis hotlines for the suicidal where trained counselors can help a person over the moment or telephone others for help.

You should ask the doctor whether it is advisable to keep a suicidal parent at home to be treated with medication and/or therapy, or whether you must consider hospitalization. Even if the physician considers it possible to treat your parent at home with medication, ask yourself whether you are willing and able to establish the support system necessary to insure 24-hour monitoring until the crisis is passed. If you and the physician in charge have ascertained that the suicidal threat is real, psychiatrists believe the hospital is the better place for such a patient, especially if a serious physical illness is also involved.

"Whether or not the family has hospitalized the patient or followed an unsuccessful course of treatment, it is difficult," says Dr. Shamoian. "People feel guilty no matter what. The important thing for family members to remember is that if they have done all that is possible, they really shouldn't feel guilty. [But] guilt is a normal phenomenon . . . Feeling guilty doesn't mean you need therapy."

WHEN IT'S ALZHEIMER'S DISEASE

The devastating loss of the mind that characterizes senile dementia of the Alzheimer's type and its increasing prevalence in our older population have stimulated increasingly intensive research in the neurosciences.

Until a decade or so ago, Alzheimer's disease was the diagnosis for younger patients said to be suffering from presenile dementia. This and senile dementia were subsequently determined to be the same, and Alzheimer's disease, or dementia of the Alzheimer's type, are the names currently used. In the disease, chemical and neurotransmitter changes are evident in the brain; there are measurable metabolic differences between normal aged and Alzheimer's patients; there are indications that some genetic factor may make some families more susceptible than others. Recent studies show that the familial type of Alzheimer's is indeed inherited.

There are innumerable strands of solid data leading scientists to conclude that they are making progress in finding the markers that will help them to zero in on Alzheimer's disease. But to date, no one has yet found the way to halt or alter the course of the affliction.

Diagnosis

Alzheimer's has a gradual onset, as opposed to dementia caused by a massive stroke, wherein normal brain tissue is suddenly destroyed and the resulting deficits are immediately apparent. Alzheimer's is progressive and increasingly destructive to the victim's ability to function.

When healthy brain tissue is lost to a stroke or accident or when a tumor is present, these are evident in X rays, CAT scans or other advanced radiological techniques. The damage done by Alzheimer's—the nerve tangles, plaques, and other microscopic physiological brain changes that characterize it—are not readily seen even by these hi-tech methods. Biopsy to detect Alzheimer's, in use elsewhere in the world, is not currently a common procedure in this country. The brain changes characteristic of Alzheimer's are therefore identified here only in autopsies. That is why most specialists still regard diagnosis of Alzheimer's as a diagnosis of exclusion—one that can only be made with reasonable confidence after all the other possible causes of dementia have been carefully ruled out.

It sometimes takes a long time to diagnose Alzheimer's because its onset is gradual and it is marked at first by ambiguous symptoms: memory loss, which can happen to any older person, and confusion, which can accompany numbers of other conditions.

Diagnosis in recent years has improved greatly, "from a 10 to 50 percent error rate to at least a 90 percent assurance of accuracy,"[3] thanks to the development of better tools for determining mental status and cognitive loss and to increased clinical experience of physicians and others observing the patterns of degeneration in Alzheimer's patients.

There is considerable variation among individuals with Alzheimer's, but there is general agreement that Alzheimer's patients travel a downhill road from independence on a progressive, irreversible path of declining function.

Not too many years ago it was estimated that Alzheimer's victims lived for about five years after diagnosis. Today estimates vary from five to ten years, sometimes longer, often depending on when the disease is diagnosed, and whether it appears at a younger or later age. Early onset usually indicates a more rampant path and earlier death. Seven years is now seen as an average survival time for Alzheimer's patients. The longer life span is generally attributed to better medical care for conditions other than Alzheimer's. Whatever the length of the course, it is a very long time for a spouse, child, or family group to be involved with the daily care an Alzheimer's patient requires. Studies have shown that 50 percent of relatives caring for Alzheimer's patients eventually suffer from depression.

Some Problems of Caregivers

The Alzheimer's Disease and Related Disorders Association (ADRDA), through a vigorous media campaign, has made the public more aware of senile dementia as a major illness—a silent epidemic—requiring funds for research and services for the victims and their families, but serious problems involving services, respite, and long-term care continue.

"We must treat the patient and we must treat the family," is the consensus of physicians who witness not only the progressive deterioration of the patient, but also the toll taken on the individual or families taking care of a stricken loved one.

Care for an Alzheimer's victim can become overwhelming, no matter how much help any individual can marshal to share the burdens. Most Alzheimer's victims are cared for by their spouses, themselves generally elderly people who may have their own chronic illnesses, although their problems of personal health may seem small compared to the devastation wrought by Alzheimer's disease. The spouse of an Alzheimer's patient must deal not only with the symptoms of the partner's decline but with the personal loss of demonstrated love, companionship, and intimacy that is in some ways more cruel than death itself. The physical person of the spouse is present, with ever-increasing need for care, while the essence of the person departs, lost forever.

As in all of life, different people respond in different ways to similar conditions. Some husbands or wives are enormously angry and bitter at finding themselves hostage to a totally dependent spouse, especially if their previous relationship was troubled. Yet they may at the same time reject help from others and use their martyrdom as a way of assuaging guilt for their part in old conflicts.

Other spouses may be overcome with guilt that they have survived intact, while their beloved partners are so ill, and pay for this guilt by rejecting any help from others.

"Many people regard any mental condition as a stigma," says Dr. Shamoian. "They are afraid to let outsiders know what is happening within the confines of their home; they are ashamed and even frightened that others will discover their secret shame."

Some parents try to spare their children and take too much on themselves. Some children, in their own pain, rush in to take charge and help in their own fashion. Says Susan Cohn, coordinator of the Respite Program for the Brookdale Center on Aging,

> Often, children have an idea of what's best for the parent to do that isn't in sync with what the parent feels is right. A son may be very anxious for his father to keep his ill mother at home, while the husband is totally worn down and feels he must consider institutionalizing his wife. Conversely, the children may say 'Put mom away so that you can have a life of your own.' But that's not what the husband wants to do. The children need to recognize that the spouse is the one who must make the decision. It's still the spouse that lives with the person day in and day out. And the children need to support that decision in whatever way they can.[4]

HOW ALZHEIMER'S PROGRESSES

Most professionals distinguish between the early, middle, and late stages of the disease, or mild, moderate, and severe symptoms, and have observed the general patterns described below. Your relative may not follow these patterns exactly—the progression of the disease is highly idiosyncratic—but they will give you some idea of what to expect if your elder has been diagnosed as having Alzheimer's. You can then begin to make the plans necessary to carry you and your family through. The examples of what you can do at each stage are merely illustrative. More detailed and helpful strategies for you to follow can be obtained from the helping sources named in the Appendix.

Early Stage

Memory The most obvious symptom is loss of memory for recent events and names of people or places. The person may have difficulty finding the right word for an object or may forget a thought in process. Trouble finding familiar objects, such as keys and glasses, becomes more frequent; appointments are forgotten; phone messages are garbled or forgotten. Finding one's way, even to familiar places, becomes a problem.

What you can do: Help set up a routine so that familiar things are always in accustomed places and appointments written down. Have an identification bracelet made that cannot be removed.

Cognitive Ability Tasks at home and at work become difficult: paying bills, keeping or balancing a checkbook, making change, playing bridge, writing reports. This is usually the point at which denial sets in, the psychological mechanism that protects one from consciously accepting the truth that something terrible is happening. Thus, if a child asks on the telephone, "How are you?" the answer may be "Fine." This is particularly a problem for children at a distance, who have no idea that anything is wrong until a utility turns off the service, or a neighbor, the police, or a hospital telephones to report a crisis.

What you can do: Once you know that the problem exists, try to simplify tasks so that your elder can continue to do as much as possible independently. You or someone else can assist with some of the normal tasks of living: pay the rent and utility bills and arrange for a third party notice if bills aren't paid; help with banking and checkbooks. Suggest that this may be a good time to retire from active employment and relax. Your suggestion will probably be welcomed if it comes as a loving thought rather than as a judgment. Consult a lawyer about establishing a conservatorship, or ask social agencies for help on this. Make the best financial plans you can for long-term care.

Coordination/Motor Skills These do not appear to be impaired, although the ailing person may begin to have traffic accidents, going through red lights or stop signs and exhibiting a marked slowing of reaction time. Gait and physical health appear to be relatively normal.

What you can do: If and when auto safety becomes an issue, consult your physician to determine whether he or she believes this is a suitable time for you to inform the motor vehicle office and request suspension of the driving license. This is a difficult decision. Hiding keys to the car and garage are what some people do under these circumstances to deter the patient from driving. Don't act hastily in this matter. So long as the person can drive safely, or do anything else competently, do not hurry him or her into dependence. Encourage exercise and recreation.

Ability to Live Independently Washing, dressing, bathing, and eating are carried on with little difficulty. Some assistance may be required in carrying out financial tasks and to insure safety. Ordinary activities that require several steps may become too complex for the person to deal with. For example, the person may at this stage be able to write a letter but then forget to address the envelope or put on a stamp or mail the letter.

What you can do: Provide assistance as required. Simplify the environment and break down the ordinary activities of daily living into steps the person can accomplish: for example, if a letter is written, suggest the envelope be addressed, then stamped, then mailed. Try to be gentle in your guidance, not officious.

Communication While interaction with others may decline somewhat, speech continues to be relatively normal. Use of language begins to change, however. You may be more aware that your elder has increased difficulty finding words, or that a previously rich vocabulary is no longer used. Conversations may be interrupted by irrelevant or inappropriate comments.

What you can do: Keep communication as full as possible. Simplify your own vocabulary as it becomes necessary to help the impaired person understand whatever you wish to convey. Similarly, help them convey their thoughts and wishes to you if a word or thought is lost. With the help of experienced advisers, you can learn how to do this effectively without harming the dignity of the person you're trying to assist.

Mood and Behavior The person may become moody and depressed, suffer mood swings, and be less able to concentrate. He or she is now easily distracted, withdrawn from friends and family, and appears "flat," less spontaneous, less sociable, and less likely to take the initiative. Forgetful or confused, the person will nevertheless deny that anything is wrong. New experiences, places, or people are likely to be shunned in favor of the familiar.

What you can do: Talk to the doctor about what you observe. At this stage, antidepressant medication may alleviate some of the symptoms and make it possible for the patient to enjoy what he or she is still quite capable of enjoying. Try not to shrink the social circle or avoid social occasions with old friends and family. While some friends and family may become uncomfortable, others will rally to your side if you help them to understand what is happening. You can still travel together if you're willing to take full responsibility for all the arrangements and to accompany the traveler for all activities. Don't isolate the Alzheimer's patient, but don't insist on "new and exciting" things to do. There is comfort in the routine. It's important to stimulate an Alzheimer's patient to do what is still possible and to enjoy feelings of accomplishment, but watch for the fine line between stimulating and overwhelming.

Take care of yourself, and while you increasingly routinize the day for your patient, be sure to include some routine time away for yourself. It will help you to protect this time later when you will really need it. Don't shun opportunities to enjoy yourself or feel guilty when you do. This is a good time to find some outside help to spell you while you're away and to introduce this person into the normal routine of the household for whatever number of hours or days you can afford. Consider joining a support group to help you through the more difficult days ahead. Others who know what you're going through can help you with their experiences of how to cope. Investigate the day-care programs in your area, where planned activities as well as medical and social services are available. Make a list of services or people you may need for ongoing help or in a crisis. Keep names and addresses handy.

Middle Stage

Memory Recent memory is largely gone. The patient is unable to form or store the memory of recent events or experiences and is therefore unable to learn new things. Long-term memory capacity is still in evidence, as the Alzheimer's patient is still able to recall the distant past. The people and events of chidhood are recalled, not what happened this morning or yesterday.

What you can do: Understand that memory has a great deal to do with how we function, and its loss isn't uniform. You may ask, "If she can remember this, why can't she remember that? It doesn't make sense." Increasing memory loss will demand more care and attention from you. If you understand that memory is involved in everything we do—how to eat, bathe, dress, or use the toilet, how to find your way home—you will understand better why these "simple" activities of life involve too many steps for the impaired person to carry out independently. With a little guidance and supervision from you (break down the steps involved in performing the task) your loved one may be able to perform some tasks.

Because the Alzheimer's patient may start wandering and get lost, an identification bracelet is essential. Also, keep up-to-date photos on hand to help others find your elder if he or she becomes lost. Do not be ashamed to inform close neighbors of your situation. You will be encouraged by their willingness to "keep their eyes open." If you consider and practice quick and safe procedures for fires or medical emergencies, you can then lock your doors and put the key out of reach so that an impaired person cannot leave the house independently, but never leave such a person alone under these circumstances.

Find old photo albums to bolster the positive benefits that come when an impaired person recognizes the people of the past, or play old records, or sing old songs. Enjoy memories of happy times together—it will help give you some moments of pleasure and some perspective on your life.

Cognitive Ability Making choices or decisions becomes a problem. Thus your impaired relative may not be able to choose clothing for the day, or may put on two or more sets of clothes, or dress in the wrong clothes for the time of day or season. By now he or she may be unable to do simple arithmetic or follow a story or conversation. At this stage there is commonly a loss of orientation to place, time, or season. A formerly sensible person with Alzheimer's will at this stage exhibit poor judgment. He or she will be unable to distinguish between a hot or cold water faucet and may develop a fear of bathing.

What you can do: You will need to participate in all the simple activities of daily living, break each activity down into the simplest steps, and guide the impaired person through each of them. Thus, you choose the clothing for the day and help the person dress, select and prepare the food and help the person eat, guide him or her through all the procedures of toileting. You will need to learn how to manage urinary and fecal incontinence, which also occur at this stage. Regular toileting and diapers will help. It is a good idea to discard carpeting and upholstered furniture so that stains and smells do not linger. Make the physical space as easy to clean as possible. You will need to help the person bathe and keep clean or get help if you are physically unable to cope with this task. For safety, remove all poisonous cleaning materials, sharp knives, and other dangerous or inflammable objects from the impaired person's access. Find out from your utility company how to secure the stove.

Coordination/Motor Skills A previously well-coordinated individual may now fall down easily, have difficulty walking, and bump into things as coordination and balance become impaired. Gait may change and writing become illegible. The patient is not losing basic motor function but rather the cognitive ability to command the body to perform.

What you can do: Be sure the living space is as simple, uncluttered, and safe as possible. Remove any carpets or rugs that slip; any lamp cords, coffee tables, baskets, plants, or other objects in a pathway that can cause a tumble or hurt a falling person. Be sure rooms are well lighted. Check with the doctor to make sure that hearing and vision problems are not also complicating your patient's coordination. You can put railings along the wall between bedroom and bath and grab bars in the bathroom to reduce chances of accident. When you walk together, keep a gentle hold on an elbow or arm to forestall falls. Follow an exercise program together that will help you as well as the person you are caring for. Consult the doctor or a physical therapist for advice on this, or follow the suggestions in *Caring,* a guidebook from the New York City Alzheimer's Resource Center (see Appendix).

Ability to Live Independently At this stage, independent living is untenable. Assistance is required for all the activities of daily living.

What you can do: Be sure all the legal and financial arrangements are in place for whatever may follow. Arrange for as much help as you can afford, because care for the impaired person can now become overwhelming. If living at home with assistance is no longer possible, investigate nursing homes and begin to make the necessary arrangements for admission. Understand that Medicare does not cover custodial care; therefore costs for home care or institutional care must be borne by the individual or the family. Medicaid will cover such care if the patient meets the eligibility standards of the state. Every effort should be made to protect the financial security of a surviving spouse while attending to the ill person's needs. Pauperization is a real threat and avoiding it may require expert legal action (see chapter 6 for a general discussion of legal and financial planning). Consult a lawyer, the Area Agency on Aging legal services office, a social service agency, or your local ADRDA chapter for specific advice.

Communication The ability to use and understand words is significantly diminished. Speech is less frequent, slower, halting, fragmented and disjointed, repetitive, and may be senseless as well. Whatever is said may be frequently revised. Sentences may be reduced to two or three words or may not be used at all as difficulty in constructing a sentence increases.

What you can do: Do not give up on communicating your love and respect to this impaired person who has meant so much to you. Try to adjust your language and vocabulary to his or her level of comprehension. Don't say too many different things at once. Help find the lost word, not by correcting mistakes but by supplying a lost word or asking specific questions: "Do you want (this) or (that)?" Or help the person "talk around" the word, or write it down if that is still possible, or tell you what it's like. Don't allow frustration to build up if you can supply the word yourself. Nonverbal communication is also understood: anger, impatience, frustration. Communicating these will probably complicate your problems. Using nonverbal techniques can also help you: communicate approval, pleasure, patience. Touch the person to get his or her attention, stroke an arm, give a kiss. Closeness and a smile communicate love, and words aren't necessary.

Mood and Behavior Wandering becomes a serious problem at this stage. Agitation, sleeplessness, aggressiveness, paranoia, delusions, and hallucinations are now more common, as well as increased self-absorption and insensitivity to others. Accusations of theft, insults, and obscenities reflect growing loss of the ability to control what is thought and said and to make judgments based on reality. Mood swings are more frequent.

What you can do: Stay in touch with the doctor. Antidepressant drugs, because of their side effects, can make things worse at this stage; some tranquilizers may help. Medication must be carefully monitored and changed if necessary or eliminated depending on what is occurring. Small doses may be better than large ones. Do not take personally the insults or accusations that may come your way. If you cannot deal with this, seek the help of a counselor or therapist. If the impaired person becomes a danger to you or him or herself, 24-hour supervision is essential. You may have no choice but to seek placement in a nursing home. You should not feel guilty about this or think you have failed in your responsibilities. Care for yourself and seek whatever counseling or therapy can help you cope with the enormous stress you are experiencing. In some families, a mourning and grieving process peaks at this point, and people can then accept the reality that they have indeed lost the person they once knew.

Late Stage

Memory All memory of recent or past events is apparently gone. Spouse and children are no longer recognized.

Cognitive Ability All intellectual function is lost.

Coordination/Motor Skills The ability to walk, sit, and even smile or swallow are gone. The patient eventually recedes into stupor or coma.

Ability to Live Independently The patient is totally dependent on others for survival.

Communication Speech may be reduced to one or two words or be lost entirely. One word may do for all needs, calls for attention, or responses to questions. Music may still be enjoyed even when speech is gone. A grunt may be the only vocal communication finally left.

Mood and Behavior The patient is frequently agitated but oblivious to surroundings and people.

What you can do: A nursing home is the best place for the patient at this stage unless 24-hour nursing care can be provided at home, not a realistic solution for most families. Some nursing home administrators will tell you that a senile patient feels neither pleasure nor pain, that you should not be concerned that the patient is unhappy. It is the family that feels the pain, says Dr. Mattis: "It is quite true that pleasure and pain can be defective in demented people. There is a point at which the quality of humanness seems to be lost. But it is hard to say where that is. Some behavior seems to be reflexive; there is a primitive system operating and a pinprick will bring withdrawal, and stroking may seem to give pleasure. It is very difficult for families to deal with this."

Your patience will be strained, your frustration high, unless you learn to accept the reality: that this once intelligent, caring individual is no longer capable of understanding what you mean, carrying out the simplest tasks, or communicating what he or she feels; that if he or she seems able to understand one thing and not another, perversity and obstinacy are not the causes. If you expect yourself to be a saint or a martyr and become one in fact, your patient will be unaware of how much you have done or sacrificed on his or her behalf. You may yourself be experienceing explosive outbursts, shame and guilt, crying, depression, anxiety, sleeplessness. Increased physical and mental illness are not uncommon among people giving care to Alzheimer's patients. To avoid or reduce these negative effects on your own physical and mental health, talk to the doctor who is managing your impaired relative's problems. He or she should also be prepared to help you discover and use good coping strategies. There are also social workers and counselors available to help you in the aging agencies, the family service agencies, and those working with members of the local chapters of the ADRDA.

ADULT DAY-CARE FOR ALZHEIMER'S PATIENTS

Society is becoming increasingly aware of the incidence of Alzheimer's disease, of the severity of impact on its victims and their families, and the necessity to provide an alternative to institutionalization. Day-care is a useful and humane alternative. Properly organized and staffed day-care programs fill a need which allows family structures to remain intact sometimes for years after the diagnosis of dementia. It provides a dignified environment for afflicted patients, gives them an opportunity to socialize, which temporarily avoids the inevitable social isolation experienced by the victim and the family. Day-care provides an important opportunity for retraining and behavior modification which often help make an individual, no matter how demented, socially acceptable. Family involvement in the program has allowed staff to provide meaningful psychological support for the nonafflicted.[5]

Adult day-care has two purposes: benefit to the patient and respite for the person providing care for the impaired adult. Respite for you is not an indulgence. If your loved one is eligible for admission to a day-care program and a good one exists in your vicinity, make every effort to take advantage of what it offers. "It is very hard for some families to give up care of their loved ones to strangers" was an opinion voiced at a workshop for social workers offering counsel at adult day-care programs. If you feel this way, you should talk to some of the families whose relatives participate in a good day-care program and discover how they dealt with similar feelings. Of course you will want to visit and investigate the facilities, staffing, and program of the centers you are considering. Then choose what is best for you.

What to Look For

All the criteria for a good day-care center described in chapter 2 apply as well to good day-care centers for dementia patients. They should be clean, professionally staffed, and offer appropriate programs; the physical environment should be safe and tailored to the needs of the participants; toilets should be clean and accessible and have buttons to summon help. Temperatures should be even and comfortable for the older person, neither too hot nor too cold. The hours and arrangements should be convenient for you, the caregiver.

More than this, however, is important for the dementia participant. Dr. Laurie Barclay, Director of Clinical Services of the Dementia Research Service at the Burke Rehabilitation Center in White Plains, New York, advises families to pay particular attention to two other criteria:

1. There should be a high ratio of staff to patients. At Burke, the day hospital for dementia patients has one staff member to two patients. The staff should be professionally trained to deal with dementia patients.
2. A doctor should be on the premises as part of the professional team, to monitor and advise on medication, to treat injuries, and to deal with such medical emergencies as chest pains and breathing difficulties.

The day hospital at Burke has become a model for other facilities around the country. In the manual prepared at Burke by John Panella, Jr., and Dr. Fletcher H. McDowell, the following additional factors are highlighted: the physical space should be large enough to accommodate the various needs of the day and provide opportunities for freedom of movement without being too large and making it difficult for the patient to focus on the activity at hand. Movable partitions help to accomplish this. Furniture should be comfortable, uncluttered, preferably plastic for easy cleaning.

Distances between arrival (or departure) points and the designated day room area should be as short as possible. Appropriate barriers should be used at entrances and exits and at outdoor activity space to protect the wanderers without making them feel trapped or uncomfortable. Staff should never leave a participant unattended. There should be direct physical transfer of patient from family to staff and from staff to family at arrival and departure.

Safety hazards should be avoided, such as glass doors or large windows, stools and hassocks or other small objects on the floor, sharp or protruding corners of furniture, uneven or waxed floors. Floor surfaces should be easy to clean (to avoid mess and unpleasant odors) and left uncarpeted. Fire extinguishers should be available for trained staff to use. Fire drills appropriate to the condition of the patients should be a regular feature.[6]

If a doctor is not directly on the premises of the facilities you visit, then you should ascertain (1) whether the staff has been trained in CPR (cardiopulmonary resuscitation) and first aid and has had basic instruction in recognizing reactions to common drugs and basic physical signs of illness and (2) whether a doctor is on call and how long it takes him or her to arrive for emergencies.

What Happens at a Day-Care Center

The activities at a good day-care center are designed to promote the highest function of which the patient is capable: to encourage social activity, to provide exercise and release of tension, to provide activities that are pleasurable and give emotional benefit, to train for better performance in the activities of daily living, and to provide cognitive stimulation. At each step along the way, trained staff ease the transition from one activity to another, and a variety of specialists organize and conduct the assigned activity. Most activities are conducted for groups, although a quiet room should be available to separate an agitated or ill patient from the others. Psychologists, social workers, or other trained therapists conduct psychotherapy sessions for those with enough cognitive function to benefit from exchanging feelings and receiving treatment. Medical services should include administration and evaluation of medication and direct communication with the personal physician in charge of the patient.

Costs

Costs will vary according to your locality. At Burke, as of 1987, the program operated five weekdays a week, with most patients attending two or three (four if they could afford it) days a week. Costs were $70 a day for participation, usually borne by the individual or family. Medicare does not cover day-care center programs for dementia patients, though Medicaid-eligible participants may be reimbursed, or sliding scale fees may apply under other entitlements. Some corporate programs offer adult day-care benefits to employees under "cafeteria" benefit packages.

Criteria For Admission

Criteria will vary from community to community. To be admitted to Burke Day Hospital the patient must (1) be ambulatory, (2) not require full-time assistance (one to one), (3) not be combative or agitated, and (4) be at an appropriate level of cognitive impairment. Dr. Barclay explains:

> If he or she is functioning at too high a level, the patient may become depressed or upset at observing and being with others who are worse off and whose losses are substantially greater. On the other hand, as function continues to recede, there is a hard-to-define moment when it is a good idea to introduce the patient to the facility, group activity, and routines of the day before function becomes too limited to permit a satisfactory adjustment to the program. If deterioration is too far advanced, so that the patient no longer recognizes anyone and is unable to verbalize, then the day hospital is no longer a suitable placement.

TEMPORARY PLACEMENT AWAY FROM HOME

No matter how dedicated and devoted you may be, for your own health you need a break from your ceaseless tasks, and this may be possible if you can find a facility where your dependent elder can live for a short period. Such a placement may even become necessary if an emergency makes it impossible for you to provide care. If you investigate the possibilities in your locality in good time, then you will be ready in an emergency, or you may be able to take a needed vacation, attend to your own urgent personal medical needs, visit a child at school or camp, or do something you would enjoy doing, knowing that your afflicted elder is in good hands.

There may be local nursing homes that admit impaired patients on a short-term basis to provide respite to families. There may be a local hospital with a section of unused beds converted to respite care that will give temporary care to the impaired person in your family.

There are even individual families in some communities who take Alzheimer's patients as one would take a foster child and care for them within their own families for a fee. Social workers report that some moderately demented patients do very well in families with young children, where their performance is not that different and the pressures to conform to normal standards are lessened.

Some communities have established special respite homes that offer care for a few hours or overnight. Not enough such facilities are available as yet, but the need is growing, and families working together are helping to expand their own sources of assistance.

The best way to take advantage of temporary respite care outside your home is to introduce the patient to it before there is an emergency, so he or she can become familiar with the surroundings and the personnel and enjoy some pleasant activities there. Then, when the house is used for temporary residence, the patient will be able to adjust more quickly and with less confusion and agitation than might otherwise occur when a change in environment is made abruptly and without preparation. Your local ADRDA or AAA will know about the alternatives available to you for respite.

When behavior becomes hard to live with, your doctor can help. Antidepressants, tranquilizers, and sleeping pills each have their role. Used inappropriately they can make matters worse. All medication must be closely monitored. Any illness should be promptly treated, since accompanying illness can compound the cognitive deficits of Alzheimer's patients.

When the doctor is unable to maintain a patient at home on suitable medication, if the patient becomes a danger to him- or herself or to others, or if you can no longer tolerate the regimen and the stress or feel in control of the situation, then you should consider a nursing home as the best and safest place for your loved one to be. There you can visit and provide the loving caresses and emotional support, the recreational and social activities that speak your love and devotion, perhaps more than you can at home when so many other burdens of care wear you out.

Some Alzheimer's patients may need to be admitted to an inpatient medical-psychiatric geriatric unit to be treated for medical, behavioral, and emotional problems. If you are having difficulty deciding about nursing home or other placement, the team helping you care for your afflicted patient can help you. See also chapters 6 and 7 and Appendix.

LEGAL AND FINANCIAL PLANNING

Families of Alzheimer's patients and spouses in particular need expert advice in setting up plans that will minimize the difficulties they may encounter in trying to use the impaired person's assets for his or her own benefit, in seeking benefits or entitlements under various government programs, or in trying to avoid pauperizing a surviving spouse or other members of the family whose financial resources for their own future are at serious risk when long-term care of an Alzheimer's patient is involved.

Because of the nature of this disease, it is foolhardy for any family to hope that their beloved afflicted member will somehow avoid a devastating loss of intellectual function. Others will ultimately have to act in his or her behalf in all legal and financial matters. The financial drain on a spouse and/or family can be considerable and potentially devastating. Some financial aid may be available through various entitlements. Some actions can be taken to protect a portion of the couple's resources for the benefit of the other spouse. The sooner you consult an experienced lawyer and/or financial advisor, the better. See chapter 6.

TEN

SUCCESSFUL AGING

There is no magic spell to halt the inevitable process of aging, but some people are more successful than others in making their later years rewarding. As the old song says, you've got to accentuate the positive. You can encourage the elements of your parent's lives that can make their later years enjoyable.

What kind of people age successfully? Researchers have been raising this question for years. The biological scientists look at cells and tissue and mark successful aging in terms of health and survival. The social scientists mark successful aging in terms of individual attitudes and activity. They generally agree on some common characteristics.

Successful older people seem to accept the natural processes of the life cycle. They recognize the changes taking place in their physical capacity and energies and organize their lives to accommodate these changes, foregoing activities that are too difficult or stressful to accomplish and choosing new activities that may be challenging but are not stressful. Having altered the structure and conditions under which they expect to operate, they can function smoothly and without constant frustration. They learn how to substitute new satisfactions for old ones now impossible to achieve. Making this accommodation is not simple—it is a discipline that requires great effort for some people—but those who succeed in the effort take responsibility for their own well-being and do what is possible to maintain it.

Older people with healthy attitudes judge themselves by criteria that reflect their current lives, not relics of a more energetic, more ambitious past. They learn new roles and unlearn old ones. They integrate new values and goals into their personalities. They perform some useful function and are involved with other people or a consuming task, maintain their self-esteem at a high level, and win the approval of others.[1]

According to Dr. Bernice L. Neugarten, gerontologist and professor of human development at the University of Chicago, older people who find life good

- take pleasure from their daily activities
- regard their lives as meaningful and take responsibility for them
- feel they have reached their major goals
- have a positive self-image
- are optimistic in attitude and moods[2]

These are broad precepts, stated more than a decade ago, but they define the aura that surrounds the present activities of millions of older people who are actively engaged in the business of living.

MAKING THE MOST OF A NEW STAGE OF LIFE

When people died younger, the time between the end of formal work and the end of life was relatively short. If they were lucky and had enough money, they enjoyed a few "golden years of leisure" called retirement. As the life span lengthened, and Social Security or other pensions increased, retirement held promise for greater numbers of people. But it has slowly become apparent that consigning mature adults to a nonproductive life for as long as thirty years or more may not be very satisfactory for the individuals involved or for the society deprived of their rich resource of experience and talent. Endless rounds of golf and bridge can pale into endless hours of boredom. Money can run short. Therefore mature people have begun to carve out new, more satisfying approaches. Their productivity, zest, and flowering have been beacons to others to join them in pioneering new paths for a new stage of life, different from any other in history. Volunteer or paid work, travel, recreation, and other interests pursued at home and in company with others are some of the activities that nourish the mind and sustain the sense of well-being.

NEW CAREERS

A new career certainly makes for an active mature life. Enforced retirement, economic necessity, or just plain boredom may send your parent into a search for a new job opportunity. Breaking in is a tough business at any stage of life and especially tough when the older person bucks up against the business world's preference for young comers who have "new ideas," lots of energy, and command a lower salary. Nevertheless, while the pressure to retire early continues unabated as companies make themselves "meaner and leaner," postretirement job opportunities for older people are in fact expanding in some fields, especially in parttime work.

Some companies, such as Travelers Insurance, are offering part-time work to their own retirees as temps for vacations, busy periods, or when permanent staff become ill. In Florida a corps of retired physicians helps care for the burgeoning elderly population. Elsewhere, retired pharmacists give young ones time with their families by working in the drug store evenings or weekends. Accountants find plenty of work at tax time. One retired but once prominent lawyer does research for his ambitious lawyer son: "He's the only associate in the office with his own law clerk." The fast food industry—which pays minimum wage—has seen merit in older workers' steadiness, graciousness, and greater respect for their uniforms and the customer. Your parent may or may not be interested in dishing out hamburgers, but some may enjoy the liveliness of such a restaurant for a few hours a day or week.

The plumber who opens a nursery because he loves plants, the editor who opens a catering business because he always loved to cook, the housewife who turns realtor, counselor, taxi dispatcher, cashier, or entrepreneur—all are doing something different because they enjoy the new experience and because they want to work. And if your parent goes back to school to earn credentials for a new professional or business career, he or she will no longer feel out of place in class; many other older people will be there too.

Older people need only open their hearts and minds to new dreams and use their old experience to find their ways into new careers. Plenty of groups and organizations stand ready to help them. Organizations like the AARP, OWL, and local colleges and universities sponsor workshops for adults who want to explore new avenues of work. Community organizations also sponsor retraining programs for those who need to brush up on old skills or acquire new ones. The library will have a shelf of books on retirement in which your mother or father may find help deciding on a new field of work and taking the proper steps to make this new venture successful.

Finding a New Job

Many cities and counties have senior employment and counseling services that maintain banks of full- and part-time job openings for older people. The Area Agency on Aging will have information about the Community Senior Service Employment Project for low-income people. The state employment offices throughout the country operate a computerized job bank. Private employment agencies may have opportunities, particularly in department stores and banks. Older salespeople often relate better to other older people, and managers of sales forces understand and appreciate this. Banks have found that older people often make the customer happier: they dress better and are more polite.

Job Fairs are sometimes conducted in regions where employers are looking for good and experienced employees. In Syracuse, New York, for example, the Metropolitan Commission on Aging, with help from an insurance company and Syracuse University, sponsored a job fair where major corporations, small businesses, and nonprofit organizations ran booths at which older people could meet prospective employers in a relaxed atmosphere, find out about training programs for older workers, sharpen their job-seeking and interview skills, and attend workshops on resume writing, coping with stress, job search, and reentering the labor market. There may be similar activities in your parent's community, or your parent might help to organize them.

The law prohibits job discrimination on the basis of age, and activists may be interested in making a case on their own behalf or on behalf of others. The local Area Agency on Aging will help with this.

Starting a New Business

Many couples dream of starting a business together after retirement—a bookshop, a motel, an art gallery, or a restaurant. Many succeed. But there are bound to be problems in entering a new field of activity. Caution commands that thorough investigation precede any capital investment, and risks for older people are more serious if the required investment is taken from their security fund. Investigation of potential partners who paint glowing pictures of quick profits is especially important. Your mother or father may have good business experience and sound judgment and not require these cautions; but many people retiring from long-held professional jobs have not had entrepreneurial experience and do not fully realize the effort, organizational skills, or risks involved.

Careful analyses of the economic climate of a community, the choice of location, the required capital, available credit, likely costs, and potential income are only the beginning of the kind of evaluation that should precede any decision to open a business. Your parent's lawyer and accountant can help with advice about potential problems, as can people who have been in a similar business and know the pitfalls. The Small Business Administration (SBA) in Washington, D.C., and its regional offices have a great deal of useful information available for the asking. Members of the Service Corps of Retired Executives will also provide counsel, answer questions, and may be able to direct your parent to help with financing.

See the Appendix under Retirement.

VOLUNTEER WORK: A TWO-WAY STREET

More volunteers for community and charitable work in this country come from the older population than from any other age group. They bolster paid staffs of hospitals and clinics, senior centers, museums, and schools; they drive the old, the ill, or the handicapped who require transportation; they transcribe books into braille and read to the blind; they visit the homebound and set up and participate in telephone reassurance programs and hot-line counseling; they volunteer their services in schools and day-care centers to add an extra dimension of personal caring for children who are deprived or in trouble. Even older people who live in sheltered residences teach children, such as the residents of Kitay House in the Bronx who once a week meet in their communal rooms with children from a local school to tutor them, hug them, and teach them to read, write, do arithmetic, sew, or paint. One Puerto Rican child said that his mother loved the recipe "my Jewish grandmother taught me to cook."

Retired businesspeople offer guidance on business problems for entrepreneurs starting out, accountants help out in free tax preparation programs, lawyers contribute legal services to poverty law centers or legal service groups, doctors staff free clinics in community health centers, and other professionals through the senior sections of their professional societies find other ways to help. When mature people free of job commitments volunteer their time on a regular and sustained basis, they make an enormous contribution to improving the quality of life for others and enriching their own.

Many corporations are enhancing their retired employees' eagerness to work for their communities by providing them with office space, meeting rooms, and even funding. In Minnesota, Elva Walker, chairman of the Purity Soap Company and an officer of the National Council on Aging, describes Project Vie. This volunteer program in the Twin Cities involves retired employees of seventeen corporations, including Pillsbury, 3M, General Mills, and Control Data, who use their experience to contribute to acknowledged community needs. Technical experts from one corporation worked with the disabled to develop instruments that would help them function. An energy expert helped the local hospital reduce its energy costs. A camera group filmed community projects.

In Cocoa Beach, Florida, older residents come into the hospital as respite workers over the weekend so that hard-pressed family caregivers can have some time to themselves free of their wearing responsibilities.

Jack Ossofsky, president of the National Council on the Aging, describes the Family Friends Program, in which older volunteers work in the homes of severely disabled or chronically ill children. Their presence helps to keep these children out of institutions if the parent is working. They may receive a stipend for their services.

Thousands of Volunteers with Vision across the country are learning to transcribe braille books and articles, which the Library of Congress provides to the blind through its Division for the Blind and Physically Handicapped. The Library of Congress itself teaches braille transcription in a free correspondence course, and many local social clubs and religious groups conduct classes for volunteers. Some volunteers transcribe books printed in small type so that the partially sighted can continue to read. Others with good enunciation and well-pitched voices record books on tape. Musicians can help by transcribing musical notation, by lending a talented voice, or by giving technical advice.

There's almost no service agency of any kind that doesn't need some volunteer help. Politics is a fertile area for interested volunteers—there's no candidate or political club that won't bless the volunteer who comes to campaign headquarters to offer assistance. Groups working on civil liberties, human rights, environmental protection, and other basic issues could not exist without solid phalanxes of volunteers.

The possibilities are limited only by one's interests and talents. Some years ago, a retired 65-year-old, a former bank vice president, came to the office of WGBH, Boston's public television station. He said he was retired and wanted a volunteer job, was there anything he could do at the station? The station management, short of both staff and money, was trying at that moment to mount its annual fund-raising drive and gladly turned the project over to him. He put into place and worked for years at organizing the successful week-long auctions that have become models for public television fundraisers across the country. He worked eleven months of the year, attracting hundreds of auction items, thousands of bidders, and enormous publicity in the large area the station serves.

Many men and women don't want scheduled activity. There are individual activities that work just as well to stimulate the healthy juices of life. In large city apartment houses where so many of the widowed live, and in retirement villages and communities, residents volunteer their services to each other. One helps with income taxes, another with shopping, another keeps the books of the residents' association. The point of it all is to be involved with other people, doing something that provides personal satisfaction and wins someone else's approval.

Many elderly people would be happy to participate as volunteers if only someone would show them the way. If your mother or father is too shy or reluctant to be among the active volunteers in the community, you might be helpful in introducing them to an enthusiastic volunteer.

Government-Sponsored Volunteer Programs

ACTION, a federal government agency, is the overall umbrella for a group of volunteer programs that bring older people in large numbers into community service.

RSVP (Retired Senior Volunteer Program) is perhaps the best known of the government-sponsored programs for older volunteers. Elderly people are recruited to work in federal hospitals, courts, libraries, and day-care centers. They help with the Tax Counseling for the Elderly program. They may work as teaching assistants, tutors, counselors, bookkeepers, or arts and crafts instructors. Some work in local offices on aging.

The Peace Corps still takes older men and women for overseas assignments. Miss Lillian, President Carter's mother, was perhaps the most visible representative of this group and often told of her Peace Corps experiences in India. VISTA (Volunteers in Service to America) is also open to older volunteers, offering assignments in underpriviledged communities within the United States. Under SCORE (Service Corps of Retired Executives), retired business and corporate executives counsel on managerial problems.

Some of the elderly poor have been recruited into the Foster Grandparents and Senior Companion programs. Lured by the prospect of a small stipend to augment their Social Security checks, this corps of volunteers has made dramatic contributions toward meeting the extraordinary needs of millions of children in schools, day-care centers, and hospitals. In New Rochelle, New York, where an especially active Foster Grandparents program flourishes, a drop-in visit quickly shows what a boon this is to the surrogate grandparents as well as to the children. Meeting as a group to be trained for their work, the older people extend their social ties, make new friends, enjoy the expansion of their lives, and demonstrate an esprit de corps hard to find elsewhere in our cynical society. A middle-class grandparent could do the same kind of work without being paid.

In addition to such national programs, there are numerous opportunities within any state or local government agency. A telephone call to the state or Area Office on Aging will provide specific information on current opportunities.

See the Appendix under Volunteers.

CONTINUING EDUCATION

One 70-year-old in Florida enrolled in a doctoral program while his wife took courses in creative writing at a local university. A New York woman started a law career at 60 and worked full-time until she was 72. A chemical engineer went to law school at 50 and became a distinguished partner in a patent attorney's firm. A woman who had worked all her life at factory and clerks' jobs went to college at night after she became a grandmother to get a better job and improve her retirement benefits. The stories are becoming commonplace, but many individuals growing older may still be reluctant to join the academic crowd without some outside encouragement. You may be the one who can open a classroom door for your parent. Research studies have demonstrated that older people without impeding disease and disorders can maintain intellectual and learning ability at a high level.

Many schools and colleges offer a broad menu of courses to older people at little or no tuition. Many universities permit alumni to audit courses at no fee. Some offer home study courses for a fee, using taped lectures and a reading list to stimulate an old grad's interest in a new field of learning. Some offer an alumni college week, after commencement and reunion, to restart the engines of learning. One elderly city couple rents a home in a university town from a vacationing faculty family each summer to enjoy the summer academic program and cultural activities in a relaxed setting. Your parent might inquire from the administration if any faculty members are looking for responsible summer renters or house sitters.

The Institute for Retired Professionals at the New School for Social Research in New York City has become a model for such university programs in other parts of the country. In San Francisco, at Nova University in Florida, and at dozens of other locations, retired professionals teach each other in courses that cover the sciences, the humanities, and the arts.

City and suburban campuses are usually accessible by public transportation, but getting to a class may be a problem in rural or less populated areas. There are probably drivers among these older students, however, and car pools for seniors are as natural as car pools for kids. It's also possible that a local agency or the school itself will provide a bus.

To find out about education prospects, get in touch with

local colleges and universities, the city or county board of education, the state board of higher education, and national associations of higher education.

RECREATION AND ENTERTAINMENT

Whether it occupies all or part of your parent's time, recreation is an essential respite from work, worry, and responsibility. It is at once a channel for using one's energies creatively and for receiving the satisfactions that recharge those energies.

Should you ever visit a residential hotel or home for the aged, you'll be struck by the fact that the residents who seem alert and relatively content are actively engaged in doing something: playing cards, taping an oral history, discussing current events, embroidering or needlepoint, even carpentry or painting. There are others who sit alone, their hands still, their faces vacant. True, they may lack the physical or mental resources for entering into some kind of activity, but perhaps they were never inclined to do anything beyond the requirements of their working or homemaking careers and never learned skills to engage the attention of the others. One middle-aged woman said, "I've never played bridge in my life, but after visiting my mother-in-law in a senior residence, I decided to learn now, as a protection for my old age." Good idea!

Recreation can be a strong link with other human beings, a major source of self-satisfaction and feelings of self-competence. It is both pleasure and necessity to learn how to use leisure time so that it nourishes. Reading and television can fill time for the nongregarious, but in an important sense—and especially for the shy and insecure—these diversions are nonproductive. Developing new interests, improving one's deftness at a game or a craft, joining a movie or theater club or a group at a public library are among the ingredients for continuing intellectual health. Participating in groups assures companionship and the stimulation of new people and new situations that are essential to maintaining emotional good health.

Someone who has always been a joiner will probably continue to be one unless a strong shock—loss of a spouse, a severe illness, deepening money problems—knocks him or her off course. In good time, however, these people can be helped to reestablish old connections. If your parent has always been a loner, antigroup, anti–new experience, you may have a tough time, but don't give up too quickly; use your ingenuity to find the person or group that just might entice your parent out of the house: someone in the apartment building or neighborhood who needs advice or help getting to some recreational activity; someone who needs a companion for a trip to a city museum, a fourth at bridge or to borrow a sewing machine—whatever may spark your parent to do something with other people.

City or county recreation departments, senior centers, religious centers, public schools, and Ys have excellent programs emphasizing arts and crafts, photography, and other skills, which don't require extraordinary talent but still enable the participant to turn out attractive and satisfying results. Church groups and fraternal and professional organizations are other sites where your parent may find outlets for pursuing interests and hobbies with congenial companions.

If your parent doesn't want to expose her or his early learning attempts to public view, private lessons may be an option. Another way to learn in private is by renting or buying videotapes or borrowing them from the library. There are catalogs available showing hundreds of skills demonstrated through this popular medium.

Museums may feature reduced fees or free admission for senior citizens and offer programs of lectures and special events. These are especially interesting for people who never before had the time to learn about and enjoy art, science, history, or anthropology. Many museums also host concerts and movie series.

While rock music may irritate rather than soothe the older

ear, many social dancing classes for older people are conducted with the familiar music of the big band era. One young band leader takes his van of musicians across the country playing "old-style popular music" to sellout crowds of older folks. If your father claims he has two left feet and can't count, but your mother has been longing to join a dance group just for fun, suggest she do exactly that. Your father may change his mind and gain confidence when he sees others perform. And there are always aerobics classes to jazz at the Y or community center.

Entertainment outside the home can sometimes be expensive, but discounts at movies, theaters, sports events, and concerts are becoming routine for people with senior citizen cards, and there may be free concerts and plays. Rehearsals of these are sometimes free and open to the public.

If entertaining at home is costly, a more sedentary version of the old progressive dinner party may work. Each person or couple is responsible for a course, so the cost to the host is minimal. Everybody takes a turn at hosting. What is important is not how much the meal costs but that there is company to share it.

There are endless possibilities for recreation at little or no expense. If your parent(s) need a nudge, put their names on some mailing lists for information about what is happening in their communities, and perhaps they'll take it from there.

TRAVEL

Domestic and foreign travel has become a reality for hundreds of thousands of older people who dreamed of faraway places while they were growing up. Senior travel clubs, recreation vans, and reduced senior fares for bus, rail, and air travel have propelled older people to destinations from Paris to the Khyber Pass. If your parents are not taking advantage of these opportunities, they are surely missing out on one of the great benefits of being an older person with time to travel.

There's no part of the country without accessible resorts,

interesting natural phenomonena, museums, and historical landmarks. If your parents haven't been accustomed to travel, it's much easier to encourage a trip if both are living and not too old, so that they have each other as companions. The widowed or really elderly may be apprehensive about traveling. For them, group travel arrangements take most of the burden away and provide congenial companionship. Your parent can enjoy a day's or weekend's junket arranged under group auspices. Traveling under such circumstances becomes an appealing rather than awesome adventure.

Trailer Travel

House trailers and campers are a relatively inexpensive way to transport and shelter a couple exploring the country. There are good facilities in all regions of the nation for people traveling in this fashion. Older people on limited incomes find it much less expensive than paying for hotels and restaurant meals and a good way to meet congenial company.

The trailer or camper can lead to a variety of recreational experiences. In Florida, for example, it's not unusual to see a land-sea recreation combination: a trailer park next to a waterway, with a trailer for home, a car parked for shopping and chores, and a boat in the water for fishing or cruising. In Maine, an elderly carpenter has converted his pick-up truck into a vacation resort: with foam mattress, battery boat lamps, portable grill, folding chairs, table and other necessities, he takes his wife from camp to camp, to fish, trap lobsters, take photographs, and enjoy the outdoors. In the West, the national parks fill early with everything from modest campers to luxurious traveling homes, as all strata of older people take to the roads.

Traveling with camper or trailer may be easier for two persons than for one because distances can be great and require long hours of driving. But if your parent enjoys driving, he or she may enjoy the variety, flexibility and economy this do-it-yourself kind of travel makes possible. For information consult one of the automobile clubs, the National Park Service, or a state tourist bureau.

Travel Programs

Wherever one travels around the country and around the world these days, older Americans are very much in sight and very obviously enjoying themselves. For a lover of ancient history, the Acropolis is just as compelling at 70 as at 20, and the streets of London just as exciting for a student of English literature.

The adventurous and affluent can plan their own journeys through an individual travel agent or link up with one of the hundreds of package tours offered regularly by domestic and foreign airlines, church, business and professional groups, and college and university alumni associations.

Group tours organized especially for older people and catering to their needs might be more satisfying for some. The national associations of older people organize many varieties of tours geared to a range of budgets and personal tastes. These tours are plotted at the slower pace older people usually prefer to follow, and allow plenty of time for rest and refreshment.

Elderhostel and Saga are organizations exclusively focused on senior travel and educational experiences. Elderhostel combines inexpensive travel with learning. Participants are housed in colleges, universities, convents, or other institutions, and weeklong courses are taught by the host college faculty in settings where participants can also play golf or other sports. Moderate fees cover food, housing, and tuition. The range of possible courses is practically infinite. Sites are at campuses all over this country and overseas. Saga features trips for older people at home and abroad all through the year, for short or longer periods and at a full range of comfort and cost.

If your elderly parent plans to travel, suggest he or she ask the doctor about special precautions, take along an abbreviated medical history or copy of an EKG, wear a tag for allergies, and keep a wallet copy of any special instructions so that physicians in other places can act promptly and appropriately. Check health insurance for coverage away from home. An extra pair of glasses and plenty of hearing aid batteries will avoid unpleasant surprises. It is also wise to take out travel insurance in case paid-for trips have to be canceled or your parent must return home earlier than the group.

See the Appendix under Travel.

ELEVEN

YOUR PARENT AT A CROSSROAD

Life-Changing Events

Profound life events don't happen to an individual alone—they happen to his or her family as well. The chronic or catastrophic illness of a parent carries the family along in the trauma. Agonizing decisions—and guilt—about using or foregoing life-prolonging technologies are shared by spouse, children, and grandchildren. Grief at the death of a parent is a family experience. The aftermath of a parent's retirement or remarriage can spark strong reaction from adult children. Some families cope better than others with these life events. They cope when they have personal resources, access to outside resources if these are needed, and the knowledge that there are no perfect solutions. There are some ways to make these events less painful and less disruptive than they might be. The following is intended to help you and your family through these periods of change.

RETIREMENT: BLESSING OR BLIGHT?

Not so very long ago, a gold watch was a prized possession, an expression of appreciation for years of satisfactory and respected service to a business enterprise or professional career. In its ritualistic way, it marked for the retiree the end of a long, fruitful era. And nobody thought much about what beginning it signaled.

A retirement ceremony today has different overtones. A videotape recorder is more likely to be the gift, or a set of tools, a trip to a far-off place, or a computer—something that symbolizes activity rather than the marking of time. People think about the problems and challenges that lie ahead and have plenty of books and articles written by psychologists and counselors to guide them to a fruitful future. Nevertheless, the retiree who is feted, no matter how well read or organized, often feels that this moment marks the first step toward the end of his or her life.

Retirement or loss of formal work for men is often so profound a life-changing event that it can precipitate depression and even suicide. Women who retire from work appear to make significantly better adjustments than men, perhaps because they are already geared to household activities and can transfer some of their creative energies to them more easily or because they feel relieved finally to have only one, not two jobs, to do. The woman who has worked mainly in the home, however, faces her own brand of woes when the last child leaves home or a married child moves, taking grandchildren far away. This woman too suffers the psychological deprivation that attacks her retired spouse. Even women who have been exhausted by caring for an aged parent or in-law face profound loss when death robs them of this responsibility.

Each spouse has to deal not only with his or her own reactions to a new or difficult period, but with the undercurrents of the other's. Retirement, coupled with other events, can disrupt not only the life of the individual but the relationship of the married couple. Studies of the impact of retirement on families indicate that couples who have previously adapted successfully to their marriage relationship will make a better adaptation to retirement than those who enter the retirement years with unresolved marital conflicts. A smaller income, more time together, fewer outside opportunities for satisfactions, and possible health worries can threaten even a good marriage. Your parent's sense of self-esteem may dwindle. You may hear a sudden upsurge of stories about past glories that signal how little satisfaction your parent is deriving from current activity. One parent may not know how to give the other the support he or she needs. Each will need support.

You should be sensitive to the atmosphere between your parents at this time. Perhaps you can help with suggestions for new work or recreation, shared or separate (see chapter 10). You cannot be a counselor for their problems with each other, but if these problems are temporarily destructive of their relationship, you might want to suggest that they seek professional counseling.

Anything you can do in anticipation of your parent's retirement may soften the transitions. A sampling of resources is listed in the Appendix under Retirement.

Voluntary Retirement

Those who retire voluntarily may believe they are better prepared for it than those who feel they've been pressured to retire. Except among the professions and top executive layers, most working people look forward to the release from work, especially if it has been arduous or not especially stimulating. As people grow older, many want to try something different, and many tired managers say there is no such thing as too much golf. Professional people and the self-employed have almost always chosen the time of their retirement unless poor health dictates an earlier date than they had envisioned. The act of choice gives them a sense of control over their lives that others may envy.

But once the initial glow fades, like other older people, they may miss the chat over the coffee machine, the schedule that tells them where to be, when, and with whom, the network of colleagues with whom they shared so much for so long. The neighbor in the apartment house, the couple in the condo across the lane may not share the same interests and certainly not the same history. Holing up in the woods for blissful solitude may turn sour when it is unrelieved by other activities.

Your parent may be among those who see retirement as a positive, not a negative, state—one that permits a more relaxed pattern of life and new opportunities. "I am becoming hungry for privacy, for the opportunity to savor life at my own gait, and I am choosing, hopefully, to attain a bit of serenity," said an Ohio congressman who chose to retire at 70. "I am the right age and in the right mood to retire, and it's better to retire too soon than too late."[1]

Those who usually adjust well to retirement

- have shown skill previously in handling major problems
- have looked forward to retirement as an opportunity to pursue interests that were out of reach before.
- have made realistic postretirement plans
- have been involved in a number of regular activities, which include some emphasis on helping others
- are flexible and willing to adjust course as the need occurs.

Nevertheless, the hardy and creative are sometimes as shocked by the reality of a suddenly unstructured life as those with fewer resources.

The Shock Absorbers

Large corporations, professional societies, labor unions, and other groups offer planning seminars for employees about to retire. Sometimes these are led by professional counselors, sometimes by retired employees who come to share their personal experiences. All aspects of retirement are explored: psychological problems, housing needs, financial management, the productive use of leisure time, community needs and opportunities for volunteer work, considerations of different or part-time paid employment. In some corporations, spouses are encouraged to join the seminars. Some local hospitals and civic organizations, in cooperation with the local Social Security office, present preretirement seminars. Many colleges and universities schedule periodic retirement workshops, which bring in batteries of psychologists, lawyers, and counselors to help new retirees carve out a new life. Check nearby campuses.

What is always important, no matter what course your parents pursue, is that they enlarge, not tighten, their circle of friends and acquaintances. This circle becomes a network of support. In times of pleasure they enhance each other's lives. In times of crisis they are part of each other's lifeline.

Your Role

Your greatest contribution can be in helping to make possible the kind of life your parents choose. Understand their decisions in terms of their past lives, personalities, and expectations for the retirement years. Perhaps your father has chosen the best move for him—for a time. Perhaps your mother's burst of activity is not too much for her heart condition. Some people remain active in retirement; others prefer to stay inactive for a long time, till they're ready for something else. In each group some are content, and others are unhappy. If your parents seem happy doing what you think is nothing, don't make them feel guilty. If you feel they're doing too much and should relax more, don't nag. Decisions about occupation and recreation after retirement are often subject to change.

Whatever choice your mother or father makes, the primary test is whether it is suitable for your parent, not you. Consider a distinguished filmmaker who says that when he retires he plans to deliver newspapers door to door the way he did as a boy. "It will be so great watching the sun come up. There won't be much traffic. I don't sleep late anymore, anyway. If I miss the toss, I'll be sure to walk the paper to the door. By the time I bicycle back for breakfast, I'll have had my exercise, be all set to sit down, read my own paper, and get ready for the next part of my day. I'll prepare my materials to help the kids in the high school who are making a movie. I'm not sure I'll take the afternoon paper route, because I don't want to tie myself down for both ends of the day, but I will absolutely do the mornings. I can't wait."

If this were your father, would you be ready to accept his decision?

CONFRONTING LIFE AND DEATH DILEMMAS

Barely a week goes by without the media drawing our attention to a lawsuit over whether life support systems should or should not be withdrawn from a patient. The issues are complex and are drawing the growing attention of lawmakers, the courts, religious leaders, philosophers, health care professionals, organizations of concerned individuals, and millions of ordinary people who are not always quite sure how they feel on this subject.

People are living longer than ever. Technology makes it possible to prolong life beyond any previous generation's imagination. Increasing cadres of older people march uncertainly toward the ends of their lives, not wanting to live a life without meaning, not knowing whether their wishes will be honored. How do you feel about this? How do your parents feel? Have you ever discussed this? Would you now?

The U.S. Senate Special Committee on Aging has prepared *A Matter of Choice: Planning Ahead for Health Care Decisions* to "help individuals understand the options available to them . . . to protect their fundamental right of personal autonomy. . . ."[2] The publication is intended for professionals who counsel families but is also useful for those who are concerned about the important process of preparing for physical or mental disability.

An individual's right to accept or forego medical treatment is based on judicial interpretations of the right to privacy. These are exemplified by decisions that state: "Every human being of adult years and sound mind has a right to determine what shall be done with his body and cannot be subjected to medical treatment without his consent"[3] and "The makers of our Constitution . . . conferred, as against the Government, the right to be let alone . . . the most comprehensive of rights and the right most valued by civilized men."[4] This right has since been interpreted to include the right to make decisions about health care and, by extension, the right to have these decisions implemented by others, if necessary. Except for some situations, such as decisions that affect the public health, a mentally competent adult has the right to decide which treatment to accept and which to refuse.

In order for your physician, hospital, and family to carry out your wishes should you become mentally or physically unable to express them, however, you must make these wishes known in advance. This is just as important if you've been in an auto accident and are in a coma as if you are in the last stages of a terminal illness.

A 1982 Harris poll revealed that only about one-third of the population had given instructions concerning how they would like to be treated in the event they were unable to make their own decisions about health care, and only one-quarter had put these instructions in writing. While physicians in this survey indicated they would not resuscitate a patient in the last stage of a painful and terminal illness if the patient had left written instructions in this regard, more recent studies indicate that most doctors do not make a practice of having this kind of discussion with their patients and are therefore unclear about their patients' wishes. Other studies have indicated that physicans often do not follow even written instructions if there is division in the family about what to do. Likewise, if the hospital is not in accord with the practice of disconnecting life support, it will not permit such actions. Whether or not a family can agree to give or deny medical treatment is determined differently in the various states, except in federal institutions.

All this is further complicated if there are questions about the patient's competence at the time he or she refuses medical treatment. Guardians can be appointed by the courts to protect the individual, but this is a time-consuming task if no prior arrangements have been made.

The American Hospital Association, which accredits hospitals, in an effort to remove some of the imponderables from a difficult situation, told hospitals in June 1987 that "it would require them to have formal policies specifying when doctors and nurses may refrain from trying to resuscitate patients who are terminally ill."[5] You should know what these policies are prior to hospitalization, if at all possible.

Two kinds of advanced directives are now recognized as mechanisms for exercising individual rights about making health care decisions. These are living wills and durable powers of attorney (see chapter 6).

How death is determined becomes a worrisome issue for families of people who have decided to donate organs. As a result, the President's Commission for the Study of Ethical Problems in Medicine proposed a model law, The Uniform Determination of Death Act. More than a dozen states have adopted such a law, which permits death to be determined on the basis of brain-related criteria, not just heart and lung function—which can be maintained by machine even when there is no brain function. According to this law, however, "it is still the physician's responsibility to determine whether an individual patient's brain has ceased to function totally and irreversibly." By stating in advance what they wish to be done in these instances, people spare their families having to make difficult decisions at a time of extreme stress.

Making a living will and granting durable powers of attorney for health care decisions are not decisions to be made impulsively. One must think through the possible ramifications of these decisions, including the possibility of changing one's mind. Especially as years pass, one's views may alter in the light of other people's experiences or one's own soul-searching. One person may become more and more convinced that he or she would not wish to live attached to machines; another might not be so sure. So long as one is competent, the option to change one's mind remains. The challenge then is to consider how one would feel about being incompetent or physically unable to express a different opinion and then to state this clearly through these documents.

The Vatican in 1981 said that the use of procedures to effect a "burdensome prolongation of life" was not necessary, and church people of many faiths are among those who support the thesis that it is acceptable to refuse such treatments. But there is also a more troublesome issue—withdrawal of nutrition and hydration from people who say they wish to die. There is a difference, says Msgr. Charles Fahey, director of the

Fordham University Center on Gerontology, between moral and ethical values and legal policy. "Dying is as natural as being born, yet it is seen as an enemy. The notion of 'dying well' is not contradictory. We need to think profoundly about the dying process. . . . The law does not speak to virtue, only to obligations. Do we have an obligation to provide food and water?" That is a question before many courts—and the issue is far from settled.

To help physicians, the American Medical Association has offered guidelines to doctors, recognizing their allegiance to life and their duties under the Hippocratic oath.

To help all people deal with these issues, the Hastings Center has been investigating the varieties of situations in which life and death decisions are made. The project has resulted in guidelines for the termination of treatment that draw on the insights of experts from the whole spectrum of fields involved in this pivotal arena: law, medicine, philosophy, religion, hospital administration, and economics.

Says Dr. Daniel Callahan, director of the Hastings Center, "Families should talk among themselves about what they are prepared to do, and by doing so avoid making decisions under crisis circumstances. They need to use the help available to them to help them think through their decisions." Help is available from the clergy, the legal profession, physicians, and therapists.

See the Appendix under Living and Dying.

COPING STRATEGIES

Coping strategies are the means people use to make themselves feel more comfortable and to enable themselves to function. Not everyone copes in the same way. Following are some of the ways people cope, as described by physician A. D. Weisman in *The Realization of Death:*[6]

- rational/intellectual: seek additional information regarding stressful situation
- shared concern: talk with others about problem

- reversal of affect: laugh it off
- suppression/isolation/passivity: don't worry, close off feelings, wait and see
- displacement: distract yourself with activities
- confrontation: take positive concerted action based on present understanding
- rationalization/redefinition: accept, rise above it, make a virtue out of necessity
- fatalism: accept stoically; prepare to accept the worst
- acting out: do something (ambiguous, impractical, reckless)
- repetition: use strategies used in the past
- tension reduction: eat, smoke, use drugs
- stimulus reduction/avoidance: withdraw socially, get away
- projection: blame others, externalize
- compliance with authority: do what you are told
- masochistic surrender: seek blame, atonement, sacrifice

Some adult children can't deal with the reality of a parent's mortality. They deny to themselves that their parent is seriously ill, is aging, and is going to die, because acknowledging this alters the whole hierarchy of family relationships. These children may cope with the daily problems, but they're looking the other way. "It's nothing," they say to the parent, "You're going to get better." The child may really believe this is true—because he or she wants to believe it.

But the parent who knows he or she has a severe condition may view things differently from the child. Even if the illness is not immediately life-threatening, the parent may believe the situation is catastrophic. It doesn't really help, if your parent holds this view, to make believe all this concern is over "nothing."

Saying "Yes, I know how you feel, it must make you miserable" is better than appearing insensitive to the depth of your parent's emotion. It is not unusual for chronically ill patients themselves to go through a denial phase at first. The process of dealing with a serious chronic illness is, in fact, similar for the patient and the family. A typical but not universal process involves first denial, then realization and acceptance of the unwelcome events, then a kind of mourning for what has been lost.

Finally the patient and the family are ready to cope. If good communications are established between the patient and the doctor, the doctor and the family, and among family members themselves, the stage is set for realistic decisions to be made.

DEATH AND DYING

Your parent may be quiet and accepting as death approaches—may even welcome it. If this is true, it may be easier for you to accept as well. But if your parent is enraged and hostile, that should be understandable to you. The professionals say that dying patients able to express this rage without fear of retribution from a doctor or disapproval from a family come sooner to an emotional acceptance of their fate than those who are encouraged to repress, who subsequently become profoundly depressed and withdrawn. The same is true of families.

Dr. Elisabeth Kübler-Ross, renowned for her work on death and dying, describes five stages of coping with death: denial, anger, bargaining, depression, and finally acceptance. If patients are permitted to proceed through these stages, Kübler-Ross believes, they can make peace with death and die with dignity and beauty. Similarly, a family that goes through them is better able to accept the outcome and then proceed with living.[7]

It is difficult in a death-denying culture to confront death as a natural phenomenon, a common fate. Only recently have efforts been made to teach children in school about the life process and the inevitability of death. Those of us who are older have not had any "death education"; it is only through the efforts of such researchers as Kübler-Ross that we are learning how to confront death instead of avoiding its reality. Many of us were left at home when a grandparent's funeral took place, shushed away from the room where adults cried or grieved. Your doctor or your parent's doctor or nurse or health aide may share the same heritage, so that you may not get as much help from them as you would normally expect from professionals at a time of great stress. Religious families, with help from their clergy, are known to have less traumatic problems with death than those who are skeptics. It has been suggested that rituals surrounding birth and death need to be designed for nonbelievers for the sake of their mental health.

Hospice

The hospice movement was initiated in Great Britain by Dr. Cicely Saunders in her work at St. Christopher's Hospice in London. There, with nursing nuns, Dr. Saunders created a haven for the terminally ill, where families were taught to work through their own fears and patients encouraged to express their feelings as they prepared for death. Together, patients and family approached the impending death with mutual emotional support.

Following Dr. Saunders's lead, Dr. Sylvia Lack opened a hospice in New Haven, Connecticut, a little more than a decade ago, with support from the National Cancer Institute. By 1987, almost 1,600 hospice programs in this country were providing care for terminally ill patients and members of their families.

Hospice is a relatively new Medicare option. In 1987 there were 320 Medicare-certified programs. Some states are making hospice a Medicaid option. Ira Bates, education director of the National Hospice Organization (NHO), reports that 6,000 to 8,000 people a year call asking for information on hospice where they live.

Hospice is not a place; it is a concept. A hospice program is led by an interdisciplinary team consisting of a physician, a registered nurse, social workers, clergy, and occupational and physical therapists. They create an individual plan of care for the patient and counseling for the family, recognizing their social, psychological, emotional, and medical needs.This may be carried out in a hospital, a nursing home, a freestanding hospice, or the patient's own home. Most hospice patients are terminally ill cancer patients within three to six months of death, but any terminally ill patient can take advantage of the program. The program focuses on controlling pain and symptoms for the patient and providing adequate medical care. Hospice honors the individual's right to choose or refuse treatment, including food and water.

Hospice patients have many choices. If they want desperately to experience an event, such as a marriage, a birth, or a graduation, vigorous treatment is pursued to keep the patient alive at all costs; but once the event occurs, the patient can ask to be left alone to die peacefully. Hospice will honor that. Hospice also focuses on creating a network of support around the family before and after death. It deals with the issues of saying goodby and helps families through the transition from before to after death. Families are followed up for one year after the death to identify any pathological grief that may be interfering with normal recovery from their loss. Those in need of further help are referred to a mental health center.

To find out about hospice programs in your area, ask your parent's physician, check the telephone book, or write or call the NHO. The National Consumers League publishes *A Consumer Guide to Hospice Care,* designed to help patients and family decide whether hospice is for them. See Appendix under Hospice.

Burials and Funerals

Families who have never thought about burials and funerals can suddenly find themselves in a totally unanticipated whirlwind if someone unexpectedly dies. Even if they've considered alternatives but never resolved their thoughts into a plan of action, they're likely to have trouble. The most thoughtful elderly people get their paperwork done ahead of time, leaving clear-cut instructions about their preferences. If this is done, the family is spared having to decide whose wishes to follow if there is disagreement among members.

As one psychologist says, "Everybody is in the same boat.

Everyone is going to die. Not being able to discuss your funeral or burial arrangements is really denying you're going to need them."

If discussing this with your parent is painful and difficult, you've got a problem. You'll have to decide such matters as burial versus cremation, religious services or not, whether your generation will insist on a less traditional service or cater to the more traditional preferences of older relatives, whether you honor the wishes of the deceased or the preferences of the living. Can you live with your decision, or will it be a constant source of guilt?

These are very personal problems that require personal solutions. If you have not already done so, now is the time to start thinking about them.

See chapter 3 on the consumer aspects of purchasing funeral and burial services.

Grief

How we deal with death tells a great deal about us—what we've faced and what we've avoided. Death is the ultimate crisis, the continuing mystery. The death of one parent leaves the other in jeopardy. The death of both parents leaves you an orphan. It puts you on the line; you're on your own.

No matter what you've imagined before you've experienced the death of a parent, when it happens it is unique, overwhelming, elemental, and powerful. Everything in you surfaces—the love, the hate, the guilt, what you will miss, what you are free of. If you grieve, so much the better; if you repress your emotion, so much the worse. If you grieve too long, you're in trouble.

There is now a great deal of research on grief, particularly on how it affects the mental health of survivors. Ethnic and religious groups differ in how they grieve and for how long. The Puritans frowned on displays of emotion, and those raised in that tradition have more psychological problems, it appears, than those who are free to express their emotions according to the mores of their group. The Catholics with their wake and the Jews with their shiva generally emerge with fewer psychological scars. Freedom to cry without shame, to show resentment and anger—to express whatever it is one feels—is what liberates us from ceaseless mourning.

Children in mourning for one parent should try to understand the needs and feelings of the remaining parent as well as their own. For example, some children are offended when a widow or widower expresses anger or hostility to the departed parent. They have no insight into the complex relationship that has just ended. A surviving parent, on the other hand, can similarly impose a burden of guilt on a child who expresses anger or resentment about the departed parent. Most relationships are complex, and too often in moments of stress one member of a grieving family may be too harsh in judging the others. With time and understanding, conflicting emotions can be worked through. Unless other events or conditions intervene, you and your surviving parent will ultimately emerge from this period of mourning and grief to resume your lives. That may be easier for you than for your parent.

Elderly people who lose a longtime partner may never really resume their lives. If they have been particularly dependent on each other, even when it has not been a harmonious relationship, the loss is too profound for them to overcome at an advanced age. The survivor may quickly become ill and pass away or become too frail or listless to maintain an independent life. But people with stronger emotional and physical resources, even quite old people, can still find the motivation to pick up and carry on or to seek the help they require to map out a new course for themselves.

Widows and Widowers

Being able to share one's sense of bewilderment and loss is an important part of the healing process for widows and widowers, and this is often accomplished better with other people similarly situated than it is with one's children. For that reason, retirement groups, family service associations, and mental health centers offer workshops, self-help sessions, and personal counseling for people who need a little extra boost to deal with their problems.

One widow who leads a clinic on widowhood calls the initial period of being alone a time of dealing with dilemmas. It may also be a time to start a new way of life, build a new personality, become a new person. "Should I feel guilty about enjoying something my husband hated or found boring—like the ballet? Or should I continue to deprive myself of that pleasure for his memory?" Anger is the probable outcome of that debate, says workshop leader Fannie Bakst. If widowed people don't get rid of these conflicting feelings of anger and guilt, they end up with physical disabilities, which are manifestations of their inner turmoil. Children should not hinder the healthy efforts of an adult parent to achieve a new life appropriate to his or her new state.

Whose advice to take is another dilemma. Is your father being told one thing by you, another by his friends, and still another by his sister? Should he learn how to cook, move into a hotel, go on a cruise, or start looking for a new wife? Denying that anything is different is a way of saying that dealing with the difference is too much to face. Many widows and widowers tend to hang on to familiar patterns, afraid to take the next step. But sooner or later the next step has to be taken.

For women it is harder. Women really do suffer more as widows. The fifth woman at a couples dinner party is a fifth wheel; the fifth man is a social coup. Attitudes on this may be changing, but not fast enough for most widows. Women have a slim chance of remarrying compared to men. And older widows are likely to have fewer coping skills in addition to fewer financial resources. Many never learned to drive, never had advanced education or interests or work outside the family to sustain them. Even if they are financially secure, they may need advice and help from lawyers, banks, and stockbrokers, to manage their affairs prudently. And if they are not, widowhood can become a period of real poverty.

Intimate relationships with children seem to be different also. Fathers tend to interfere less in their children's affairs than mothers. A widower will criticize much less than a widow the way the grandchildren are being brought up or the way a daughter is running the house. Grandpa doesn't "feel slights" as much as Grandma does, is less sensitive to hurts inflicted by unthinking children. Widowed men are less likely to depend on their children for emotional or social sustenance.[8]

The eminent Swedish gerontologist Dr. Alvar Svanborg reports that men are at greater risk than women of dying in the first three lonely months following loss of a spouse. The male risk of dying increases by 48 percent during bereavement, while the increased risk for women is at 22 percent. Dr. Svanborg says it is not just depression and suicide that are involved during this period, but also the "parameters of physiological aging accelerate during bereavement." There are measurable changes in heart, autoimmune, and other vital functions.

If your mother or father is having a hard time, encourage her or him to join a widows and widowers group. Ruth Lowensohn's *Survival Handbook for Widows* can help your mother make a healthy transition and help you see things from her viewpoint.

Children cannot live their parents' lives, but they can help to make them better. They can treat their parents with respect, help them to have access to new opportunties for social activity, soothe some of the aches and pains, help to sustain them in crisis, and not get in their way when they adjust themselves to the new condition.

See the Appendix under Widows.

REMARRIAGE

Families can certainly get stirred up when a parent remarries. Primal jealousies and more mundane problems of money and inheritance can spiral to distasteful levels when a new husband or wife takes up residence in a parental home.

How would you feel if your parent remarried? Matters of money and inheritance can readily be handled through marriage contracts and other arrangements, if people so desire, but can you view your parent as a private individual with needs and desires separate from the relationship with you? If you asked one of your own children to describe you to a stranger, would you be satisfied with the description or would you think, "What do they really know about me and how I feel?"

Children can be severely judgmental about their parents. Just as you wanted your parent to have confidence in your choice of spouse, so should you have confidence in your parent's, unless the choice is obviously absurd or destructive. Even then, you may have to bite your tongue and be silent, as many a parent has been when a child insisted on a disastrous marriage.

Of course old people make mistakes. There's no fool like an old fool, the saying goes, and it is perfectly possible that an aged man will fall victim to a scheming "gold digger." It is equally likely that an elderly woman, starved for companionship and affection, will fall into the arms of a clever con man who can divest her of all her assets. But neither event is the rule.

Adult children do get upset about money—upset for themselves and their children and upset when they think back on the sacrifices the dead parent made to accumulate the nest egg now being enjoyed (squandered?) by a stranger. A thoughtful parent should discuss with his or her children any contemplated financial commitment to a new partner and should make a will that states clearly what portion of the estate will go to the new spouse and what portion to children and grandchildren. Without such an arrangement made in advance, it is important to remember that state laws give spousal rights to married couples, and the new spouse will be entitled at least to the legal portion if there is a contest. A friendly question from you is not out of order to determine that what your parent really intends has been legally secured.

In many families, the remarriage of a parent is a warm and welcomed event. Adult children accept that the parent is an independent adult who is lucky enough to have found affection and companionship from another person. Or, more selfishly, children may be happy that the new spouse will relieve them of the burden of thinking about their parent's life or feeling guilty when they don't. They may or may not have a good relationship with the new spouse, but at least their love for their own parent dominates the situation and softens any hostile feelings toward the stepparent that may emerge from time to time. Problems arise when all the relationships are in disarray. Then petty problems become major problems. Major problems cause total rifts. If you are having trouble accepting a stepparent who is honorable and decent, kind and loving to your parent, then perhaps you are the one who needs help. You should seek it before you attribute venal motives to a person who is adding a new and positive dimension to your parent's life.

Less easy for adult children to accept, even in these days of high divorce rates, are the events that cause one parent to divorce the other in order to remarry. Even understanding adult children are uneasy in the face of a parent's marital problems, uncomfortable with the implications of a new late-life passion, with acts of disloyalty, with the problems of the rejected spouse. More often than not, it is the mother who has been left for a new love and it is the mother who has fewer options for remaking her life. Even when the new stepparent turns out to be a person with whom the adult child can spend enjoyable time, rarely is that time entirely free of past images of a different family. And on major family occasions—births, graduations, marriages, even funerals—each encounter of old and new family reopens old wounds. Adult children are torn between father and mother, hoping against hope that no overt confrontation or sullen or tearful behavior will intrude on the event. To avoid such confrontations, children are sometimes asked to bar the offending parent. That is an unfair task to impose on a child with deep links to each parent. Friendly repairings of older people do occur, but they are not the majority.

Remarriage, unfortunately, runs the risk of being of short duration, and the prospect of providing nursing care for a relatively new partner sometimes give people pause before they undertake such commitments, or induce strain when they do. You have heard older women say "I've buried three husbands" or older men say "I have no luck with wives. They die." But many are willing to try again; someone is better than no one.

Many older people are living together these days without benefit of formal marriage. Some prefer a "relationship" that permits each to maintain an independent household where they can retreat for time alone without the emotional flak such needs sometimes cause in formal marriages. Many prefer to avoid the financial complications late marriages can create. Or they may be afraid they will tire of one another or have trouble adjusting to a new relationship. They are saving themselves the trouble and expense of divorce. They may be saving you trouble as well.

GRANDPARENTS' RIGHTS

Grandparents do not have an automatic right to visit or be visited by their grandchildren should the parents of the children separate, divorce, die, remarry, or in some way lose custody of the children. This usually comes as a shock to the people involved. Following death, divorce, or remarriage the taken-for-granted visits often become rights or privileges to be bestowed or denied by a parent in custody, a new mother or father by adoption, or by the courts if it comes to that.

All fifty states have now enacted statutes to protect the rights of grandparents in visitation. These statutes are based on the best interest of the child and are not automatic passports to a continuing relationship with a grandchild. Each time there is a contest that cannot be resolved by family agreement, it is up to the courts to decide whether you can deprive a grandparent of being with the child in question.

Doris Jonas Freed, an eminent scholar and legal practitioner who has specialized in family law and grandparent's rights, notes that the courts generally recognize that animosity between parent(s) and grandparents is not reason enough to interfere with grandparents who ask for access to the child if this leads to betterment of the child. Furthermore, many states recognize that remarriage of the parent and adoption by the stepparent does not interfere with natural grandparents' rights to see the child.

In the mid-seventies a New Jersey judge reflected: "Visits with a grandparent are often a precious part of a child's experience, and there are benefits which devolve upon the grandchild which he cannot derive from any other relationship. Neither the legislature nor this court is blind to human truths which grandparents and grandchildren have always known."[9]

No matter which generation you are and what role you play, if visiting a child becomes a divisive issue in your family, it is wise to seek help and counsel as soon as possible and to look deep into your own behavior as well as that of the adult you are opposing. Make every effort to have someone all respect —perhaps a member of the clergy, a family service worker, or a trusted friend—help to mediate your differences. Try to resolve your adult differences for the real benefit of the child. Resort to the law and the courts as a last resort, but do it if it is in the interest of the child. One of the grandparents' organizations can provide information and counsel (see Appendix).

TWELVE

DOING THE BEST YOU CAN

Human felicity is produced not so much by great pieces of good fortune that seldom happen, as by little advantages that occur every day.

—Ben Franklin, *Autobiography*

This book has been written to help you help your parents as they grow older. You may, in this period of your lives, achieve a rich new relationship in which past contests are quieted and your time together is appreciated as a special gift. During this stage of life many things change. This book should alert you to the important aspects of these changes and help you to plan better for their consequences, to reduce the stress and ease the difficulties. Over time the felicitous moments may be fewer, but not necessarily. They can come even in times of great trouble, as you gain a different perspective on what is a "little advantage." You and your parent share a unique family history; your choices and decisions will grow out of that history and how much you know about your alternatives. This book is intended to help you reinforce the positive factors in your aging parents' lives, to broaden their opportunities for reward and satisfaction, as well as to help you in times of trouble. If you focus only on the problems, you will deprive yourself and them of those rich relationships that many in your position are enjoying. Each of you is concerned about control over your own lives. At each step along the way from independence to dependence, parents and children alike are called upon to be reasonable and fair. Not all can achieve that happy balance when choices are clear. It is all the more difficult when they are not. It is not always clear whose needs are most pressing or whose, by right, come first. How we resolve our inner conflicts over competing demands, how we satisfy our own aspirations and needs, and how we define our responsibilities to ourselves and others are lifelong processes, and there are no pat prescriptions.

What is clear is that the problems of your parents' old age are not your fault. You cannot keep them from becoming ill. You cannot keep them from dying. You can stretch and extend yourself in times of crisis. You can provide information, explore community resources, find assistance, and help your parents lead independent lives as long as possible. You should not shun the help that is available from the outside because of pride. Rather you should enlist as many others as possible to share what must be done. You may have to do more yourself than you would prefer. You may, for a time, sacrifice a great deal for yourself, and do so without hard feelings toward others. Talking and planning together with all the concerned family members will soften many sharp edges, but unresolved conflicts at critical points can damage goodwill for longer than your parent's lifetime. If bad feelings undermine what must be done for your parent's care, or threaten your own important relationships, experienced counselors can help. While the focus of immediate concern may be your parents' welfare, you must balance their needs against the legitimate needs of others, including yourself.

There are times when you must say no to your parent rather than no to your spouse or children or to yourself. Your parent may be unhappy with your choices; only you can decide how strongly your parent's feelings will determine how you live your life, how you will balance their needs against others', their perceptions against your own. If you are the caring child of a caring parent, your parent may make fewer demands on you than you do on yourself. If you have done all that is reasonable, all that is possible within the circumstances of your own life and your parent's, that is all anyone can ask. You will have done the best you can.

PLANNING AHEAD

As you progress through the passages of your parent's later years, certain parallels to your own life may emerge which you should not dismiss. You are living in a time of great new knowledge, some of which may be too late to affect your mother's or father's life dramatically but which may make a big difference in yours. Some people are so traumatized by the events of their parents' lives that as soon as their immediate responsibility ends, they want not to think about it again for a long, long time. Others become obsessed with the tragedies they have seen and cheat themselves of the pleasures of their healthy years by worrying constantly about their own old age. Neither is a productive route.

You can use the experience of these years to plan better for your own later years. Keep a diary as you proceed, and note what is important to you, what plans you can make at whatever age you are now to fulfill your hopes for your own later years, to protect yourself financially and emotionally for what may come, and to enjoy the new opportunities. Know, from your own experience, what you will probably be able to count on, and know what you have learned is a chimera. When you buy your house, lease your apartment, take out a mortgage, make out your will, neglect or care for your own health, think about what this means for ten or twenty years from now. Make a plan for what you want, but don't just put it in a drawer. Review it every few years, and see what holds and what must be changed. Do not underestimate the length of your life. It may be longer than you think.

APPENDIX A: RIGHTS OF HOSPITAL PATIENTS, NURSING HOME RESIDENTS, AND HOME CARE RECIPIENTS

Most state departments of health publish bills of rights for patients in hospitals and nursing homes, and you can obtain copies from your own state health department. Federal law requires Medicare- and Medicaid-certified nursing homes and home health agencies to grant nursing home residents and those receiving care at home extensive individual rights. You and your parents should be familiar with these rights. In general, they follow those printed here.

A PATIENT'S BILL OF RIGHTS*

The American Hospital Association presents a Patient's Bill of Rights with the expectation that observance of these rights will contribute to more effective patient care and greater satisfaction for the patient, his physician, and the hospital organization. Further, the Association presents these rights in the expectation that they will be supported by the hospital on behalf of its patients, as an integral part of the healing process. It is recognized that a personal relationship between the physician and the patient is essential for the provision of proper medical care. The traditional physician-patient relationship takes on a new dimension when care is rendered within an organizational structure. Legal precedent has established that the institution itself also has a responsibility to the patient. It is in recognition of these factors that these rights are affirmed.

* Reprinted with permission of the American Hospital Association, copyright 1972.

1. The patient has the right to considerate and respectful care.

2. The patient has the right to obtain from his physician complete current information concerning his diagnosis, treatment, and prognosis in terms the patient can be reasonably expected to understand. When it is not medically advisable to give such information to the patient, the information should be made available to an appropriate person in his behalf. He has the right to know, by name, the physician responsible for coordinating his care.

3. The patient has the right to receive from his physician information necessary to give informed consent prior to the start of any procedure and/or treatment. Except in emergencies, such information for informed consent should include but not necessarily be limited to the specific procedure and/or treatment, the medically significant risks involved, and the probable duration of incapacitation. Where medically significant alternatives for care or treatment exist, or when the patient requests information concerning medical alternatives, the patient has the right to such information. The patient also has the right to know the name of the person responsible for the procedures and/or treatment.

4. The patient has the right to refuse treatment to the extent permitted by law and to be informed of the medical consequences of his action.

5. The patient has the right to every consideration of his privacy concerning his own medical care program. Case discussion, consultation, examination, and treatment are confidential and should be conducted discreetly. Those not directly involved in his care must have the permission of the patient to be present.

6. The patient has the right to expect that all communications and records pertaining to his care should be treated as confidential.

7. The patient has the right to expect that within its capacity a hospital must make reasonable response to the request of a patient for services. The hospital must provide evaluation, service, and/or referral as indicated by the urgency of the case. When medically permissible, a patient may be transferred to another facility only after he has received complete information and explanation concerning the needs for and alternatives to such a transfer. The institution to which the patient is to be transferred must first have accepted the patient for transfer.

8. The patient has the right to obtain information as to any relationship of his hospital to other health care and educational insti-

tutions insofar as his care is concerned. The patient has the right to obtain information as to the existence of any professional relationships among individuals, by name, who are treating him.

9. The patient has the right to be advised if the hospital proposes to engage in or perform human experimentation affecting his care or treatment. The patient has the right to refuse to participate in such research projects.

10. The patient has the right to expect reasonable continuity of care. He has the right to know in advance what appointment times and physicians are available and where. The patient has the right to expect that the hospital will provide a mechanism whereby he is informed by his physician or a delegate of the physician of the patient's continuing health care requirements following discharge.

11. The patient has the right to examine and receive an explanation of his bill regardless of source of payment.

12. The patient has the right to know what hospital rules and regulations apply to his conduct as a patient.

No catalog of rights can guarantee for the patient the kind of treatment he has a right to expect. A hospital has many functions to perform, including the prevention and treatment of disease, the education of both health professionals and patients, and the conduct of clinical research. All these activities must be conducted with an overriding concern for the patient, and, above all, the recognition of his dignity as a human being. Success in achieving this recognition assures success in the defense of the rights of the patient.

NURSING HOME RESIDENT'S BILL OF RIGHTS*

Preamble

The dignity of the individual is never more important—and never more at risk—than in old age. With its traditional concern for the older person, the American Association of Homes for the Aging believes the elderly are entitled not only to high standards of social and physical care, but to the exercise of inherent human rights that contribute to individual dignity.

To emphasize this belief, the association recommends this Bill of Rights for residents in homes for the aging in the hope that it will

* February 1987 revision reprinted with permission of the American Association of Homes for the Aging.

contribute to their physical and mental well-being, personal growth, and the reaffirmation of their humanity.

The rights of a resident fall into several categories. In each, however, the older person retains one overriding claim—his or her right to be treated in all respects as an intelligent and sensitive human being. The older person has the right to religious and civil liberties and the widest possible freedom of choice, consistent with the standards, rights and obligations of the provider of care.

Personal Rights

The resident has the right to courteous and equal consideration from all with whom he or she comes in contact.

The resident has the right to choose among the various options for personal privileges provided by the facility. He or she also has the right to expect that the means for enhancing personal needs will be made available.

The resident has the right to privacy and to confidential communication by mail and telephone.

The resident has the right to keep a reasonable number of personal mementos.

The resident has the right to explore the limits of his or her potential growth, in terms of interpersonal relationships, opportunities for service in the community, and opportunities to revitalize old skills or develop new ones and channel them into creative current uses. He or she has the right to expect that physical, psychological, and spiritual counsel will be available to help achieve this growth.

The resident has the right to have his or her suggestions considered by staff and administrators through means such as a residents' council and has the right to present grievances without fear of reprisal.

The resident has the right to manage his or her own finances.

The resident has the right to the same dignity in dying as in living.

Environmental Rights

The resident has the right to safe physical accommodations and environment. Wherever reasonable, this should include aesthetically tasteful surroundings in addition to the basic amenities. Areas for socialization and for entertaining family and friends should be provided.

The resident has the right to physical security. This includes adequate protection against natural disasters such as fire and storm, and the right to secure storage space for personal belongings.

Health Rights

The resident has the right to health care, including full information regarding his or her medical condition, diagnosis and treatment (unless medically contraindicated); prompt care by qualified and competent personnel; privacy during care and confidentiality of all medical records consistent with adequate treatment; and the right to retain a personal private physician for consultation with staff doctors.

The resident has the right to be free of physical or chemical restraint, except when medically authorized.

The resident has the right to give or withhold informed consent for nonemergency treatment after the implications of that choice have been explained.

HOME CARE PATIENT'S BILL OF RIGHTS*

As a consumer you have the right:

- to receive considerate and respectful care in your home at all times;
- to participate in the development of your plan of care, including an explanation of any services proposed, and of alternative services that may be available in the community;
- to receive complete and written information on your plan of care including the name of the supervisor responsible for your services;
- to refuse medical treatment or other services provided by law and to be informed of the possible results of your actions;
- to privacy and confidentiality about your health, social and financial circumstances *and* what takes place in your home;
- to know that all communications and records will be treated confidentially;
- to expect that all home care personnel within the limits set by the plan of care will respond in good faith to your requests for assistance in the home;

* Reprinted with permission of the National HomeCaring Council Division of the Foundation for Hospice and Homecare and the Council of Better Business Bureaus, Inc., from *All About Home Care: A Consumer's Guide*, 2nd ed. (New York: National HomeCaring Council; Arlington, Va.: Council of Better Business Bureaus, 1983), 25.

- to receive information on an agency's policies and procedures including information on costs, qualifications of personnel and supervision;
- to home care as long as needed and available;
- to examine all bills for service regardless of whether they are paid for out-of-pocket or through other sources of payment;
- to receive nursing supervision of the paraprofessional if medically related personal care is needed.

APPENDIX B: RESOURCES

GOVERNMENT AGENCIES

(Consult local telephone books for Social Security, Medicare, IRS.)

Federal

Administration on Aging, 200 Independence Avenue, S.W., Washington, D.C. 20201; (202) 245-0742.

House Select Committee on Aging, 712 House Office Building Annex No.1, Washington, D.C. 20515; (202) 226-3375.

Senate Special Committee on Aging, Room G-33, Dirksen Senate Office building, Washington, D.C. 20510; (202) 224-5364.

State

For assistance in finding local Area Agencies on Aging:

Alabama
Commission on Aging, State Capitol, Montgomery, Alabama 36130; (205) 261-5743.

Alaska
Older Alaskans Commission, Department of Administration Pouch, C-Mail Station 0209, Juneau, Alaska 99811; (907) 465-3250.

American Samoa
Territorial Administration on Aging, Office of the Governor, Pago Pago, American Samoa 96799; 011 (684) 633-1252.

Arizona
Aging and Adult Administration, Department of Economic Security, 1400 West Washington Street, Phoenix, Arizona 85007; (602) 255-4446.

Arkansas
Office of Aging and Adult Services, Department of Social and Rehabilitative Services, Donaghey Building, Suite 1428, 7th and Main Streets, Little Rock, Arkansas 72201; (501) 371-2441.

California
Department of Aging, 1020 19th Street, Sacramento, California 95814; (916) 322-5290.

Colorado
Aging and Adult Services Division, Department of Social Services, 717 17th Street, P.O. Box 181000, Denver, Colorado 80218-0899; (303) 294-5913.

Connecticut
Department on Aging, 175 Main Street, Hartford, Connecticut 06106; (203) 566-3238.

Delaware
Division on Aging, Department of Health and Social Services, 1901 North DuPont Highway, New Castle, Delaware 19720; (302) 421-6791.

District of Columbia
Office on Aging, 1424 K Street, N.W., 2nd Floor, Washington, D.C. 20011; (202) 724-5626.

Florida
Program Office of Aging and Adult Services, Department of Health and Rehabilitation Services, 1317 Winewood Boulevard, Tallahassee, Florida 32301; (904) 488-8922.

Georgia
Office of Aging, 878 Peachtree Street, N.E., Room 632, Atlanta, Georgia 30309; (404) 894-5333.

Guam
Public Health and Social Services, Government of Guam, Agana, Guam 96910; 749-9901, ext. 423.

Hawaii
Executive Office on Aging, Office of the Governor, 335 Merchant Street, Room 241, Honolulu, Hawaii 96813; (808) 548-2593.

Idaho
Office on Aging, Statehouse Room 114, Boise, Idaho 83720; (208) 334-3833.

Illinois
Department on Aging, 421 East Capitol Avenue, Springfield, Illinois 62701; (217) 785-2870.

Indiana
Department of Aging and Community Services, 251 North Illinois Street, P.O. Box 7083, Indianapolis, Indiana 46207-7083; (317) 232-7006.

Iowa
Department of Elder Affairs, Jewett Building, Suite 236, 914 Grand Avenue, Des Moines, Iowa 50319; (515) 281-5187.

Kansas
Department on Aging, 610 West Tenth, Topeka, Kansas 66612; (913) 296-4986.

Kentucky
Division for Aging Services, Department of Human Resources, DHR Building, 6th Floor, 275 East Main Street, Frankfort, Kentucky 40601; (502) 564-6930.

Louisiana
Office of Elderly Affairs, P.O. Box 80374, Baton Rouge, Louisiana 70898; (504) 925-1700.

Maine
Bureau of Maine's Elderly, Department of Human Services, State House, Station No. 11, Augusta, Maine 04333; (207) 289-2561.

Maryland
Office on Aging, State Office Building, Room 1004, 301 West Preston Street, Baltimore, Maryland 21201; (301) 225-1100.

Massachusetts
Department of Elder Affairs, 38 Chauncy Street, Boston, Massachusetts 02111; (617) 727-7750.

Michigan
Office of Services to the Aging, P.O. Box 30026, Lansing, Michigan 48909; (517) 373-8230.

Minnesota
Board on Aging, Metro Square Building, Room 204, 7th and Robert Streets, St. Paul, Minnesota 55101; (612) 296-2544.

Mississippi
Council on Aging, 301 West Pearl Street, Jackson, Mississippi 39203-3092; (601) 949-2070.

Missouri
Division on Aging, Department of Social Services, 505 Missouri Boulevard, P.O. Box 1337, Jefferson City, Missouri 65102; (314) 751-3082.

Montana
Community Services Division, P.O. Box 4210, Helena, Montana 59604; (406) 444-3865.

Nebraska
Department on Aging, 301 Centennial Mall–South, P.O. Box 95044, Lincoln, Nebraska 68509; (402) 471-2306.

Nevada
Division on Aging, Department of Human Resources, Kinkead Building, Room 101, 505 East King Street, Carson City, Nevada 89710; (702) 885-4210.

New Hampshire
Council on Aging, 105 Loudon Road, Building No. 3, Concord, New Hampshire 03301; (603) 271-2751

New Jersey
Division on Aging, Department of Community Affairs, 363 West State Street, P.O. Box 2768, Trenton, New Jersey 08625; (609) 292-4833.

New Mexico
State Agency on Aging, 224 East Palace Avenue, 4th Floor, La Villa Rivera Building, Santa Fe, New Mexico 87501; (505) 827-7640.

New York
Office for the Aging, New York State Plaza, Agency Building No. 2, Albany, New York 12223; (518) 474-4425.

North Carolina
Division on Aging, Kirby Building, 1985 Umpstead Drive, Raleigh, North Carolina 27603; (919) 733-3983.

North Dakota
Aging Services, Department of Human Services, State Capitol Building, Bismarck, North Dakota 58505; (701) 224-2577.

Northern Mariana Islands
Office of Aging, Department of Community and Cultural Affairs, Civic Center–Susupe, Saipan, Northern Mariana Islands 96950.

Ohio
Department on Aging, 50 West Broad Street–9th Floor, Columbus, Ohio 43215; (614) 466-5500.

Oklahoma
Special Unit on Aging, Department of Human Services, P.O. Box 25352, Oklahoma City, Oklahoma 73125; (405) 521-2281.

Oregon
Senior Services Division, 313 Public Service Building, Salem, Oregon 97310; (503) 378-4728.

Pennsylvania
Department of Aging, 231 State Street, Harrisburg, Pennsylvania 17101-1195; (717) 783-1550.

Puerto Rico
Gericulture Commission, Department of Social Services, P.O. Box 11398, Santurce, Puerto Rico 00910; (809) 721-3141 or 722-0225.

Rhode Island
Department of Elderly Affairs, 79 Washington Street, Providence, Rhode Island 02903; (401) 277-2858.

South Carolina
Commission on Aging, 915 Main Street, Columbia, South Carolina 29201; (803) 758-2576.

South Dakota
Office of Adult Services and Aging, Kneip Building, 700 North Illinois Street, Pierre, South Dakota 57501; (605) 773-3656.

Tennessee
Commission on Aging, 715 Tenessee Building, 535 Church Street, Nashville, Tennessee 37219; (615) 741-2056.

Texas
Department on Aging, 1949 IH 35–South, P.O. Box 12786 Capitol Station, Austin, Texas 78741-3702; (512) 444-2727.

Trust Territory of the Pacific Islands
Office of Elderly Programs, Community Development Division, Government of TTPI, Saipan, Mariana Islands 96950.

Utah
Division of Aging and Adult Services, Department of Social Services, 150 West North Temple, Box 45500, Salt Lake City, Utah 84145-0500; (801) 533-6422.

Vermont
Office on Aging, 103 South Main Street, Waterbury, Vermont 05676; (802) 241-2400.

Virgin Islands
Commission on Aging, 6F Havensight Mall–Charlotte Amalie, St. Thomas, Virgin Islands 00801; (809) 774-5884.

Virginia
Department on Aging, James Monroe Building, 18th Floor, 101 North 14th Street, Richmond, Virginia 23219; (804) 225-2271.

Washington
Aging and Adult Services, Department of Social and Health Services, OB-43G, Olympia, Washington 98504; (206) 753-2502.

West Virginia
Commission on Aging, Holly Grove–State Capitol, Charleston, West Virginia 25305; (304) 348-3317.

Wisconsin
Bureau of Aging, Division of Community Services, One West Wilson Street–Room 480, Madison, Wisconsin 53702; (608) 266-2536.

Wyoming
Commission on Aging, Hathaway Building–Room 139, Cheyenne, Wyoming 82002-7010; (307) 777-7986.

Also:

National Association of Area Agencies on Aging, 600 Maryland Avenue, S.W., Suite 208, Washington, D.C. 20024; (202) 484-7520.

National Association of State Units on Aging, 800 Maryland Avenue, S.W., Washington, D.C. 20024; (202) 785-0707.

DENOMINATIONAL SOCIAL WELFARE AGENCIES

Check local telephone book listings for organizations, such as Catholic Charities; Jewish Family or Community Service or Services to the Aging; Protestant, Lutheran, or other welfare agency; and Family, Community, or Aging Services.

NATIONAL HELPING ORGANIZATIONS

(Write or telephone to find nearest local agency and for general information and pamphlets.)

American Red Cross, 17th and D streets, N.W., Washington, D.C. 20006; (202) 737-8300.

Corporate Angel Network, Westchester County Airport, New York 10604; (914) 328-1313. Free air transportation to treatment centers for selected cancer patients.

Family Service America, 11700 West Lake Park Drive, Milwaukee, Wisconsin 53224; (414) 359-2111.

National Association of Private Geriatric Case Managers, Box 6920, Yorkville Station, New York, New York 10128; (212) 831-5582 (office), (212) 831-5101 (messages).

National Association of Social Workers, 7981 Eastern Avenue, Silver Spring, Maryland 21910; (301) 565-0333.

Salvation Army in the USA, 799 Bloomfield Avenue, Verona, New Jersey 07044; (201) 239-0606.

Volunteers of America, 340 West 85th Street, New York, New York 10024; (212) 873-2600.

NATIONAL ORGANIZATIONS OF AND FOR OLDER PEOPLE

American Association of Retired Persons, 1909 K Street, N.W., Washington, D.C. 20049; (202) 872-4700.

American Society on Aging, 833 Market Street, Suite 516, San Francisco, California 94103; (415) 543-2617.

Asociación Nacional Pro Personas Mayores (National Association for Hispanic Elderly), 1730 West Olympic Boulevard, Suite 401, Los Angeles, California 90015; (213) 487-1922.

Gray Panthers, 311 South Juniper Street, Philadelphia, Pennsylvania 19107; (215) 545-6555.

National Association of Mature People (NAMP), 2212 N.W. 50th Street, P.O. Box 26792, Oklahoma City, Oklahoma 73126; (405) 848-1832.

National Association of Retired Federal Employees, 1533 New Hampshire Avenue, N.W., Washington, D.C. 20036; (202) 234-0832.

National Association for Spanish-Speaking Elderly, 1412 K Street, N.W., Washington, D.C. 20005; (202) 393-2206.

National Caucus and Center on Black Aged, 1424 K Street, N.W., Suite 500, Washington, D.C. 20005; (202) 637-8400.

National Council of Senior Citizens, 925 15th Street, N.W., Washington, D.C. 20005; (202) 347-8800.

The National Council on the Aging, 600 Maryland Avenue, S.W., West Wing 100, Washington, D.C. 20024; (202) 479-1200.

National Indian Council on Aging, P.O. Box 2088, Albuquerque, New Mexico 87103; (505) 766-2276.

National Interfaith Coalition on Aging, 298 South Hull Street, P.O. Box 1924, Athens, Georgia 30603; (404) 353-1331.

National Pacific/Asian Resource Center on Aging, 1341 G Street, N.W., Suite 311, Washington, D.C. 20009; (202) 393-7838.

Older Women's League, Suite 300, 730 Eleventh Street, N.W., Washington, D.C. 20001; (202) 783-6686.

NATIONAL HEALTH ORGANIZATIONS

(Write or telephone for information on health matters and for the addresses and telephone numbers of local chapters and affiliates.)

American Academy of Ophthalmology, P.O. Box 7424, San Francisco, California 94120-7424.

American Cancer Society, 261 Madison Avenue, New York, New York 10016; (212) 599-3600. Moving to Atlanta, Georgia, in late 1988. Check information operator for correct telephone number.

American Dental Association, 211 East Chicago Avenue, Chicago, Illinois 60611; (312) 440-2500.

American Diabetes Association, 2 Park Avenue, New York, New York 10016; (212) 683-7444.

Diabetes Information Center, 1660 Duke Street, Alexandria, Virginia 22314; (800) ADA-DISC or (800) 232-3472.

American Dietetic Association, 430 North Michigan Avenue, Chicago, Illinois 60611; (312) 899-0040.

American Foundation for the Blind, 15 West 16th Street, New York, New York 10011; (212) 620-2000.

American Heart Association, 7320 Greenville Avenue, Dallas, Texas 75231; (214) 750-5300.

American Hospital Association, 840 North Lake Shore Drive, Chicago, Illinois 60611; (312) 280-6000.

American Lung Association, 1740 Broadway, New York, New York 10019; (212) 245-8000.

American Medical Association, 535 North Dearborn Street, Chicago, Illinois 60610; (312) 751-6426.

American Optometric Association, Communications Division, 243 North Lindbergh Boulevard, St. Louis, Missouri 63141; (314) 991-4100.

American Podiatric Medical Association, 20 Chevy Chase Circle, N.W., Washington, D.C. 20015; (202) 537-4900.

American Society for Geriatric Dentistry, 271-11 76th Avenue, New Hyde Park, New York 11040; (212) 343-2100, ext. 260. Inquire here for information on special dental requirements of Alzheimer's patients.

Association of Sleep Disorder Centers, 604 2nd Street, S.W., Rochester, Minnesota 55902; (507) 287-6006.

American Speech-Language-Hearing Association, 10801 Rockville Pike, Rockville, Maryland 20852; (301) 897-5700.

Blue Cross–Blue Shield Association, 676 North St. Clair Street, Chicago, Illinois 60611. For general information telephone in the East: (914) 683-5800; in the West: (312) 440-5798.

Medic Alert, Turlock, California 95381; (800) 344-3226. For bracelets with personal medical information. Also, this organization will make your medical data available for emergency help.

National Arthritis Foundation, 1314 Spring Street, N.W., Atlanta, Georgia 30309; (404) 872-1000.

National Association for Ambulatory Care, 5151 Beltline Road, Suite 1017, Dallas, Texas 75240; (214) 788-2456.

National Association of Rehabilitation Agencies, 1700 K Street, N.W., Washington, D.C. 20009; (202) 842-0440.

National Association of the Deaf, 814 Thayer Avenue, Silver Spring, Maryland 20910; (301) 587-1788.

National Easter Seal Society, 1350 New York Avenue, N.W., Suite 415, Washington, D.C. 20005; (202) 347-3066.

National Health Information Clearinghouse, (800) 336-4797.

National Information Center on Deafness (NICD), Gallaudet College, 7th and Florida Avenue, N.E., Washington, D.C. 20002; voice: (202)

651-5109; TDD: (202) 651-5976. A full resource for information, devices, education, training, law, and technology. Referrals.

National Institutes of Health, 9000 Rockville Pike, Bethesda, Maryland 20014; (301) 496-2433.

National Institute on Aging: (301) 486-9265.

National Cancer Institute: (301) 496-5651. Cancer Information Service: (800) 4-CANCER. See resources for Cancer for additional telephone numbers.

National Eye Institute: (301) 496-2234.

National Heart, Lung and Blood Institute: (301) 496-4236.

National Institute of Arthritis, Diabetes, Digestive and Kidney Disease: (301) 496-5887.

National Institute of Neurological and Communicative Disorders and Stroke: (301) 496-3167.

National Kidney Foundation, 2 Park Avenue, New York, New York 10016; (212) 889-2210.

National League for Nursing, 10 Columbus Circle, New York, New York 10019; (212) 582-1022. Includes regional Visiting Nurse associations.

National Mental Health Association, 1021 Prince Street, Arlington, Virginia 22314; (703) 684-7722.

National Rehabilitation Information Center, (800) 34-NARIC or (202) 635-5826 from 9 to 5 EST, Monday through Friday.

National Society to Prevent Blindness, 500 East Remington Road, Schaumburg, Illinois 60173-4557; (312) 843-2020.

Parkinson's Disease Foundation, 640-650 West 168th Street, New York, New York 10032; (212) 923-4700 or (800) 457-6676.

Stanford Sleep Disorder Center, 701 Welch Road, Suite 2226, Palo Alto, California 94304; (415) 723-8131.

United Parkinson Foundation, 360 West Superior Street, Chicago, Illinois 60610; (312) 664-2344.

NATIONAL MENTAL HEALTH ORGANIZATIONS

American Association for Geriatric Psychiatry, 1440 Main Street, Waltham, Massachusetts 02254-9132; (617) 894-7030.

American Association for Marriage and Family Therapy, 1717 K Street, N.W., Washington, D.C. 20009; (202) 429-1825.

American Association of Pastoral Counselors, 9508A Lee Highway, Fairfax, Virginia 22031; (703) 385-6967.

American Psychiatric Association, 1400 K Street, N.W., Washington, D.C. 20005; (202) 682-6000.

American Psychological Association, 1200 17th Street, N.W., Washington, D.C. 20036; (202) 955-7600.

National Clearinghouse for Mental Health Information, Public Inquiry Section, National Institute of Mental Health, 5600 Fishers Lane, Rockville, Maryland 20857; (202) 436-4515.

SPECIFIC RESOURCES

Alcohol

Alcoholics Anonymous (AA), P.O. Box 459, Grand Central Station, New York, New York 10163. Write for information on programs and local chapters. Free pamphlet: *Time to Start Living.*

The Food and Drug Administration sends free single reprints of article "Liquor May Be Quicker, But . . ." Send postcard to FDA, HFE-88, 5600 Fishers Lane, Rockville, Maryland 20857.

National Clearinghouse for Alcohol Information, P.O. Box 2345, Rockville, Maryland 20802; (301) 468-2600. Distributes written materials and answers public inquiries.

National Council on Alcoholism, 733 Third Avenue, New York, New York 10017. Write for information and referrals for treatment services in your area.

Alzheimer's Disease

Alzheimer's Disease and Related Disorders Association (ADRDA), 70 East Lake Street—5997, Chicago, Illinois 60601; (800) 621-0379 or (800) 572-6037 (in Illinois). A basic resource for information and help in the states and cities. Write for pamphlets, including: *Alzheimer's Disease and Related Disorders, a Description of the Dementias; Legal Considerations for Alzheimer's Disease; Memory and Aging.*

American Society for Geriatric Dentistry, 271-11 76th Avenue, New Hyde Park, New York 11040; (212) 343-2100, ext. 260. Inquire here for information on special dental requirements of Alzheimer's patients.

Family Survival Project, 44 Page Street, Suite 600, San Francisco, California 94110; (415) 626-6556. Write for *Family Survival Handbook: A Guide to Financial, Legal and Social Problems* ($1.50) and free fact sheets.

The National Institute on Aging (NIA), Bethesda, Maryland 20205; (301) 486-9265. Write for information and resources: for example; *Q's and A's: Alzheimer's Disease.*

The New York City Alzheimer's Resource Center, 280 Broadway, Room 214, New York, New York 10007. Mail a check for $10.00, payable to Fund for Aging Services, to receive a copy of *Caring: A Family Guide to Managing the Alzheimer's Patient at Home.*

More to Read

Aronson, Miriam K., ed. *Understanding Alzheimer's Disease*. New York: Scribner's, 1987. Available from ADRDA.

Cohen, Donna, and Carl Eisdorfer. *The Loss of Self: A Family Resource for the Care of Alzheimer's Disease and Related Disorders*. New York: Norton, 1986.

Mace, Nancy L., and Peter V. Rabins. *The 36-Hour Day: A Family Guide to Caring for Persons with Alzheimer's Disease*. Baltimore: Johns Hopkins University Press, 1981.

Reisberg, Barry, *A Guide to Alzheimer's Disease: for Families, Spouses and Friends*. New York: The Free Press, 1981.

Cancer

American Cancer Society (see National Health Organizations) local affiliates (see local telephone books) offer help, information, referrals.

Cancer Information Service (800) 4-CANCER; in Alaska, (800) 638-6070; in Hawaii on Oahu, (808) 525-1234; other Hawaiian islands call this number collect. Spanish-speaking staff available during daytime hours in California, Florida, Georgia, Illinois, northern New Jersey, New York, and Texas.

National Cancer Institute, Publications Order, Office of Cancer Communication, Building 31, Room 10A18, Bethesda, Maryland 20892. Write for free publications (some in Spanish).

More to Read

Holleb, Arthur I., ed. *The American Cancer Society Cancer Book*. Garden City, N.Y.: Doubleday, 1986.

Caregivers

Aging Network Services, 4400 East West Highway, Suite 907, Bethesda, Maryland 20814; (301) 657-4329. For help with parents at a distance.

Children of Aging Parents, 2761 Trenton Road, Levittown, Pennsylvania 19056; (215) 547-1070. Information, local support groups.

The National Association of Private Geriatric Care Managers, Box 6920, Yorkville Station, New York, New York 10128. Write for national directory of private geriatric care managers (individuals: $17.50; not-for-profit organizations: $20.00; companies: $25.00).

National Council on Aging, Publications Department, 600 Maryland Avenue, S.W., Washington, D.C. 20024. Write for *Family Home Caring Guides*, eight booklets, $4.00 per set, order #2023, and *Caregiving Tips*, six brochures, $3.00, order #2032.

National Support Center for Families of the Aging, P.O. Box 245, Swarthmore, Pennsylvania 19081.

New York State Office for the Aging, Empire State Plaza, Agency Building No.2, Albany, New York 12223; (518) 474-5731. *Manual for Caregivers* available.

U.S. Department of Health and Human Services, Washington, D.C. 20402. Available publication: *Where to Turn for Help for Older Persons: A Guide for Action on Behalf of an Older Person*.

Video

Media Assistance Project, The Brookdale Center on Aging of Hunter College, 425 East 25th Street, New York, New York 10010. Write for information about *In Care Of: Families and Their Elders*, a 55-minute video hosted by Hugh Downs.

More to Read

Hoffman, Nancy. *Taking Care*. New York: The Free Press, 1986.

Horne, Jo. *Caregiving (Helping an Aging Loved One)*. Washington: AARP; Glenview, Ill.; Scott, Foresman, 1985.

Communications Help

Medical Alert Communications Systems: call local Area Agency on Aging or social service agencies for local, reliable systems.

AT&T offers a free catalogue of products for special needs in communication. Call (800) 233-1222 for voice communications or (800) 833-3232 for teletypewriter communications.

The Mount Sinai Medical Center Communi-card helps you communicate with chronically impaired (or non-English-speaking) individuals through pictographs and the alphabet and helps them communicate their medical, physical, and emotional needs. The Mount Sinai Medical Center, Communi-card, Box 852, One Gustave Levy Place, New York, New York 10029; (212) 650-7724 or (212) 650-6920.

Consumers

Consumer Credit Counseling Services, National Foundation for Consumer Credit, 8701 Georgia Avenue, Suite 601, Silver Spring, Maryland 20910; (301) 589-5600.

Consumer Products Safety Commission, 5401 Westbard Avenue, Washington, D.C. 20207; (800) 638-2772.

Council of Better Business Bureaus (CBBB); 1515 Wilson Boulevard, Arlington, Virginia 22209; (703) 276-0100.

Federal Trade Commission, Bureau of Consumer Protection, Washington, D.C. 20580; (202) 523-3598.

National Citizens' Coalition for Nursing Home Reform, 1825 Connecticut Avenue, N.W., Washington, D.C. 20009; (202) 797-0657.

National Consumer's League, 815 15th Street, N.W., Suite 516, Washington, D.C. 20005; (202) 639-8140.

More to Read

AARP Consumer Affairs Section. *A Consumer Education Bibliography for Older Americans*. Resources listed for ten topics. Free from AARP, Consumer Affairs Section, Program Department, 1909 K Street, N.W., Washington, D.C. 20049.

National Futures Association. *Before You Say Yes: 15 Questions to Turn Off an Investment Swindler*. Available free from Consumer Information Center, P.O. Box 100, Pueblo, Colorado 81002.

U.S. Congress. House. Select Committee on Aging. *Consumer's Choices to Funeral Planning*. Com. Pub. 99-541, 1986. Write to Superintendent of Documents, GPO, Washington, D.C. 20402.

U.S. Office of Consumer Affairs. *Consumer's Resource Handbook*. Available free from Consumer Information Center, Pueblo, Colorado, 81009.

Crime

AARP Criminal Justice Services, 1909 K Street, N.W., Washington, D.C. 20049; (202) 872-4700.

Federal Crime Insurance Program, P.O. Box 41033, Washington, D.C. 20014; (800) 638-8780. In Maryland and D.C.: (301) 652-2637. Provides insurance against burglary and robbery to those whom private carriers will not insure.

The National Crime Prevention Council, The Woodward Building, 733 15th Street, N.W., Washington, D.C. 20005. Write for crime prevention tips.

National Organization for Victim Assistance (NOVA), P.O. Box 11555, Dept. BHG, Washington, D.C. 20008; (202) 232-8560. Can provide help and information on the 37 states (and the Virgin Islands) that have Crime Victim Boards. In other locations call the state attorney general for help.

More to Read

Persico, J.E., with George Sunderland. *Keeping Out of Crime's Way.* Washington: AARP; Glenview, Ill.: Scott, Foresman, 1985.

Dental Health

American Dental Association Health Education, 211 East Chicago Avenue, Chicago, Illinois 60611. Write for pamphlets such as *How to Keep Your Smile in the Later Years, How to Be a Wise Dental Consumer, Periodontal Disease (Don't Wait till It Hurts).*

Discounts

Southwestern Bell (800) 252-6060 (8 A.M. to 4:15 P.M.). *The Silver Savers Passport* (discount directory).

Education

American Association of Community and Junior Colleges, One Dupont Circle, N.W., Washington, D.C. 20036; (202) 293-7050.

American Association of State Colleges and Universities, One Dupont Circle, N.W., Washington, D.C. 20036; (202) 293-7070.

Employment and Work

Check local telephone books for Senior Employment, the local State Employment Office, and the Area Agency on Aging.

Small Business Administration, 1441 L Street, N.W., Washington, D.C. 20005; (202) 655-4000. For SCORE inquiries, (202) 634-6200.

Falls

Falls and Immobility Clinic, The Mount Sinai Medical Center, New York, New York 10029; (212) 241-5561. Write for referrals in your area. Also, see more under Safety.

Fitness

Center for the Study of Aging, 706 Madison Avenue, Albany, New York 12208; (518) 465-6927.

The President's Council on Physical Fitness and Sports, 450 5th Street, N.W., Washington, D.C. 20001; (202) 272-3430.

Funerals

More to Read

Nelson, Thomas C. *It's Your Choice: The Practical Guide to Planning a Funeral.* Washington: AARP; Glenview, Ill.: Scott, Foresman, 1983.

U.S. Congress. House. Select Committee on Aging. *Consumer's Choices to Funeral Planning.* Com. Pub. 99-541, 1986. Write to Superintendent of Documents, GPO, Washington, D.C. 20402.

Geriatric Physicians

American Association for Geriatric Psychiatry, 1440 Main Street, Waltham, Massachusetts 02254-9132; (617) 894-7030.

The Ritter Department of Geriatrics and Adult Development, Box 1070, Mount Sinai Medical Center, One Gustave L. Levy Place, New York, New York 10029, will send you a list of doctors who see geriatric patients that includes all states except Hawaii and Alaska. Copies are $5 to individuals. Include a check payable to the Department of Geriatrics with your request.

Health and Wellness

HealthFare USA, 9411 Connecticut Avenue, Kensington, Maryland 20895; (301) 942-6601. Promotes health awareness and information on healthier lifestyles through community-based programs.

Healthy Older People Program; Office of Disease Prevention and Health Promotion, Public Health Service, Bethesda, Maryland 20205; (800) 626-5433.

More to Read

The Dartmouth Institute for Better Health, Dartmouth Medical School. *Medical and Health Guide for People over Fifty.* Washington: AARP; Glenview, Ill.: Scott, Foresman, 1986.

University of California, Berkeley, Wellness Letter. A subscription is $15 a year. Subscription Department, P.O. Box 109211, Des Moines, Iowa 50950.

Warach, Benjamin. *The Older American's Survival Guide for Better Health and a Longer Life.* Englewood Cliffs, N.J.: Prentice-Hall, 1981.

Hearing

American Speech-Language-Hearing Association, 10801 Rockville Pike, Rockville, Maryland 20852; (301) 897-5700.

National Association of the Deaf, 814 Thayer Avenue, Silver Spring, Maryland 20910; (301) 587-1788.

National Information Center on Deafness, Gallaudet College, 7th and Florida Avenue, N.E., Washington, D.C. 20002; voice: (202) 651-5109; TDD: (202) 651-5976. Information, devices, education, manufacturer information on telecommunications devices, training, law, referrals.

Self Help for Hard-of-Hearing People, 4848 Battery Lane, Suite 100, Bethesda, Maryland 20814; voice: (301) 657-2248; TDD: (301) 657-2249.

Home Care

Foundation for Hospice and Homecare, 519 C Street, N.E., Washington, D.C. 20002; (202) 547-6568. For accredited/approved agencies prepared by the National HomeCaring Council (nonprofit) and for their publications.

Home Health Services and Staffing Association (proprietary), 2101 L Street, N.W., Suite 800, Washington, D.C. 20037; (202) 775-4707. Information on local agencies.

National Association for Home Care, 519 C Street, N.E., Stanton Park, Washington, D.C. 20002; (202) 547-7424. Write for *All About Home Care: A Consumer's Guide.* ($2.00) and *How to Select a Home Care Agency* (free).

More to Read

Nassif, Janet Zhun. *The Home Health Care Solution—A Complete Consumer Guide.* New York: Harper & Row, 1985.

HMOs

Medicare and Prepayment Plans. Washington: GPO, 1985. HCFA publication #02143. Available from your Social Security Office.

More Health for Your Dollar: An Older Person's Guide to HMO's. Washington: AARP, 1983.

Hospice

National Consumers League, 815 15th Street, N.W., Suite 516, Washington, D.C. 20005; (202) 639-8140. Write for *A Consumer Guide to Hospice Care.*

National Hospice Organization, 1901 Fort Meyer Drive, Suite 307, Arlington, Virginia 22209; (703) 243-5900.

Housing and Homes for the Aging

American Association of Homes for the Aging, 1129 20th Street, Washington, D.C. 20036; (202) 296-5960.

American Health Care Association (nursing homes and allied facilities), 1200 15th Street, N.W., Washington, D.C. 20005; (202) 833-2050.

National Center for Home Equity Conversion, 110 East Main Street, Madison, Wisconsin 53703. Write for information and publications.

National Institute of Senior Housing, National Council on the Aging, 600 Maryland Avenue, West Wing 100, Washington, D.C. 20024; (202) 479-1200.

National Shared Housing Resource Center, 6344 Greene Street, Philadelphia, Pennsylvania 19144; (215) 848-1220. Publishes a directory.

Volunteers of America National Housing Corporation; 3939 North-Causeway Boulevard, Metairie, Louisiana 70002; (504) 837-2652.

More to Read

Boyer, Richard, and David Savageau. *Places Rated Retirement Guide.* Chicago: Rand McNally, 1987.

Dickinson, Peter. *Sunbelt Retirement.* Washington: AARP; Glenview, Ill.: Scott, Foresman, 1987.

National Directory of Retirement Facilities. Phoenix: Oryx Press, 1986. Lists more than 12,000 state-regulated facilities by state and city and alphabetically. See your library.

Raper, Ann T., ed. *National Continuing Care Directory: Retirement Communities with Prepaid Medical Plans.* Washington: AARP; Glenview, Ill.: Scott, Foresman, 1984.

Sumichrast, Michael, Ronald G. Shafer, and Marika Sumichrast. *Planning Your Retirement Housing.* Washington: AARP; Glenview, Ill.: Scott, Foresman, 1984.

See also Nursing Homes *and* Retirement.

Incontinence

The Mount Sinai Treatment Program for Incontinent Adults, 5 East 98th Street, New York, New York 10029; (212) 996-7213.

More to Read
National Institute on Aging. *Age Page: Incontinence.* Washington: GPO, 1982.

Insurance

Call your state insurance office for information on carriers and regulations within your state, as well as for general information. In some states there is coverage under a high-risk sharing pool to provide hospital, surgical, and medical care coverage to people who cannot obtain insurance anywhere else.

Inquire from the appropriate national health organization about special insurance problems for people with special diseases or disorders. For example, the Arthritis Foundation and the American Diabetes Association provide guidance on insurance.

Health Insurance Association of America, 1025 Connecticut Avenue, N.W., Suite 1200, Washington, D.C. 20036; (202) 223-7780.

Insurance Information Institute, 110 William Street, New York, New York 10038; (212) 669-9200.

Older Women's League, 1325 G Street, N.W., Lower Level-B, Washington, D.C. 20005. Information on continuation of health insurance for spouses, unemployed workers, and dependents.

More to Read
Chasen, Nancy H. *Policy Wise: The Practical Guide to Insurance Decisions for Older Consumers.* Washington: AARP; Glenview, Ill.: Scott, Foresman, 1983.

Legal Problems

ABA Commission on Legal Problems of the Elderly, 1800 M Street, N.W., Washington, D.C. 20036; (202) 331-2297. Write for *The Law and Aging Resource Guide,* a directory to legal resources in the 50 states.

American Bar Association, 1155 East 60th Street, Chicago, Illinois 60637; (312) 988-5000.

Institute on Law and the Rights of Older Adults, Brookdale Center on Aging of Hunter College, 425 East 25th Street, New York, New York 10010; (212) 481-4433.

National Health Law Center, 1302 Eighteenth Street, N.W., Washington, D.C. 20036; (202) 887-5310.

National Senior Citizens Law Center, 1302 Eighteenth Street, N.W., Washington, D.C. 20036; (202) 887-5280. Also 1636 West 8th Street, Los Angeles, California 90017; (213) 783-6686.

Living and Dying, Ethics, Living Wills.

Concern for Dying, 250 West 57th Street, Room 831, New York, New York 10107; (212) 246-6962.

The Hastings Center, Hastings-on-Hudson, New York 10706. Write for *Guidelines on the Termination of Life-Sustaining Treatment and the Care of the Dying*, $14.50, or see your library.

New York State Task Force on Life and Law, 33 West 34th Street, New York, New York 10001-3071.

Society for the Right to Die, 250 West 57th Street, New York, New York 10107; (212) 246-6973.

For organ donations: consult state motor vehicle departments; or write to The Living Bank, P.O. Box 6725, Houston, Texas 77265; or see form in House Select Committee on Aging, *Consumer Choices to Funeral Planning*, Com. Pub. 99-541, 1986.

More to Read
U.S. Congress. Senate. Special Committee on Aging. *A Matter of Choice: Planning Ahead for Health Care Decisions*. 99th Cong., 1987. Serial no. 99-M.

Medicare and Social Security

United Seniors Health Cooperative, 1334 G Street, N.W., Suite 500, Washington, D.C. 20005; (202) 393-6222. Write for their easy-to-read *Guide to the Medicare Maze* and Medical Bill Organizer. Includes expandable file with nine dividers. $19.95 for complete set.

More to Read
AARP, Health Advocacy Services. *Medicare's Prospective Payment System: Knowing Your Rights—Check Out the Facts Before You Check into the Hospital*. Washington: AARP, 1985, revised 1986 and August 1987. Write for this booklet: AARP, Stock #D 12330 Fulfillment, 1909 K Street, N.W., Washington, D.C. 20049.

Telephone your local Social Security Office or write to the Health Care Financing Administration, Department of Health and Human Services, 6325 Security Boulevard, Baltimore, Maryland 21207 for the most recent Medicare and Social Security pamphlets, such as those listed in the bibliography under Health Care Financing Administration.

Nursing Homes

American Association of Homes for the Aging, 1129 20th Street, Washington, D.C. 20036; (202) 296-5960.

American Health Care Association; 1200 15th Street, N.W., Washington, D.C. 20005; (202) 833-2050. Free pamphlets on various aspects of nursing homes. Directory of members.

National Citizens Coalition for Nursing Home Reform, 1825 Connecticut Avenue, N.W., Suite 417-B, Washington, D.C. 20009; (202) 797-0657.

Nursing Home Information Service, National Council of Senior Citizens, National Senior Citizens Education and Research Center, Inc., 925 15th Street, N.W., Washington, D.C. 20005; (202) 347-8800. *Long-Term Care Directory for the Metropolitan Washington Area* ($2.50) can help provide a framework for help in your area. Also, *Nursing Home Patient's Bill of Rights, Presented in Pictures.*

U.S. Department of Health and Human Services, Public Health Service, Office of Nursing Home Affairs, 5600 Fishers Lane, Rockville, Maryland 20857.

Consult State Health Department in your locality for specific information.

More to Read

Directory of Nursing Homes, 2nd ed. Phoenix: Oryx Press, 1984. Information on admissions, certification, level of care, ownership, affiliations, and staffing. Listed by state and city and alphabetically. Does *not* evaluate.

The editors of Consumer Reports Books. *Who Can Afford a Nursing Home?* New York: Consumers Union, 1988.

How to Select a Nursing Home, Consumer Information Center, Department 152-M, Pueblo, Colorado 81009. ($4.75)

Pacific Northwest Long-Term Care Center. *Choosing a Nursing Home: A Guidebook for Families.* Seattle: University of Washington Press, 1985.

Quacks

Federal Trade Commission, 6th and Pennsylvania Avenue, N.W., Washington, D.C. 20580; (202) 523-3598.

Food and Drug Administration, Office for Consumer Communications, 5600 Fishers Lane, Rockville, Maryland 20857; (301) 443-3170.

National Consumer's League, 815 15th Street, N.W., Suite 516, Washington, D.C. 20005; (202) 639-8140.

More to Read

The Big Quack Attack: Medical Devices, HHS Pub # (FDA) 84-4022. Order from Public Health Service DHHS, 5600 Fishers Lane, Rockville, Maryland 20857.

Respite

Inquire about local respite from Agency on Aging and social service organizations.

National Council of Catholic Women, 1312 Massachusetts Avenue, N.W., Washington, D.C. 20005; (202) 638-6050. List of respite services.

Retirement

Information on preretirement planning can be obtained through corporations, labor unions, community colleges, and professional and business groups and from the National Council on the Aging and the AARP through their Pre-Retirement Planning Programs.

More to Read

Fromme, Allan. *Life After Work: Planning It, Living It, Loving It.* Washington: AARP; Glenview, Ill.: Scott, Foresman, 1984.

Looking Ahead: How to Plan for Your Successful Retirement. Washington: AARP; Glenview, Ill.: Scott, Foresman, 1988.

Weaver, Peter, and Annette Buchanan. *What to Do with What You've Got: The Practical Guide to Money Management in Retirement.* Washington: AARP; Glenview, Ill.: Scott, Foresman, 1984.

Weinstein, Grace W. *Life Plans.* New York: Holt, Rinehart and Winston, 1979.

Safety

AAA Foundation for Traffic Safety, 2990 Telestar Court, Suite 100, Falls Church, Virginia 22042.

National Safety Council, 444 North Michigan Avenue, Chicago, Illinois 60611. Write for addresses and telephone numbers of local affiliates.

U.S. Consumer Product Safety Commission, Washington, D.C. 20207. Free hot line: (800) 638-CPSC or (800) 638-2772. TTY including Alaska and Hawaii: (800) 638-8270; TTY Maryland only: (800) 492-8104.

More to Read

American Red Cross. *Home Safety*. Independent Living Series 4104. Washington: ARC, 1984.

Brenton, Myron. *The Older Person's Guide to Safe Driving*. Public Affairs Pamphlet 641. New York: Public Affairs Committee, 1986. ($1.00)

The National Safety Council. *Falling! The Unexpected Trip: A Safety Program for Older Adults*. Chicago: undated. 10M 1283—stock no. 599.02.

U.S. Department of Health and Human Services. *Rape and Older Women: A Guide to Prevention and Protection*. Washington: GPO, 1981. No. ADM 81-734.

U.S. Product Safety Commission. *Home Safety Checklist for Older Consumers*. Washington: GPO, 1985. 475-981: 32202.

Self-Help

Alcoholics Anonymous, P.O. Box 459, Grand Central Station, New York, New York 10163.

National Self-Help Clearinghouse; Graduate School and University Center/CUNY, 33 West 42nd Street, New York, New York 10036; (212) 840-7606.

Self Help for Hard-of-Hearing People, 4848 Battery Lane, Suite 100, Bethesda, Maryland 20814; voice: (301) 657-2248; TDD: (301) 657-2249.

The Self-Help Institute, Center for Urban Affairs, Northwestern University, 2040 Sheridan Road, Evanston, Illinois 60201.

More to Read

Help Yourself. Free from The Blue Cross Association, 840 Lake Shore Drive, Chicago, Illinois 60611.

La Buda, ed. *The Gadget Book (Ingenious Devices for Easier Living)*. Washington: AARP; Glenview, Ill.: Scott, Foresman, 1985.

National Institute on Aging. *Self-Care and Self-Help Groups for the Elderly: A Directory*. Washington: GPO, 1985.

Packet on Aging. 26 booklets on concerns of older people, $11.70. Individual booklets $1.00. Write for catalog of titles to Public Affairs Committee, 381 Park Avenue South, New York, New York 10016; (212) 683-4331.

Sex and Marriage

American Association for Marriage and Family Therapy, 1717 K Street, N.W., Washington, D.C. 20009.

More to Read

Brecher, Edward R., and the editors of Consumer Reports Books. *Love, Sex and Aging*. Mount Vernon, N.Y.: Consumers Union, 1984.

Butler, Robert N., and Myrna I. Lewis. *Love and Sex After Sixty*. Revised ed. New York: Harper & Row, 1988.

Sex, Romance and Marriage After 55. Order pamphlet from Publications Office, Andrus Gerontology Center, University of Southern California, University Park, Los Angeles, California 90007.

Taxes

AARP Tax Aide program, 1909 K Street, N.W., Washington, D.C. 20049; (202) 872-4700.

Internal Revenue Service, 1111 Constitution Avenue, N.W., Washington, D.C. 20224; (202) 488-3100 or (202) 566-5000.

IRS publications: (800) 224-FORM

Information on a variety of tax topics: IRS Tele-Tax (800) 544-4477

Tax Counseling for the Elderly Program, Taxpayer Service Division: (202) 566-4904

For TTY equipment: (800) 428-4732; in Indiana only: (800) 382-4059

See local telephone books for local offices, for assistance and pamphlets.

U.S. Senate Special Committee on Aging, Washington, D.C. 20510. Tax information publications.

Travel

Elderhostel, 80 Boylston Street, Suite 400, Boston, Massachusetts 02116. Registration: (617) 426-8056; administration: (617) 426-7788.

Saga International Holidays, Ltd., 120 Boylston Street, Boston, Massachusetts 02116; (617) 451-6808.

More to Read
Massow, Rosalind. *Travel Easy: The Practical Guide for People Over 50.* Washington: AARP; Glenview, Ill.: Scott, Foresman, 1985.

Veterans

American Legion, 1608 K Street, N.W., Washington, D.C. 20006; (202) 861-2700.

Disabled American Veterans, 807 Maine Avenue, S.W., Washington, D.C. 20024; (202) 554-3501.

Veterans Administration, 810 Vermont Avenue, N.W., Washington, D.C. 20420. See local telephone books for toll-free numbers to VA regional offices and hospitals.

Veterans Group Life Insurance, Office of Servicemen's Groups Life Insurance, 213 Washington Street, Newark, New Jersey 07102. This is the place to submit beneficiaries claims.

Veterans of Foreign Wars, 200 Maryland Avenue, N.E., Washington, D.C. 20002; (202) 543-2239.

Vision

American Council of the Blind, 1010 Vermont Avenue, N.W., Suite 1100, Washington, D.C. 20005; (800) 424-8666.

American Foundation for the Blind, 15 West 16th Street, New York, New York 10011; (212) 620-2000. Help and information on services for aging blind people.

The Carroll Center for the Blind, 770 Centre Street, Newton, Massachusetts 02158; (617) 969-6200. *Aids and Appliances Review,* issue no. 13, summer 1984, includes information on various products to help those with impaired vision.

The Lighthouse National Center for Vision and Aging, 11 East 59th Street, New York, New York 10222; (212) 355-2200. Hot line: (800) 334-5497. A resource and information unit of the New York Association for the Blind. Call for information on eye/vision care, rehabilitative services, local resources.

The National Eye Care Project, Foundation for the American Academy of Ophthalmology, P.O. Box 6988, San Francisco, California 94101-9970; (800) 222-3937. Information about free eye care.

The National Library Service for the Blind and Physically Handicapped, The Library of Congress, Washington, D.C. 20542. Apply for free library service in your area. Books, magazines in braille, discs, and cassettes. Materials sent free and returned by postage-free mail.

National Society to Prevent Blindness, 500 East Remington Road, Schaumburg, Illinois 60173-4557; (312) 643-2020. Hotline: (800) 221-3004. National information and Referral Center answers questions on eye health and safety and makes referrals. Free pamphlets.

Vision Foundation, 2 Mt. Auburn Street, Watertown, Massachusetts 02172; (617) 926-4232. Free Vision Inventory List of information on products and services for visually impaired people.

Volunteers

ACTION/OAVP. 806 Connecticut Avenue, N.W., Washington, D.C. 20525; (202) 634-9355. Coordinates all federal volunteer programs. Also check regional offices of RSVP, VISTA, SCORE, Foster Grandparents, The Peace Corps, Senior Companions.

Voluntary Action National Center, 1111 North 19th Street, Suite 500, North Arlington, Virginia 22209; (202) 276-0542. Free pamphlets.

Widows

Inquire from local social service agencies and Area Agency on Aging for local support groups or write to:
AARP Widowed Person's Service, 1909 K Street, N.W., Washington, D.C. 20049; (202) 872-4700.

More to Read

Kushner, Harold S. *When Bad Things Happen to Good People*. New York: Schocken Books, 1981.

Loewinsohn, Ruth Jean. *Survival Handbook for Widows (and for Relatives and Friends Who Want to Understand)*. Washington: AARP; Glenview, Ill.: Scott, Foresman, 1984.

Women

American Association of University Women (AAUW), 2401 Virginia Avenue, N.W., Washington, D.C. 20037; (202) 785-7700.

Federation of Business and Professional Women's Clubs, 2012 Massachusetts Avenue, N.W., Washington, D.C. 20036; (202) 293-1100.

National Organization for Women, 1401 New York Avenue, N.W., Washington, D.C. 20005; (202) 347-2279.

Older Women's League, Suite 300, 730 Eleventh Street, N.W., Washington, D.C. 20001; (202) 783-6686.

Women's Equity Action League, 1250 I Street, N.W., Suite 305, Washington, D.C. 20005; (202) 898-1588.

More to Read

Feltin, Marie. *A Woman's Guide to Good Health After 50*. Washington: AARP; Glenview, Ill.: Scott, Foresman, 1987.

Seskin, Jane. *Alone, Not Lonely*. Washington: AARP; Glenview, Ill.: Scott, Foresman, 1985.

NOTES

Information drawn from interviews is not individually cited. All those interviewed are listed in the Bibliography.

INTRODUCTION

1. Elaine M. Brody, " 'Women in the Middle' and Family Help to Older People," *The Gerontologist* 21, no. 5 (October 1981): 471–80.

CHAPTER 2

1. National Association for Home Care, Division of Research, *Home Health Overview* (Washington: NAHC, 1984), 1.
2. House Select Committee on Aging, *The "Black Box" of Home Care Quality*, 99th Cong., 2nd sess., 1986, Com. Pub. 99-573, 1.
3. National Association for Home Care, *How to Choose a Home Care Agency: A Consumer's Guide to Home Care* (Washington: NAHC, 1987).

CHAPTER 3

1. Margaret Clark and Barbara Gallatin Anderson, *Culture and Aging: An Anthropological Study of Older Americans* (Springfield, Ill.: Charles C Thomas, 1967), 211–22.
2. Judith Rodin, "Aging and Health: Effects of the Sense of Control," *Science*, September 1986, 1271.
3. Raymond Harris, "Improving and Maintaining Health and Per-

formance Through Exercise, Nutrition and Stress Reduction," *Medical Times*, in press.

4. Alvar Svanborg, "The Brain: New Plasticity/New Possibility," (Remarks delivered at *The Promise of Productive Aging*, an international conference sponsored by the Japan Shipbuilding Foundation, Washington, D.C., 28 April 1987).

5. Raymond Harris, "Health and Fitness," a column for *Seniority*.

6. HealthFare USA, "You're in Charge of Changing Images," *Health Focus* worksheet (Wheaton, Md.: HealthFare USA, 1986).

7. National Safety Council, *Older American Accident Facts, Age 65 and Over* (Chicago: National Safety Council, 1985).

8. Myron Brenton, *The Older Person's Guide to Safe Driving*, Public Affairs Pamphlet No. 641 (New York: Public Affairs Committee, 1986), 23.

9. House Select Committee on Aging, *Crime, Violence and the Elderly*, 99th Cong., 1st sess., 1986, Com. Pub. 99-547, 35.

10. "Prepaid Funerals—Not the Way to Go," *Consumer Reports*, February 1986, 75.

CHAPTER 4

1. Senate Special Committee on Aging, *Developments in Aging—1985*, Vol. 1, 99th Cong., 2nd sess., 1986, 292.

2. Ibid., 285.

CHAPTER 5

1. American Association of Retired Persons and the Administration on Aging, *A Profile of Older Americans, 1985* (Washington: AARP and AoA, 1985), 13.

2. Ibid., 4.

3. Adapted from Jean Barron Nassau, *Choosing a Nursing Home* (New York: Funk and Wagnalls, 1975) and advice of the National Council of Senior Citizens, Association of American Homes for the Aging, and American Health Care Association.

4. Beverly A. Yawney and Farrell L. Slover, "Relocation of the Elderly," *Social Work* 18 (1973): 90–91.

5. The National Academy of Sciences 1986 study reported in the *New York Times*, 17 January 1988, L1 and L18.

CHAPTER 6

1. *New York Times*, 16 January 1987, A10.

2. John Regan, *Tax, Estate and Financial Planning for the Elderly* (New York: Matthew Bender, 1986), Sec. 9:11[2].

3. Older Women's League, "Give 'Em Health Alert—1987" fact sheet (Washington: OWL, 1987).

4. The Pennsylvania Department of Aging, *Do You Really Need This Additional Insurance? An Insurance Guide for Older Persons* (Harrisburg, Penn.: 1985), 4.

5. Health Care Financing Administration, *Guide to Health Insurance for People with Medicare*, HCFA Pub. #02110:ICN 48 7790 (Washington: GPO, 1986), 2–6.

6. Speech by Secretary of Health and Human Services Bowen reported in the *New York Times*, 13 September 1987, L43.

7. Senate Special Committee on Aging, *Developments in Aging—1986*, Vol. 1, 100th Cong., 1st sess., 1987, 275.

8. Regan, *Tax, Estate and Financial Planning*, Sec. 6:02.

CHAPTER 7

1. Francis W. Peabody, quoted in William Morgan and George L. Engel, *The Clinical Approach to the Patient* (Philadelphia: W. B. Saunders, 1969), 2.

2. American Association of Retired Persons, Health Advocacy Services, *Medicare's Prospective Payment System: Knowing Your Rights—Check Out the Facts Before You Check into the Hospital* (Washington: AARP, 1987).

3. Senate Special Committee on Aging, *Developments in Aging—1986*, Vol. 1, 100th Cong., 1st sess., 1987, 189.

4. United Seniors Consumer Cooperative, *The United Seniors Health Report* 1, no. 2 (July–August 1986): 1–3. (This organization is now known as the United Seniors Health Cooperative.)

CHAPTER 8

1. Senate Special Committee on Aging with American Association of Retired Persons, Federal Council on Aging, and Administration on Aging, *Aging America, Trends and Projections, 1985–1986 Edition*, 1987, 94–95.

2. Office of Technology Assessment, *Losing a Million Minds: Confronting the Tragedy of Alzheimer's Disease and Other Dementias*, April 1987, OTA-BA-323, 14.

3. Harold M. Schmeck, Jr., "Heart Blood Shortage Linked to Mental Stress," *New York Times*, 21 April 1988.

4. Raymond Harris, "Special Features of Heart Disease in the Elderly," in *Working with Older People: A Guide to Practice*, vol. 4 (Rockville, Md.: 1974), 89.

5. National Institute of Neurological and Communicative Diseases and Stroke, *Stroke*, NIH Pub. 83–222 (Washington: GPO, 1983), 1.

6. Ibid., 22.

7. National Institute on Aging, *Age Page: Stroke—Prevention and Treatment* (Washington: GPO, January 1986).

8. *Stroke*, 14.

9. Arthur I. Holleb, ed., *The American Cancer Society Cancer Book: An Overview of Cancer Today* (Garden City, N.Y.: Doubleday, 1986), 42.

10. Bruce H. Peterson and B. J. Kennedy, *Aging and Cancer Management: Clinical Observations* (New York: American Cancer Society, 1979), 329.

11. American Diabetes Association, *Diabetes—Facts and Figures* (New York: American Diabetes Association, 1986).

12. *Aging America*, 88.

13. Arthritis Foundation, *Arthritis: The Basic Facts* (New York: Arthritis Foundation, 1974).

14. National Institute on Aging, *Age Page: Osteoporosis—The Bone Thinner* (Washington: GPO, 1985).

15. National Institute on Aging, *Age Page: Constipation* (Washington: GPO, 1985).

16. Gena Kolata, "Parkinson Procedure: Fervor Turns to Disillusion," *New York Times*, 21 April 1988, Y1 and 11.

17. Arthur Kay and Rein Tideiksaar, "What Causes Falls?" *Geriatrics* 41, no. 12 (December 1986): 32.

18. Ibid.

19. National Eye Care Project, *Cataracts* (San Francisco: The Foundation of the American Academy of Ophthalmology, undated).

20. National Society to Prevent Blindness, *Living With Low Vision* (Schaumburg, Ill.: National Society to Prevent Blindness, undated).

21. American Dental Association, *Keeping Your Smile in the Later Years*, pamphlet W142 (Chicago: American Dental Association).

22. American Podiatric Medical Association, *Your Podiatrist Talks about Foot Health and Aging*, FL50 M-8/85 (Washington: American Podiatric Medical Association, 1985).

23. "Dos and Don'ts for Poor Sleepers," *Patient Care* 15 (August 1980): 131.

CHAPTER 9

1. Office of Technology Assessment, *Losing a Million Minds,* 1.

2. Robert N. Butler, "Psychiatric and Behavioral Considerations in the Aged Patient," in *Clinical Geriatrics,* 2nd ed., edited by Isadore Rossman (New York: J. B. Lippincott, 1979), 527.

3. Quoted in Dr. Robert Katzman, "Medical Progress: Alzheimer's Disease," *New England Journal of Medicine* (10 April 1986): 964.

4. Quoted in Jill Crabtree, "In Sickness and in Health: Alzheimer's Disease and the Spousal Relationship," *The Brookdale Center on Aging Newsletter* 8, no. 5 (Summer 1986): 3.

5. John Panella, Jr., and Fletcher H. McDowell, *Day Care for Dementia: A Manual of Instruction for Developing a Program* (White Plains, N.Y.: Burke Rehabilitation Center, 1983), 1–3.

6. Ibid.

CHAPTER 10

1. Margaret Clark and Barbara Gallatin Anderson, *Culture and Aging: An Anthropological Study of Older Americans* (Springfield, Ill.: Charles C. Thomas, 1967), 415–33.

2. Bernice L. Neugarten, "Successful Aging in 1970 and 1990," in *Successful Aging,* edited by Eric Pfeiffer (Durham, N.C.: Duke University Press, 1973), 13.

CHAPTER 11

1. Congressman Charles A. Mosher, Ohio, quoted in the *Wall Street Journal,* 2 January 1976.

2. Senate Special Committee on Aging, *A Matter of Choice: Planning Ahead for Health Care Decisions,* 99th Cong., 2nd sess., 1987, iii.

3. Ibid., 3 (quoting decision of Benjamin Cardozo, while judge on the New York Court of Appeals).

4. Ibid. (quoting Supreme Court Justice Louis Brandeis).

5. *New York Times,* 5 June 1987, A1.

6. A. D. Weisman, *The Realization of Death* (New York: Jason Aronson, 1974).

7. Elisabeth Kübler-Ross, quoted in *Catastrophic Illness in the Seventies* (New York: Cancer Care, Inc., 1971), 14–18.

8. Clark and Anderson, *Culture and Aging,* 279.

9. Mimkon v. Ford, Supreme Court of New Jersey 66 N.J. 426; 332 A. 2d. 199, 204–5 (6 February 1975).

SELECTED BIBLIOGRAPHY

Following are the interviews I conducted and a selection of readings, conference presentations, reports, and research papers from which I drew while writing this book.

INTERVIEWS

Susan Abbott, Consultant, former program associate for Health Promotion and the Aging, The National Council on the Aging, Washington, D.C.

May Allin, resident, La Vida Llena, Albuquerque, New Mexico.

Dr. Jerry L. Avorn, Department of Social Medicine and Health Policy, Harvard Medical School, Boston, Massachusetts.

Leo Baldwin, Housing Consultant, AARP, Washington, D.C.

Dr. Laurie Barclay, Clinical Director of Dementia Research Service, Burke Rehabilitation Center, White Plains, New York.

Ira Bates, Director of Education, National Hospice Association, Washington, D.C.

Dee Bergman, Director of ABLE, San Francisco, California.

Dayle Berke, Esq., Director of Government Affairs, National Association for Home Care, Washington, D.C.

Laura Bolotsky, Westchester County Office on Aging, White Plains, New York.

Pat Brady, Study Coordinator of Dementia Research Service, The Burke Rehabilitation Center, White Plains, New York.

Barbara Brodbar, former director of Channeling Project, Director of Home Health Agency for Miami Home and Hospital for the Aged, Douglas Gardens, Miami, Florida.

Dr. Robert N. Butler, Brookdale Professor of Geriatrics and Adult Development, Chairman of Gerald and May Ellen Ritter Department of Geriatrics and Adult Development, Mount Sinai Medical Center, New York, New York.

Mary Lou Caccavalle, Public Information, Internal Revenue Service TCE Program, New York, New York.

Barbara Cahn, Director of Education, Public Affairs Committee, New York, New York.

Margaret Carlson, Director of Riley County Seniors' Service Center, Manhattan, Kansas.

Dorothy Chafkin, Director of Senior Nutrition Program, YMCA of Greater New York, Bronx, New York.

Deborah Cloud, Manager of Communications, American Association of Homes for the Aged, Washington, D.C.

Dr. Gene D. Cohen, Director of Program on Aging, National Institute of Mental Health, Rockville, Maryland.

Nancy M. Coleman, Staff Director of Commission on Legal Problems of the Elderly, American Bar Association, Washington, D.C.

Dr. Richard T. Conrad, Chairman of Southmark Heritage Corporation, Bradenton, Florida.

Michael Cusick, Department of Social Services, New Rochelle, New York.

Dr. Kenneth Davis, Chief of Psychiatry at Veterans Administration Medical Center, Bronx, New York, and Mount Sinai Medical Center, New York, New York.

George Degnon, Public Information Officer, U.S. Public Health Service, Washington, D.C.

William Dickey, Director of Aging Services, Archdiocese of New York, New York, New York.

Dr. Rose Dobrof, Executive Director of Brookdale Center on Aging, Hunter College/CUNY, New York, New York.

Carole O'Brien Edelman, Director of Nursing, Ruth Taylor Geriatric and Rehabilitation Institute, Westchester County Medical Center, Hawthorne, New York.

Marian Emr, National Institute on Aging, Washington, D.C.

Msgr. Charles Fahey, Director of Third Age Center (The University Center on Gerontology), Fordham University, New York, New York.

Dr. James Firman, Executive Director of United Seniors Consumer Cooperative, Washington, D.C.

Dr. Edward Fischel, Chief of Staff, Northport Veterans Administration Medical Center Hospital, Northport, New York, and Associate Dean, School of Medicine, State University of New York at Stony Brook, Stony Brook, New York.

Dr. Doris Jonas Freed, Counselor-at-Law, New York, New York.

Riz Galicinao, Director of Home Health Services, Special Programs Branch, Division of Primary Care Services, U.S. Public Health Services, Rockville, Maryland.

Susan Buckley Gannon, Manager of Public Relations, Alzheimer's Disease and Related Disorders Association, Chicago, Illinois.

Dr. Ira J. Gelb, Senior Assistant Editor, *Journal of the American College of Cardiology*, and Past President of the American Heart Association—Westchester/Putnam, New York.

Lou Glasse, President of Older Women's League, Washington, D.C., and Executive Director of Project on Aging Policy, New York Community Trust, New York, New York.

Marilyn Goldaber, Director of Social Services, Miami Hebrew Home and Hospital, Douglas Gardens, Miami, Florida.

Dr. Natalie Gordon, Director of Social Services, Jewish Home and Hospital, New York, New York.

Sarah Gotbaum, sociologist, Washington, D.C.

Barbara Greenberg, Administrator of National and Community Affairs, The Travelers Corporation, Hartford, Connecticut.

Patrick Hare, Patrick Hare Associates, Washington, D.C.

Dr. Raymond Harris, Director of Center on Aging and cardiologist, Albany, New York.

Sally Harrs, Program Director of National Council of Catholic Women, Washington, D.C.

Loretta O. Havener, American Diabetes Association—Westchester/Putnam, White Plains, New York.

Angela Heath, Program Specialist, Caregivers Programming, AARP, Washington, D.C.

Dr. Charles Herrera, Medical Director of Sleep Disorders Center, City College, CUNY, and instructor in Department of Geriatrics and Adult Development, Mount Sinai Medical Center, New York, New York.

Jennifer Hirshan, National Association for Home Care, Washington, D.C.

David Hobman, Director of Age Concern and President of International Federation on Aging, Surrey, England.

Ida Isaacson, volunteer in senior center, Nyack, New York.
Victoria Jaycox, Executive Director of Older Women's League, Washington, D.C.
Christopher Jennings, staff, U.S. Senate Special Committee on Aging, Washington, D.C.
Dr. Harold Kallman, Director of Geriatric Education, School of Medicine, East Carolina University, Greenville, North Carolina.
Dr. Saul Kamen, Chief of Dental Services, Jewish Institute for Geriatric Care, New Hyde Park, New York.
Benjamin Kaplan, Director of Administration, Jewish Association for Services to the Aged, New York, New York.
Dennis Kodner, Director of Elderplan, Brooklyn, New York.
Lorraine Lidoff, Vice President of Professional and Community Services and director of Family Caregivers Program, National Council on the Aging, Washington, D.C.
Diane Lifsey, former Minority Staff Director, U.S. Senate Special Committee on Aging, Washington, D.C.
Barbara Lilliston, Assistant Director of Social Work, The Burke Rehabilitation Center, White Plains, New York.
Ruth Loewinsohn, Manager of Social Outreach and Support Program, AARP, Washington, D.C.
Charles Longino, Director of the Center for Social Research on Aging, University of Miami, Coral Gables, Florida.
Georgina I. Lucas, Director of Leadership Programs, The Travelers Corporation, Hartford, Connecticut.
Marjorie McCarty, Head of the Social Service Unit, Rockefeller University Hospital, New York, New York.
Joan Magit, Older Women's Health Project, Senior Health and Peer Counseling Center, Santa Monica, California.
Dr. Steven Mattis, Director of Neuropsychology Services, New York Hospital/Cornell Medical Center, White Plains, New York.
Alice Mehling, Executive Director of the Society for the Right to Die, New York, New York.
Cathy Michaelson, Coordinator for the National Institute on Community Long-Term Care, National Council on the Aging, Washington, D.C.
Dr. Harry R. Moody, Deputy Director of Brookdale Center on Aging, Hunter College, CUNY, New York, New York.
M. Natkin, Social Security Office, New Rochelle, New York.
Jerry Norquist, Public Information Officer, Administration on Aging, Washington, D.C.
Louise and Charles Odell, retirees, Pinehurst, North Carolina.

Jack Ossofsky, President of the National Council on the Aging, Washington, D.C.

Janice Paganelli, New York State Hospice Association, White Plains, New York.

Ricki Polisar, Coordinator of Ombudsman Service in Long-Term Care Facilities, Great Neck, New York.

Karen Presti, Arthritis Foundation, Hudson Valley Branch, Burke Rehabilitation Center, White Plains, New York.

Jeanne Priester, National Program Leader of Home Economics and Nutrition, U.S. Department of Agriculture Extension Service, Washington, D.C.

Betty Ransom, Senior Coordinator of Professional Membership Units (including National Institute on Adult Day Care and National Center on Rural Aging) for the National Council on the Aging, Washington, D.C.

Ruth Ravich, Patient Representative, Mount Sinai Medical Center, New York, New York.

John Regan, Professor of Law, School of Law, Hofstra University, Hempstead, New York.

Dr. Barry Reisberg, Clinical Director of the Geriatric Study and Treatment Program, Milhauser Laboratories, Department of Psychiatry, New York University Medical Center, New York, New York.

Dr. Robert M. Rice, Executive Vice President of Family Service America, Milwaukee, Wisconsin.

Dr. Harold Rifkin, Past President of the American Diabetes Association.

Lila Rosenthal, Executive Director of the National HomeCaring Council, New York, New York.

Charles Sabatino, Associate Staff Director of the American Bar Association, Commission on Legal Problems of the Elderly, Washington, D.C.

Janet Sainer, Commissioner on Aging, City of New York.

Daniel Sambol, Director of the Division on Aging, Federation of Protestant Welfare Agencies, New York, New York.

Linda Samuels, Director of the Food Stamp Program, Westchester County, New York.

Mal Schecter, Deputy Director of the Institute on Productive Aging, Mount Sinai Medical Center, New York, New York.

Kenneth Scholen, Executive Director of the National Center for Home Equity Conversion, Madison, Wisconsin.

Harris Schrank, Vice President, Equitable Life Assurance, New York, New York.

Annabelle Seidman, National Council of Senior Citizens, Washington, D.C.

Dr. Charles A. Shamoian, Professor of Clinical Psychiatry and Director of Geriatric Services, New York Hospital/Cornell Medical Center, White Plains, New York.

Jane Shure, Director of Public Information, National Institute on Aging, Washington, D.C.

Pat and Nelson Silva, retirees, Pompano Beach, Florida.

Al Sirrocco, National Center for Health Statistics, Long-Term Care Statistics Branch, U.S. Public Health Service, Hyattsville, Maryland.

Barbara Sklar, Chair of National Council on the Aging and President of Western Consulting Group, San Francisco, California.

Dr. Robert Sonneborn, Physician, Internal Medicine, Boca Raton, Florida.

Sidney Spector, Managing Partner of Senior Housing Associates, Cleveland, Ohio.

Dr. Perry Starer, Codirector of Treatment Program for Incontinent Adults, Mount Sinai Medical Center, New York, New York, and Chief of Geriatrics, Elmhurst Hospital, Queens, New York.

Dr. Robert Stivelman, Associate Professor of Medicine, University of California, Los Angeles, and cardiologist, Loma Linda Medical Center and Cedars Sinai Medical Center, Los Angeles, California.

Ann Stoddard, retiree, San Francisco, California.

Dr. Alvar Svanborg, Professor and Chairman of the Department of Geriatric and Long-term Care Medicine, Vasa Hospital, University of Göteborg, Sweden.

Eileen Sweeney, National Senior Citizens Law Center, Washington, D.C.

Milt Szimanski, Director of Public Relations, HealthFare USA, Kensington, Maryland.

Dr. Simeon I. Taylor, Section Chief of the Diabetes Branch, National Institute of Diabetes, Digestive, and Kidney Diseases, National Institutes of Health, Bethesda, Maryland.

Irma Tetzloff, Aging Program Analyst, Long-Term Care, Administration on Aging, Washington, D.C.

Dr. Rein Tideiksaar, Codirector of Falls and Immobility Program, Department of Geriatrics, Mount Sinai Medical Center, New York, New York.

Dr. Fernando Torres-Gil, former Staff Director, U.S. House of Representatives Select Committee on Aging, Washington, D.C.

Peggy Trahar, Director of the Day Program for Dementia, Burke Rehabilitation Center, White Plains, New York.

Theodore Wagner, Partner, Carter, Ledyard, and Milburn, New York, New York.

Elva Walker, Secretary of the National Council on the Aging and Chairman of Purity Soap Company, Minneapolis, Minnesota.

Ben Warach, Executive Director of Jewish Association for Services to the Aged, New York, New York.

John and Jane Wassung, residents, Westport, Connecticut.

Dr. T. Franklin Williams, Director of the National Institute on Aging, Washington, D.C.

Anna H. Zimmer, Director of the Media Assistance to Caregivers Project, Hunter/Brookdale Center on Aging, New York, New York.

READINGS

Abeles, Ronald P. "Social and Behavioral Research (From Research to Practice: Adding to Our Knowledge Base and Capacities)." Presentation at the National Council on the Aging, Washington, D.C., 1986.

American Association of Retired Persons. *More Health for Your Dollar: An Older Person's Guide to HMO's.* Washington: AARP, 1983.

———. *The Prudent Patient: How to Get the Most for Your Health Care Dollar.* Washington: AARP, undated.

American Association of Retired Persons and the Administration on Aging. *A Profile of Older Americans, 1985.* PF3049(1085)•D996. Washington: AARP and AoA, 1985.

American Association of Retired Persons, Health Advocacy Services. *Medicare's Prospective Payment System: Knowing Your Rights.* Washington: AARP, 1985, revised February 1986 and August 1987.

American Dental Association. *Keeping Your Smile in Later Years.* W 142. Chicago: Bureau of Health Education, 1985.

American Legion (National Veterans Affairs and Rehabilitation Commission). *The Aging American.* Washington: undated.

American Medical Association. "Introduction and Purposes." In *Guidelines, Discharge Planning.* #004170 15-M-6/84-40899. Chicago: 1984.

Arthritis Foundation. *Arthritis, Basic Answers to Your Questions.* 4001/8-86. Atlanta: Arthritis Foundation, 1986.

———. *Guide to Insurance for People with Arthritis.* 9332/8-86. Atlanta: Arthritis Foundation, 1986.

Avorn, Jerome L. "Drugs and the Elderly." *The Harvard Medical School Letter* 9, no. 8 (June 1984).

———. "Medicine, Health and the Geriatric Transformation." *Dædalus* 115, no. 1 (Winter 1986).

Avorn, J. L., P. P. Lamy, and R. E. Vestal. "Prescribing for the Elderly —Safely." *Patient Care* 16 (30 June 1982): 14–62.

Barclay, Laurie L. "Alzheimer's Disease: Update on Diagnosis, Treatment and Research." White Plains, New York: The Burke Rehabilitation Center, 1986.

Barclay, L., and J. P. Blass. "Evaluation and Treatment of the Cognitively Impaired Patient." In *Practical Geriatric Medicine,* edited by A. Norman Exton-Smith and Marc E. Weksler, 88–89. Edinburgh: Churchill Livingston, 1985.

Blass, John P., and L. L. Barclay. "New Developments in the Diagnosis of the Dementias." *Drug Development Research* 5 (1985): 39–58.

Brody, Elaine M. " 'Women in the Middle' and Family Help to Older People." *The Gerontologist* 21, no. 5 (Oct. 1981): 471–80.

The Brookdale Center on Aging, Hunter College/CUNY. *Newsletter* 8–9 (1986–1987).

Cantor, Marjorie. "Women as Caregivers: Today and Tomorrow." Presentation at annual meeting of the National Council on the Aging, Washington, D.C., 1986.

Cohen, Gene D. "Prospects for Mental Health and Aging." Presentation at the annual meeting of the National Council on the Aging, Washington, D.C., 1986.

Cuff, Claudia B. "Divorce Statistics of Older Americans." Third Age Center, Fordham University, New York.

Davis, Karen. "Economic Implications of Providing Health and Long-Term Care to an Aging Population. Presentation at the National Council on the Aging, Washington, D.C., 1986.

Fine, Alan. "Transplantation in the Central Nervous System." *Scientific American* 225, no. 2 (Aug. 1986): 52–58.

Furstenberg, Anne-Linda. "Older People's Choices of Lay Consultants." *Journal of Gerontological Social Work* 9, no. 1 (Fall 1985): 21–34.

Harris, Raymond. "Highlights of the Second International Conference on Physical Activity, Aging and Sports." *International Council of Sports Science and Physical Education Review* (1986):51–58.

———. "Improving and Maintaining Health and Performance through Exercise, Nutrition and Stress Reduction." *Medical Times.* In press.

Health Care Financing Administration. Selected pamphlets: *Guide to*

Health Insurance for People with Medicare (HCFA Pub. #02110: ICN 48 7790); *Medicare and Prepayment Plans* (HCFA Pub. #02143); *Your Medicare Handbook, 1986, 1987* (HCFA Pub. #10050, ICN-461250); *How Work Affects Social Security Checks,* January 1986 edition (SSA Pub. #05-10069); *Your Social Security,* January 1987 edition (SSA Pub. #05-10035); *Medicare and Employer Health Plans* (HCFA Pub. #02150); *SSI for the Aged, Blind and Disabled in New York State* (SSA Pub. #05-1146); *Program Highlights, Social Security Bulletin, Annual Statistical Supplement, 1986.* Washington: GPO.

HealthFare USA (formerly National Health Screening Council). "You're in Charge of Changing Images." *Health Focus* worksheet (Wheaton, Md.: HealthFare USA, 1986).

Herzog, Barbara, "Impact of DRG's on Quality of Care." Presentation at the National Council on the Aging, Washington, D.C., 1986.

Holleb, Arthur I., ed. *The American Cancer Society Cancer Book.* Garden City, N.Y.: Doubleday, 1986.

Johns, Celeste A., Richard C. Mohs, Bonnie M. Davis, Blaine S. Greenwald, Thomas B. Horvath, and Kenneth L. Davis. "Clinical Studies of the Cholinergic Deficit in Alzheimer's Disease." Paper for the Department of Psychiatry, Bronx Veterans Administration Medical Center, and the departments of Psychiatry and Pharmacology, Mount Sinai School of Medicine, New York.

Johnson, Colleen L., and Leslie A. Grant. *The Nursing Home in American Society.* Baltimore and London: The Johns Hopkins University Press, 1985.

Katzman, Robert. "Medical Progress: Alzheimer's Disease." *The New England Journal of Medicine* 314, no. 15 (10 April 1986): 964–73.

Kraemer, Ann. "The Experience of Hospitalized Older Persons and Family Members." Presentation at the National Council on the Aging, Washington, D.C., 1986.

Lilliston, Barbara A. "Psychosocial Responses to Traumatic Physical Disability." *Social Work in Health Care* 10, no. 4 (Summer 1985).

Mahoney, Charlotte. "The Impact of DRG's: What Can You Do About It." Presentation at the National Council on the Aging, Washington, D.C., 1986.

Mohs, Richard C. "Assessing Changes in Alzheimer's Disease: Memory and Language Tasks." Paper for the Psychiatry Service, Bronx Veterans Administration Medical Center.

Mohs, Richard C., and Kenneth L. Davis. "Psychopharmacology, Neurotransmitter Systems and Cognition in the Elderly." In *Experimental and Clinical Interventions in Aging,* 305–16. New York and Basel: Marcel Dekker, 1983.

Mohs, Richard C., Kenneth L. Davis, and Daniel D. Dunn. "A Medical Overview of Alzheimer's Disease." Paper for Bronx Veterans Administration Medical Center.

Mohs, Richard C., Thomas B. Horvath, and Kenneth L. Davis. "Alzheimer's Disease: VA Research Brings Hope to the Elderly." *VA Practitioner* (January 1984): 48–51.

Mount Sinai Medical Center. Gerald and May Ellen Ritter Department of Geriatrics and Adult Development. *Newsletter* (1985–1987).

Mount Sinai School of Medicine. The Center for Productive Aging. *Productive Aging News* (May–September 1987).

National Council on the Aging. *Aging in the Eighties: America in Transition*, a study by Louis Harris and Associates, Inc. Washington: 1981.

———. *Supports for Family Caregivers of the Elderly: Highlights of a National Symposium*, compiled by Lorraine Lidoff. Washington: 1985.

National Institute on Aging. *Age Page*. Washington: GPO, 1984–1986.

———. *Progress Report on Alzheimer's Disease*. Vol. 3, NIH Pub. #86-2873. Washington: GPO, December 1986.

National Institute on Alcohol Abuse and Alcoholism. Public Health Service. "Alcohol and the Elderly: An Overview," by Millree Williams. *Alcohol and Research World* 8, no. 3 (Spring 1984): 5–51.

National Institutes of Health. National Cancer Institute. *Radiation Therapy and You*. NIH Pub. #86-2227. Washington: GPO, July 1986.

National Institutes of Health. Office of Scientific and Health Reports. National Institute of Neurological and Communicative Disorders and Stroke. *Hope Through Research* pamphlets: *Chronic Pain* (NIH Pub. #82-2406); *The Dementias* (NIH Pub. #83-2252); *Headache* (NIH Pub. #84-158); *Hearing Loss* (NIH Pub. #82-157); *Parkinson's Disease* (NIH Pub. #83-139); *Stroke* (NIH Pub. #83-2222). Washington: GPO, 1982–1984.

National Institutes of Health. Public Health Service. "Medicine for the Layman: Coping with Aged Parents." Presentation by T. Franklin Williams and Carter Williams, September 1984.

National Safety Council. *Older American Accident Facts, Age 65 and Over*. Stock no. 044-218. Chicago: National Safety Council, 1985.

New York Academy of Medicine. "Symposium: The Geriatric Medical Education Imperative." *Proceedings* 61, no. 6 (July–August 1985).

New York State. Senate. Committee on Aging. *Elder Abuse: A Hidden Phenomenon*. January 1986.

New York Times. "Life Span Research Predicts Healthier, but Not Longer, Old Age." 21 October 1980, C1.

———. "Nursing Costs Force Elderly to Sue Spouses." 6 March 1986, A1.

———. "Officials Warn of Gaps in Insurance for the Aged." 16 January 1987, A10.

Panella, John, Jr., and Fletcher H. McDowell. *Day Care for Dementia: A Manual of Instruction for Developing a Program.* White Plains, N.Y.: The Burke Rehabilitation Center, Dementia Research Service, 1983.

Pennsylvania State. Department of Aging. *Do You Really Need This Additional Insurance? An Insurance Guide for Older People.* Harrisburg, Penn.: 1985.

Powchick, P., and K. L. Davis. "Psychological Side Effects of Non-Psychiatric Drugs." Paper for the Department of Psychiatry, Bronx Veterans Administration Medical Center, and the departments of Psychiatry and Pharmacology, Mount Sinai School of Medicine, New York, New York.

Regan, John J., *Tax, Estate and Financial Planning for the Elderly.* New York: Matthew Bender, 1986, and 1987 supplements.

Reisberg, Barry. *A Guide to Alzheimer's Disease for Families, Spouses and Friends.* New York: The Free Press, 1981.

Reisberg, Barry, and Steven H. Ferris. "Emergency Issues in the Assessment and Management of Alzheimer's Disease." *Emergency Health Services Review* 3 (1985): 55–76.

Reisberg, Barry, Steven H. Ferris, Mony J. de Leon, and Thomas Crook. "Age-Associated Cognitive Decline and Alzheimer's Disease: Implications for Assessment and Treatment." In *Thresholds in Aging,* edited by Bergener, Eermini, and Stahelin. London: Academic Press, 1985.

———. "Global Deterioration Scale for Age-Associated Cognitive Decline and Alzheimer's Disease." *American Journal of Psychiatry* 139 (1982): 1136–39.

Research News. "Brain Architecture: Beyond Genes." *Science,* 11 July 1986, 155.

Rodin, Judith. "Aging and Health: Effects of the Sense of Control." *Science,* 19 Sept. 1986, 1271–76.

Rossman, Isadore, ed. *Clinical Geriatrics.* 2nd ed. Philadelphia and Toronto: J. B. Lippincott, 1979.

Sabatino, Charles P. "An Advocate's Primer on Long-Term Care Insurance." *Bifocal* 6, no. 4 (Winter 1985): 1–7.

Shanas, Ethel. "Older People and Their Families: The New Pioneers." *Journal of Marriage and Family* (Feb. 1980): 9–15.

Sherman, Frederick. "Paying Physicians for Geriatric Care." Presentation at Mount Sinai Medical Center, June 1986.

Sprott, Richard L. "Biomedical Research (From Research to Practice: Adding to Our Knowledge Base)." Presentation to the National Council on the Aging, Washington, D.C., 1986.

Stone, Robyn. *Women as Caregivers: A Descriptive Profile of Caregivers from the 1982 Long-Term Care Survey.* Washington: National Center for Health Services Research, 1986.

Syracuse, N.Y. Metropolitan Commission on Aging. *Senior World* (1980–1987).

Tideiksaar, Rein. "Preventing Falls: Home Hazard Checklists to Help Older Patients Protect Themselves." *Geriatrics* 41, no. 5 (May 1986): 26–28.

Tideiksaar, Rein, and Arthur D. Kay. "What Causes Falls? A Logical Diagnostic Procedure." *Geriatrics* 41, no. 12 (December 1986): 32–50.

United Seniors Consumer Cooperative. *United Seniors Health Report* 1, no. 2 (July–August 1986).

U.S. Bureau of the Census. *Marital Status and Living Arrangements: March 1985.* 181-064:40097 Washington: GPO, 1986.

U.S. Congress. House. Select Committee on Aging. *The "Black Box" of Home Care Quality.* A report prepared by the American Bar Association. August 1986. Com. Pub. 99-573.

———. *Consumer's Choices to Funeral Planning.* A report of the Chairman. 1986. Com. Pub. 99-541.

———. *Crime, Violence and the Elderly.* 1986. Com. Pub. 99-547. GPO 56-444 0.

U.S. Congress. Senate. Special Committee on Aging. *Challenges for Women: Taking Charge, Taking Care.* Transcript of hearing by Senator John Glenn, 18 November 1985, in Cincinnati, Ohio.

———. *Developments in Aging.* 1985, 1986.

———. *The Graying of Nations II.* Transcript of hearing at Mount Sinai Medical Center, New York, 12 July 1985.

———. *How Older Americans Live: An Analysis of Census Data.* Serial no. 99-DF.

———. *A Matter of Choice: Planning Ahead for Health Care Decisions.* 1987.

U.S. Congress. Senate. Special Committee on Aging in conjunction with the AARP. *Aging America: Trends and Projections.* 1984 and 1985–1986.

U.S. Consumer Product Safety Commission. *Home Safety Checklist for Older Consumers.* 475-981:32202. Washington: GPO, 1985.

U.S. Department of Health and Human Services. *Alzheimer's Disease:*

Report of the Secretary's Task Force on Alzheimer's Disease. (ADM) 84-1323. Washington: GPO, 1984.

———. *Alzheimer's Disease: A Scientific Guide for Health Practitioners.* NIH Pub. #84-2251. Washington: GPO, 1984.

———. *Current Estimates from the National Health Interview Survey, United States, 1985 (Vital and Health Statistics).* DHHS Pub. #86-1588, series 10, no. 160. Washington: GPO.

U.S. Department of Health and Human Services. National Center for Health Statistics. *Charting the Nation's Health Trends Since 1960,* by P. M. Golden. DHHS Pub. PHS-85-1251. Washington: GPO, August 1985.

U.S. Department of Housing and Urban Development with the Federal Council on Aging and the Administration on Aging. *Proceedings: The Future Is Now—A Home Equity Conversion Conference.* Washington: GPO, January 1985.

U.S. Federal Trade Commission Office of Consumer/Business Education. *Facts for Consumers.* Washington: GPO, February 1986.

U.S. Office of Technology Assessment. *Losing a Million Minds: Confronting the Tragedy of Alzheimer's Disease and Other Dementias.* OTA BA-323. Washington: GPO, April 1987.

U.S. Public Health Service. National Center for Health Services Research and Health Care Technology Assessment. *Research Activities.* Rockville, Md.: 1986–1987.

Weisman, A. D. *The Realization of Death.* New York: Jason Aronson, 1974.

Wetle, Terrie, ed. *Handbook of Geriatric Care.* Boston: Harvard Medical School, 1982.

INDEX

COPYRIGHT ACKNOWLEDGMENTS